Realms of the Unconscious:
The Enchanted Frontier

Realms of the Unconscious: The Enchanted Frontier

by V. V. NALIMOV

Edited by ROBERT G. COLODNY

Illustrated by V. S. GRIBKOV

Translated by A. V. YARKHO

PHILADELPHIA

Published by

iSi PRESS® A Subsidiary of the
Institute for Scientific Information®
3501 Market St., University City Science Center, Philadelphia, PA 19104 U.S.A.

BF315
N3413
1982

© 1982 ISI Press

Library of Congress Cataloging in Publication Data

Nalimov, V. V. (Vasiliĭ Vasil'evich), 1910–
  Realms of the unconscious.

  Translated from the Russian.

  "This volume is a logical extension of the two previous works of V. V. Nalimov: In the
Labyrinths of Language: A Mathematician's Journey and Faces of Science"—Pref.
  Includes bibliographical references and indexes.
  1. Subconsciousness. 2. Psychology—Philosophy. 3. Science—Philosophy.
I. Colodny, Robert Garland. II. Title.
BF315.N3413 1982   154.2   82–15602
ISBN 0-89495-020-7

Printed in the United States of America

Contents

Foreword

*There are more things in heaven and earth, Horatio, than
are dreamt of in your philosophy.*
— HAMLET, ACT I, SCENE 5

*Even now, however, the brain of man, with all its in-
dividual, never to be abandoned richness, is becoming
merely a unit in the vast social brain which is potentially
immortal, and where memory is the heaped wisdom of the
world's great thinkers.*
— LOREN EISELY, THE IMMENSE JOURNEY

*A single word may be the spark of inextinguishable
thought.*

— SHELLEY

This volume is a logical extension of the two previous works of V. V.
Nalimov: *In the Labyrinths of Language: A Mathematician's Journey*
and *Faces of Science*. The trilogy thus represents a survey of the physical
cosmos and man's intellectual and emotional pilgrimage through it over
time. The work now being introduced draws heavily from the previous
studies but is self-contained. The primary ontological position is that the
world is an open one, the outcome of processes that are probabilistic in
nature and constantly the domain of novelties and uncertainties. The language in which one captures aspects of reality is itself polymorphic, metaphorical, constrained by Gödelian principles of undecidability.

It is clear that any serious study of the cognitive process will lead a
scholar to a consideration of the psychic phenomena that make *homo sapiens* unique in the cosmos. Nalimov, the co-worker of the world-re-
nowned Soviet mathematician Andrei Kolmogorov, having explored the
sources of creativity in that most rigorously logical discipline, here

pushes on to the frontiers of traditional explanation and asks radically new questions about the nature and function of the unconscious. This has been the concern of thinkers since the first thoughts flickered into awareness in the minds of our most remote ancestor. Theologians, philosophers, artists, scientists have pursued the elusive goal down the eons and it would be no exaggeration to say that, in any inventory of unfinished important tasks awaiting our species, an understanding of the substratum of mind or psyche retains primacy of place.

Our twentieth century with its enormous list of terrors and achievements may well be remembered for its explorations in these uncharted seas as an earlier age remembered Columbus, Magellan, and Captain Cook. Some of the outlines of continents and islands have been marked in with relative certainty. The great globe is round and in the ocean sea there are no monsters. But how little do we know of the eternally dark, frigid deep! Nalimov has looked deeply into the work of the schools associated with the names of Freud, Jung, James, and Piaget, *inter alia,* but his preliminary conclusions are not so much an acceptance or a commentary on any of the contending schools as they are an effort of theoretical transcendence, a search for a new set of *questions* pertaining to *what we mean* by such common terms as imagination, memory, creativity, time, and wholeness (particularly when the last term refers to our image or concept of the world). In his previous works, Nalimov has indicated that in the history of science, a prevalent, pervasive orthodoxy composed of various cognitive constructs in science, philosophy, theology, and aesthetics restricts the possibility of posing certain types of questions. Posing them evokes the charge of heresy or the attribution of idiocy! Nalimov's exposition of his tentative ideas concerning the realms of the unconscious may well be the target of this double attack. This is anticipated in his concept of progress in science being a sequence of intellectual rebellions. Consider for example the complex set of ideas which postulate a semantic field of language—within which each human creature is immersed and from which are derived consciously and unconsciously the individual's links with the external world and the interpretations thereof. To this field are attributed features associated with the field in quantum mechanics. By deepening and extending the concepts of time which have evolved from the thought of Plotinus, Augustine, Leibniz, Kant, and Einstein, Nalimov grounds a vision of the unconscious in the flux of history, not merely traditional cultural history but history in the deeper senses revealed by evolutionary theory. Some old ideas concerning ontogeny and phylogeny are reexamined and the question is posed: Do we as human creatures—each irreducibly individual—nonetheless possess fragments of a collective memory, an attribute that manifests itself through our unconsciousness? And furthermore, would not such an assumption clarify the similar experiences of mystics and visionaries across both temporal and cultural boundaries? Nalimov, mathematician, physicist, cyberneticist, remains firmly rooted in the older Russian tradition. For him, the recorded experiences of the religious mystic constitute important clues concerning the nature of the unconscious—not as a repository of primitive ignorance and superstition but as a potential guide to understanding aspects of our world that do not fit the contemporary scientific paradigms. His viewpoint is similar to the one expressed recently in the *New York Review of Books* by J. M. Cameron: "The Bible is in the Christian era a principal contributor to our visionary account of the universe and of ourselves within it. If we are to move easily within our inherited culture, knowing how to read the Bible is not something we can do without." Western readers may be particularly fascinated by the novel experiments in altered states of consciousness carried out in Soviet laboratories. The use of religious symbolism, mystical texts, and ancient art forms in place of hallucinogens or other drugs should be of immense interest. That some of the visionary experience has been recorded by participating professional painters (and reproduced here) will constitute a valuable addition to the accumulating evidence from the "Enchanted Frontier." Nalimov's use of this material reminds one of the insight of the historian of mathematics Solomon Bochner: "In a scientifically conducted psychological introspection or self-inspection, the internal object of the inspection becomes 'externalized' by the procedure itself." One recalls also the beautiful phrases of the pioneer English neuro-physiologist Sir Charles Sherrington wherein he refers to the mind as "an enchanted loom where millions of flashing shuttles weave a dissolving pattern, always a meaningful pattern, though never an abiding one."

It is almost four hundred years since Descartes inaugurated modern philosophy and bequeathed the radical dualism of extended substances and thinking substance: the familiar dichotomy of mind and body, brain event and cognitive act. Where Descartes naively sought a causal link in the pineal gland, his contemporary heirs look to molecular biology and to that strange functional asymmetry of the left hemisphere and the right. The American neuro-psychologist K. Pribram puts it this way: "In right-handed persons the left hemisphere processes information much as does the digital computer, while the right hemisphere functions more according to the principles of optical, holographic systems." Nalimov's colleague, the mathematician Yu. I. Manin, adds: "In particular, the left hemisphere contains genetically predetermined mechanisms for understanding national languages and more generally symbolism, logic—the Latin 'ratio'; the right hemisphere controls forms, gestalt-perception, intuition. Normally, the functioning of human consciousness continually displays a combination of these two components, one of which may be manifested more noticeably than the other.''

In Nalimov's synthesis, the unconscious may provide links that permit these faculties to function along unusual circuits so that sequential processes become concurrent in real time. The history of creativity in the arts as well as the sciences, including mathematics, contains innumerable examples of this form of unconscious activity. For Nalimov, human thought moves always in quest of a unitary image of the world and towards a unified image of man. This process of unification depends not so much on the gathering of empirical data with subsequent corroboration or falsification of theories. On the contrary, the ancient vision guides and shapes the cognitive process itself. The somewhat brash new community of the historians of science will find much to debate here. Nalimov is much fascinated by the influence of the arts on science as manifested for example by the relations of Coleridge, Wordsworth, and Sir William Hamilton. Alfred North Whitehead expressed this debt for all of science when he said: ''The pilgrim fathers of the scientific imagination as it exists today are the great tragedians of ancient Athens: Aeschylus, Sophocles, Euripedes. Their vision of fate, remorseless and indifferent, urging a tragic incident to its inevitable issue, is the vision possessed by science. Fate in Greek tragedy becomes the order of nature in modern thought.'' Nalimov adds the religious mystic to the list of those who have woven parts of the seamless garment of science, and in so doing increased the dimensions of what we mean by human nature.

In the pages that follow, Nalimov is not attempting to construct an exhaustive theory of the realms of the unconscious; nor is he seeking to convert the infidel. In the tradition of the early natural philosophers and without dogmatism, he asks new questions, questions that are provocative and hence productive of debate and perhaps a little wisdom.

ROBERT G. COLODNY
University of Pittsburgh

Preface

All of us are now aware of the fact that the progress of science is accompanied by explosive changes in its constituents, i.e., paradigmatic concepts (Kuhn, 1970).

Revolutions may be of different power and effect. I believe that the present revolution in science is the most serious it has ever faced.

The science of the past was above all permeated by a deep belief in rationalism. Scientific thought, as well as the world in general, was considered indubitably logical. Rationalism was the principal component of the scientific paradigm.

European thought has always contained a latent criticism of the all-embracing rationalism, but in recent decades this criticism has been acquiring a menacing strength. We have begun to see quite clearly that our consciousness is underlain by the bottomless unconscious. People are ready to see in the unconscious a source of both scientific thought[1] and social life in all the complexities of its conflicts and its ideological formations. In our everyday verbal behavior, we understand the meaning of utterances by resorting to semantic fields inherent in our unconsciousness (Nalimov, 1981a).

I regard the unconscious as the entire variety of manifestations of our consciousness situated outside its logical structure or, in other words, as the part that will remain after we mentally reject all the features of our consciousness which can be passed over to computers. The study of the depths of our consciousness makes us look at what Tillich calls the *ultimate reality* of the World. Man cannot be understood outside his participation in the World Integrity.

---

[1] The extra-rational character of science, its unrealized premises, its closeness to a myth, is the subject of many contemporary publications. The irrationalism of science in its extreme and arbitrarily dramatic form was shown by Feyerabend (1975). Similar ideas, though in a more reserved form, were developed in an earlier book (Nalimov, 1981b).

I am going to formulate a very bold idea: Why should we perceive the World only through man-made physical devices? Perhaps the depth of our unconscious is a specific receptor which opens up the possibility of direct contact with another reality closed to physical devices. Science acknowledged the validity of studying nature by means of physical devices which had been created by logic, but it did not recognize man as such a device. Man is created by nature, not by logic. According to the European cultural tradition going back to Judaism and particularly to the book of Genesis, nature cannot be outside logic or, moreover, above it.

But if people are now prone to attach such great significance to the unconscious, we have to ask: What does science know of the unconscious? The answer to this question is ambivalent: on the one hand, colossal amounts of empirical data have been accumulated during recent decades; on the other hand, no universally accepted conceptualization has ever been formulated.[2] No all-embracing definition of science can be given today, but one thing is certain: no science can exist outside all conceptions. Therefore, we can state that there is no science of the unconscious. Such a science could not have been formed if only because it was opposed by the paradigm which, on the one hand, considered as reality only that which could be reduced to physical or chemical phenomena and, on the other hand, required conceptual arrangement of the observed phenomena into a system of rigid logical structures.

Here the following question can be posed: In what way can a thing or process existing outside logic be described so that the description becomes conceptual? In trying to answer this question, one should first of all pay attention to the fact it does not follow from anything that the criticism directed against an all-embracing rationalism should turn into mere iconoclasm. I am in no way calling for the rejection of logic—one can hardly say anything significant while ignoring it. Rather, I seek an *expanded* usage which would allow us to discuss the extralogical in a language comprehensible to people brought up within the culture of logic.

In this book an attempt is made to elaborate a probabilistic approach to the construction of a conception of the unconscious. The following considerations are basic:

1. We make use of the language of a probabilistic logic, which allows us to draw conclusions directly from fuzzy, probabilistically weighted concepts.

2. Conceptualization is made to sound arbitrarily metaphorical.

---

[2] This was clearly demonstrated at the highly representative International Symposium on the Unconscious in Tbilisi, October 1979. There the scientific status of psychoanalysis was heatedly discussed. In the process of discussion, it became clear that the unconscious, in its broad meaning, also lacks scientific status though it is studied in laboratories and clinics and is discussed in scientific journals.

3. We juxtapose freely the entire range of knowledge accumulated by mankind, including mathematics, physics, psychology, psychiatry, philosophy, religious studies, culturology, anthropology, linguistics, and theology. The right to compare the incomparable is supported only by the conviction that the source for everything lies in what we call the unconscious.

4. We report on experiments in which the authors act both as experimenters and as subjects.

Methodologically, the most important for our purposes was the use of physical concepts. Philosophers are prone to claim physics to be the leader of all sciences. If this is true, it is so only in the sense that it is physics which acts as a destroyer of the paradigm [see Chapter 1 in *Faces of Science* (Nalimov, 1981*b*)]. Physics has agreed to consider randomness a carrier of knowledge, not an expression of ignorance, the latter being the way it was regarded for centuries by European thought. Physics has acknowledged the legitimacy of a reality which cannot be registered by physical devices. Physics has proved able to accommodate the paradoxes that exist within its own theories.

Physics, in the course of its development, has in the long run taught us to explain *the incomprehensible comprehensibly by the much more incomprehensible*. This is exactly what this book attempts to do.

This book is a natural completion of my two previous ones: *Probabilistic Model of Language* and *Faces of Science*. The first of these was published in the USSR in 1974 and 1979 and in the United States (under the title *In the Labyrinths of Language: A Mathematician's Journey*) in 1981; the second, a collection of previously published articles, was also published in the United States in 1981.

The first of the above-mentioned books was dedicated to the memory of A. A. Solonovich. The two later books also go back to his lectures which I, then a young man, attended in the 1920s. I was first struck by their broad natural-philosophic significance. Solonovich, being a mathematician, could show another meaning underlying mathematics. Proceeding from mathematics, he had attempted (before Gödel's proof appeared) to demonstrate the incompleteness of pure logic. He spoke of the cosmic extension of consciousness of man freed from the power of doctrines fettering him. Freedom was shown as a cosmic essence. Later, my impressions were strengthened by what I heard from his wife, Agniya Solonovich.

Acknowledgments

I am particularly indebted to J. A. Drogalina, whose contribution to this book is, indeed, great. Several chapters of the book were written in cooperation with her. She was also the leading experimenter who prepared experimental material and processed experimental results, as well as carried out the experiments.

I owe words of gratitude to the artists A. S. Dyachkov, V. S. Gribkov, N. V. Obukhov, and B. P. Safronov, who participated in our experiments and whose enthusiasm did not diminish during a collaboration that lasted almost two years. I am especially indebted to V. S. Gribkov, who also charged himself with an organizational part of the project and brilliantly succeeded in it.

I would also like to express my deep appreciation to A. V. Yarkho, the translator of the manuscript, for her responsible and creative attitude toward the text and the utmost care with which she tried to convey my ideas in English.

(10) Jesus said: I have cast fire upon the world, and behold, I guard it, until it is ablaze.

APOCRYPHAL GOSPEL OF THOMAS

LANGUAGE OF THE PROBABILISTIC VISION OF THE WORLD

On the Threshold of Part I

All the chapters of Part I are devoted to the language of a probabilistic vision which I believe can lead to a new and deeper interaction with the reality of the world. The "non-real" may become real if the limitations set by Western culture on our perception of the world are removed. These limitations have enabled the development of Western culture in all its richness and splendor. However, richness always conceals poverty within itself. A radical change in the language always signifies a radical change in the culture. This idea is attractive, but it is also fraught with certain difficulties, which may prove to be insurmountable, and with dangers lurking in unforeseen consequences. However, whether or not we wish it, the process of cardinal changes has started. The search for new languages is also going on: the language of contemporary physics cannot be compared with that of classical physics; and the response to the papers by Zadeh, devoted to fuzzy sets, would hardly have been possible even in the recent past. I have also started on this road.

The first chapter, written in an extremely laconic form, attempts to show the potentially existing universality of the language of probabilistic vision. This chapter opens up broad vistas of the probabilistic perception of the world. The second and third chapters give a detailed account of two instances of using this language to solve problems that were unsolvable in a familiar language. In the fourth chapter an attempt is made to show that the language of a probabilistic vision is a continuation of the trend in our culture which used to perceive manifoldness, made fuzzy by number, as uniqueness. This had been done by Plotinus, who seemed to follow the tradition coming from Pythagoras. Finally, the fifth chapter emphasizes the highly metaphorical character of our use of probabilistic concepts. Randomness is regarded as a synonym for the "fuzziness" treated by Zadeh.

Chapter 1

Probabilistic World: A Transition to Another Culture?[1]

Can Western Culture Have a Second Mediterranean?

A. Stereotyped Vision of the World

1. Culture is the vision of the world. This vision is determined by our language.

2. The prevailing peculiarity of earlier European culture was its *deterministic* vision of the world.

3. The language of deterministic concepts makes us perceive the world as a gigantic clockwork governed by cause-and-effect relations.

4. The hierarchy of the world—the concept of elementary particles and their blocks, the belief in the existence of general, universal laws of the world, the idea that only one consistent description of the world is possible—all this is given by our language.

5. Language based on logic made us acknowledge the *existence* of logic in the world. The principle of logical consistency acquired an ontological status. The necessity of this postulate was formulated in the thirteenth century by Thomas Aquinas (Wild, 1963), who stood at the source of European culture.

6. Within this vision of the world, a human being is nothing more than a block of matter which became so sophisticated that it managed to

---

[1] This chapter was written by V. V. Nalimov and S. V. Meyen. A part of it relating to the problems of biological taxonomy was previously published (Meyen and Nalimov, 1978); the abstract of the latter paper was published abroad (Nalimov and Meyen, 1979).

3

master the logic built into the foundation of existence. A human being was reduced to a microclock (the reflection of the macrocosm in the microcosm is a conception coming from ancient Egyptian hermetism). But the microclock has proved to be *spoiled* by the subjectivity of human behavior which cannot be described by the language of logic. The conception of a human being as a spoiled mechanism goes back to the traditions of Judaism. The Old Testament gives the Law according to which people should have lived, but real people do not obey the Law completely because original sin had broken the automatism of human behavior. The myth of the Fall always occupied the central place in the Judeo-Christian *Weltanschauung* of the Western world. At the International Symposium on the Unconscious in Tbilisi in 1979, one often heard invocations against reductionism in psychology, but then one also heard about the existence of the objective laws of the unconscious. The latter assertion is, as a matter of fact, a manifestation of the notorious reductionism, though concealed. If objective laws of the unconscious do exist and if sooner or later we discover them or at least come closer to comprehending them, the unconscious will no longer remain such, since it will be described in the formal logic expressed by the laws discovered by us, in the same way that the mechanisms created by us in the physical world are controlled by these laws. The Fall embodied in the ignorance of the true Law will be overcome by new knowledge. And man will become a controllable automaton.

7. A scientific description of the world represents the vision of the world by physical devices: photoelements, thermoelements, Geiger counters, and so forth. Quantum mechanics willingly agreed to acknowledge the role of an apparatus-like observer, but science as a whole refused to acknowledge the role of man, a spoiled mechanism, in comprehending the world. Science is supposed to comprehend the world objectively, that is, not through man but through objectively existing logic.

8. Logic is the rule for constructing true statements over symbols with a discrete, atomistic meaning. This brings forth the idea of discrete thinking and accounts for the search for physical repositories of discrete thoughts in the human brain and for a neurophysiological mechanism directly responsible for abstract thinking, including creativity.

9. In teaching a student, a professor speaks of the knowledge he has obtained, but he does not teach his pupil to obtain new knowledge.

10. In European science from the time of Aristotle up to the middle of the nineteenth century (and in the USSR up to the middle of the twentieth century), both philosophers and scientists were inclined to consider *chance* an indication of our ignorance (Nalimov, 1981a).

11. No matter what the defenders of religion would say, it does look absurdly archaic within this system of notions, since here everything is

perceived through man who is again a broken clockwork. Religion is incompatible with science because man himself in his versatility is incompatible with science.

B. Probabilistic Vision of the World

> God has *"arranged all things by measure and numbers and weight."*
>
> THE APOCRYPHA
> "THE WISDOM OF SOLOMON," 11:20

1. Any flourishing culture seems to be always pregnant with a counterculture whose sprouts pierce the surface of culture and, if they are numerous, can give birth to a new culture.

2. I believe that the sprouts of the counterculture of our epoch are forming a single, *probabilistic* vision of the world.[2]

3. In the language of probabilistic concepts, we say that a random variable is known if its distribution function is known. This is to say that we may quite deliberately reject the cause–effect interpretation of the observed phenomena. We may be satisfied with a purely *behavioral* description of the phenomena. A distribution function describes the behavior of a random variable without any allusion to its cause. Thus, we receive the right to describe phenomena simply as they look. In other words, we describe them in their *spontaneous* manifestation and acknowledge their freedom of manifestation: phenomenologically, it looks as if a coin has a free will and makes a decision whether it will fall heads or tails. Probabilistic description becomes fuzzy: a continuous random variable after its realization (e.g., as a result of measurement) has any given value with zero probability. There can only exist a non-zero probability for a random variable to lie in an interval of values. The principal peculiarity of the probabilistic language is *fuzziness* of description. In a more general way, we could say that randomness is a synonym for semantic fuzziness of a concept, and the distribution function of probabilities is a measure of this fuzziness (Nalimov, 1981*b*, Chapter 5). If we pass now from the probabilistic interpretation of the results of measurements to the probabilistic comprehension of the fundamental concepts of our culture, they will also be described *fuzzily*. This will be profusely illustrated later.

4. It has suddenly become clear that *words*, on which our culture is based, do not and cannot have an atomistic meaning. It has become pos-

---

[2] The language of probabilistic concepts in its broad sense was elaborated in my two previous books (Nalimov, 1981*a*, *b*).

sible and even necessary to consider words as possessing fuzzy semantic fields over which the probabilistic distribution function is constructed and to consider people as probabilistic receivers (Nalimov, 1981*a*).

5. It has become clear that a *metaphor* is not a lifeless rudiment but an essential component of our language. A metaphor embodies the rejection of formal logic or, to be more correct, the rejection of one of its principal laws, the law of the excluded middle. Bohr's principle of complementarity signifies the open recognition of the necessity of metaphorical thinking in science (Nalimov, 1981*a*). Moreover, any scientific concept is but a metaphor: the phenomenon under study behaves as the theory predicts and at the same time *not quite so* (Hutten, 1956).

6. What are verbal meanings? They are single objects, their properties and relations, and the classes of objects, properties, and relations. The totality of all this forms the typology of the world in all its diversity. Every word is put in correspondence with a domain in the world typology. The fuzziness of this domain has always been perceived as a deficiency of our language. No matter whether we deal with jurisdiction or with science, we strive to outline the domain as clearly as possible, implying that not only are individuals discrete, but taxa as well. The ideal is to put discrete taxa into one-to-one correspondence with discrete words. This quest for verbal unambiguity starting with Aristotle passes via the scholastics to modern logical positivism.

7. A probabilistic model of language accepts fuzzy semantic fields. It may be the capitulation of language before the complexity of the world— the complexity of its typology and its numerous taxa. But it also may be the reflection of the properties of the world typology. Are taxa discrete? Or are they probabilistic by their nature? An affirmative answer to the second question leads to a new outlook on the world and to the counter-culture of the probabilistic world. What we are considering is not merely the probabilistic *vision* of the world stemming from its infinite complexity but inwardly deterministic "in fact." We mean the probabilistic world where probability lies at the core of the world. We mean probabilistic ontology of the probabilistic world, not probabilistic epistemology of a deterministic world.

8. Are taxa probabilistic by their nature? Here are a few illustrations. Biologists always tend to define exactly the genus and the species of an organism, being quite confident that these taxa are discrete. Any deviation from the norm is an abnormality and is not the object of taxonomy but of a special discipline called teratology. Only seldom is it understood that the abnormality has properties which are not normally characteristic only for a given taxon, but which are normal and common for other taxa (Krenke's rule; see Meyen, 1973). On the other hand, several taxa may have similar abnormalities, and thus their variational tails interlace. Ex-

ceptions link the rules. But if so, taxa of organisms are not discrete aggregates determined by a stable list of attributes, but fuzzy sets differing from one another by the frequency of manifestation of attributes, and we would like to emphasize that it is often *manifestation* of attributes and not their appearance anew which takes place.

9. At the opposite pole from the living organisms is the kingdom of minerals. Their taxa are expressed by discrete chemical formulas and seem to be ideally suited for objective taxonomy. But if we start to take into account lesser quantities of elements which are traditionally considered as contamination of a mineral ("chemical abnormality"), we shall by and by reach the level of the "omnipresence of elements." On this level minerals cannot be distinguished on the basis of the list of elements they contain. Natural minerals (in contrast to those described in textbooks) differ not by the list of elements they contain but by the proportions in which these are present.

10. An acquaintance with taxonomy in other branches of knowledge leads to the following hypothesis: taxa probabilistic by nature are neither an exception to nor a result of deficiency of our cognition; they are the rule and an immanent property of the world. In this way the old typological antinomy is removed. All attempts to discover the natural system of organisms or the natural typology of the world failed because of dubious demarcation lines between taxa. That gave rise to a skeptical attitude and a tendency to treat all taxa as artificial units since there are no clear-cut boundaries between them which would make taxa natural. In the probabilistic world everything is vice versa: clear-cut boundaries and the absence of "transitional forms" testify to a reduction in completeness. If we are dealing with a differential distribution function, for a continuous variable the probability of coming across a point-like, exactly defined (deterministic) value equals zero.

11. But if taxa are not discrete, then probably natural individuals are discrete? Recall again discussions where one individual ends and where another begins: in space or in time?

12. From biology we know of the pleiotropic action of genes. Each gene is responsible for a number of properties, e.g., blue-eyed cats are always deaf. It is obvious that a gene is connected with various properties by the distribution function of probability. In the particular case, if the probabilities are distributed evenly for all the properties, the species will be stable in all its polymorphism. Biologists know of the stable polymorphism of populations. It is restored even after a severe selection for uniformity. In the history of culture, such selections have also taken place. Burning books, as well as the destruction of outstanding thinkers (Anaxagoras was jailed, Socrates was forced to suicide, Bruno was burned), was an effort to maintain uniformity and orthodoxy of culture

(Nalimov, 1981*b*, p. 229). But again variety rose from the ashes of the burned books. The present variety is, however, but a small part of the potential variety.

13. We are accustomed to the idea that evolution means the appearance of something absolutely new. The truly new thing is a new taxon or a new archetype. But within the world of probabilistic taxa, archetypes, and individuals, evolution may take another course: it suffices to redistribute probabilities. A rare deviation becomes the norm, while the norm becomes an abnormality, an atavism. But potentiality still exists. If so, we again come to the idea of unchangeable biological species: however, this constancy differs from what pre-Darwinian naturalists believed. What we keep in mind is the constant potentiality which underlies various probabilities of manifestation. And in culture, too:

> In vain you believe, oh artist,
> You are the creator of things.
> For ages they roved in the air
> Invisible for our eyes.
> A. K. TOLSTOY

14. But still, it is impossible to accept the idea of evolution being only a redistribution of frequencies in the initially given potentialities. We believe in the expansion of potentialities, in absolute creativity. The fundamental question of evolution, whether it is the evolution of galaxies, of biological species, or of cultures, is how much of it is mere redistribution of probabilities and how much is absolutely new. How can these two components be divided, and where can one find answers to these questions? Absolute creativity means the appearance of new principles which cannot be reduced to old ones. So the new principles are absolutely random. We are already accustomed to the regularities of chance, but can we become accustomed to the aporia: "randomness of the principle" in a truly evolutionary world, randomness having a direction. The creative agent of nature, the Christian God, should possess absolute randomness.

15. Our world perception starts with image perception. This is a probabilistic task where an answer indicates the taxon. This taxon is probabilistic by nature (see above, paragraph 10). The concept corresponding to the taxon will naturally be probabilistic as well. Having chosen a taxon, we look for the word corresponding to it. Here the probabilistic model of language comes into force. Thus we pass all the angles of Frege's triangle, from the reality to the concept and term or in the opposite direction. Both the angles and their relations are penetrated with probability. It is hardly necessary to prove the significance of Frege's triangle,[3] which outlines our perception of the World and, therefore, our culture.

---

[3] Frege's triangle is a semantic triangle establishing the relations among the external side of the word

16. Culture is a deep *collective consciousness* whose roots go far back into the remotest past. It forms a fuzzy mosaic of concepts with the distribution function of probabilities given over it. This is a view from the standpoint of a neutral, hypothetical metaobserver. Real people have their own individual filters of perception, i.e., probabilistic ones. Collective consciousness passing through an individual filter generates *personal* perception of culture, again probabilistically given. The part of the concepts within our consciousness which have small probabilities may be interpreted as the collective unconsciousness (in the sense of Jung). It is revealed either in dreams, when the filters of perception cease to function, or in peculiar situations when these filters become selective.

17. Society is divided into *clusters* which embrace people whose personal perceptions of the collective consciousness are similar. We shall call these clusters, if a bit conventionally, *psychic genotypes*. The varieties of social life—political, intellectual, and religious schools worshipping an authority, the striving for limitless power or its rejection—are all manifestations of different psychic genotypes. In particular, this makes it clear that class ideology of the proletariat is formed and realized in no way by its representatives.

18. In a probabilistic sense, man is *never free*: he is always dominated by the past stored in the collective consciousness. At the same time he is *free* because the genotype does not rigidly (biologically) determine the probabilistic structure of an individual filter of perception; it only gives certain possibilities for its formation. Great religious teachings—Oriental religion and early (gnostic) Christianity—were primarily directed at liberating man from the collective consciousness of the past, since without that all the rest is closed. The history of Christianity has shown that the new wine was put into old wineskins.

19. One of the specific features of our time is the emergence of nationalistic movements all over the world. They have shifted to the background those things hitherto perceived as manifestations of class struggle. This phenomenon cannot be understood from the traditional standpoint but is easily interpreted on the basis of our conception presented here. The culture generated by a comparatively small region of the Earth, as a result of its technological power, started to exercise an intolerable pressure over other people of the world, who were not historically prepared to absorb it. And so there appeared a wide gap between the *collective consciousness* of peoples and the ideology promoted by the mass media, which were literally penetrating all aspects of their lives. This may ac-

---

(phonetic word, *a symbol*), the object denoted by this word (meaning, *referent*), and sense (*signifier*, i.e., information contained in the word); graphically these relations are represented by an equiangular triangle at whose angles the three above characteristics are placed and whose sides are arrows indicating connections between them.

count for the unstable psychology of some of these groups with its well-known extreme manifestations, as well as for the growing self-consciousness concerning the specific role of one's nationality in the historical process. Thus, an illusion is created that the collective consciousness is still preserved within the all-embracing and domineering modern culture.

20. The notion of a *paradigm* in science introduced by Kuhn (1970) can be interpreted as the functioning of a fuzzy field of axioms which determines our attitude as to what is considered either scientific or non-scientific in the science of today. For this field the probability distribution is set. Besides, each scientist has his individual filter which determines his personal views and ideas. This might explain astonishingly different evaluations of a basically new work. Incidentally, cowardly scientific "managers" have learned to make use of this fact: they have always at their disposal a list of rigid-minded reviewers who are sincerely ready to condemn any interesting, novel—and therefore dangerous—work.

21. Outstanding scientific and philosophical concepts always proceed from a fuzzy, probabilistically weighted set of axioms constructed over ideas without a precise meaning.[4] Later, individual filters of perception enter the game. This accounts for the ramification of teachings: neo-Kantians; Darwinians, Lysenko among them (this also happens sometimes); and Marxists of various shades and colors, including here the Chinese version as a projection of Marx's theory on the collective consciousness of an utterly different culture. Individual filters of perception brought about by the cultural peculiarities may so radically change the initial premises that the text elucidating them will become new not only in its form of exposition but also in its content. Without a probabilistic conception it is hardly possible to explain the fact that such different structures are obtained from the same original prerequisites by means of formal logic. (The mechanism of interaction between the initial probabilistically weighted information and the filter of the person perceiving it is considered in detail in later chapters.)

22. Human drives are determined by personal values. *Value* is not a category of formal logic. The object of logic is to determine whether an assertion is true or false and in no way to estimate its value. Value categories stem from fuzzy probabilistic notions which are part of the general cultural consciousness. Here again, I would like to mention individual filters of perception which, on the one hand, depend on new *goals* and, on the other hand, are exposed by the faculties of human genotypes. Goals emerge and spread in societies like infectious diseases (Nalimov,

---

[4] Matters stand otherwise only in mathematics, where mathematical *structures* are formulated unambiguously over symbols which, according to Hilbert, are finite objects and do not serve to signify anything different from themselves; this accounts for the absence of semantic fuzziness.

1981*b*). To pursue the metaphor, just as the development of immunity causes mutation of the viruses and bacteria, the boredom of old ideas provokes new ones. However, new goals simply purloin old layers of the collective consciousness: "brand new" hippies restored the ancient mysteries; communism stirred the age-old dream of the paradise lost, which surfaced now in the Charters of Kumran communities, now in Albigensian and Hussite heresies. The philosophy of the absurd, which is now linked with the name of Kierkegaard, also stems from this source.

23. All human activity is based on *forecasting*: by leaving our house, entering a college, taking a job, or marrying, we are constantly forecasting our future. Forecasts are always probabilistic. Past experience is represented by a fuzzy, probabilistically weighted mosaic of notions. Again, much depends on the individual filters of perception determined by the task set and on genotype peculiarities which reflect such properties as courage or cowardice. Seemingly strange rites of such sober people as the Greeks, e.g., the strange prophecies of the Pythoness, were quite meaningful: psychologically, they helped to focus the too fuzzy contours of presentiments.

24. Let us look at the probabilistic aspects of the physical nature of humans. A human embryo (as well as that of any multicellular organism) develops along a trajectory in the space of attributes determined by the evolutionary pre-history of mankind. In this space a distribution function of probabilities is given. The embryo's development can be treated as a reconstruction and shifting of this function. Some attributes are suppressed (have very low probability) while others become dominant. The space of attributes represents a fuzzy domain in the space of attributes of all other organisms since the nature of the taxon *Homo sapiens* (as well as of any other taxon) is probabilistic. In the ontogeny the spoiled distribution function brings the human embryo toward the periphery of the domain and closer to the norm of the adjoining taxa, including here the taxa of the ancestors (such atavisms as a tail, entire hairiness, and others), or, perhaps, the taxa of descendants. Human somatic individuality again depends on the peculiarities of the distribution function constructed over the manifold of attributes common for all people.[5]

25. In a similar way it is possible to construct a probabilistic model of the human ego. Human spiritual individuality can be described by the

---

[5] Meditation in a museum: The idea that *Homo sapiens* is only a patch on the field of attributes of the entire animal world seems to have been shared by ancient Egyptians. This becomes obvious when one strolls in the Egyptian Department of the Bode Museum in Berlin: semi-human, semi-animal creatures strike the observer with their grandeur. One cannot help feeling their wisdom and serenity lost by our people. Perhaps these creatures embody the integrity of the world. Egyptians seem to have perceived the whole field of attributes on which the patch of human attributes drifted, and by force of their fantasy sought the possibility of revealing new forms for thinking creatures shifting the distribution function over this field of attributes. Are we not coming back to the ancient vision of the world?

distribution function of probabilities over a field of attributes common for all people. I am going to call this field semantic. The distribution function can be needle-shaped, fuzzy, or asymmetrical, and its shape determines human types. A bimodal distribution function can account for a sharply marked split of personality. During one's lifetime the distribution function seems to undergo perpetual change. A rigidly discrete consciousness of one's ego typical of a needle-shaped distribution function might lead to the state in which a person would feel minor deaths while passing from one moment to another. This also accounts for the concept of black holes in psychopathology, the pathological fright of life and death (for more details see Welwood, 1977*a*).

26. The semantic field connected with the human ego and human somatics contains the suppressed memory of the pre-historic past. The return to the remote past related to the anomalous redistribution of the probability function is interpreted as a psychic disease. Some Western psychiatrists (see, for example, Sall, 1976) agree with some mystic writers of the past, e.g., Swedenborg (see Dusen, 1974), in treating certain psychic diseases as a "demon possession," but perhaps what actually happens is the splitting of a personality which results in the extreme shift of the distribution function so that a person becomes controlled by his remote past. Probably the entire astral world does not exist independently but is inherent (with negligibly small probabilities) in every person as his evolutionary past. And it also may be that the entire, evolutionarily probable future is contained in the person's present, but again with negligibly small probabilities.

27. The foregoing probabilistic model of the psychic domain allows us to explain many ancient religious ideas in modern language. It elucidates the ancient Indian teaching of the illusory nature of our ego and of metempsychosis—a peculiar interpretation of vague awareness of sequential links in the evolution of the probabilistic distribution function constructed over the field of the entire diversity of psychic states. (Chapter 16 is devoted to the phenomenon of reincarnation recollections.) However, matters are more complicated with the interpretation of the Christian *inferno*. The structure of the distribution function largely depends on culture with all its trends and values, but when death comes, culture (at least in its external, verbal form) can no longer influence a person who then has to face the transcendence of the cosmos.[6] Does everybody have the strength to stand this trial or are some people doomed to return into their pre-human past? It seems to explain the con-

---

[6] Reanimated people describe their experience as "life after life." The widely known books by Moody (1975, 1977) are devoted to this problem. Contemporary medicine, having made reanimation really possible, paradoxically made the scientific component of European culture consider facts which previously were part of deep religious experience.

cept of *inferno* as a state of unpreparedness. In the Middle Ages, Western Christians shared a somewhat similar idea of inferno, as exemplified by the *Divine Comedy* and the paintings of Bosch and Breugel. On the fragment of Breugel's "The Fall of the Rebellious Angels," one can see a reptilian man. I believe this to be a symbolic representation of man's return into his pre-human past. Are not modern mental hospitals a prototype of the inferno?

28. We are constantly speaking of the continuous nature of our consciousness. The notion of the discrete manifestations of an *altered state* of consciousness introduced by the well-known transpersonal psychologist Tart (1975) can be interpreted as a description of the phenomena accompanying the shift and reconstruction of the probabilistic distribution function which determines the open comprehension of separate areas of the continuous mosaic of the mind. Our conception of the unity of the mind has much in common with that of Welwood (1977b), who introduced the concept of psychological spaces.

29. From the probabilistic model of language, it follows that the continuous consciousness cannot be reduced to the discreteness of language (Nalimov, 1981a). Phrases constructed over discrete symbol–words are always interpreted at the continuous level. This is an explanation of the principal difficulties of constructing artificial intelligence. A person is always *in contact with his continuous consciousness*, even in everyday verbal communication. But the entrance to this consciousness is realized by means of words. Direct entrance into the continuous consciousness is provided by an altered state of consciousness. An instant entrance into the continuous consciousness is an *insight*. This allows us to interpret scientific creativity as an insight, a response to the problem formulated at the discrete logical level.

30. The attempt to simulate thinking by means of the discrete elements of computers seems futile. Contemporary neurophysiology pins all its hopes to encephalograms, which are allegedly a direct record of thinking. Neurons are regarded as small transistors or other elements of computer hardware functioning in two or a few regimes and receiving and transmitting discrete commands. However, all these models lack the principal component: the probabilities of occurrence as evaluated by a person who recognizes patterns while listening, speaking, or thinking about the world.

31. In the physics of the microworld, the wave function determines only the *possibility* of a certain behavior of an electron under given macroconditions; subatomic particles do not exist with certainty at definite places but rather show "tendencies to exist" (Heisenberg); at the level of the microworld, events do not occur with certainty but rather have tendencies to occur: within this world any observed phenomenon does not

exist separately but only as an interaction of the process of the preparation of the experiment and the measurement itself. Here the contemporary probabilistic vision of the world has an amazing amount in common with Eastern concepts (Capra, 1975, 1976).

32. The "bootstrap" concept in physics, with its rejection of elementary particles, universal constants, and general laws of nature, again signifies the transition to a fuzzy description of the world in its universal interrelations.

33. The American physicist Chew (1968), discussing the problem of integrality in physics, writes to the point:

> Carried to its logical extreme, the bootstrap conjecture implies that the existence of consciousness, along with all other aspects of nature is necessary for self-consistency of the whole. Such a notion, although not obviously non-sensical, is patently unscientific. (p. 763)

Perhaps we should be more cautious and speak not of consciousness of the world but of the semantic field of universal significance through which the world we know as divided is restored in its wholeness. Is there any other way to imagine the world in its integrality?

34. In contemporary science, *chance* has turned from the expression of our ignorance into the expression of our knowledge. In terms of the so-called algorithmic theory of probability (Nalimov, 1981*b*; for more details, see Fine, 1973), a random sequence of symbols is a sequence which cannot be recorded by means of an algorithm in a form shorter than the sequence itself. In other words, such a sequence has *maximum complexity*—it cannot be transmitted through communication channels by a brief record. But the notion of maximum complexity ceased being synonymous with ignorance. This is the *cardinal* change in our *Weltanschauung*. It took our culture *more than twenty centuries to achieve it*.

35. As was pointed out by Monod (1972), phenomena at the gene–molecular level can and must be described only in terms of chance. But chance is maximum complexity. Then this is, perhaps, reading from the complex Text that mainly cannot be recorded in a form shorter than the Text itself. The idea of the random nature of deep biological processes is in agreement with the conception of directed evolution of Teilhard de Chardin (1965) and Berg (1969). (For more details see Nalimov, 1981*b*.)

36. If all the taxa of our culture, despite their uniqueness, are but various translations of one Text (this idea is brilliantly expressed by Paz, 1975) and biological species are various translations of another Text, then it is quite plausible that they all are the translation of one and the same Text. It might be the reading from the cosmic fields of consciousness at one time in the language of human cultures and at another time in the language of the genetic code. The ecological crisis is, perhaps, a conflict of two languages which suddenly came into too close contact.

37. When we acknowledge the legitimacy of the idea that the world can be represented fuzzily, by its probabilistically weighted facet, we add power to our consciousness, emphasizing its uniqueness and difference from logically arranged machines.

C. Can It Be That the Probabilistic Vision of the World Gives Rise to the Culture of Not-Doing?

1. Each of the past cultures selected a narrow strip from the entire spectrum of human consciousness, thus directing human activities to a definite goal and using resources with thrift.

2. In moments of crisis, when cultures have exhausted their potentialities, they start mixing and blending with one another. This is what happened in the Mediterranean regions when the teaching of Christ blended with Judaism, Hellenism, ancient Egyptian religion, and the collective consciousness of the peoples who were to undertake the development of the new culture. This is also true of Byzantium. Syncretism is not eclectic. The individuality is determined here by the distribution of probabilities, and the dynamics of its progress is determined by its restructuring.

3. The breakthrough to ultimate domination over nature became possible when European culture sharply narrowed the strip of perception of the spectrum of human consciousness. For the first time in human history, the logical structure of consciousness became the cultural dominant. This has led to a rapid depletion of natural resources and to a crisis; one of the manifestations of the latter is the ecological impasse. The ecological problem has acquired an eschatological overtone.

4. Can it be that Western culture is now having its second Mediterranean?

5. The spectrum of human consciousness is again opening up in all its broadness. The field of vision now embraces even what has previously been rejected, including the entire diversity of religious experience. The East rushes into Western culture. Cosmopolitanism of ideas results.

6. Nobody can tell how the weights will be distributed over the mosaic of the newly revealed expanded consciousness. Only one thing seems to be obvious: the opening of all human faculties to gain the new awareness of the world acquires a major significance. This means a holistic vision of the world which is made integral through interaction with the semantic field—the world viewed not only semiotically but also semantically. But what *is* the semantic field of the world? The answer to this question remains to be discovered. How can the fuzzy, probabilistically weighted vision of the world be combined with formal logic, which we cannot afford to reject? And if a direct, conscious contact with the se-

mantic field becomes possible, is this to say that pupils can now be taught how to obtain new knowledge?

7. The formation of a new culture will make us face new problems. Some of them are already emerging. The first problem is that of *language*. One of the peculiar features of modern culture which accounts for its schizophrenic nature is the gap between the continuous thought and the discrete language. Words now are only keys opening the way to a continuous comprehension of speech. Only rhythmical texts allow us direct access to the continuous consciousness: in rhythmical texts, as a result of a semantic rhythm, non-synonymous words merge into semantic fields, as happens, for example, in the transcendental poetry of the Russian poet Marina Tsvetayeva or in religious texts, or even in the paradoxes of Wittgenstein's *Tractatus* (Nalimov, 1981*a*). However, any rhythm, including here the semantic rhythm of a text, is now perceived as archaic.

Thus, if human consciousness operates with fuzzy, probabilistically weighted fields of concepts, is it possible to introduce this system of concepts directly into our language? The experience of statisticians, representatives of the subjective probability interpretation, shows that it is extremely difficult, if at all possible, to extract from people prior, probabilistically given ideas of some familiar phenomenon. Though such fuzzy knowledge almost certainly exists, people for some reason or other will not, or perhaps cannot, transfer it to others. This barrier is erected by our culture: it is not customary to reveal the process of thinking; hence, communication goes on at the discrete level.

8. It seems that Western culture is now ready to accept the fact that one phenomenon can be explained by several scientific hypotheses. However, there is still a tendency to evaluate these hypotheses and to select the only true one. If this cannot be done, the situation is evaluated as obviously unsatisfactory. Is it possible to act otherwise, i.e., to perceive the phenomenon through a *field of hypotheses*, without their discrimination? Such an approach now becomes unavoidable even in simulation by computers (Nalimov, 1981*b*). But shall we be able to cope with this at the psychological level: is our mind ready for this vision of the world?

9. As long ago as at the dawn of Christianity, the gnostics proclaimed power to be the protection of *ignorance*. Indeed, if knowledge is expressed by a system of rigid, discrete notions, it will necessarily become more and more fuzzy.[7] The desire to preserve its purity will immediately result in forcible restraint of free thought. And this is a source of tragic aspects in the history of European culture. From the time of the most an-

---

[7] The mechanism of this phenomenon may be explained by proceeding from the theoretico-probabilistic concepts. This question is considered in detail in Chapter 18, section D.

cient priesthoods to the twentieth century, not only books were burned, but their authors as well (as mentioned earlier).

10. It is hard to tell with confidence what is immanent in human nature and what comes from the historical norms of European culture, "non-obligatory" for human nature. The cult of unique knowledge, or unique belief, formed in Western culture and supported by Christian dogmatism, and later by scholastic schools and the deterministic attitude of the Renaissance, does not give either credit or respect to any doubts, hesitation of thought, or probabilism of any kind. In Western culture probabilism is regarded either as a consequence of insufficient knowledge (or shaky belief) or as a superfluous, and therefore reprehensible, sophistication.

11. A schizophrenic aspect of culture is primarily revealed in the necessity to *act*. What makes people act is the discreteness of good and evil, beauty and ugliness, truth and falsity. However, any action is preceded by a *decision*. And this process is always trying; it always leads to bifurcation. Any decision is, perhaps, absurd, since it is an attempt to represent discretely a fuzzy situation which is by no means necessarily determined by a needle-shaped function of the distribution of probabilties. This gives rise to all kinds of stipulations and corrections. Opinion and decision are related as meaning and word. For this reason, just as "a thought, once uttered, is untrue" (Tyutchev), any ultimate categorical decision is erroneous, and to form an opinion on the basis of the decision is simply absurd.

12. Discrete concepts and, moreover, formulations of the *goal, victory, or defeat* are no less absurd (Nalimov, 1981*b*). History is full of examples of a victory turning into a defeat. One of them is the victory of the allies in World War I: without making a detailed analysis of the events that took place afterwards, we still can ask whether perhaps it was this victory that led to the horrible tragedy of Nazism. In the endless human attempts to transform the earth, victory often turned into defeat: the transformed nature turned into a lifeless space. There are also many examples of a goal being too straightforwardly chosen, leading to wild perversions and turning from the coming blessing into an everyday burden.

13. Perhaps the culture of the continuous vision of the world will become "the culture of not-doing," where preference will be given to spontaneous development, and not to the unreserved and destructive activities in the name of a goal to which we are ascribing an unconditional value. But can we possibly imagine such a culture of "not-doing"? Some knowledge has come to us from the Oriental outlook. Something is written in the Gospels: the parable of the birds in the air who neither sow nor reap. We have also read something to the point in the teachings of the

Mexican sorcerer Don Juan recorded by Castañeda (1972). Still, what is "not-doing"? It must not be confused with idleness. The culture of not doing is actually that of "soft" doing. The slogan "Knowledge is power" proclaimed by Francis Bacon needs a more profound interpretation. The power of knowledge should not be suicidal. We have by now accumulated sufficient experience showing that rigid non-probabilistic knowledge generates blind and stupid force. Action in the probabilistic world does not signify a stubborn violation of the world but a collectively comprehended risk that presupposes ways of retreat or changes from the course originally outlined. This is the only way to act when we attempt to change nature. Contemporary technology tempts us to invent and realize grandiose projects. However, ecological forecasts, if possible at all, can only be made in a soft, probabilistic form. Is it not safer to act more cautiously, by introducing into the projects beforehand ways of retreat? Perhaps this is also true of social activities in their broad meaning. Is such a culture of soft doing possible at all? Only the progress of the continuous vision of the world will bring us closer to the answer.

14. And one more sad thought. If rigid logical formulations of assertions did not save humanity from the mighty sweep of wild doctrines, and irrationalism, in its vulgar form, started to serve Nazism, then to what will lead an unrestrained and direct access to the continuous aspects of consciousness by an unprepared person? However, this is quite a separate problem, namely, the heterogeneity of society which will be the carrier to the integral culture.

Must we remark that we are not proving anything? Our task is more modest; we would like to demonstrate that such an approach is also possible.

Chapter 2

Free Will in the Probabilistic World

No idea can be so rightly called undetermined,
polysemantic, open for greatest misunderstandings and
therefore actually subject to them as the idea of
freedom.

G. W. F. HEGEL

Indeed, the antinomy of freedom and necessity has been the concern of European thought at least since the Middle Ages. Thomas Aquinas (1225–1274) believed consistency to be a self-evident and indubitable principle of thinking and existence. Freedom was always unavoidably opposed to necessity. This followed naturally from the rigid determinism of the rationalistic vision of the world. The French scholastic Buridan (1300–1358) believed the problem of free will to be logically unsolvable. His arguments seem to have greatly affected the further evolution of this problem. In any case, well known is the paradox (which, incidentally, does not belong to Buridan) of Buridan's ass which, not having logical grounds for making a decision, starves to death between two identical stacks of hay. By the way, this paradox is a brilliant illustration of how the problem of free will merges with the concept of chance. Indeed, a metaobserver could not tell the manifestation of free will from random behavior if he observed, on the one hand, the fall of a coin (which can fall down heads or tails) and, on the other hand, the real ass which does not actually starve to death between two identical stacks of hay but in the sequence of similar situations chooses one — sometimes the right one and sometimes the left one. The metaobserver would describe both cases by the same binomial distribution function. The coin may be claimed to possess free will to the extent that Buridan's ass does. In other words, what is called random in the physical world in psychology seems to us an instance of free will.

Attempts to remove the antinomy "freedom versus necessity" are still

19

being made, in Marxism (this will be elucidated elsewhere) and in positivism. As an example I would like to quote an elegant paper by Gill (1971) in which freedom is considered within a calculus: to define freedom, three postulates are introduced, and then two theorems are formulated. Naturally, when a calculus is constructed, chance has to be excluded:

> If a given command is contingent, its contradictory opinion is necessary—cannot be rejected without self-contradiction. The agent cannot control himself if he commands or permits an inconsistency. If a prohibition is contingent—not necessary—its contradictory permission is necessary (p. 9).

However, we find such reasoning fairly artificial.

A probabilistic vision of the world removes the problem of free will from consideration, and its dramatic quality disappears. Everything is explained in a very simple way.

This can be illustrated by the perception of verbal meanings. In an earlier book (Nalimov, 1981a) I claimed that the perception of verbal meanings is determined by two distribution functions, namely, $p(\mu)$, the prior distribution function of the meaning of the word μ, and $p(y|\mu)$, the filter arising in the person's mind when he analyzes the meaning of the word μ in a phrase y. During comprehension of the phrase y, the prior distribution function of the word's meaning is reduced by the filtering function according to Bayes's theorem

$$p(\mu|y) = kp(\mu)p(y|\mu)$$

and we get the posterior distribution function[1] of the word μ that determines its meaning in the new concrete phrase y. Distribution functions $p(\mu)$ and $p(y|\mu)$ are both individual, and in this sense they manifest a person's free will. At the same time, they are to some extent determined by the culture in which the person lives, by his social status and upbringing. This is the manifestation of non-freedom, or of the notorious necessity. Manifestations of freedom are not absolute. Freedom exists in the possibility of varying the distribution functions determined to some extent by the culture to which the person belongs.

In my earlier book (Nalimov, 1981a) I introduced a scale of languages which determines the degree of freedom in comprehending texts. For hard languages there is less freedom and for soft languages there is more. But even for such a hard language as that of physics, texts can be interpreted with a certain amount of freedom. In quantum mechanics the

---

[1] Here k is a constant of normalizing: the area limited by the abscissa and the curve $p(\mu|y)$ must be unity.

constructions are compared to experimentation in a certain definite way, but at the same time metastatements on quantum mechanics are very different. This is well illustrated by the collection of statements by physicists and philosophers quoted previously (Nalimov, 1981*a*) on the meaning of the ψ function, compiled by the American philosopher Abel (1969). In soft languages the freedom in comprehending texts is uncommonly great. Capra (1975) describes the freedom in comprehending Ancient Chinese texts as follows:

> Both the Confucian Analects and the *Tao Te Ching* are written in the compact suggestive style which is typical of the Chinese way of thinking. The Chinese mind was not given to abstract logical thinking and developed a language which is very different from that which evolved in the West. Many of its words could be used as nouns, adjectives or verbs, and their sequence was determined not so much by grammatical rules as by the emotional content of the sentence. The classical Chinese word was very different from an abstract sign representing a clearly delineated concept. It was rather a sound symbol which had strong suggestive powers, bringing to mind an indeterminate complex of pictorial images and emotions. The intention of the speaker was not so much to express an intellectual idea, but rather to affect and influence the listener. Correspondingly, the written character was not just an abstract sign, but was an organic pattern — a "gestalt" — which preserved the full complex of images and the suggestive power of the word.
>
> Since the Chinese philosophers expressed themselves in a language which was so well suited for their way of thinking, their writings and sayings could be short and inarticulate, and yet rich in suggestive images. It is clear that much of this imagery must be lost in an English translation. A translation of a sentence from the *Tao Te Ching*, for example, can only render a small part of the rich complex of ideas contained in the original, which is why different translations from this controversial book often look like totally different texts. As *Fung Yu-Lan* has said, "It needs a combination of all the translations already made and many others not yet made, to reveal the richness of the *Lao-tzu* and the Confucian Analects in their original form." (p. 103–104)

In language, free will is expressed by a stratum of polymorphous words forming fields of meanings which are sometimes fuzzy to such a degree that they include even antonyms:

> **spare:** (1) additional to what is usually needed or used; in reserve for use when needed ⟨∼ cash⟩ ⟨∼ parts⟩ ⟨∼ room⟩ ⟨∼ time⟩; (2) small in quantity ⟨∼ diet⟩.
>
> **to bless:** (1) ask God's favor for; consecrate; make sacred or holy ⟨to ∼ oneself⟩ ⟨to ∼ one's stars⟩; (2) to praise, to call holy; (3) be fortu-

nate in having; (4) (iron. or euphem.) used for a word of opposite meaning, "curse, damn," etc. I'm blest — expresses surprise.

to abstract: (1) take out, separate; (2) to separate in mental conception; to consider apart from the material embodiment or from particular instances; (3) to make an abstract of; to summarize; (4) (colloq.) steal.

Antonyms express, perhaps, the maximal degree of polymorphism, its completeness. I would venture to suggest that the most semantically developed words are characterized by the presence of antonyms in their semantic field. The conclusion seems to be as follows: antonyms are the manifestation of free will in the language or even the property of free will in its verbal form.

Since we have started to speak of the East, let us consider here the problem of *karma*. I would like to emphasize that this concept is rigidly deterministic, which is rather non-typical of the free Oriental outlook which we find so attractive. In any case, this concept is in obvious discordance with the game model of the world which is so explicit in all Ancient Indian conceptions. It seems quite probable that the concept of karma came into Ancient Indian consciousness from the remotest past and is unavoidably marked by the lack of alternatives peculiar to magic thinking. It has created a specific situation: this concept has preserved its archaic content, and it has also entered the soft system of concepts of the later outlook. A European thinker always tries to divide everything. Manifestations of karma must be rigid. Otherwise, what is its meaning?

However, the probabilistic vision of the world allows us to perceive the law of karma as a fuzzy one which admits the existence of free will. I consider it relevant here to draw a parallel with the physical picture of the microworld presented by Born (1949):

> [in quantum mechanics] we have the paradoxical situation that observable events obey laws of chance, but that the probability for these events itself spreads according to laws which are in all essential features causal laws. (p 103)[2]

---

[2] In quantum theory causality is expressed by the famous Schrödinger equation. Its simplest form is as follows:

$$i\hbar \frac{\partial \psi}{\partial t} = \mathbf{H}\psi$$

Now if we deal with a quantum ensemble exhaustively described by a set of dynamic variables $q_1, q_2, \ldots$, which are measured simultaneously and independently, the probability of finding a definite value of the set is determined by the probability density

$$W_M(q) = |\psi_M(q)|^2$$

The wave function ψ_M is explicitly given as a function of the coordinates q. It determines the *statistics* of any measurement of the microsystem compatible with a macrosystem M which dictates the conditions for

Perhaps the effects of karma should be described by a similarly paradoxical system of notions in order that its principal idea be understood by a European. Indeed, personal possibilities may be said to be determined by a field of elementary events. Karma determines a distribution function of probabilities on this field of potentially possible events [the function $p(\mu)$ in our terms] for each person and in each birth. The distribution function evolves according to the karmic predetermination, but this latter proves to be fuzzy, or probabilistically weighted. In each concrete situation a person can make his *own* decision. This latter can again be represented by a fuzzy, probabilistically weighted filter [our function $p(y|\mu)$]. Then we can apply the Bayesian theorem which explains the way the potential possibility determined by the past interacts with the freedom of actions. Freedom exists in the possibility of redistributing the weights in the karmic situation. And though this state of things is much more complicated than in the case of Buridan's ass, it is also describable within the system of probabilistic notions. Whereas in the case of Buridan's ass free will may be represented as a generator of random binary numbers, people facing the karmic predetermination respond by generating the probabilistic filter of perception, and this is, as a matter of fact, the manifestation of their individuality. Within this model, overcoming the karmic predetermination will unavoidably lead to the elimination of individuality. Indeed, if μ, the function of the karmic predetermination, degenerates into an untruncated (tending to infinity) uniform distribution, then the interval cut off on the ordinate by the straight line determining this distribution will tend to zero, and generation of any filtering function will become an utterly useless task. It will turn into nothing or into everything, if this everything is void of selective abilities (attachments or preferences). This is exactly *nirvana* expressed in the language of probabilistic notions.

In the terms of the American protestant theologian Paul Tillich (1955), $p(\mu)$ is a fuzzily determined destiny, $p(y|\mu)$ is an ethical constituent in overcoming one's destiny in a situation y, and $p(\mu|y)$ is a reduction of destiny by the ethical constituent.

And now a few words on the game model of the world. A European who has just begun his acquaintance with the East is most of all puzzled by the concept of the world as a game: to his mind this idea is humiliating, and arbitrarily flimsy. But matters stand differently in the probabilistic interpretation. A game is a fuzzy, probabilistically weighted situation which enables us to overcome the karma of individuals and en-

---

the changes in the microsystem (Blokhintsev, 1966). It is possible to speak of a probabilistically determined potential for a certain behavior under certain macroconditions even for a single electron. Potentiality may be said to be a probabilistically determined limit of freedom given to an electron.

tire peoples. The advent of the spiritually elevated aeon on the Earth can only change the distribution of probabilities but in no way determines the rigid way of evolution. This is what happened during the advent of Christ.

And the last thing is Theodicy,[3] the poignant problem of rationalistic theology. In the probabilistic vision of the world it merely disappears, as follows from all said above. Christ refused to take the power from the tempting devil and thus let the world retain its spontaneity. However, something very important in the world did change, and different people could perceive these changes differently.

Everything said above concerns the partial, relative manifestation of freedom. According to Indian concepts, its complete realization becomes possible only when a person overcomes his karma and, according to Christianity, when he learns the truth. But to leave the cycle of births is the same as to learn the truth: this means communion with God. Freedom proves to be the *synonym* for God, but God then becomes the *synonym* for nothing—nirvana.

Stated another way, for a person in a state of absolute freedom, the meaning of the concept "freedom" is lost. Is there any sense in asserting the freedom of choice of the filter $p(y|\mu)$ if the function $p(\mu)$ becomes a specific case of the rectangular distribution with the ordinate tending to zero? (Strictly speaking, if the argument tends to infinity, the concept of rectangular distribution loses the probabilistic meaning.)

*   *   *

I am quite aware of the fact that the ideas presented in this chapter may irritate many readers. The probabilistic vision of the world does not solve the poignant problems of European philosophy and theology; it only withdraws them from consideration. All the problems underlying our culture turn out to be merely pseudoproblems. Indeed, it has suddenly become obvious that European thought came to a standstill in dealing with the following dichotomous concepts generated within its culture:

subjective	objective
mind	matter
continuity	discreteness
chance	necessity
freedom	predetermination

---

[3] Theodicy is the justification of God. The term, introduced by Leibniz in 1710, unites numerous doctrines which attempt to coordinate the idea of the benevolent God, who rationally rules the world, with the existence of evil.

dialectics	logic
gnosticism	agnosticism
spontaneity	regularity
infinite	finite
life	death
good	evil
truth	falsity
conscience	duty
mercy	punishment
God	atheistic mechanisticity of the world

If we make these concepts fuzzy, the dichotomous oppositions will disappear: each opposition will merge into one semantic field and, moreover, all the oppositions will turn out to be synonymous. All the problems thus disappear. But will new, real problems arise? In other words, will a new culture emerge?

It is noteworthy that European culture emerged while solving problems which actually were unsolvable. Did the Orient solve real problems? And what are real problems?

Chapter 3

Probabilistic Approach to Describing the Evolution of Texts

> *Jesus took them all by stealth, for he did not reveal himself as he [really] was, but he revealed himself as they would be able to see him . . . he revealed himself to them . . . to the great as great . . . little as little . . . to angels as an angel, and to men as a man. Because of this his logos hid itself from everyone. Some indeed saw him, while they thought they were seeing themselves, but when he appeared to his disciples in glory on the mount he was not small. He became great, but he made the disciples great, that they might be able to see him in his greatness. He said on that day in the thanksgiving (εὐχαριστία): Thou who hast joined the perfect, the light, with the Holy spirit, unite the angels with us also, the images.*
>
> THE APOCRYPHAL GOSPEL OF PHILIP

No matter what we are, scholars, poets, or unbiased observers scrutinizing the surrounding world, we are seeking in it clarity, order, and harmony. The world is seen as a text. And through texts accessible to our consciousness we interact with the world.

The integrity of the world finds its expression in *language* which unites all individual manifestations of life *as the Whole*. This may account for the temptation to describe by a single model both the evolution of the texts of our culture and that of the texts of the biosphere.

Proceeding from Monod's (1972) interpretation of evolution as a process generated by distortions overlaying the initial biological text, Ivanov and Toporov (1975) made a theoretical–informational reformulation of the evolution of mythological texts. They wrote:

> Various transformations of the initial text (a myth, in particular)

26

are considered as leading to a distortion of the text, the invariant scheme being preserved. (p. 50)

Such a transformational approach to the description of evolution in its broad meaning is undoubtedly attractive. But in order to make it meaningful, one has to answer the question of whether the distortions affect the process additively or multiplicatively. Because it is so important, the answer to this question will have the status of an initial premise. If we acknowledge the multiplicative character of distortions, we shall lose the formal criterion separating signal and a distortion,[1] and we shall be tempted to perceive what we have called a distortion as an incomprehensible text.

If we view the world non-linearly (i.e., we assume that the noise and the signal are multiplied, not added), we shall have difficulties in naming one of the interacting factors a text (a signal) and the other a distortion (noise).

Using the Bayesian approach (Nalimov, 1981a), I proceeded from the multiplicative nature of interaction of the two probability distribution functions $p(\mu)$ and $p(y|\mu)$, regarding the first one as an initial text and the second as a preference filter. But the rules of the language game allow us to change the interpretation as well. The object under consideration requires such a re-interpretation. It is difficult to imagine the evolution of a structure—a manifestation of something new—as an additive process formed by the ceaseless additions of small noise components, besides unstructured. The idea of evolution as a transformation can be comprehended only by means of a multiplicative model that enables us to see the change of the existing pattern as a whole affected by another pattern. As to the additive character, only the microevolution of a text can be such. It seems possible to select a weak form of transformational evolution and a strong one. We shall confine ourselves to the latter.

If we consider biological evolution as an example, the species undergoing evolution[2] can be viewed as an initial text whose constituents (with respect to their significance) are described by the prior distribution function $p(\mu)$ while the changeability acts as a noise filter $p(y|\mu)$ showing the way an attribute y which belongs to the field of attributes μ can be modified. However, this may be interpreted otherwise if we assume that a completely new text $p(y|\mu)$ has appeared in the field of evolutionary potentialities; this text is to be transformed through the filter $p(\mu)$ determined by the existing species. Evolution is a series of sequential passages of the type $p_0(\mu) \rightarrow p_0(\mu|y) \rightarrow p_1(\mu) \rightarrow p_1(\mu|y), \ldots$; i.e., the posterior

[1] If the effect of distortions (noise) is additive, the criterion will be the insignificance of its contribution.

[2] In Chapter 1 I spoke in detail on the possibility of the probabilistic approach to biological taxonomy (see also Meyen and Nalimov, 1978).

distribution function turns into the prior at the next step—it turns into a new filter. Otherwise, we proceed from the idea of directed evolution. At the initial, zero stage of evolution there exists an initial text symbolically recorded as $p_0(\mu)$. In the process of evolution this text proves to be a receiver ready to perceive a text $p_0(y|\mu)$ existing as a potential power directing the evolution in the situation y. In such an interpretation function $p_0(\mu)$ may be regarded as a filter of the receiver. As a result of the interaction with the initial text $p_0(y|\mu)$ determining the evolutionary process, there emerges the posterior text $p_0(\mu|y)$ which immediately becomes a filter for the second evolutionary impetus. Symbolically we record it as $p_0(\mu|y) \rightarrow p_1(\mu)$. *It is not the initial text but the filter which changes in the process of evolution.* If this change proves unfavorable, i.e., the filter does not acquire a capacity favorable for the new text $p(y|\mu)$ (here the variable y denotes changes occurring in the medium undergoing evolution), the species is either extinguished or reaches a deadend. Perhaps insects[3] turned into such a blind-alley branch: the number of their species reaches millions, but the species themselves are strikingly conservative.

Within our system of concepts, noise is no longer an evolutionary factor though description remains probabilistic. The major role is played by the emergence of a new text given by the function $p(y|\mu)$. We can use the term "probabilistic nomogenesis" [though, as created by Berg (1969), it was of a purely deterministic character; Teilhard de Chardin (1965), proceeding from different premises, also developed the concept of directed evolution as tending to the point Ω]. Representing evolution as a process determined by the probabilistic effect of a new text, we politely introduce into biological science the concept of consciousness, without which, according to Efron (1977) "biological science suffers from a progressive and potentially fatal epistemological disorder."

The same seems to be true of the evolution of any text, including myths. The initial myths may be said to act as filters distorting the new texts whose mechanism of formation is rather incomprehensible. The history of Christianity may also be regarded as a ceaseless filtration of the completely new text through the initial pagan notions which have undergone a slight evolution. Is it possible to say that the depths of the Christian *Weltanschauung* have resulted from the addition of noise to pagan myths?

It is noteworthy that ancient thinkers were quite aware of the fact that new texts could only be perceived to the extent that their listeners were

---

[3] We may suppose that the evolution of insects could have gone toward the development of the central nervous system which would have unavoidably been connected with a general increase in their size, but beetles, for example, have a very delicate chitinous coat, and this could have created an obstacle to the increase of their size.

prepared to do this: evidence for this can be found in the fragment quoted at the beginning of this chapter.

It is relevant to draw the reader's attention to the recent emergence in the West of the fashion of depriving a man of ideology and mythology: this brought about the cult of the "naked man" freed from his cultural past (see, for example, Brune, 1973). But, as follows from what was said in the preceding chapter, the prior distribution function $p(\mu)$ was going to degenerate into the untruncated (going to the infinity) rectangular distribution, while the segment cut by the straight line on the ordinate would tend to zero. And, according to the model based on Bayes's theorem, the new text with the semantics given by the function $p(y|\mu)$ will simply not be perceived. A person removed from society goes down to the level of an animal which does not understand our texts as a result of its semantic unpreparedness. We find the result obtained non-trivial. However, what is said here is true only for the endless consciousness with infinitely stretched semantic field. Comparing the contents of this chapter and the preceding one, we may draw the following conclusion: the idea of the *absolutely free person is senseless*. The concept of *free will* can be comprehended only for an *unfree* person. Here lies the paradox of freedom.

The progress of science also consists of the endless filtration of new ideas through the filter of paradigmatic criteria carried by past conceptions. And if the filters prove unable to evolve to more plastic forms, they are overthrown by revolution. In the history of Western Christianity, this found its expression in religious and ideological wars and revolutions, and in science, in the revolutionary change of paradigms so brilliantly described by Kuhn (1970). This explains Bakunin's words: "The destroying spirit is a creative spirit."

Note that it is not the initial set μ which is destroyed, but the probability distribution function given on it which plays the role of a filter with respect to the new text probabilistically given on the same set. I would like to emphasize that the perception of new texts always requires softening of the old filters, though not their complete destruction. Evolution also presupposes succession though it is sometimes accompanied by explosions.

New texts are always a result of free creativity realized on a probabilistic set which may be regarded as an unexposed semantic universe or *nothing*, the semantic vacuum or, metaphorically, an analogue of the physical vacuum. Here we have to deal with the problem of *nothing* which stimulated thinkers both in the East (nirvana) and in the West (gnostics: Eckhart, Boehme, Schelling, Sartre, Heidegger, Jung, Tillich). I am going to devote three chapters to this important subject.

The transfer of Monod's concepts onto culturological ground can be quite easily traced historically; it turns out to be a peculiar experiment falsifying the former (in terms of Popper). We might as well say that this is an example showing the legitimacy of using a single approach to study seemingly incompatible texts of evolution.

And now a few words clarifying my methodology.

A text, as follows from the meaning of the term, has two facets: discrete (semiotic) and continuous (semantic). In the texts of everyday language, the discrete elements are words; in nucleic texts, they are codons. But both words and codons are only triggers starting a mechanism that manifests itself on the continuous level. Words may be said to be semantically polymorphous, while with respect to texts of the animate world one can speak of the pleiotropy of genes. The continuous nature of everyday language finds its expression in the limitless divisibility of the verbal meanings, while the continuous nature of the morphology of the animate world is expressed by the impossibility of constructing a discrete taxonomy.[4]

There is a tendency to consider verbal (or codon) manifestation of both languages — that of the anthroposphere and that of the biosphere — as the initial cause for the semantic manifold contained in their texts. But another approach is also possible, in which everything taking place on the discrete level is considered only as one facet of a complicated process far from determining its complete evolution. We are prone to believe that everything taking place on the continuous level can be described by a multiplicative model rather than by structural–combinatorial models of an additive effect.

Imagine an operator sitting in front of a control board and mixing fragments of musical texts with the hope of forming a new text. Now assume that he gets tired of varying the turnings of the handles and starts to turn them always according to a certain pattern but sometimes makes mistakes due to fatigue and boredom. The model of the bored Demiurge reduced to the level of the generator of randomness, developed by Monod, is, as a matter of fact, no less theological than all other models of the origin of essentially new texts (though the theological nature of certain models is camouflaged by the conception of evolution as a way to perfection). However, its deficiency lies not in the least in its theological nature but in its incompleteness: the phenomena are described only on the level of triggers. And an attempt to describe the evolution of texts on

---

[4] The existing discrete biological taxonomy is but a rough approximation to reality. Using this classification, one constantly comes across borderline cases when no unambiguous decision can be made, though logical foundations of the system do not preview such possibilities. Rigid discreteness of classification generated the idea of abnormalities in the animate world, and this, in its turn, brought about the necessity to systematize and study these phenomena. This was discussed in detail in Chapter 1.

the level of triggers seems to represent reductionism to the computerized vision of the world.

What is said above is nothing more than an attempt to describe by symbols the phenomenologically observed facts. Like any other scientific description, it does not explain the essence of things but only produces new problems or, to be more cautious, deepens the old ones.

Chapter 4

The Language of Numerical Vision of the World in Ancient Times

Dialectics of the Continuous vs. Discrete in Plotinus's Tractatus *On Numbers*

> *Christ is he who is measured.*
> THE APOCRYPHAL
> GOSPEL OF PHILLIP

The probabilistic vision of the world being developed here may be regarded as a realization of the dream of Pythagoras and Plotinus[1] of describing the world in its integrity and fuzziness through *number*. In his tractatus *On Numbers* Plotinus attempted to reveal the meaning of the Universe through the analysis of the single notion of *number*. As the reader can easily see, Plotinus was a true *dialectician*, a representative of the Ancient Greek dialectics which Hegel strove in vain to restore. Perhaps this dialectics is connected with Ancient Egypt via Pythagoras.

We find the tractatus to be manifold, though verbose despite the laconic and fragmentary style of some propositions. Strange as it may seem, the idea is much more clear as expressed by fragmentary, often paradoxical formulations than in the subsequent verbose explanations. Below I quote certain excerpts from this wonderful tractatus which seem to me most interesting. The tractatus is difficult to understand. It is an expanded *koan*. Dialectical analysis of the koan in no way signifies that its meaning is revealed in a deductive way. Plotinus many times reformulates one and the same proposition as applied to different problems. This enables us to perceive the koan at various angles. The reader must be able

---

[1] Biographical information on Plotinus is given in the appendix to Chapter 7.

to unite features which cannot be united logically and to see them in their manifoldness. This is exactly dialectics, dialectics of seeing the world in one word. To comprehend the tractatus, one must enter a specific, altered state of consciousness. I hope that the previous chapter has helped to create an adequate tuning.

A thing, in fact, becomes a manifold when, unable to remain self-centered, it flows outward and by that dissipation takes extension: utterly losing unity it becomes a manifold, since there is nothing to bind part to part; when, with all this overflowing, it becomes something definite, there is a magnitude.

. . . a thing is itself not by being extended but by remaining, in its degree, a unity: through expansion and in the measure of the expansion, it is less itself; retaining unity, it retains its essential being.

What, then, of the "Number of the Infinite"? To begin with, how is Number consistent with infinity?

Objects of sense are not unlimited and therefore the Number applying to them cannot be so. Nor is an enumerator able to number to infinity; though we double, multiply over and over again, we still end with a finite number; though we range over past and future, and consider them, even, as a totality, we still end with the finite.

Are we then to dismiss absolute limitlessness and think merely that there is always something beyond?

No; that more is not in the reckoner's power to produce; the total stands already defined.

. . . we make a man a multiple by counting up his various characteristics, his beauty and the rest . . .

Whatever is in actual existence is by that very fact determined numerically.

. . . approach the thing as a unit and you find it manifold; call it a manifold, and again you falsify, for when the single thing is not a unity neither is the total a manifold . . . Thus it is not true to speak of it (Matter, the unlimited) as being solely in flux.

It is inevitably necessary to think of all as contained within one nature; one nature must hold and encompass all; there cannot be as in the realm of sense thing apart from thing; here a sun and elsewhere something else; all must be naturally present within a unity. This is the very nature of the Intellectual-Principle . . .

. . . But within the unity There, the several entities have each its own distinct existence.

. . . It is surely inconceivable that any living thing be beautiful failing a Life-Absolute of a wonderful, an ineffable beauty; this must be the Collective Life, made up of all living things, or embracing all, forming a unity coextensive with all, as our universe is a unity embracing all the visible.

When it takes lot with multiplicity, Being becomes Number by the fact of awakening to manifoldness; . . .

We may be told that unity and monad have no real existence, that the only unity is some definite object that is one thing, so that all comes to an attitude of the mind towards things considered singly. But is this attitude, this concept itself, a unity or a manifold? When we deny the unity of an object, clearly the unity mentioned is not supplied by the object since we are saying it has none; the unity therefore is within ourselves, something latent in our minds independently of any concrete one thing.

If, then, unity is more pronounced in the continuous, and more again where there is no separation by part, this is clearly because there exists, in real existence, something which is a Nature or Principle of Unity.

If by division the one identical mass can become a duality without loss of quantity, clearly the unity is possessed and by this destructive division lost was something distinct. What may be alternatively present and absent to the same subject must be classed among Real-Beings, regardless of position; an accidental elsewhere, it must have reality in itself whether it be manifested in things of sense or in the Intellectual—an accidental in the Laters but self-existent in the higher, especially in the First in its aspects of Unity developing into Being. We may be told that Unity may lose that character without change in itself, becoming duality by association with something else; but this is not true; unity does not become two things; neither the added nor what takes the addition becomes two; each remains the one thing it was; the duality is predictable of the group only, the unity remaining unchanged in each of those unchanged constituents.

. . . while continuous quantity exists, discrete quantity does not—and this though continuous quantity is measured by the discrete.

. . . the Intellectual-Principle by its very nature contains all intelligences as several members within itself. Now all this means Number There. Yet even in Intellect Number is not present primally; its presence There is the reckoning of the Acts of Intellectual-Principle; it tallies with the justice of Intellectual-Principle, its moral wisdom, its virtues, its knowledge, all whose possession makes that Principle what it is.

The Number belonging to body is an essence of the order of body; the number belonging to Soul constitutes the essence of souls.

By this analysis and totalling you get quantity; but there are two objects under consideration and each of these is one; each of the unities contributes to the complete being and the oneness is inherent in each; this is another kind of number, number essential; even the duality so formed is no posterior; it does not signify a quantity apart from the thing but the quantity in the essence which holds the thing together. The number here is no mere result of your detailing; the things exist of themselves and are not brought together by your reckoning, but what has it to do with essential reality that you count one man in with another? . . .

The Number inherent apart from any enumeration has its own manner of being, but the other, that resulting upon the appearance of an external to be appraised by the Number within yourself, is either an Act of these inherent numbers or an Act in accordance with them; in counting we produce number and so bring quantity into being just as in walking we bring a certain movement into being.

When you enumerate two things—say, animal and beauty—each of these remains one thing; the number is your production; it lay within yourself; it is you that elaborate quantity, here the dyad. But when you declare virtue to be a Tetrad, you are affirming a Tetrad which does actually exist; the parts, so to speak, make one thing; you are taking as the object of your act a Unity-Tetrad to which you accommodate the Tetrad within yourself.

It appears then that Number in that realm is definite; There every being is measure; and therefore it is that all is beautiful.

In virtue of this Essence it is that life endures, that the Intellectual-Principle endures, that the Beings stand in their eternity; nothing alters it, turns it, moves it; nothing, indeed, is in being beside it to touch it; anything that is must be its product; anything opposed to it could not affect it. Being itself could not make such an opposite into Being; that would require a prior to both and that prior would then be Being, so that Parmenides was right when he taught the identity of Being and Unity. Being is thus beyond contact not because it stands alone but because it is Being. For Being alone has Being in its own right . . . every soul and every intellect seeks to be its Being; but Being is sufficient to itself.

The tractatus *On Numbers* finishes with the last proposition quoted above. Reading it, I could not help wondering whether my paper written in co-authorship with S. V. Meyen (see Chapter 1 of this book) is but a contemporary comment on Plotinus's reflections on the organizing role of a number. Our basic concept is the probabilistic vision of the world. In the tractatus by Plotinus, everything is "determined numerically"; "every being is measure"; "the Number . . . has its own manner of being"; number "constitutes" both our soul and our body. At the same time, Plotinus understood that the numbers which determine Beings in multiplicity somehow differ from those which are used in a numerical process. Perhaps he guessed vaguely that what he had in mind was a probabilistic measure which weighs multiplicity and creates unity, Being. Again, the past in the present!

We can continue our comparison: our concept of the continuous fields of consciousness is in resonance with Plotinus's ideas of the Intellectual Being and Intellect Number which cannot be measured. Thus he expressed a clear-cut, almost contemporary concept of continuity which cannot be counted by a countable set (these two sets cannot be put into one-to-one correspondence).

In §14 of the Tractatus, the author introduced the concept of infinite divisibility: "while continuous quantity exists, discrete quantity does not—and this though continuous quantity is measured by the discrete." In contemporary set theory the continuum is still described by discrete points, though a point is considered a degenerate continuum.

It seems relevant to remind the reader of our interpretation of human speech as discrete symbols charged with continuous semantics. According to Plotinus, the whole visible world represents discrete symbols of the text generated by the continuous power of the First Existent.

In conclusion, I would like to compare Plotinus's views with gnosticism. The Gnostics wrote of the omnipresence of Christ. Plotinus expressed holistic ideas of the unity of the world penetrated or, more accurately, constituted by universal wisdom and universal intellect. In a certain sense both Plotinus and the gnostics proceeded from a single vision of the world, but the gnostics made their outlook known through a myth whereas Plotinus expressed it in a koan on numbers. The language of our culture makes it easier for us to speak of the probabilistic vision of the world, this time in a new manner, but again through a koan of numbers.

However, hermeneutics is but the art of seeing the new in the old, and this viewpoint is, of course, utterly personal.

Chapter 5

On the Metaphorical Nature of the Language of Probabilistic Concepts

I feel that what is said in the previous chapters needs some comments. Having consciously rejected the accepted techniques of constructing mathematical models, I started developing a language that makes a metaphorical use of mathematical notions; I assumed that this was the way to overcome seemingly insurmountable difficulties in comprehending the nature of human consciousness.

Psychologists, especially those who are engaged in studying the problems of language, thinking, and consciousness, are at the moment seriously troubled by the failures to construct traditional mathematical models. It is possible to claim that mathematical models have been fruitfully applied in psychophysiology (see, for example, Leonov, 1977), but the psychology of thinking, as well as that of the unconscious, has remained non-mathematized. In these fields too, there have been a few attempts at mathematization. The reader might be referred to numerous papers by Chudakov (e.g., 1977) and Chavchanidze (e.g., 1970, 1974) and also to the paper by Stuart et al. (1979) aimed at constructing a quantum-mechanical model of informational–psychological processes, but, to my mind, these papers do not seem to attract the attention of psychologists because they are extremely physicalistic and, therefore, far from the real psychological problems. As to linguistics, well known are papers on mathematical linguistics leading to the theory of context-free languages (see, for example, Ginsburg, 1966). But they regard language as a formal system alienated from the peculiarities of human thinking. It is not without reason that the Large Soviet Encyclopaedia even claims that *mathematical linguistics* does not belong to linguistics in general. Though this claim is perhaps too categorical, it is nevertheless true to a certain degree.

The Russian psychologist Brushlinsky (1979) thoroughly discussed the requirements a psychologist studying the problems of thinking could make for mathematical models. Here are some of them: non-disjunctivity, i.e., inseparability of cognitive and affective aspects of thinking; non-additivity of the stages of the process of thinking; ability to reflect aspects of behavior which are beyond logic (people come to the conclusion that something is true not only by means of pure logic); fuzziness of concepts—the absence of clear-cut boundaries between the classes to which an object of study may belong. The ontological problem of whether the world is a class of distinctly differentiated objects is being seriously discussed.

Is our existing mathematics sufficient to satisfy all these requirements? In discussing this question, Brushlinsky draws the reader's attention to the words of another Russian psychologist, Bernshtein (1965), on the necessity to develop new biological branches from the very essence of the problems which the life sciences have to face. I have come across similar ideas in other papers discussing the specific demands made on mathematical models in life sciences [see, for example, the concluding article by M. Williams in the collection of papers edited by Solomon and Walter (1977)].

Indeed, if the problem is considered more broadly and the question is formulated as "What have we achieved by mathematical models in biology?" the answer will be quite optimistic: special journals, numerous publications and monographs, even guides to models [see, for example, Holden (1976) or Sampath and Srinivasan (1977)]. However, these activities are around biology rather than within it. This is true in part because throughout the world biologists are not taught mathematics to the degree that would enable them to understand these models. But if they are not taught, this means there is no necessity to teach. Is this possible, for example, in physics?

However, mathematicians (and this was noted by Brushlinsky as well) did not answer the call to create mathematics specially oriented for describing life processes. This is only natural since this call did not contain any new mathematical idea.

I believe that the difficulties of constructing mathematical models may be largely explained by the fact that biologists and psychologists try to construct them in order to obtain a literal, mechanistic interpretation of phenomena. This is what happened in early physics. Newton had created an easily perceived model of the discrete world. Mechanics acted as the universal law of motion of the material particles which seemed to construct the entire variety of objects existing in the world. Bodies affected one another at a distance (long-range interaction) without any intermediary. However, this clear and obvious picture of the world started to dissipate after Faraday and Maxwell introduced the concept of a field in order to describe the effect of electric and magnetic forces. There emerged the concept of the physical continuum. It became possible to speak of short-range interaction: the charged point modifies space around itself. When the field evolves, its characteristics change simultaneously in an infinite number of points. The famous equations of Maxwell initiated the new vision of the world. And the mathematical models of modern physics, as was brilliantly shown by Hutten (1956), are metaphors. They lack physical vividness of presentation. The phenomenon described behaves similarly to, but not the same as, the model. A model is required only to *resemble*, not to be identical. The resemblance may be achieved by introducing into the model speculative symbols which have no direct and unambiguous interpretation in terms of the physical world. Such a symbol is the well-known ψ function in quantum mechanics. The American philosopher Abel (1969) compiled an interesting and extremely heterogeneous collection of statements by physicists on the ontological meaning of this function. [This collection is partly reproduced in my earlier book (Nalimov, 1981*a*)]. His article concludes by asking whether we can say we know something which we have been unable to put into words. I believe that we can if the scientific concept turns from a familiar scientific term with a rather unambiguous meaning into an extremely semantically polymorphous *symbol* with a metaphorical flavor. A word, a sign of our language, is contrasted here to a symbol since these two notions are not completely synonymous.

A metaphorical problem may be constructed for a specially invented situation which can be imagined but does not actually take place. Constructing such models turns into a kind of art: the modeller must become a symbolist–poet. He creates a model–symbol by means of which he does not so much actually describe the phenomenon as consider it from a new angle. The model proves to be nothing more than a hint. It makes use of the ability inherent in people from the days of yore to control their consciousness through symbols.

It was mentioned above that quantum-mechanical models of thinking had not been made use of by psychologists; perhaps this happened simply because their metaphorical content was not rich enough. They could not make psychologists see things from a new angle and, therefore, could not set new problems in front of them. Psychologists might find essential what follows from the von Neumann interpretation of quantum mechanics, namely, the necessity to acknowledge the existence of consciousness in nature, able to change the impulse and energy of a particle. What we have in mind is the experiment in which energy and impulse of the particle change when, moving from the source to the receiver, it passes through the hole in the sphere surrounding the source. On its way the particle does not interact with the field or other particles, and consequently, according to von Neumann, the change in energy and impulse occurs as a result of the awareness of the fact that the particle had flown through a hole. This is not to assert the direct influence of consciousness on the energy and impulse transfer, but only to emphasize the change in the probability of the realization of certain events. Consciousness thus proves as fundamental as, for example, electromagnetic field.

Below, an attempt is made to illustrate what is meant by speaking of the metaphorical use of probabilistic notions in the psychology of thinking. Note, by the way, that metaphorical use of mathematical and physical notions in psychology is in no way new. The concept of psychological spaces (Welwood, 1977*b*), of the spectrum of consciousness (Wilber, 1977), or the holographic model of transpersonal consciousness (Anderson, 1977), as well as my concept of continuous thinking, are but metaphors. We are quite aware of the fact that semantic fields of consciousness do not represent the numerical continuum, but in some sense they behave so as to enable us to speak of the continuous nature of consciousness. An abstract mathematical idea of the continuum acquires a metaphorical resonance.

In the first three chapters of this book, as well as in my earlier book (Nalimov, 1981*a*), I was constantly using certain semantic manifolds whose separate fragments differ in value. For example, in a bilingual dictionary words explaining the meaning of an entry are arranged in a sequence corresponding to their accepted values within our culture. In the Large Ancient Greek-Russian dictionary the concept λογος is first of all translated as "word, speech," and its meanings "number" and "calculus" occupy, respectively, the thirty-second and thirty-third positions. We thus forget that in the Hellenic world the famous beginning of the Gospel according to St. John could be interpreted as follows: "In the beginning was the Number, and the Number was with God, and the Number was God." The explanatory words in dictionaries are only marks on the scale μ. Dictionaries do not provide us with numerical values for the degrees of preference which our culture ascribes to various segments on the scale μ, but we proceed from the assumption that in the depths of our consciousness such numerical values do exist. Otherwise, how could we be able to ascribe any meaning at all to a text? I assume such a manifold to be metrically ordered on the axis μ representing either the straight line or a segment of it. Ascribing different weights to different segments, we obtain a weighting function which determines the fuzziness of the manifold in question.

After normalization (the area under the curve is unity), we are dealing with the distribution function of probabilities (the remaining axioms of the probability theory can be accepted without special notice), and in our psycho-semiotic research we were constantly making use of the weighting function interpreted as the distribution of probabilities. Note that the concept itself of a non-normalized weighting function is absurd; non-normalized weighting functions remain incomparable. A normalized weighting function can be regarded as a two-dimensional analogue of the familiar one-dimensional concept of *percentage*. Note also that my conception of the nature of freedom elaborated in Chapters 2 and 3 follows from the requirement of normalization. Otherwise, the paradoxical nature of the concept of *freedom* is implicitly contained in the idea of the incomparable weighting of our value concepts.

It turns out that the distribution function of probabilities may be regarded as a measure of fuzziness of the set where it is given. Thus fuzziness is here *synonymous* with chance. Recall that a random value is determined if its distribution function is determined. Thus, determination of a random value is the determination of fuzziness of the set of elementary events, whose values the random value may take. Such an interpretation of randomness is unusual but, nevertheless, quite legitimate. If we analyze attentively the practice of applying the probability distribution function, all our misgivings disappear. Imagine that we are repeatedly weighing an object on an analytical scale. Consider the set of all possible results coming from unavoidable experimental errors. More often than not, the experimental results are grouped around the deviation center; significant deviations also take place, but their frequencies of occurrence are small. Frequencies interpreted as probabilities will be the measure of deviation or, in other words, the measure of fuzziness of the experimental results. And when we say that the error of measurement is *random*, this is only to say that, by means of probabilistic concepts, we are able to determine only the potential possibility of an error falling in a certain interval of the scale of measurements.

More than once I have drawn the reader's attention to the fact that the notion of *chance* is of an epistemological nature rather than an ontological one (Nalimov, 1981*b*): there are phenomena which have to be described as random, though the ontological meaning of this concept is not exactly clear.[1] From this viewpoint I believe that the opposition of the distribution of possibilities and that of probabilities introduced by Zadeh (1978) is a misunderstanding: if the former is normalized, we automatically obtain the latter and do not need to invent a new grammar to operate with fuzzy sets. This problem is explored in detail in my earlier book (Nalimov, 1981*b*). I would only like to mention that the interpretation of the mathematical notion of probability as the frequency of occurrence of

---

[1] It is noteworthy that the commonly accepted axiomatics of probability theory, proposed by A. N. Kolmogorov, lacks the notion of chance. It is also true, however, that in the so-called algorithmic theory of probability, also connected with the name of Kolmogorov, the notion of chance plays the leading role, but randomness is interpreted as maximum complexity.

an event is not the only one possible: any weighting function answering certain axiomatic requirements may be called the distribution function of probabilities. Trying to explain the difference between the distribution function of probabilities and that of possibilities, Zadeh considers an example of Hans eating eggs for breakfast. The frequency of eating a certain number of eggs is interpreted as probability, and the degree of ease with which they are eaten is interpreted as possibility. But if the area of the weighting function determining the degree of ease with which various numbers of eggs are eaten is normalized to unity, we then deal with the distribution function of probabilities, though these latter will have a different physical interpretation than the frequencies.

In European culture the twenty-century long fight against chance interpreted as a manifestation of ignorance at the same time had been a fight against the fuzziness of our concepts. Zadeh made an attempt to introduce the concept of *fuzzy sets* and thus avoid the idea of chance. Although Zadeh's approach had a wide exposure and we must keep it in mind, we should also realize that we have no reason to oppose fuzziness and randomness.

And now a few words on the Bayesian theorem to which we resort constantly when describing phenomena occurring on the levels of our consciousness that are not logically structured. We have two fuzzily given premises $p(\mu)$ and $p(y|\mu)$ from which we obtain the corollary $p(\mu|y)$, also fuzzily given.

A broad use of probabilistic logic requires overcoming a very serious obstacle predetermined paradigmatically. Common, non-metaphorical usage of the language of probabilistic concepts demands that both the space of elementary events and its metrics should be given. But, strictly speaking, the semantics we have to deal with when studying the psychology of thinking *cannot have any metrics*: we cannot order our semantic concepts on the axis μ and do not know how to determine the distance between two points on this scale. If we look through the papers making use of Bayesian statistics, we easily see that they are confined to problems with well-metricized variables, e.g., those of quality control, etc. This makes it quite obvious why the Bayesian approach, in its traditional form, has so insufficiently penetrated linguistics and psychology.

The metaphorical approach allows us to overcome the difficulties stemming from the fact that semantics does not yield to metricization. We reject the parametric analysis of the distribution function of probabilities and limit ourselves to their *qualitative* consideration.[2] The curve determining the distribution function proves mathematically *inexpress-*

---

[2] It would seem relevant to draw a parallel with the so-called qualitative theory of differential equations which allows one to obtain information on the behavior of the solution of a system of equations without solving them and, consequently, without knowing the numerical values of parameters.

ible, but mentally imaginable, and this is sufficient for constructing a system of reasoning and drawing certain conclusions. All of my earlier book (Nalimov, 1981*a*), as well as the preceding chapters of this book, was written from this viewpoint. In my earlier book I did not explicitly make use of the model based on Bayes's theorem though I kept it in mind while speaking of the probabilistically given filter through which our system of value concepts, also given probabilistically, passes. For example, it is easy to imagine the way functions $p(\mu)$ and $p(y|\mu)$ should look in order to enable the emergence of the form of Darwinism proposed by Lysenko (see Chapter 1). The entire system of judgments is easily traced on the qualitative level.

Thus, we see that a mathematical language for describing the psychology of thinking, which would answer the requirements formulated by Brushlinsky (1979), can actually be created. This language enables us to describe continuous phenomena; its notions are fuzzy, and the measure of fuzziness is representable; it is non-disjunctive (several overlapping distribution functions of probabilities can be constructed on one and the same field of elementary events); finally, it is non-additive, since it allows multiplicative interactions. As follows from Chapter 1, in this language it is possible to answer the major question formulated by Brushlinsky: whether the real world is a class of distinctly differentiated objects. The answer has proved to be negative: the probabilistically fuzzy description of the world looks much more realistic than the familiar discrete description with distinct differentiation.

I would like to emphasize once more that my attempt to formulate uncommonly broad use of probabilistic concepts seems possible only on the qualitative level. Then the actual models are perceived only as metaphors.

It is noteworthy that the metaphorical use of mathematical and physical concepts (in the chapters to follow) made it unnecessary for me to invent my own terminology. All the philosophers of the world seem to have come across the same problem: each of them had to invent his own *thesaurus,* and this made their ideas incomparable.

PART II

INTERNAL TIME

On the Threshold of Part II

For a person who wishes to comprehend the world, there is, perhaps, no more important task than to understand the nature of Time and learn to control one's internal Time.

The problem of Time has often attracted the attention of philosophers and naturalists. Recently, interest in this subject has become noticeably more acute, and numerous books and articles devoted to this topic have appeared. Among the books are those by Fraser (1975, 1978), the founder of the International Society for the Study of Time, that by Doob (1971), which contains a reference list of 887 titles, including 169 book titles, and those by Gale (1968), Prior (1968), Eiseley (1960), Gardner (1979), Grünbaum (1962, 1973), Molchanov (1977a, b), Kazaryan (1980), and Vernadsky (1975). Extremely interesting articles on the problem of Time in modern physics have been published in the journal *Foundations of Physics* (Schlegel, 1977; Capek, 1975; Browne, 1976; Roxburgh and Tavakol, 1978; Edmonds, 1975; McCollum, 1978; Duffey, 1975), and these were reviewed by Panchenko (1980). Of interest are the conceptions of Time inherent in other cultures (Schayer, 1938; Tarthang, 1977), including cultures in the earlier stages of development (Lee, 1977). It seems that special attention should be paid to the role played by the problem of Time in existentialism: the concept of the "axis" Time by Jaspers through which the epochs and philosophical traditions are linked represents the fraternity of thinkers of all Times. Heidegger (1960) elaborated the concept of indivisible integrity in which the interpenetrating constituents of Time—past, present, and future—acquire their specific qualities. For Heidegger philosophy is the way to existence, and for this reason the problem of Time in his conception acquires a major significance.

The above list is certainly no more than a selective sample from the enormous body of works which consider the problem of Time from different angles. A brief and comprehensible account of all that has ever been said about Time is hardly possible.

Neither can we embrace the problem of Time in its completeness. My task is much more modest. I am going to consider two aspects of the problem: that of personal, psychological time and the concept of Time as the grammar of the Texts of the World.

The first aspect is important because it opens up the possibility of comprehending how a person can alter his or her state of consciousness at will. The second aspect is essential for understanding the nature of Nothing—a concept to which any attempt to comprehend the World in its integrity converges.

Chapter 6

Time: A Dialogue with a Metaobserver

The disciples said to Jesus: "Tell us how our end will be." Jesus said: "Have you then discovered the beginning so that you inquire about the end? For where the beginning is there shall be the end. Blessed is he who shall stand at the beginning, and shall know the end and he shall not taste death."

APOCRYPHAL GOSPEL OF ST. THOMAS

Metaobserver: I have come to the Earth from another World which lacks the concept of Time, and it seems to me that I have comprehended all terrestrial concepts except this one. Could you explain for me what "Time" is?

Author: It seems quite impossible. There are no words to explain it.

M.:   Why is it impossible? In your dictionaries you manage in some incomprehensible way to explain the meaning of a word by using other words alien to the explained one.

A.:   Well, I could try, but I hardly expect to succeed. Time is, first of all, something which one wishes to measure; one can understand this concept to a certain degree only through the analysis of its measures and of the explanatory words accompanying these measurements.

M.:   But you people seem to be able to measure anything, even the taste of brandy.

A.:   The point is that Time should be measured and comprehended in quite a special way, always referring to the Past, Present, and Future.

M.:   But in speaking of the taste of brandy, you can also refer to the Past and Present.

A.:   Yes, but only because the taste of brandy is related to Time. We believe the behavior of its taste to be time-like.

M.:   So what is, in your opinion, the Present, Past, and Future?

A.:   Here lies the core of the problem, since nobody can explain it

47

clearly. However, let us agree to assume the Present to be simply the realized *Doing*, or a state of Doing.

M.:   And what about the Past and the Future?

A.:   The Past is also Doing but, once done, it cannot be undone. In other words, this is frozen Doing, petrified like architecture. As to the Future, it is the Doing which lies in store, the potential of Doing. All the difference is only in the states of Doing. And Time here is but a grammatical category which serves to express various states of Doing.

M.:   This is not quite clear.

A.:   Well, I could also define the Present operationally, but such a definition will unavoidably be subjective. If Ego exists, that means there exists a certain field of potential Doings for me. Different plots of the field have different significance for me; in other words, the field of potential Doings is characterized by a weight function. We shall normalize it and call it the function of the distribution of probabilities. But this is only my potential, extra-present existence. This happens, for example, in a deep sleep: Ego exists but does not act, and therefore the Present does not exist for me. Perhaps in such a sleep Ego exists only in the Future. Potential existence becomes real when Ego starts to interact with its field of potential Doings. This interaction is multiplicative: my Free Will is realized as a filtering function (also probabilistic) which is laid over the distribution function of potential Doings. Making use of the Bayesian theorem (see Chapter 2), we obtain the probability distribution function characterizing the Actual Ego of a person. Manifestations of my Free Will divide the entire field of potential Doings into two parts. To the right there is again a field of potential Doings but with a new function of the distribution of probabilities, and to the left is the field of rejected potentialities with many dead Egos. This seems to account for the illusory nature of Ego. It turns out that Ego is merely Doing. Ego expressed by Doing is not an object, but a state, or a *process*. And this brings forth the necessity of the concept of Time.

M.:   But is the Past always frozen in your culture? Is it always cut off from the Present?

A.:   Yes, the paradigm of our culture is such that it always seems to be frozen, though one can come across facts which refute this paradigm. But within our paradigm we must treat such facts with utmost distrust, ascribing these phenomena to hallucinations (this is a very convenient term for eliminating all the unaccountable facts). We keep in mind very rare states which make a person aware of the previous incarnations, and this awareness is accompanied by the possibility of a repeated identification with them. The following is one such description borrowed from Stevenson (1977):

> It is also worthy of note that unusual behavior shown by such a

child [children, usually between two and four years old, who claim to remember that they have lived before and who sometimes make accurate statements about previous lives] that appears to derive from behavioral memories of a previous life sometimes appears in more or less discrete "attacks." During these "attacks" the child appears to be living in a "present time" for him that is nevertheless a "past time" for the persons watching him. On other occasions, however, the same child may show awareness of the passage of time and have the experience then of remembering, as if from his own past, the previous life in which, at other times, he seems still to be living. Furthermore, behavior seemingly derived from the remembered previous life, such as a tendency to miserliness, may manifest simultaneously with behavior presumably derived from the influences of the "present life."

Here a very interesting phenomenon is revealed, namely, the possibility of simultaneously living in different Times. And calling this phenomenon a hallucination does not help much: it still takes place in reality and is similar to all other human psychic phenomena. It is only its rarity which makes us consider it abnormal, but only by examining rarely occurring phenomena do we become aware of the rich potentialities of our psychic life.

M.:   How do the matters stand with the measurement of Time?

A.:   In our cultural traditions, psychological events are ordered according to the physical Time which arises from physical Doing. The concept of Time allows us to describe physical Doing by the velocity dS/dt, acceleration, and differential equations. Regularity (rhythm) of a physical Doing aptly coincides with a swing of a pendulum. In our everyday life the Sun is also regarded as a pendulum. However, from a purely psychological point of view, we would like to speak not of the track covered by Time but of the velocity of Time changes estimated by what is Done: dt/dS. Now S is no longer the track covered by a body in motion, but a scale of Doing. Psychological Doing changes our Ego. Psychological Time is the feeling of the dynamics of changes in our psychological space estimated with respect to the changes of our Ego. We all know that our psychological Time is felt differently in different periods of life. This may also be affected by some external conditions. Solitary confinement or simply standing in a line for something oppresses us because here the natural course of Time is violated. Life without a possibility of Doing is merely waiting in line for Death. The speed of psychological Time changes simply because the scale of Doing is transformed: either expanded or compressed. Otherwise, *the metric of space*, in which the velocity of Time changes is estimated, *alters*. Note that in some incomprehensible way the dynamics of our psychological space radically changes our state of consciousness. The transition to "altered states of consciousness'' is realized either by rhythmic exercises or by meditation, which alters the scale of Doing, or it may be a result of complete isolation, e.g., in a submarine chamber. The well-known auto-training is also directed at making the person stop Doing: the guide tells you, "Your arm is becoming heavy, very heavy . . ." and, indeed, you cannot raise it. Now even physical Doing is impossible for you. Thus, the altered state of consciousness turns out to be directly related to the rate of the course of Time which is made use of in the practice of esoteric teachings.

M.:   But has your science ever faced the necessity to describe the change of the concept of Time in connection with the change of Doing in the physical world?

A.:   Yes, it has, though there is a tradition not to mention the fact. Everything remains implicit. However, one might quote the words of M. I. Podgoretskii (1978), an atomic physicist, on the troubles accompanying the attempts to construct a theory of quantum measurements:

> Hence [from the von Neumann theorem] unavoidably follows the conclusion of the existence in quantum mechanics of two quite different types of processes: dynamic processes developing in time according to the Schrödinger equation and measurement processes which do not yield to a dynamic description and occur instantaneously (in any case, very quickly as compared to the periods of time characteristic of the corresponding dynamic processes). . . . the interval of time necessary for the dynamic compression of the wave function into a small region occupied by the counter does not correspond to the actual working time of real counters.

The fragment quoted discusses the fact that the measurements are taken by the counter within intervals which are many orders of magnitude less than the time necessary for the dynamic reduction of the wave packet. This is perhaps evidence for the fact that the functioning of the counter is the Doing by which physical Time is measured.

The second example relates to cosmogony with one of its unanswered questions: what was there before the emergence of the Universe? In the literature you may come across such expressions as "Hubble time" or "Friedmann time."[1] They reflect the attempts to determine theoretically the time of existence of the Universe after the explosion, when the nature of our world took its present form. But what had there been before the initial explosion? The Soviet physicist V. L. Ginsburg (1970) refuses to acknowledge the existence of Time before the start of the Universe. His arguments are both physical and philosophical:

> Indeed, if it had been possible to speak of time "before" the Uni-

---

[1] Named after Alexander Friedmann, a Russian mathematician who, in 1922, gave a nonstatic solution of Einstein's equations.

verse started to evolve, and if the Universe had not existed, we should have assumed the "creation of the world." . . . On that ground it seems consistent to assume the finite character of Time in the past, while the "beginning" of Time in the models by Friedmann and the like, can be comprehended as a "singular" state of the infinite density [of matter]. Many cosmologists believe this approach to be generally satisfactory . . .

To our mind, the most promising theoretical models of today are those with "singularities" in the past, and the region of the "singularity" should be regarded with reference to quantum effects. Thus Time in the past is indefinite rather than finite. The advantage of such models is that they are not fraught with the difficulties typical of the models with infinite Time. (p. 100–103)

On the manifestation of singularity in the past, see Misner, Thorne, and Wheeler (1973):

. . . all the universe as being from time to time "squeezed through a knot-hole," drastically "reprocessed" and started out on a fresh dynamic cycle. (p. 1214)

It is natural to speak here of the cyclic nature of time, which is discussed again in Chapter 15 (p. 252).

In his book *The First Three Minutes* Weinberg (1977) discusses the initial Time somewhat more calmly:

At about one-hundredth of a second, the earliest time about which we can speak with any confidence, the temperature of the universe was about a hundred thousand million (10^{11}) degrees centigrade. This is much hotter than in the center of even the hottest star. (p. 5).

This can be re-interpreted as follows: before the initial explosion there had not been the physical Doing which exists now, and, consequently, there could not have been the Time which exists now. However, both situations described above are rather exotic: one of them relates to the microworld, and the other, to the macroworld. They are obviously insufficient to make us reject the familiar naive concept of physical Time which exists substantially and independently of all the events of our everyday world. The important thing to be noted here is that the concept of physical Time also lacks consistency and unanimity.

M.: Are the notions of the Past, Present, and Future also essential for the physical Time?

A.: I do not think so. If a pendulum swings with a period $T = 2\pi\sqrt{l/g}$, where is its Present? And when a volcano erupts, one feels like speaking of the Present moment of Time. But these seem to be anthropomorphisms. From the viewpoint of an observing Ego, a pendulum also has its Present that divides the Time scale into two parts, the Past and the Future.

M.: But if so, maybe Time does not exist at all?

A.: Indeed, if the concept Time denotes quite different things, maybe it does not denote anything at all. Time can hardly be imagined as an independently existing object. Rather, this is a concept necessary to describe something happening to the Ego or within the Ego and then transferred to describe events of the world. Kant realized that the concept of Time did not come from experience. Before Kant, it was Leibniz who elaborated the concept of Time as the order of phenomena coming one after another or of states of bodies. (I return to Leibniz's conception of Space and Time in Chapter 7, p. 61–62.) Therefore, this category is purely linguistic. It is noteworthy that this concept proved to be grammatically invariant for almost all the languages of the Earth.

However, different languages specify this concept with different degrees of accuracy. The English language with its 16 tenses describes Time very thoroughly. In Russian the sequence of tenses is expressed more fuzzily: it is well known that subtle shades of sequential events described in English cannot be adequately translated into Russian. But maybe in the polysynthetic languages of American Indians the concept of Time is lost. Sometimes it is said that in such languages without grammar all the words are verbs, or all the words are nouns to which verb-forming elements are added. The familiar European phrase "A man yonder is running down the long street" in a polysynthetic language will consist merely of predicative lexemes "one," "man," "yonder," "traverse," "street," "long" (for more details, see Whorf, 1956). It seems that post-Kantian philosophers and anthropologists must have answered the following questions: What called forth the necessity of this grammatical invariant? Why was it this invariant which had proved crucial for the structure of our vision of the world? To what extent is the temporal vision of the world convenient for the perception of the entire spectrum of the observed phenomena? In what way is the vision of the world changed in languages without grammar? We are quite aware now that, in the words of Wittgenstein, "the limits of my language are the limits of my world." None of these questions has been answered: moreover, the questions themselves have not been formulated precisely enough. But our conjecture is that the category of Time arose from the necessity to overcome the barrier between the deep inner sensation of the continuous nature of the World and the discrete representation of its verbal expression. Besides, the possibility of Doing, which determines our psychological Time, had been generated by the dichotomous discreteness of the basic concepts of our culture: for instance, it seems rather plausible to assert that social activity is based on the definite and unconditional (though deeply personal) opposition of good and evil, truth and falsity, etc. It is noteworthy in this respect that in the ancient Oriental philosophies the rejection of the dichotomous vision of the world leads to the rejection of Doing, and, therefore, to the disappearance of Time.

M.: But does Death exist without Time?

A.: Death is the end. But what can we say of the end if we do not know the Beginning? (I am merely repeating the words of Christ given at the beginning of this chapter.) Our World can be represented by a Wilson cloud chamber (or a bubble chamber) in which only charged particles leave a trace. Imagine a naive observer looking at the picture taken in this chamber. He sees something without a beginning appear in the chamber, leave a trace, and then disappear into nowhere. The concepts of the beginning and the end result here from the incomplete vision of the phenomenon. But is not this what is happening in our psychological space? The model of a Wilson chamber accounts for the transcendence of history as well: invisible energies from the cosmos leave a visible trace, and this might explain the fact that previously quite ordinary people, having absorbed colossal energy after a collision with the invisible carrier of astral energy, change their way in the world and become outstanding personalities, and then, also suddenly, become mediocrities again: remember, for instance, Napoleon Bonaparte. Wars and revolutions act as colossal accelerators that help to reveal the unknown in history. But can a naive observer see all this?

M.: But you, the people of the Earth, attach some exclusively great significance to death. Why is this so?

A.: For us death means an instant and complete cessation of any possibility of Doing and, consequently, it means the disappearance of Time. The rate of Time flow equals zero. The greatest shock comes from the suddenness of the cessation: it is a break in the natural course of the permanently changing process. Note that if a person (or, perhaps, a better example is a social structure or even a scientific concept) starts aging and declines gradually, this is perceived as a natural process: the scale of Doing is expanding gradually, and death may be described simply as a second passage to the limit (assuming that the velocity of Time change is finite in all points):

$$\lim_{k \to \infty} \frac{dt}{dkS} = 0$$

where k is a parameter of the scale S expansion. There is no break here: the velocity of Time change equals zero only in the limit case.[2] This can

---

[2] In the above example concerning measurements in the microworld, it seems relevant to assume that, at the instant when the measurement is taken by the counter, the scale S tightens, perhaps nonlinearly (e.g., logarithmically). But this is an object of a separate study.

be illustrated by the following example from real life. None can tell at what moment of historic time the people of the Roman Empire disappeared. The Romans, who had subdued the entire world, disappeared gradually and without a trace. At present, the technique of reanimation has developed to the point that it is possible to make a statistical inquiry of reanimated persons en masse (see, for example, Moody, 1975, 1977). I have also heard reports of clinical death from people who have gone through it. Actually, there is no death, though it is stated to occur on the physical level of existence: the possibility of Doing now opens up in the psychic plane. This is indicated by people who have come close to death. And now imagine that a person during his earthly life learns to exercise his free will outside our bubble chamber world; e.g., he gains the possibility of consciously controlling deep dreams. This would radically change the concept of death, but we know of such skills only from vague legends. Perhaps they came from the contemplation of the problem we are trying to discuss.

M.:   But what is the difference between death and dream?

A.:   Death means the loss of both the Present and the Future, whereas in dreams the Present ceases or almost ceases to exist but the existence in the Future is preserved. In other words, the deeper the dream is the more the scale *S* expands. But this does not lead either to passage to the limit or to a break in the course of Time change. Note that dreaming is graded according to its depth, but our culture lacks gradations for the state of death. True, the recent practice of reanimation has started to destroy this ideology. Recall that in the practice of esoteric teachings whose roots lie in Ancient Egypt one of the initiations consisted of the experience of death. An adept of this school was warned that he might well not survive deep death-like dreaming. By the way, the episode of Lazarus's resurrection may describe the return from this state. In this episode the line dividing death and dream seems to be erased.

M.:   And what about the concept of reincarnation?

A.:   Above I spoke about the model of a bubble chamber. For the naive observer the bubble tracks come from "Nothing" and go into "Nothing." But the physicist, who sees another reality behind the visible "Nothing," would interpret this picture in a different manner. If we are allowed such an analogy, then the concept of reincarnation would correspond to the interpretation by the physicist who sees another reality behind "Nothing." Note that there recently began scientific, strictly documentary research of situations (very rarely occurring) in which phenomena can be explained only by proceeding from the concept of reincarnation (Stevenson, 1975).

M.:   Could you tell me anything else about the concepts of Time and death in the past cultures of the Earth?

A.: This is a very difficult question. I don't know whether anybody has even tried to collect and systematize such material, but I feel that the concept of death in other cultures must reflect extraordinary, significant experience. Each culture allows us to perceive the world from a new angle, now by revealing something to our consciousness, now by keeping silent about something. I'll try to speak of what I know well. First of all, I would like to draw your attention to the fact that it was typical of early Christianity, and especially of gnosticism, to emphasize the possibility of another, higher form of life realized outside the Earth concept of Doing and, therefore, outside the Earth-bound Time. The gnostic God is non-existent, unborn, indestructible, unknowable, incomprehensible, super-celestial, immutable, self-begotten (Jonas, 1958). In the apocryphal Gospels of Nag Hammadi, Christ is called "the Son of Silence." Below I quote the Gospel of the Egyptians:

> He brought   /praise/   to the great, /in/ visible, virginal (παϱθενιϰόυ) Spirit (πνευμα), /the silence (οιν)̈ / of the /Father/ in a silence (   )³ /of the/ living silence (   ) /of silence/ /the/ place where the man rests.

In the Canonical Gospel according to St. John, Christ, talking to the Jews, descendants of Abraham, spoke of his extratemporal nature:

> Jesus said to them, "Truly, truly, I say to you, before Abraham was, I am." (St. John, 8:59)

We are inclined to perceive this as an attempt to describe the lost experience of life outside Doing. This experience is manifold and exists in many mystic teachings; its practice is elaborated in detail: its roots are found in the ancient pre-gnostic epoch.

Now I would like to say a few words of the perception of Time in the slavonic paganism which still exists today. A philologist studying Polesie (some areas in Byelorussia famous for their remnants of the pagan outlook) has told me a legend which he heard quite recently on the relativity of Time:

> A wedding procession. On the way to the church the groom recalls that he wanted to invite his friend. But his friend has died. The procession passes the cemetery where he has been buried. "Wait a minute, I'll visit my friend in the cemetery," says the groom. He comes up to the grave; the grave is dug up, and he sees there a table and a bench. His friend sits on the bench waiting for him. On the table there is a bottle of vodka and a pack of cigarettes. "Have a drink," says the dead friend, and let's have a chat." "I'm in a hurry," answers the groom. "There is my wedding. I've come only for a mo-

---

³ Lacunae in the text.

ment." "All right, smoke one cigarette and go." The groom smokes a cigarette and runs to catch up with the wedding procession, but there is no wedding procession. He runs to the church, but there is no church either—only its ruins overgrown with moss.

This parable dramatically shows that Time can be quite different. Especially prolonged is sepulchral Time. The physical measure of Time, the smoking of a cigarette, cannot also be a measure coordinating different Times. (Versions of this parable exist in the folklore of many peoples.) At present I don't feel like speaking any longer about the perception of Time in different cultures, though perhaps I should mention the Egyptian and Tibetan books of the dead. But this subject requires a separate study. I would only like to emphasize that the study of Time is a brilliant illustration of how the world's ontology is revealed through the study of human psychology. We see the world through man and not through physical devices.

M.:   Do you happen to know of any problems which arise now in your society from the conscious desire to change one's Time?

A.:   I would like to quote here the Russian folk saying: "What are you doing this for?" "Just to *stir up* Time." So sometimes Time may, and even should, be stirred up, or it will die away. This simple saying is fraught with obvious interpretation of the Game Model of the Oriental world: in order to realize the world in Time there must exist an occupation which would help the psychological time to acquire a non-zero speed. From the standpoint of the Metaobserver, such an occupation is nothing more than a Game. This is philosophical relativism brought to the extreme limit of thought. It deprives history of the simple meaning we are anxious to discover.

Having retired, aged people immediately change the tempo of their life: they expand the scale S and enter another Time. They coexist with their relatives, living in a slackened Time, and in this Time, as well as in the previous one, they have no Time. They say that retirement often leads to an unexpectedly rapid death: bodily functions cannot quickly accommodate themselves to the sudden transformation of the psychological Time.

And the last remark: the genre of the many-volumed novel, once so popular, with its measured rhythm and unhurried flow of events, is becoming more and more out-of-fashion. Why is this so? The answer seems to be simple: in a traditional novel the scale S is deliberately expanded. Crucial events happening with large intervals are interspersed with seemingly unimportant details. When reading such a novel, we must enter another Time, alien for us. Just try to make an adolescent read *War and Peace*. Will you have success? This, by the way, accounts for the popularity of the cinema: you can see all the events during a single showing and the course of Time is familiar for you.

M.: If I understand you correctly, you claim that psychological time is related to psychological space through its metric.

A.: Well, yes. As demonstrated above, it is the change of metric of the space of Doing that changes the sensation of Time. We would like to emphasize here that many people are psychologically ready to change their notion of Time. This is vividly seen in experiments with LSD (Grof, 1975):[4]

> Distortions in the perception of time and space are one of the most striking and constant aspects of LSD sessions. The perception of time is quite regularly altered; most commonly a short time interval is experienced as being much longer, although sometimes the opposite is true. In the extreme case, minutes can be experienced as centuries or millennia, or, conversely, a long time period in the session can be perceived as lasting only several seconds. Occasionally, time is changed not only quantitatively but also as a dimension. It can stop completely, so that the sequential nature of events disappears; past, present, and future are experienced as juxtaposed. A special category of time change is the experience of regression to various periods in the individual's history. (p. 10)

It should be noted that LSD does not specifically affect people. According to Grof, LSD has a low level of toxicity and a wide range of safety. This drug performs the role of a trigger and then of an intensifier, bringing to the surface and intensifying what exists within the subject's deep consciousness. Thus we see that the possibility of the modified, *temporal state of consciousness*, different from that accepted in our culture, is built into us. Perhaps Kant divined this when he asserted that space and time are forms of sensory contemplation given to us outside our experience.

M.: What is, then, the philosophy of earthlings?

A.: First of all, philosophy is Doing. This was well expressed by Wittgenstein (1955): "Philosophy is not a theory, but an activity" (*Tractatus*, 4.112). It may be, of course, that he implied something very different, but does it matter? In some narrower sense philosophizing means the constantly renovated reinterpretation of our knowledge of the world which comes from our psychological experience. Reinterpretation is made in new languages, and each new reinterpretation is an invention of

---

[4] Stanislac Grof began his research into psychedelic drugs in his native Czechoslovakia in 1956. Since 1967, he has been working in the United States, at the Esalen Institute in Big Sur, California. Being mainly an expert in LSD therapy, he is at the same time a scholar who uses LSD as a flashlight to illuminate the deep levels of consciousness. His books have a philosophical flavor.

a new myth. In previous epochs people created myths derived from the common concepts: love, hatred, or perfidy. Now we can create myths derived from scientific concepts. I have demonstrated this possibility above: does it appeal to you? The concept of Time is a structure which has come to us from very ancient myths. And it cannot be overcome since it has deeply penetrated the consciousness of earthlings.

M.:   Now I see why Doing has become so difficult for earthlings. They cannot work their way through the thick bushes of their myths and grow new species by multiplying phantoms. Farewell. I wish you luck in this mad activity.

A.:   Farewell. Tell the people of other planets that it was said about Doing on our Earth: "You will know them by their fruits" (St. John, 5:17). And we never forget this. We remember also the words from the Bhagavad-Gita: "This world is linked by Doing" (III.9). Perhaps it would have been better not to have started our conversation about Time.

Chapter 7

Time as Grammar of Texts of the World

Contemporary Concepts of Time vs. Plotinus's *On Time and Eternity*

> *What is Time? Time does not exist, time is a number, time is: the ratio of being and non-being.*
> FROM THE ROUGH NOTES OF DOSTOEVSKY
> TO THE NOVEL *CRIME AND PUNISHMENT*

Earlier, we compared the probabilistic vision of the world to the tractatus *On Numbers* by Plotinus (see Chapter 4); now the time has come to compare our conception of Time, through which we try to comprehend the nature of Nothing, to his tractatus *On Time and Eternity* found in the Third Ennead (Plotinus, 1956).

Recall that Plotinus inherited not only the ideas of the entire Mediterranean, but also those of Persia and India. (See the appendix to this chapter.) We may think he was the first philosopher to comprehend critically and re-integrate the experience of perception of the world by ancient people. This experience could be called religious, since it was opened through a direct contact with the unconscious. We should be aware of the fact that Plotinus's writings are implicit rather than explicit: in order to understand what he was speaking about, one had to ask questions. At his conferences he encouraged such a form of studies. But whom can we ask now? Only ourselves.

We are naturally going to speak here not of direct parallels but of the echoes of ideas.

The following are excerpts from the tractatus *On Time and Eternity:*

Eternity, thus, is of the order of the supremely great; intuition identifies it with God: it may fitly be described as God made manifest, as God declaring what He is, as existence without jolt or change, and therefore as also the firmly living. (p. 226)

Thus a close enough definition of Eternity would be that it is a life limitless in the full sense of being all the life there is and a life which, knowing nothing of past or future to shatter its completeness, possesses itself intact forever. To the notion of a Life (a Living-Principle) all-comprehensive add that it never spends itself, and we have the statement of a Life instantaneously infinite. (p. 227)

We must then have, ourselves, some part or share in Eternity.

Still, how is this possible to us who exist in Time?

The whole question turns on the distinction between being in Time and being in Eternity, and this will be best realized by probing to the nature of Time. (p. 228)

Movement Time cannot be . . .

In a word, Movement must be distinct from the medium in which it takes place.

And, with all that has been said or is still said, one consideration is decisive: Movement can come to rest, can be intermittent; Time is continuous. (p. 229)

Would it, then, be sound to define Time as the Life of the Soul in movement as it passes from one stage of act or experience to another? (p. 234)

Here I make a break in the quotations and draw the reader's attention to the fact that the last of the above excerpts could be made an epigraph for Chapter 6. Alternatively, this chapter linking psychological Time with Doing can be considered as an explication of this excerpt.

But let us return to Plotinus:

If, then, the soul withdrew, sinking itself again into its primal unity, Time would disappear: the origin of Time, clearly, is to be traced to the first stir of the soul's tendency towards the production of the sensible Universe with the consecutive act ensuing. This is how "Time"—as we read—"came into being simultaneously with" this All: the soul begot at once the Universe and Time; in that activity of the Soul this Universe sprang into being; the activity is Time, the Universe is a content of Time. No doubt it will be urged that we read also, of "the orbit of the stars" being Times: but do not forget what follows; "the stars exist," we are told, "for the display and delimitation of Time," and "that there may be a manifest Measure." No indication of Time could be derived from (observation of) the Soul; no portion of it can be seen or handled, so it could not be measured in itself, especially when there was as yet no knowledge of counting; therefore the Demiurge (in the Timaeus) brings into being night and day; in their difference is given Duality—from which, we read, arises the concept of Number. (p. 236)

It follows from this text that Time is ascribed a Demiurgic role: The world manifests itself through Time. In other words, Time becomes the synonym for existence. Furthermore, the double-faceted nature of Time is emphasized: it is astronomic Time which is perceived directly; the other kind of Time, which I have called psychological, unregistered by devices, is not felt. Then follows an extremely interesting speculation on the nature of Time:

> Time itself is not a measure . . . Time, then, serves towards measurement but is not itself the Measure; the Movement of the All will be measured according to Time, but Time will not, of its own nature, be a Measure of Movement: primarily a Kind to itself, it will incidentally exhibit the magnitudes of that movement. (p. 236)

Recall that Plotinus (see Chapter 4) held that the world manifests itself through number, or, in my terms, through the distribution function of probabilities. In his system Time turns out to exist outside the number, i.e., outside measurement; it is only a means through which measuring becomes possible. In other words, this is to say that ontologically Time is outside Existence, though it makes Existence possible.

We face Existence as a Text (see the beginning of Chapter 3) whose semantics we wish to learn, to comprehend, and to experience. And if we see the world as a Text, then Time is only its *grammar*. Grammar is outside the Text; it only arranges it—similarly to Time, which is outside the world Existence; it only rhythmically arranges the Texts of the World through which we contact it. My formation of such a conception of Time has been affected by Plotinus, though he used different words when speaking about Time.

The tragical search for the nature of Time which has been going on for twenty centuries stems from the desire to describe Time in terms of Existence, but Time has not the self-sufficiency of Existence: it exists only as an organizing idea. Plotinus has long remained uncomprehended. It was Leibniz who came back to his ideas at the beginning of our scientific era. For Leibniz, Space is but an *order* of mutual arrangement of a set of bodies which exist independently of one another, and Time is an *order* of events or states of bodies replacing one another. The idea of Space as an order proves applicable only to a set of bodies, and the idea of Duration, though applicable to an individual phenomenon, is such only because it exists as a link in a single chain of events. The term *order* introduced by Leibniz can be regarded as a synonym for the term *grammar*. The latter is more meaningful for us since now we know a lot about the role of grammar as the structure of language.

I would like to quote Leibniz as well

> Time, strictly speaking, never exists, since it never exists as a whole
> because its parts do not exist together. (quoted from Mayorov, 1973,
> p. 164)

Indeed, if we attempt to consider Time as it is, outside any events happening within it, we shall not be able to present it as composed of constituents. It is in this sense that Time (not reduced to space) is unmeasurable as it is. In contrast to a physical field, it has no attributes which could be measured. Plotinus understood that Time is outside numerical estimation. Here lies its non-existence. For example, the category of generic case is also something non-existent, not composed of constituents, unmeasurable.

If Time is but a grammar of Existence, many related problems disappear. For example, the well-known paradox of McTaggart[1] is not valid because of the absurdity of speaking about the dynamism of Time: the term "dynamism" is borrowed from the concept of Existence. It is similarly absurd to ask whether Time existed before the original explosion in which our Universe was born. This question, discussed in Chapter 6, is as absurd as it would be to ask what the grammar of our human language was like before the texts of this language appeared. Grammar can emerge only together with the texts and can be perceived by us only through them: the theory of context-free languages (see Ginsburg, 1966) is nothing more than an abstract, purely mathematical discipline close to the theory of finite automata.

Leibniz proved to be the first thinker of modern times who opposed the idea of the substantial existence of Time and Space, but his views did not influence natural sciences in the eighteenth and nineteenth centuries: the ideas which reigned at the time were the naive theories of Newton, and it was only contemporary physics which first started to view Space and Time from a new angle close to that of Leibniz. [It is of interest whether Leibniz, who was briefly a scientific secretary of the Rosicrucians (Mayorov, 1973), introduced into European culture ideas borrowed from ancient esoteric teachings.]

The Kantian notion of Time as an inner form of sensual contemplation given a priori can be easily put in accord with the concept of Time as grammar. Kant spoke of an a priori grammar of the language we use to generate texts that reflect our interaction with the world. We see now that there may be many such languages: this possibility is potentially in-

---

[1] The paradox emerges when Time is ascribed a kinematic nature. In order to describe the course of Time, new second-order Time should be introduced with respect to which the course of the first-order Time will be noticeable. But then the same should be done for the second-order Time and so on to infinity (for more details, see Gale, 1968*a, b*).

herent in the depths of our consciousness. I would like to draw the reader's attention to the search for new formulations of the concept of Time in physics. Below are quoted short fragments from articles on time published in the journal *Foundations of Physics:*

> Time, instead of being a substratum entity which controls all physical phenomena, must now be regarded as a concomitant or measure of physical process. (Schlegel, 1977, p. 252)

> Einstein's choice of a curved space-time on which to plot events is not inevitable, but merely a convention with certain advantages (Browne, 1976, p. 458).

> The general theory of relativity makes use of the "curvature" of spacetime denoting the entity which exists independently of anything, though in fact this provides only a convenient mathematical representation of the physical theory. (Roxburgh and Tavakol, 1978)

> The programme of the spacetime code[2] has in view a construction of the quantum theory of processes rather than spacetime objects. The problem of space and time is considered operational and is answered as follows: spacetime is macroscopic and statistical (analogy: temperature); it emerges in the limit of many monads and is unacceptable on the level of an individual monad, since on this level there are neither clocks nor rods. (McCollum, 1978)

> A new relativistic formalism must make use of a hypercomplex number system. Under these postulates the mass of elementary particles is the eigenvalue of a fifth momentum operator component. The fifth dimension is identified with cosmic time, . . . particles can reverse their time direction only along the ordinary time axis. (Edmonds, 1975)

> Tachyons—hypothetical objects travelling at superluminal speed . . . A coordinate system can be selected in which a tachyon appears and disappears instantaneously, existing for a moment as an endlessly extended spacelike structure. (Duffey, 1975)

The above excerpts show that an intensive search for new grammars, for the new language, is going on, necessitated by the fact that physicists have started to face a reality earlier closed for people. It is possible to sketch a succession of internally similar though externally different conceptions of Time: Plotinus, Leibniz, Kant, contemporary physics.

Scientists dealing with the history of the Earth seem to face a similar problem in the immediate future. The brilliant book by the paleobotanist Meyen (1981) is written in a critical mode: the author asserts that there is no validly reconstructed past. If an attempt is made to restore it, this brings about the problem of Time:

---

[2] This is a reformulation in contemporary language of the ideas of Leibniz concerning space and time.

> Studying the past of the Earth, we practically have no clock. (p. 150)

The researcher can determine geological time only by proceeding from the changeability of the objects under study. But then

> The observer notes that the changeability of objects-individuals is different, i.e., the processes occurring in different objects are different. In accordance with the classes of objects, classes of processes and, therefore, classes of times can be selected. (p. 151)

This seems to account for the difficulties in registering the past. The general impression given by Meyen's book is as follows: events on the cosmic scale, as well as events occurring in the microworld, cannot be described with the familiar concept of Time. Time, as we perceive it, is not a grammatical category of the universal language of the World.

In the preceding chapter we discussed personal, psychological Time and introduced the concept of the velocity of the course of this Time. Now, after what has been said here, we may claim psychological Time to be nothing more than a grammar by means of which various states of our consciousness are represented as a comprehensible Text. The idea of the velocity of personal, psychological Time is a *measure* arranging various states of consciousness. The introduction of such a measure enables us to speak of the control over states of consciousness in a comprehensible language. This is a good illustration of Plotinus: the possibility of measuring psychic states is opened by introducing another kind of Time, namely, psychological time.

Varying this measure in meditation experiments, we, as will be shown below, in Part IV, change the grammar of consciousness and obtain new, unfamiliar Texts. Note as well that many authors indicate that mental diseases may be accompanied by violations of natural (for us) ideas of Time (these works are reviewed by Doob, 1971). A disease is represented as a violation of the grammar of our psychic condition. Perhaps psychiatrists' observations are an indirect proof of the validity of the Kantian conception of Time as an a priori given form of our internal contemplation.

It is relevant to quote here another fragment from Plotinus:

> Suppose that Life, then, to revert—an impossibility—to perfect unity: Time, whose existence is in that Life, and the Heavens, no longer maintained by that Life, would end at once. (p. 237)

In our experiments (described in detail in Part IV) reincarnation memories—the passage to the impossible—come to the fore when we strive to stop or at least slow down personal Time.

And, finally, a quotation from the last page of the tractatus:

> Simply, that the Soul-Movement has for its Prior (not Time but) Eternity which knows neither its progression nor its extension. The descent towards Time begins with this Soul-Movement; it made Time and harbours Time as a concomitant to its Act. (p. 238)

The tractatus finishes with the following lines:

> And, as with Man's Soul, so with the Soul of the All. Is Time, then, within ourselves as well?
> Time is in every Soul of the order of the All-Soul, present in like form in all; for all the Souls are the one Soul.
> And this is why Time can never be broken apart, any more than Eternity which, similarly, under diverse manifestations, has its Being as an integral constituent of all the eternal Existence. (p. 238)

It is time to sum up.

The idea of the grammar of the world is, probably, the conception of the universal harmony, when the world is represented as a spontaneously developing text.

The problem of the world ontology has been reduced within our culture to the problem of Time.

But Time as it is does not exist independently.

The problem of Time, after its critical consideration, may seem to be a pseudoproblem. But, remaining within the consciousness of a participant of this culture, it is not easy to avoid this problem.

APPENDIX

On the Life of Plotinus (According to Porphyry)

The information on the life of Plotinus (205–270 A.D.) is meager. He was born at Lycopolis (in Egypt). At twenty-seven he was caught by the passion for philosophy, but the highly reputed professors to be found in Alexandria did not satisfy him. At last he became a disciple of Ammonius Sakkas, a Greek philosopher, and he passed eleven years under him. At thirty-eight he became eager to investigate the Persian methods, and so Plotinus joined the army of the Emperor Gordian, who was at that time preparing his campaign against Persia. When Gordian was killed in Mesopotamia, it was only with great difficulty that Plotinus came safely to Antioch. At forty he settled in Rome and began his Conferences where everyone could attend. He used to encourage his hearers to put questions. Erennius, Origen, and Plotinus had made a compact not to disclose any of the doctrines which Ammonius had revealed to them, but later the compact was broken.

Plotinus's Enneads are six treatises, each consisting of nine parts (literally, Ennead means "the number of nine"). The translation of the Enneads into English proved to be the life cause of Stephan MacKenna (1872–1934). The text of the Enneads is far from being mythological. Their external style may be characterized as philosophically speculative, but they possess an enchanting inner rhythm concealed by the arbitrary carelessness of the logical course of his thoughts.

The reader is struck by sudden expressions. Some of them sound enigmatic, and the reader gets the impression that the author had obtained knowledge which cannot be explicitly explained, for an adequate language is lacking.

And now I would like to quote a few fragments from the book by Guilyarov (1919) to characterize the epoch formed by both early Christianity and Neo-Platonism:

> In the fourth century dogmatism reigned in the East; dogmatic disputes come out in the streets, they excite the crowd not less than the fight between parties in the circus. According to a mocking remark by Gregory Nissky (b. 331, died at the end of the century), money-changers, before changing money, started to discuss whether or not Christ had been born; a baker, failing to answer how much a loaf of bread was, speculated on the relation between the Father and the Son and said that the Father was more important than the Son; a bath-

66

house attendant, when asked about the bath, answered that it had emerged from NOTHING. Nevertheless, even when dogmatism reigned, the mystic stream did not dry up. (p. 62)

The role of Neo-Platonism in the evolution of European culture is hard to trace. I shall confine myself to quoting Guilyarov:

> In 529 Justinianos closed the philosophical schools in Athens. The property of the neoplatonic school was confiscated . . . Neoplatonism continued to live only as an echo in Christian philosophy and in Mohammedan Sufism.
>
> In the fourth century neoplatonism was reproduced in a broad synthesis by the first medieval scholastic and mystic Johannes Scotus Erigena whom extreme realists and mystics of the seventh and eighth centuries joined directly or indirectly. About the ninth century neoplatonism mixed with the teaching of Aristotle, formed the Mohammedan philosophy, and colored one of the major monuments of the Jewish philosophy, Cabbala . . . In the "new times" Leibniz, on the basis of Plotinus's guide, wrote his *Theodicy*, a dull copy of the luminous model.
>
> Kant is also indebted to neoplatonists . . . Hegel's dialectical method is a modified method of Proklos. Hegel's view of nature as a defection from the Fundamental Principle is neoplatonic. Bergson, with his so popular teaching is indebted to neoplatonists and other philosophers of the Decline more than to himself (p. 91–92).

Chapter 8

Metaphorical Nature of the Concept of Psychological Time

Present-Momentness of Past and Future

Our conception of personal, psychological time is as deeply meta-phorical as that of the probabilistic vision of the world. It would be naive to assume the velocity of personal time to be just the value inverse to the psychical rate. The notion of personal time becomes meaningful only after the scale S of Doing is introduced. This scale is far from being iden-tical to the scale S in physics which measures the route covered by a point in time; in some sense, however, the two scales have similar properties. We can speak, for example, of the change of metrics of the scale of Do-ing though these words will be rather metaphorical, and one should not forget that they are.

I am often asked: What is the correlation between personal time and physical time? I do not consider this a legitimate question—actually we deal not with different manifestations of a substance, but with grammars of two languages, close to one another but still different.[1]

Our conception of psychological time, on the one hand, and, on the other hand, the conception of an individual as a probabilistically deter-mined manifestation of integrality allow us to construct the spatial model for manifestations of *Past–Present–Future*. Human doings are only pos-sible in a three-dimensional space. Our past is not separated from us by

[1] Naturally, changes in Personal Time leading to changes of the inner psychic state result in distortions of estimating the length of physical Time. This can be observed in certain mental diseases. For example, before attempting suicide people had an impression that the rate of physical Time had increased. Perhaps an attempt to commit suicide is an urge to restore the lost Time through the expansion of the whole life which happens during a few moments preceding death. For a moment the scale S narrows down, and Time quickens, giving an illusion of full life.

Time: it coexists with us in a space of a larger dimension. The Past, the already *done* is constantly projected onto our three-dimensional space from the space of a larger dimension as a pattern determining our behavior. Everything new in our life is perceived through the old. In creating something anew, we actually do away with the old which is not given to us directly: it represents another reality not subject to us. In many of my papers I have emphasized that the evolution of any culture in its seemingly new and unexpected aspects always proves submerged in the pattern of the past though it can hardly be discerned in the new clothes.

In Chapter 2, considering the problem of Free Will, we based our reasoning on Bayes's theorem and introduced the concept of the probabilistically determined fate component in our behavior. This, if you like, is exactly a probabilistically weighted description of a pattern projected onto the Present from the Past.

If we acknowledge as correct what has been said of the Past, there immediately arises a new question: How should we see the Future? It may also be thought to coexist with our Present, i.e., to exist in the space of a larger dimension and be projected on the space of a lesser dimension where Doing is possible. If we turn again to Chapter 2, we see that the distribution function determining the ethical aspect of our behavior may be regarded as a manifestation of the Future in the Present. Free Will makes the choice through which the Future, existing as a set of possibilities, affects the Present. We may speak of the present-moment existence of the Past and the Future. Both exist unmanifested and are manifested in Doing realized through Free Will. I would like to quote once more the Bhagavad-Gita: ". . . this world is linked by Doing . . ." (III, 9).

Here, as in modern physics, the role of the experimenter becomes important. Through him in the Present are revealed the Past and the Future, the latter existing in its versatile potentiality.

Here another interpretation is possible: it is through people that Consciousness penetrates into the world. The activity of a conscious man, i.e., a free man, his Doing, signifies the ability to change the situation by asking a question. A possible answer is implied by the question. Explicitly the answer develops through interaction with the situation to which it is directed. Realization of the answer in Doing is a creation of a new situation. To elucidate that said above, it would again be relevant to resort to Bayes's theorem, which can be regarded as a formula that allows us to obtain the answers to questions while working with fuzzy concepts.

Assume that $p(\mu)$ is a value orientation in a situation generated by our Past; $p(y|\mu)$ is the question posed from the Future to the existing situation and related to the new problem y; $p(\mu|y)$ is an answer realized by the emergence of a newly weighted value orientation. Hence it follows that, within the system of our values (see again Chapter 2), ethical attitude is a question posed to the fate component of our life. Or, in other words, the Future expressed in ethics through man poses a question to the Past identified with the fate component. Thus, the *Future* affects the *Past* through the *Present*. The specific role of the Present consists in the fact that only here is Doing possible, by which the Future affects the Past. In this way we reveal the qualitative difference between the Time constituents which was spoken about by Heidegger.

Our ideas of the interaction of structural constituents of Time, naturally following from the probabilistic vision of the world, have amazingly much in common with the ideas of Heidegger (1960). In his terms, the Past is not something which no longer exists—it can always be found in the Present and determines both the Present and the Future. The future is of special significance in his conception of Time integrity: it is the concentration on the Future which makes "here-being" authentic. The mode of the Future is "forestalling." This qualitative characteristic of the Future coincides with our idea of the filter $p(y|\mu)$ as a question freely chosen out of the manifold of the potential Future. The probabilistic vision of the world proves to be the language which helps to reveal Heidegger's conception.

All said above seems to support the view that the categories Past, Present, and Future are only grammatical categories of the text through which we are interacting with Existence. This grammar familiarly dissects the whole into its components. It determines the direction of our Existence in the World. And we have become so accustomed to it that we regard it as natural and as the only possible mode of thinking. However, one could equally well assume the possibility of interaction with the world through Texts with a different grammar. It is thus that we assume the possibility of different cultures.

The qualitative difference of the three constituents of Time is manifested only psychologically: it is solely through *free* will that the Present becomes a specific qualitative moment in which the Past is converted by the Future. For an ideal pendulum, as stated earlier, Past, Present, and Future are indistinguishable: the pendulum lacks Free Will through which this difference could be manifested. Only Free Will generates Texts whose development proceeds from the trinity of the qualitatively different categories of Time grammar.

I would like to compare the ideas expressed in this chapter with the words of Karamsin, an outstanding Russian writer and historian of the eighteenth century, from his article published in the newspaper *Moskovskie Vedomosti* in 1795 (No. 89):

> They say that time passes; as for me, I think it is we who pass, while Time does not move.
> Our error in this reasoning is akin to the impression of people sail-

ing down the river that hills and trees on the banks are moving. Night and day are as they were, their sequence does not change: only elements, only bodies are subject to changes. Minutes and centuries measure not time, but the motion of perishable creatures: for time is infinite and differs from eternity only by its name.

The past is an abyss into which all temporal things fall; while *the future* is another abyss inpenetrable for us; the latter incessantly flows into the former. We are between them and so feel the flow of *the future into the past*; this feeling is what is called *the present* which makes our whole life. (quoted from Vinogradov, 1961, p. 268)

Have we since gained much more understanding of the nature of Time?

PART III

NOTHING

We have seen elsewhere that the Good,[1] the Principle, is simplex, and, correspondingly, primal—for the secondary can never be simplex: that it contains nothing: that it is integral Unity.

PLOTINUS, THE ENNEADS, II, 9.1

On the Threshold of Part III

Dialectically, non-existence should be concurrent with existence.

The ontology of the world would be incomplete if we did not consider non-existence.

Existence is given to us through Time, and the passage from existence to non-existence can be comprehended (if comprehended at all) only through the comprehension of Time.

Non-existence is given only as a hint. It is not given through experience since it is outside Time—the grammar forming the Texts through which man interacts with the world.

Man shares in everything which is *Being* and which is *no-Being* through non-existence undivided by Time.

Non-existence is the ultimate reality of the world.

[1] Plotinus's Good is one of the names of the first facet of the Higher Divine Triad. It is also called the First, the One, the Simple, the Absolute, the Transcendence, the Infinite, the Unconditioned, the Father.

Chapter 9

Semantic Vacuum as the Analogue of the Physical Vacuum

Comparative Ontology of Two Realities— Physical and Psychic

Does a dog have the Buddha nature? Nothing!
ZEN KOAN

It is of interest to trace the evolution of the physical concept of matter by the beginning of the twentieth century. The world was considered as consisting of the two complementary essences: discrete elementary particles and fields, the latter being physical systems continuous by their nature: physical values characterizing them have a continuous space distribution. There is also a specific state of the field, namely, physical vacuum, and its zero fluctuations are virtual particles (which cannot be registered by instruments).

Physical vacuum, the basic concept of quantum field theory, is in no way an empty space, but a state with important physical properties manifested in actual physical processes. For example, the vacuum state of the electromagnetic (photon) field is its lowest energetic state: the field of photons does not cease to exist when the number of photons in it equals zero. The field ceases to be observable since it stops emitting energy. But if a photon vacuum is given sufficient energy, then a photon will come into being, and the vacuum state will become observable. Thus, contemporary physics has come close to the concept of *non-existence* (the unobservable state) as a potential basis for *reality* (the observable state).

The possibility of giving a single, discrete-wave description of the phenomena of the microworld is realized in quantum field theory by intro-

75

ducing a new concept, the *secondary quantization*.[1] In such a description the physical field is put into correspondence with discrete entities—quanta characterizing various possible states of the field. The quantized field preserves the role of the interaction carrier, the interaction looking like an exchange of the field quanta: photons transfer the electromagnetic interactions between charged particles, and π-mesons transfer the nuclear interaction between nucleons.

We cannot help being surprised when we notice that our attempts to describe psychic phenomena at a very deep level linked to the unconscious remind us of the modern ideas of quantum field theory. Though, of course, we can speak here only of their metaphorical similarity.

Above (see Chapter 1) we dwelt on the fact that a person we consider in a discrete, individual state can also be regarded as a selective, probabilistically given manifestation of the semantic field. The discrete and the continuous are again not different sources of psychic existence but only different manifestations of it. Or, in other words, a person proves to be *one of the possible states* of the semantic field.

Note that the semantic field, like a physical one, plays the role of the medium in which the interaction takes place. A person interacts with himself or other people by means of discrete words or symbols. This process is realized through generating words (or symbols) and through their comprehension. Both aspects are realized through contact with the semantic field. In terms of physics, it could be described as emission and absorption of the semantic field quanta. However, there is a fine point here: the possibility itself of interaction between particles in quantum field theory (realized through absorption and emission of virtual particles) stems from the Heisenberg uncertainty relation giving the fuzziness of the state of a physical system.[2] Something of the kind is true of psychic reality as well: semantic interaction between people which we describe by a model based on Bayes's theorem is possible only as a consequence of semantic fuzziness of both the human psychic domain and verbal semantics. If a person's concepts had been rigidly given once and forever, he would have been absolutely incapable of understanding others.

By the way, this makes clear the insistent statement of Jung (1965) that the archetype is determined only by its form and not by its content. The archetype is but a symbol acting as a key to the Semantic Universe, but

[1] Secondary quantization is a special method of describing fields (systems with an infinite number of degrees of freedom) by means of operators representing the absorption or emission of the field quanta.

[2] In classical physics a free particle cannot either emit or absorb another particle since this would violate either the law of conservation of energy or the law of conservation of momentum. The uncertainty principle removes this limitation. Interaction of real particles becomes possible as a result of the participation of virtual particles which exist for a short period of time during which the energy is not fixed.

we can each time enter it to the degree we are prepared for this, as it is selectively manifested by our semantic fuzziness.

The archetype seems to be able to degenerate and turn into something analogous to virtual particles. This opens up the possibility for humans to interact with the *semantic vacuum* through unobservable (virtual) vacuum manifestations. Just as any physical particle constantly emits and absorbs virtual particles of various types, very similar processes go on in the psychic domain too. The latter may be described as a constant fluctuation of the probability distribution function determining a person's individuality on the semantic field. A human being never remains frozen and unchanged. We do not feel our participation in the semantic vacuum in the everyday tumult, but in a deep sleep, a sleep without dreams, this participation sometimes makes itself noticed. Rather incomprehensible phenomena, such as presentiments, telepathy, or insight, can be interpreted as an interaction of a human psyche with the fluctuations of the semantic vacuum. There is at least an external similarity to the interaction between physical particles and fluctuations of the physical vacuum. Such similarities please us if only because they reconcile us with what we do not feel like accepting.

A view of the *semantic vacuum* as a specific state of the *semantic universe* seems quite natural. This is a state of the absolute lack of semantic manifestation (or, in physical terms, an unobservable state) which must be complemented by the idea of *potentiality* as a source of semantic manifestation.

Jung (1965) described his perception of the semantic vacuum as follows:

> The dream is a little hidden door in the innermost and most secret recesses of the psyche, opening into that cosmic night which was psyche long before there was any Ego consciousness, and which will remain psyche no matter how far our Ego consciousness may extend . . . All consciousness separates; but in dreams we put on the likeness of that more universal, truer, more eternal man dwelling in the darkness of primordial night. There is still the whole and the whole is in him, indistinguishable from nature and bare of all egohood. Out of these all-uniting depths arises the dream, be it ever so infantile, ever so grotesque, ever so immoral (p. 394).

The idea of *Nothing* as a non-manifestation is easily reproduced in the probabilistic language as well. If the selective manifestation is smoothed down and passes into a uniform untruncated distribution, then, by force of the normalizing conditions, the ordinate will tend to zero. We shall face Nothing, or everything, with equal zero weights (see Chapter 2).

As already indicated, Existence is represented by Texts, while Nothing, as follows from what was said in Chapter 3, cannot hear the Text. Nothing is alienated from Existence: this idea had been formulated by the gnostics. For them, God existed outside Time, the grammar of the world, and was thus alienated from the world. It is useless to address Nothing with a textual prayer: it cannot be heard.

It is, however, a much more complicated problem to comprehend what *potentiality* is: psychologically, we are prepared for this concept and feel limitless potentialities within ourselves, but there does not exist a ready-made, easy-to-understand image.

If now we turn to the history of the evolution of religious and philosophical thought, we shall find the means for the clarification of these two concepts: the eternal Nothing and Potentiality.

We are going to briefly remind the reader of these attempts. In Hinduism this is the concept of moksha:

> . . . *moksha* is a state of consciousness in which the whole varied world of nature vanishes from sight, merged in a boundless ocean of vaguely luminous space. (Watts, 1974, p. 58)

Noteworthy are the expressive literary means used in the Upanishads to describe the hidden:

> [the *atman*] is more subtle than what is subtle, greater than what is great.

> It moves, it is motionless. It is distant, it is near. It is within all, it is without all this.

The non-manifested is described by Plotinus in very similar words. Here is how Paul Henry conveys this description in his preface to *The Enneads* (Plotinus, 1956):

> The One is the One and nothing else, and even to assert that it "is" or that it is "One" is false, since it is beyond being or essence. No "name" can apply to it; it eludes all definition, all knowledge; it can neither be perceived nor thought. It is not in movement, nor is it at rest. It is infinite, without limits, and since it has no parts, it is without structure and without form.

The God of the gnostics is also non-manifested. He is described by the following attributes:

> indestructible, unnameable, ineffable, super-celestial, immutable, unknowable, non-existent.

Note: He exists as non-existent.

In the apocryphal Gospel of the Egyptians (Böhlig and Wisse, 1975), one finds the following lines:

> . . . O God of silence. I honor thee completely. Thou art my place of

rest, O son . . . the formless one who exists in the formless ones. . . .
(p. 160)

Indeed, the conception of the fundamental principle of the world as Nothing is much more profound and spiritual than the primitive notion of the personalized, omnipotent, and exacting God, which came into our culture from the Old Testament.

And now a few words on the concept of *potentiality*. It seems to be most vividly expressed in Tao (Needham, 1954–76; Watts, 1974). Tao is the process of the world, the way of life. It is the harmonious exposition of life through its spontaneity. In the book by Watts, the following remarkable lines from Lao-tsu are quoted:

> The great Tao flows everywhere,
> to the left and to the right.
> All things depend upon it to exist,
> and it does not abandon them.
> To its accomplishments it lays no claim.
> It loves and nourishes all things,
> but does not lord it over them. (p. 38)

> The Tao is something blurred and indistinct.
> How indistinct! How blurred!
> Yet within it are images.
> How blurred! How indistinct!
> Yet within it are things.
> How dim! How confused!
> Yet within it is mental power.
> Because this power is most true,
> Within it there is confidence. (p. 36)

The above lines represent a striking attempt to describe what is inexpressible through the concept which can be expressed neither through an image nor through a myth.

If we again turn to the gnostics, we find in their teaching numerous attempts to express the idea of *potentiality* generating life from Nothing which is identified with silence, e.g., existence outside Texts. Below we quote two fragments from the above-mentioned apocryphal Gospel of the Egyptians:

> Three powers came forth from him; they are the Father, the Mother and the Son, from the living silence, what came forth from the incorruptible Father. These came forth from the silence of the unknown Father. (p. 54)

> . . . the Father of the light of everything, he who came forth from the silence, while he rests in the silence, he whose name is an invisible symbol. A hidden, invisible mystery came forth. (p. 66)

Here the words *came forth* are synonymous to *potentiality*. Another way to comprehend *potentiality* is through the conception of the omnipresence of Light in Matter. This gave birth to the gnostic image of the "possible Jesus" (Manichaeism): He "hangs from every tree," "is served up bound in every dish," "every day is born, suffers and dies" (Jonas, 1958, p. 229).

Plotinus (1956) tended to positively oppose the Potential and the Actual. In the fifth tractatus of the sixth *Ennead*, entitled "Potentiality and Actuality," the following lines appear:

> As Potentiality, then, it is not any definite thing but the potentiality of everything . . .
> Thus, since the very reality of its Nature is situated in Non-Being, it is in no degree the Actualization of any definite Being. (p. 122)

Is not this to say that Potentiality for Plotinus is neither a model nor a pattern for reality, but quite another thing radically different from reality? If we learn anything about the nature of reality, it is only from the acuteness of the problem formulation. Note that in his argument with the gnostics[3] Plotinus (1956) opposed the idea itself of the creation of the cosmos since opening a discussion of this idea will bring about a lot of other problems, much more difficult:

> 8. To ask why the Soul has created the Cosmos, is to ask why there is a Soul and why a Creator creates. The question, also, implies a beginning in the eternal and, further, represents creation as the act of a changeful Being who turns from this to that. (p. 139)

This fragment shows us very clearly how difficult the idea of the original creation is for our mind. The concept of potentiality has nothing in common with the act of the original creation. These lines are again much wiser than the Book of Genesis.

The problem of Nothing continued to be the subject of intensive attention of many Western thinkers, among them Eckhart, Boehme, Schelling, Sartre, Heidegger, Jung, and Tillich. I shall confine myself to a few quotations to the point from Boehme, Jung, and Tillich. I begin with the book by Boehme[4] (1969):

> For in the nothing the will would not be manifest to itself, where-

---

[3] Tractatus 2.9 "Against the Gnostics: or, Against Those that Affirm the Creator of the Cosmos and the Cosmos Itself to be Evil."

[4] Jacob Boehme (1575–1624) was a German protestant mystic and theologian. A shoemaker without any official education, he proved to be an outstanding personality who greatly affected the evolution of European thought, perhaps including Hegel, whose teaching of the triad, thesis-antithesis-synthesis, repeats Boehme's idea that all things are contained in YES and NO. We state with amazement that Boehme, after Eckhart, restored the gnostic ideas, especially in the pantheism of his Christianity. This came to him as an insight. It is noteworthy that the Russian philosopher-existentialist Nikolai Berdyaev said that these two thinkers had a major influence on his outlook (Berdyaev, 1949).

fore we know that the will seeks itself, and finds itself in itself, and its seeking is a desire, and its finding is the essence of the desire, wherein the will finds itself.

Courteous reader, observe the meaning right; we understand not by this description a beginning of the Deity, but we shew you the manifestation of the Deity through nature; for God is without beginning, and has an eternal end, which is himself, and the nature of the inward world is in the like essence from eternity.

We give you to understand this of the divine essence; without nature God is a mystery, understand in the nothing, for without nature is the nothing, which is an eye of eternity, an abyssal eye, that stands or sees in the nothing, for it is the abyss; and this same eye is a will, understand a longing after manifestation, to find the nothing; but now there is nothing before the will, where it might find something, where it might have a place to rest, therefore it enters into itself and finds itself through nature.

In these laconic and whimsical words which can hardly be translated into another language, we find exposed the concept of *Nothing* as the basis for all things, coexistent with God, of the *Will* as *Potentiality* (perhaps, Schopenhauer's "The World as Will and Representation" stems from here), and of *Nature* as manifested *Nothing*. We have here the *Ontological triad*. The reader can see that the above text thus turns out to be very rich semantically. But what has made it so compact?

Now I quote much simpler lines from Jung's "Septem Sermones ad Mortuos" ("Seven Sermons to the Dead") included as an appendix in his book *Memories, Dreams, Reflections* (Jung, 1965):

Harken: I begin with nothingness. Nothingness is the same as fullness. In infinity full is no better than empty. Nothingness is both empty and full . . .

This nothingness or fullness we name the PLEROMA.[5] Therein both thinking and being cease, since the eternal and infinite possess no qualities . . .

CREATURA is not in the pleroma, but in itself. The pleroma is both beginning and end of created beings . . .

Yet because we are parts of the pleroma, the pleroma is also in us.

The question ariseth: How did creatura originate? Created beings came to pass, not creatura; since created being is the very quality of the pleroma, as much as non-creation which is the eternal death. In all times and places is creation, in all times and places is death. The pleroma hath all, distinctiveness and non-distinctiveness.

Distinctiveness is creatura. It is distinct. Distinctiveness is its essence, and therefore it distinguisheth. Therefore man discriminateth because its nature is distinctiveness. Wherefore also he distinguisheth

---

[5] Pleroma is a gnostic concept (this text is written by Jung in the name of the gnostic Basilides).

them out of his own nature. Therefore must he speak of qualities of the pleroma which are not. (p. 379–380)

It seems rather odd that the text written by the major contemporary psychologist (though composed at a comparatively early period of his work) looks like a slightly vulgarized retelling of Jacob Boehme, a religious thinker who had lived three centuries earlier and had no formal education. It is only the terminology that had changed: *Pleroma* instead of *Nothing*, *Creation* instead of *Will*, *Formation* instead of *Nature*—again, the ontological triad. It is noteworthy that *Will* and *Creation* in both theories have an independent existence.

In quoting Tillich, I confine myself to the etymological analysis (his favorite method) of the word *existence* (Tillich, 1951–63)

> Summarizing our etymological inquiry, we can say: Existing can mean standing out of absolute non-being, while remaining in it; it can mean finitude, the unity of being and non-being. And existing can mean standing out of relative non-being, while remaining in it; it can mean actuality, the unity of actual being and the resistance against it. But whether we use the one or the other meaning of non-being existence means standing out of non-being. (p. 21)

Thus we see that the meaning itself of the term *being* (existence) unavoidably presupposes the *non-being* contained in *being*. This is so because we are unable to perceive anything otherwise than through opposition. Manifested *Being* must be divided, and this forms our perception.[6] We simply cannot perceive anything if it is not divided.

Within our system of concepts, all the phenomena of being, including here man—each individual person—are but a selective manifestation of the semantic field which can also be called the Semantic Universe. If selectivity vanishes and we have to deal with the uniform distribution function of probabilities determining our existence, then the Semantic Universe turns into the Semantic vacuum. But the latter is coexistent with us: both distribution functions, selective and uniform, are constructed on one and the same set of elementary events. As was said above, the fluctuations of the Semantic vacuum preserve the possibility of our permanent interaction with it. In the words of Tillich (1951–63), "The universe works through us as part of the universe" (p. 42). So, using the language of probabilistically weighted concepts, we discuss the subject which Tillich discussed. However, there is a fine point here: the language of prob-

---

[6] This assertion can be profusely exemplified. For example, *truth* can be thought of only because there exists falsity, and this latter must be contained in the truth; otherwise it would have been incomplete. If there had not existed the idea of non-truth, we could not have comprehended that of *truth*. Similarly, the idea of *health* is possible only inasmuch as there exists *non-health*, etc.

abilistic concepts makes obvious the smooth transition from the selectively expressed manifestation to non-being as non-manifestation.

The following striking words by Tillich (1951–63) also become clear: "In terms of the eschatological symbolism it can also be said that Christ is the end of existence" (p. 119). Tillich calls Christ the New Being: the end of existence is Non-being as Being in the completeness of its non-manifestation. The idea of God as Nothing may arouse strong opposition in a Christian reader, but let me repeat here the words of Eckhart (1941): "God is something that must transcend being" (p. 218). God in his transcendence of being is a depersonalized God, turning into Nothing. The personoclastic tradition[7] seems to have always been smoldering in the underground of the European culture, and this makes the latter closer to the Orient.

Tillich (1955) made an attempt to reveal dialectically the unity of the discrete and continuous aspects of God's existence. God is personalized in his existential being, and he is out of personalization in his essential being. Thus, man is divided from God only by the fact of his existential being. This softened personalization removes the basis for the opposition between the Western religions and Eastern ones. Tillich uttered a new word that destroyed the rigidly discrete perception not only of physical reality but also of psychic reality. However, what was said by Tillich is nothing more than a reflection of the softened opposition between the discrete and the continuous which has recently emerged in contemporary science.

When describing physical reality, physics, like philosophy and theology, has to deal with the same *triad*: *nothing* (physical vacuum), its manifestation (Matter), and potency (the laws of nature).

As a matter of fact, physicists cannot say a lot about the physical vacuum—what cannot be directly observed proves difficult to describe by a theory. There has accumulated a colossal body of infomation concerning matter, but this empirically obtained knowledge came to an impasse because of our ignorance of the basic principle: the concept of the initial bricks of the Universe has turned out to be an illusion. Everything is far from being clear with the laws of nature as well. The ontology of the law

---

[7] Of interest in this respect are the protocols in interrogations of the trial of Templars (Lizerand, 1964). One of the principal accusations at the trial (beginning of the fourteenth century) was persistent indications that the adept of the order in the process of initiation had to spit on the Cross. If this fact had been reported truly (the testimony was given under torture), this can hardly be explained otherwise than by the crudely medieval instance of personoclasm: the Order itself remained deeply Christian; it was formed at the epoch of Crusades for the defense of the Holy Sepulchre. In almost all of the Gnostic Gospels the image of Christ is significantly less personalized than in the Canonical Gospels. In one of the most mystic Gospels, the Gospel of the Egyptians, Christ is only given cosmogonically, non-manifested on the Earth. Recall the well-known Zen koan: "If you meet Buddha, kill him." Can we say these to be also instances of the personoclastic tendency?

is not and cannot be the object of the study. These are rather constructs of our consciousness that emerge from the attempt to comprehend what is observed as being manifested. It is senseless to discuss the ontology of the laws of nature. The question of their origin has never been discussed. They were always perceived as something which is given and whose origin is not to be discussed. The task of science was to reveal this phenomenon with the status of the fundamental principle. From a purely logical standpoint it is quite clear that no basis for the fundamental principle can be looked for. Certain physicists now doubt the existence of universal laws[8] and constants. In the concept of "bootstrap," an attempt is made to set the world potentiality through the S-matrix, allowing us (in a four-dimensional formalism) to describe the properties of hadrons in terms of probabilities of the interaction establishing relations between particles and processes.

Ontologically, the only thing we can say is that the potentiality of the physical world, no matter how it is expressed, in laws or constants or in the probabilistically given "tendency to occur," should be thought of as an independently existing essence. Potentiality in contemporary physics should be thought of as substantiated in certain primary matter. Of interest in this respect is the article by Aharon Kantorovich (1973), an Australian philosopher and historian of science:

> If quarks[9] are not discovered or even at least come to be understood as fundamental constituents of hadron matter, we may say that the physical conception is transformed from the atomistic picture to an Aristotelian conception of primary matter on which form is potentially imprinted . . . If we try to specify more concretely the primary hadronic matter, we may attribute this name to the unobservable vacuum of Dirac, or to the store of $q\bar{q}$ [quark-anti-quark] pairs . . . , to the fundamental "stuff" out of which the deformable sphere is made.
>
> But could not we identify *energy* with primary matter? It is true that matter is transmutable into energy and vice versa. But the Aristotelian hyle is unknowable and unobservable. Energy, on the other

---

[8] The conception of universal laws has come to European culture from the tradition of the Old Testament. If man, according to the Book of Genesis, is made in the image of God, and lives in a society governed by the Law, is it not to say that the World created by God must also be governed by the Law? The Old Testament by several ages of its dominance psychologically prepared Europeans to expect the scientific description of the world to be given through potentiality expressed by Law. The history of the evolution of the concept of Natural Laws is described in detail by Needham (1954–76), who also presents a substantial bibliography on the subject. And the possibility of constructing the model of world origin recognized by contemporary science follows from the Old Testament tradition.

[9] Quarks are hypothetical particles constituting all known hadrons (hadrons are a general name for the elementary particles participating in strong interaction). The word "quark" has a literary origin. It was borrowed from the novel *Finnegans Wake* by James Joyce, where it denotes something mystic and indefinite.

hand, is a quantitative concept; hence it is knowable even without having any specific material form. It seems, therefore, that energy cannot be considered as the analog of primary matter. (p. 347–348)

It would be natural to ask: How can the common ontology of physical and psychic reality be explained? The answer seems to be quite evident: by our faculty to see the world in this way. We have no grounds for asserting that the physical and the psychic worlds are constructed according to one and the same pattern. It would be more plausible to assume that in the depth of our consciousness there exists only one rigid pattern for the world perception. Psychologically, by our inner experience, we are prepared to see the World through the *triad*: *Nothing*, *Nature*, and *Potentiality*. And to these three essences we willingly add the fourth, a purely linguistical essence: *Time*. This last proves to be the state of our psyche or, in Kant's terms, the inner form of contemplation which allows us to see the World in its ceaseless, constantly changing splitting. The word splitting in the sense in which it is used here is a synonym for the word *Nature*. Space does not form a separate essence as a result of its inseparability from Time: the contemporary concept of the four-dimensional spatial-temporal continuum is but one of the possible ways to express our idea that space and time are two manifestations of the same essence.[10]

We view the World as fourfold. Note that Jung (1965) emphasized the universal character of the symbol of quaternity in our consciousness:

> The quaternity is an archetype of almost universal occurrence. It forms the logical basis for any whole judgment. If one wishes to pass such a judgment, it must have this fourfold aspect. (p. 397)

Historically, it seems relevant here to draw the reader's attention to the great interest displayed for many years by Sir William Rowan Hamilton in triads and quaternions, both philosophically (triads and triplets as aspects of harmony between thought and nature) and mathematically. He was engaged in the study of the algebra of numerical couples (at the same time as Grassmann) and gave a precise formal exposition of the theory of complex numbers; then, trying to generalize the results obtained, he had been long and in vain trying to solve an unsolvable problem—to construct an algebra of triplets—and, at last, he created a specific system of numbers, quaternions, which later turned out to be one of the sources of vector calculus.

We are naturally far from thinking that the World is actually made in this way. It seems *not to be made in any specific way*: everything is as it

---

[10] In Chapter 6, speaking of the psychological Time, I linked its velocity with the metric of the spatial scale, the scale of Doing, *S*. Thus, space and time turned out to be manifestations of one essence.

is. The quaternity of the World essences is nothing more than the way to view the World given by our consciousness. The history of human thought, revealed in mythology, religion, philosophy, or science, demonstrates that no matter how far our ideas wander away from this notorious quaternity, sooner or later they return to it. Contemporary physics also returned to it.

Nowadays we seem to have ample grounds for believing that all scientific knowledge is based on certain patterns of our unconscious. This was well understood by Pauli, one of the major theoretical physicists of our century. The following quotations are from his paper (Pauli, 1952) devoted to the analysis of how archetypic concepts affected the formation of Kepler's theories:

> Whether we speak of the "reflection of things in ideas" or of the "essence of metaphysical things, e.g., things in themselves," the relation between sensory perception and idea still follows from the fact that the soul of the cognizing person and what he learns through his sensations obey a certain order which is considered to be objective. (p. 137)

> In this world of symbols archetypes act as *ordering* operators and forming factors; simultaneously, they perform the role of the necessary bridge between sensory perception and ideas. Therefore they are significant prerequisites for the emergence of natural scientific theories (p. 138).

Below, in Chapter 11, section G we shall return once more to considering the role of the unconscious grounds for scientific creativity.

And now let us recall what we began with: the epigraph to this chapter. In the World of Texts the dog does not possess the Buddha nature. The answer to the question contained in the koan is "no." But "no" is Nothing where their nature is the same. So the koan is explained by the koan itself:

Does a dog have the Buddha nature?
Nothing!

Chapter 10

How Can We Contact
Semantic Nothing?

In the preceding chapter, when describing the world of psychic phenomena, I used broad concepts of these phenomena. The present chapter is limited to the aspects of our inner world which can be described only by concepts inherent in it.

From our own experience we know that the entrance into Nothing is signified by the stopping of our personal, psychological Time. Slowing down Time may imitate death. This was brilliantly expressed by the famous Russian actor Michael Chekhov (1953) in his passage against the naturalistic scenes of death on the stage:

> Death on the stage should be shown as a slowing down and disappearance of *time*. The actor portraying death must so arrange the rhythm and meter of his role as to enable the audience watching him to feel the slowing down of time and unnoticeably approach the point when the slowed down tempo seems to stop for a moment. And this stopping gives an impression of death.

Chekhov himself skillfully used this technique. I remember seeing him play Hamlet. In the death scene the rhythm of time was slowing down. The banners were lowered over the body of the dying Hamlet in the same slowed down rhythm. Nothing special seemed to be happening on the stage, but the spectators were bewitched: they felt the contact with Nothing. It was not an ordinary performance, but a mystery. Watching that performance was my first encounter with another reality. This memory of my youth seems to have predetermined much in my life.

All other techniques of contacting Nothing are also based on various methods of slowing down personal Time. One of them is meditation, which is described in detail in Chapter 11. Here I would like to say only

87

that the mystery played by Chekhov was an attempt to involve the whole audience in collective meditation.

A second way is the slowing down of Time that occurs in love. The nature of love has excited philosophers from time immemorial. Here I again turn to Plotinus, a philosopher completing the epoch of pre-Christian thought. He began his tractatus "Love" with a noteworthy question (Plotinus, 1956):

> What is Love? A God, a Celestial Spirit, a state of mind? Or is it, perhaps, something to be thought of as God of Spirit and sometimes merely as an experience? And what is it essentially in each of these respects? (p. 191)

At the end of the tractatus we find an amazingly simple answer to this question:

> Then Love is, at once in some degree a thing of Matter and at the same time a Celestial spring of the Soul's unsatisfied longing for the Good. (p. 201)

Plotinus had comprehended the whole complexity of the nature of love: both its material side and its urge towards contact with Nothing (recall that the Good of Plotinus is one of the names of the first facet of the higher Trinity which, by force of its simplicity, should not contain anything in itself).

Now, having enriched ourselves by the experience of many cultures, we are able to interpret Plotinus's brief but expressive assertion. Within our contemporary culture, love is primarily seen in its material, purely instinctive manifestation. In Freud's conception this instinct, being socially suppressed, leads to a pathology of personality and at the same time proves to be the principal impetus in the evolution of culture. Freudianism turned out to be a caricatural completion of the many centuries of Christianity—the culture of love aimed at merging with God, personified in Christ, through love. In Christianity love was seen in its non-physical, ascetic, and simultaneously deeply romantic facet.

Consider the way love was seen in other cultures. The East has the tradition of *tantrism*. There Love is revealed through intercourse which, transcending, acquires mystic significance. It is preceded by thorough and prolonged preparation, including the self-cleansing procedure and meditation directed at inseparable union of the couple in their psychological spaces. [For more details on tantrism, see Gold and Gold (1978).]

Thus, love was revealed differently in different cultures—sometimes submerged into matter, sometimes aimed at what we are ready to call God.

Psychologically, it is important to emphasize that love, like any other temporal process, can pass through stages of evolution, but having achieved its *fullness* it passes into an extra-temporal state.

Love in its fullness is existence outside Doing, free existence or, in other words, existence which could be called non-existence, since it occurs when the personality is dissolved in the original semantic vacuum. Non-existence signifies leaving Time. Love makes Being and Non-Being come together; it transfigures Death. But we may also say that love becomes a synonym of Death.

I have been surprised to find that certain attempts to reveal the nature of love in its fullness are also being made in the West. The quotations presented below are from an issue of the *Journal of Humanistic Psychology* completely devoted to the philosophy of love.

> Love as a way of stopping time, or entering eternity. Sex and the atemporal mystical continuum. (Keen, 1979)

> . . . love is an integral part of existence and of our individual lives. . . . We have the choice to experience love or not to experience love. We are always choosing to experience ourselves as a function of love or as loveless beings living in a meaningless universe

> Now the difficulty is that we are a consumer society. We have a grabbing and holding mentality; to go out and make, create, and build. We think that if we don't run the house, business, spouse, and children, it's all going to fall apart. We are convinced that we have to *do* in order to justify our *being*. . . .

> There is something basically wrong, and it has to do with the way we relate to nature. It has to do with the way we believe we have to create those things that are good in our lives. What we want in life we see in terms of activity, doing. But love is not a function of doing; love is a function of being, of simply what you are. That's what it means to speak of it as a substratum. It is the energy from which you are made, from which you come. . . .

> You suddenly can't have sex with anyone other than the beloved. Just as in sex two bodies become one, so in love, suddenly, two minds become one. There is a merging of the minds. Some transformation has taken place.

> When the substratum of love energy reaches the mind, flowering there in its own way and becoming love, you have a whole new series of trials before you, for love is the destroyer of ego. . . .

> Now notice that two things are frightening, and they both have to do with love. Sex is frightening because we lose control. Love is frightening because we lose the independence and autonomy of mind. We lose the capacity to control in love. When you are in love you are crazy. . . .

> . . . love is a great opportunity. It is the greatest thing going in the Human Potential Movement. We've forgotten about it. We have

techniques, facilitators, and workshops. Love, I am telling you is the greatest of these. It is what is called in India a *Sadhana*, a personal spiritual discipline. Love is a way to come to God. But it requires a constant purification. (Veereshwar, 1979)

Recall that above (see Chapter 6) we said much about personal, psychological time being generated by Doing. In the article by Veereshwar quoted above, love is the exit from Existence, Doing, i.e., a return to the extra-temporal unmanifestation which for him proves to be God.

And now a few words on tantrism from Dychtwald (1979):

> In the tantric lovemaking experience, which is called "Maithuna," the lovers undergo a variety of meditations and rituals before they actually make physical contact. These rituals and preparations are designed to create a strong spiritual bond between the two lovers and also to generate a mood of deep mindfulness and respect for the sexual joining which is to follow. Once the preparatory meditations have been completed, the two lovers proceed to make genital contact while maintaining the strong spiritual link that they have worked so devotedly to create. (p. 56-57)
>
> As the intensity and focus of the experience builds toward orgasm, the psychic space between the lovers continues to expand, allowing each partner the feeling of openness and godliness. In tantric yoga, the lovers do not try to achieve orgasm. Actually, if they are trying anything at all, they are trying not to have orgasms.[1]
>
> Instead, the tantric lovers are attempting to draw the building forces of Kundalini energy upward through their bodyminds, thus releasing the power of the various chakras. (p. 57)
>
> Once again, we see that from this eastern perspective the emphasis is not on the body and sexual release as ends in themselves, but rather as channels through which the development of self may proceed. (p. 58)

Thus we see that the East, in its anthropocentrism, which had allowed it to concentrate on the experimental study of man, managed to lift the veil of the mystery of sex and showed that the act following a series of meditations can be a means of stopping time. The act begetting life can also be regarded as begetting its end; in other words, it transcends life into another state.

The ultimate closeness of the two proves to be a crucial point on the life–death spiral—here lies the revelation achieved by the East. And that is why one can often hear there that life and death are one.

The West in its cosmocentrism has revealed something else—the trans-

---

[1] In a footnote to the quoted article, its author remarks that there are different attitudes to orgasm in different tantric traditions. In any case, if it occurs within the tradition that does not seek it, this does not cause a negative attitude. For details about the techniques of Tantrism see Gold and Gold (1978).

forming power of Love, unconditioned and acting momentarily. Recall the episode from the Gospel about the robber crucified together with Christ. His Love for Christ momentarily transfigured him. No preparations, no meditations. And before he had been just a robber.

Within the contemporary culture submerged in the world of things and success, love seems to be revealed in all its fullness only in tragic moments of ultimate tension. I would like to quote here Victor Frankl[2] (1963), who was a prisoner in a Nazi camp:

> A thought transfixed me: for the first time in my life I saw the truth as it is set into song by so many poets, proclaimed as the final wisdom by so many thinkers. The truth—that love is the ultimate and the highest goal to which man can aspire. Then I grasped the meaning of the greatest secret that human poetry and human thought and belief have to impart: *The salvation of man is through love and in love.* I understood how a man who has nothing left in this world still may know bliss, be it only for a brief moment, in the contemplation of his beloved. In a position of utter desolation, when man cannot express himself in positive action, when his only achievement may consist in enduring his sufferings in the right way—an honorable way—in such a position man can, through loving contemplation of the image he carries of his beloved, achieve fulfillment. For the first time in my life I was able to understand the meaning of the words, "The angels are lost in perpetual contemplation of an infinite glory."
>
> Another time we were at work in a trench. The dawn was gray around us; gray was the sky above; gray the snow in the pale light of dawn, gray the rags in which my fellow prisoners were clad, and gray their faces. I was again conversing silently with my wife, or perhaps I was struggling to find the *reason* for my sufferings, my slow dying. In a last violent protest against the hopelessness of imminent death, I sensed my spirit piercing through the enveloping gloom. I felt it transcend that hopeless, meaningless world, and from somewhere I heard a victorious "Yes" in answer to my question of the existence of an ultimate purpose. At that moment a light was lit in a distant farmhouse, which stood on the horizon as if painted there, in the midst of the miserable gray of a dawning morning in Bavaria. "Et lux in tenebris lucet"—and the light shineth in the darkness. For hours I stood hacking at the icy ground. The guard passed by, insulting me, and once again I communed with my beloved. More and more I felt that she was present, that she was with me; I had the feeling that I was able to touch her, able to stretch out my hand and grasp hers. The feeling was very strong: she was *there*. Then, at that very moment, a bird flew down silently and perched just in front of

---

[2] Victor Frankl is a leading European psychiatrist, the founder of the theory of logotherapy.

me, on the heap of soil which I had dug up from the ditch, and looked steadily at me. (p. 63–64)

If we started to speak of the opposition of Christianity and the East, we should emphasize the possibility of dialectical interpretation of the evangelic teaching. Being is revealed through personal Time generated by Doing; non-being comprehended as a free, extra-personalized existence not generated by Doing is revealed through love. Christ's sermon proved to represent dialectical unity of these two opposed essences. Two themes permeate the Gospels: the preaching of Love and the preaching of Doing: "Wherefore, by their fruits ye shall know them" (St. Matthew, 7:20).

The Christian comprehension of the essence of love is its manifestation through Doing. And if we are going to speak of Christ's new word, following the historical tradition, such a new, unprecedented word was the *dialectics* of manifestation of Love through Doing. Christ is revealed for everybody in the canonical Gospels through Doings of everyday Judean life. The mystic part of Christ's teachings is primarily contained in the apocryphal Gospels which seem not to have been intended for everybody. In the Gospel of the Egyptians, Christ is the son of silence. Silence, the synonym of non-being, is manifested on the Earth through Doing generated by love.

The European Middle Ages retained the tradition of Christian Doing. I only mention here the words of Eckhart (for details see Chapter 11, section D) that every man on the Earth should perform his Deed. The Middle Ages generated the romantic image of the knight, the cult of the Beautiful Lady—a peculiar transcendence of sexuality, and legends of the Temple of the Holy Grail in which the Cup with Christ's blood is kept. Then came religious wars and revolutions and the formula: Freedom, Equality, Fraternity. The East knew nothing of the kind. It was typical of the East to go away from life, and of the West, in contrast, to enter it. However, there cannot be clear-cut boundaries: hermits also existed in the West. The entire history of the Western world is a test of whether humanity is prepared socially to contact what had been called Silence.

The most vivid and passionate preaching of Doing in the East is contained in the Bhagavad-Gita; there Doing is existence itself. It is Doing born of an inner drive, without a particular goal or concern for its fruit. But the nature of the inner drive remains unrevealed. The succession of ideas is made prominent if we assume that the predecessor of the Gospels is the Bhagavad-Gita rather than the Old Testament. The Gospels reveal what was hidden in the Bhagavad-Gita. Note, however, that the ideal of knighthood was generated by the Gospels and in no way by the

Bhagavad-Gita, though it seems at first sight that it would be natural to expect just the opposite.[3]

And now let us make a comparison of the basic notions of Christian culture. The synonym[4] of love is freedom, since love is always a rebellion, an urge towards freedom. Love does not obey ego and thus destroys it. Similarly, it does not obey social and religious institutions and thus destroys them.

The personal rebellion may join the social one—and this makes clear why revolution with its romantic aspects is a purely Western phenomenon. In the Gospel of John we read: ". . . and you will know the truth, and the truth will make you free" (St. John, 8:32). So freedom also becomes a synonym for knowledge, the inner knowledge which the gnostics attempted to restore. The elements of the synonymous *circle* are: love, freedom, and knowledge. However, we already said above that death is also a synonym of love. The same is true of freedom: our subjects who meditated over the word *freedom* (see Chapter 13) constantly had the images of weightlessness, bodilessness, flight, leaving the Earth. So the synonymous circle is closed through silence akin to death. The four words love, freedom, knowledge, silence are discrete, the apices of a square circumscribed by a circle. The words are synonyms; their semantics smoothly flows from one into another. Our consciousness, prone to see the world divided, breaks the circle and the semantic links between words, making us see them as divided and different.

Above we spoke about a quaternity, and here we see another one. Perhaps, taken together, they form an eightfold pattern, the great Ogdoad of the gnostics.

The entrance into Nothing and contact with it is opened through each of its four facets: through *love* in the Christianity of the Gospels and in tantrism, through *freedom* in the Buddhist liberation of personality, through *knowledge* in gnostic Christianity, and through *silence* in meditations which seem to be known to all cultures. But it is only through Love that Nothing contacts human physical nature directly.

[3] Note that nowadays the attempt to resurrect the ideal of a free Warrior, whose inner drive remains unrevealed, is made by Carlos Castañeda in his bewitching books, especially in *Journey to Ixtlan* (Castañeda, 1972).

[4] Recall (see Nalimov, 1981a) that we call synonyms two words whose rank correlation coefficient for the succession of explanatory words ordered according to their importance is close to unity, or at least significantly differs from zero. If the coefficient approaches unity, the words become identical, semantically indistinguishable. Synonym does not mean identity.

PART IV

EXPERIMENT

On the Threshold of Part IV

The experimental data on which research on the unconscious can be based are extremely diverse. In efforts to understand what the unconscious is, everything relating to human activity in all its variety, both in the present and in the historical past, can be used. In this sense both the life of an individual and the history of humanity may be regarded as a gigantic experiment. And though only a small part of this experiment has been recorded, even those records retained in cultural monuments are boundless.

However, there is always a desire to carry out, apart from this spontaneous experiment (no matter how big it is), an active experiment which could give an answer to concrete questions.

The contents of the chapters that follow reflect the specific interests of the authors and represent their rather peculiar viewpoint.

The first and longest chapter of this part is devoted, on the one hand, to the description of meditation as a technique of entrance into specific, altered states of consciousness, achieved at will, and on the other hand, to the consideration of meditation-like states which a person enters spontaneously in everyday life.

The second chapter is devoted to the problem of symbols, signs by means of which consciousness comes into direct contact with the semantic field.

The next three chapters contain a description of the directed experiments carried out by the authors.

The contents of these five chapters have in view the comprehension of the nature of *imagination*. *Imagination* is a synonym for the unconscious. Wishing to grasp human nature, people of past ages tried to evaluate their difference from other creatures. Animals seemed to be the creatures closest to people, and philosophers of the past were persistently seeking the principal difference between man and animal. In our time, the closest and most comprehensible creature is a computer, and we ask: What is our principal difference from a computer? Primarily, it is the fact that we have imagination. This book could as well be entitled *A Probabilistic Model of Imagination.*

Chapter 11

Meditation[1]

A. Introduction: Meditation as an Entrance into Altered States of Consciousness

Freud must be acknowledged to have been the first scholar in contemporary European culture who started to develop experimental data for the study of the unconscious. Before him, everything said and written about the unconscious in Western psychology and philosophy had been largely speculative. Freud understood that people experimented with themselves while sleeping and specifically recorded the experimental results in dreams. The important thing was to learn how to interpret them. However, the entire Freudian interpretation of the unconscious proved to be projected onto a psychological subspace of a small dimension—all the axes of this subspace were only sexually charged. Adler and Jung expanded the dimensions of the psychological subspace, and our conception of the unconscious became more meaningful.

Later, it became evident that the mystic experience of esoteric aspects of Eastern and Western religions can also be interpreted as an experiment aimed at conscious penetration of the unconscious. Rhythmic exercises with breathing, severe asceticism, and ritual coition in Tantrism are all merely techniques of a psychological experiment directed at the deliberate entrance into the unconscious. Occultism and magic, so much despised by science, may prove an interesting object of study for a psychologist, as has happened with dreams. Religious experience is again a projection of the unconscious on the psychological subspace with a very peculiar choice of coordinate axes. Some researchers managed to discover in religious traditions results of experimental studies of the unconscious systematically carried out for ages.

[1] Written in cooperation with J. A. Drogalina.

97

Another experimental device directed to the same end was the use of psychedelic drugs. From time immemorial they had been used in many religious systems to provide the easiest way of entrée into the unconscious.[2] In our time the synthesis of LSD gave psychiatrists an extremely powerful means for exerting a directed influence on the human psyche. Of special interest in this respect is the book by the Czech researcher Grof (1975), now working in the United States, which describes a 17-year clinical experience of applying LSD to deliberately provide the entrée into the unconscious (later in this book we discuss his results).

Now we can state with some surprise that the entrée into the unconscious seems to be able to occur in response to any extreme somatic state, including sport (Murphy and White, 1978), as discussed below.

It has also become clear that altered states of consciousness can be brought about by more or less common somatic changes, such as those listed by Ludwig (1966):

> . . . disordered metabolism, sensory deprivation, intense emotional arousal, and induced relaxation. Sensory deprivation of the type encountered during prolonged voyages at sea may produce altered states of consciousness. These experiences may also occur as a manifestation of acute psychoses, hypnotic trances, anesthesia, or convulsive seizures.

Altered states of consciousness are also recorded in the recollections of reanimated people (Russell, 1974).

The experience accumulated up to the present moment—namely, similarity of descriptions of the phenomena in the unconscious state reached by various techniques, common semantic symbols of the unconscious, their profoundly archaic nature, invariance toward the entire variety of cultures—as well as other facts illuminated below allow us to claim that we are dealing with a phenomenon integral in its nature and related not to individuals but to humanity as a whole. Hence, it seems to follow that experimental procedures directed at selecting this phenomenon should also have much in common. However, we have to state that so far nobody has studied this problem in such a broad formulation.

We have entitled this chapter by the single word *meditation*. In European languages this word was derived from the Latin *meditatio*, which in English and French turned into *meditation* or *méditation* with the single meaning contemplation. Not very long ago, the meaning of this term was very distinct. It was used to denote some thoroughly developed techniques of contemplation that enabled individuals to enter the so-called *altered states of consciousness*, which we are now prone to identify with the manifestations of the unconscious without losing physical equilibrium.

---

[2] A faint echo of this in Orthodoxy is the use of a censer with aromatic smoke.

In other words, meditation techniques were elaborated so as to allow individuals to return easily and naturally into the familiar, waking state of consciousness.

Recently, intensive and many-sided studies of the unconscious showed that the altered states of consciousness which can be entered as a result of the above-mentioned natural, spontaneous somatic processes may also be identified as meditation. Here we would include as well the states arising under the effect of psychedelic (or, in other terminology, hallucinogenic) drugs. The meaning of the word *meditation* and especially of its derivative *meditative state* has been extraordinarily expanded.

Modern psychology and psychiatry, at least in the United States, are gradually getting accustomed to this term and the conceptual notions underlying it. However, up to now this trend of psychology has been nothing more than an appendix; its basic channel in the West still contains only two trends, psychoanalysis and behaviorism. William James, one of the most outstanding personalities of American psychology of the recent past (Taylor, 1978), who can be regarded as a predecessor of Transpersonal Psychology, also remained outside the basic channel.

There exists a voluminous literature devoted to meditation, mostly in English.

If we confine ourselves to the most primitive description of meditation, we can say that the goal of meditation is leaving the logically structured consciousness in order to attempt an interaction with the world not through speculation but *directly*, entering it and merging with it. According to Salinger, a poet is not a person who can write verse but one who *has an ability of direct knowledge of things*. Inspiration, not addition.

In meditation this ability is realized. So meditation can be said to be a poetical perception of the world through direct contact with the world of things.

To give a deeper definition, meditation is a means of broadening the limits of consciousness, of expanding its scale. In other words, meditation is a *journey* into the unknown depths of our consciousness. In interpreting meditation in this way, we naturally proceed from the fact that our consciousness is incomparably broader than the part that manifests itself in the waking state. We have to presume that, metaphorically speaking, human consciousness is cosmic, and we formulate the concept of a *semantic universe* of which we are a part. Such a holistic conception may look like a challenge to the paradigm of modern culture, but if we become afraid of our own idea, we shall have to reject the study of man in all his complexity. This is exactly what modern psychology prefers to do, at least in its major trends.

There exist many different meditation techniques, but at the initial stages the teaching is often brought down to concentration and holding attention on the object of meditation (deep contemplation) without resisting the continuous stream of images and without attempting to keep or recognize them. Recognition in this case would be the acquired constant habit of accommodating, or adapting, the world to our mentality. And if the World resists this (i.e., the process of accommodation is not mechanical), then this accommodation is carried out by force. This is a result of ceaseless inner dialogue accompanied by constant conceptualization, by "looking" at the world from outside. "Seeing" the world, interacting with it from within proves possible only when the inner dialogue is stopped, when conceptualization, i.e., giving names, finishes. This is important not because it is so erroneous to seek explanation but because it is erroneous to ceaselessly seek adequate explanations.

As a psychosomatic criterion of the cessation of the inner dialogue, a state of weightlessness, of soaring, may serve. Here is an illustration from the book by Castañeda (1974):

> My entire thought processes had stopped and I had felt I was practically suspended, floating. . . . I've told you that internal dialogue is what grounds us . . . (p. 22)

In our experiment to be described in detail in the Chapters 13–15, we stopped the inner dialogue of our participants by means of auto-training (AT), relaxation achieved by self-regulation and provoked by suggestive influence on the patient (or subject). This process results in a de-automatization of consciousness, by removing logical structuring. The cessation of the inner dialogue is a stage preceding the meditation proper.

Panke and Richards (1969) enumerate the following nine categories of meditation states: (1) undifferentiated unity of consciousness; (2) insightful knowledge or illumination about being or existence in general that is felt to be truly or ultimately real, in contrast to the feeling that the experience is a subjective delusion; (3) transcendence of space and time; (4) the feeling of spirituality and sacredness of an individual; (5) the feeling of joy and peace; (6) paradoxicality: perception of the world through the violation of the laws of Aristotelian logic; (7) inexpressability by means of the available linguistic symbols; (8) temporary duration of mystical consciousness and return to usual state of everyday consciousness (in contrast to psychosis); (9) increase of one's faith in one's own potential for creative achievement. These are, of course, only descriptions of the states of meditation in their simplest manifestations.

Literature on meditation is unusually rich and diverse. A regional–historical approach enables us to divide the practice of meditation in Buddhism, Yoga, Tibetan Buddhism, Zen, Sufism, Hesychasm, in West-European Monastic and Order Mysticism, etc. We can also speak of *transcendental meditation* in its modern application for therapeutics, with a broadly ramified system of paid courses in the United States, of meditation for children, and of experimental meditation in clinics.[3]

The publications by Goleman (1972, 1977), with a bibliography of 126 titles, are devoted to the classification of meditation techniques. The author bases his work on Visuddhimagga, the Buddhist source of the fifth century B.C.:

> At a first step in a systematic investigation of the myriad meditation practices, the Visuddhimagga roadmaps serve here as the skeleton of a typology allowing the sorting out of techniques in terms of their mechanics, despite the conceptual overlay that accompanies them. (p. 152)

In this literature the reader often comes across the classificational dichotomy: *concentration* versus *insight*. On this topic Goleman (1972) says:

> In the realm of mind, the method is the seed of the goal: the state of consciousness one reaches is contingent upon how one chose to get there. Just as each meditation subject is consequential in the level of absorption for which it serves as vehicle, so does one's technique determine whether one will follow the path of insight or of concentration. If the mind merges in samadhi with the meditation subject, and then transcends its subject to even higher levels of jhana, then one traverses the path of concentration. On the path of insight, mind witnesses its own workings, coming to see finer segments of mind–moments and becoming increasingly detached from its workings to the point of turning away from all awareness in nirvana. The great traditions evolved from these two paths can be broadly distinguished by their goal: whether to be the "One" or the "Zero." The One is the path of samadhi, of mind merging with its object, of self dissolving into Self in union. The Zero is the path to nirvana, mind taking itself as object, where all phenomena, including mind, are finally known to be voidness, where ego–self dissolves into nothingness.
>
> There is a third path, which combines the One and the Zero; *vipassana* as described in the Vissuddhimagga is itself perhaps the best example of practices integrating concentration and insight. When concentration and insight are combined in a meditation system, the combination is not simply additive, but rather *interactive*. Concentration multiplies the effectiveness of insight; insight-borne detachment fa-

---

[3] We do not give here the bioliography on the techniques of meditation since this would have made our book too cumbersome. A solid, thoroughly annotated bibliographic source may be the guide of the bookshop Yes! in Washington, specializing in books on inner development (Popenoe, 1976). *The Journal of Transpersonal Psychology,* published in the United States twice a year since 1969, is devoted mainly to the problems connected with states of meditation. The book edited by Tart (1963) contains a bibliography consisting of 1,000 titles.

cilitates concentration. This interaction can occur only when concentration is held to the access level—in jhana there can be no insight. In systems that combine the two, the outcome is a nirvanic state and consequent ego reduction. In terms of the One and the Zero, the formula that best expresses this interactive dynamic is: $1 \times 0 = 0$.

Integrated: *The One and the Zero* Concentration and insight combine and interact, ending in nirvana; $1 \times 0 = 0$.

Concentration: *The One*	**Insight:** *The Zero*
Samadhi leads through the jhanas; mind merges with the object in Unity.	Mindfulness culminates in nirvana; mind watches its own workings until cessation.

To summarize all said above, we can say that meditation is a means of entering such a state of consciousness that one can merely *Be*. To be in a state of *free* existence, in its absolute spontaneity. To be without acting, without feeling the external world, without thinking. To be without feeling one's personality, one's alienation, estrangement from the integrity of the world. To be in the unconsciousness of one's consciousness.

Humanity seems to feel always the necessity to de-automatize consciousness, at least in a temporal sense, i.e., to leave the boundaries of the culture which makes its participants view the world and act according to a certain pattern, fuzzy but still actually existing. In earlier epochs, this task was the responsibility of religion, but the latter could fulfill it only as long as it did not turn into a set of rigid dogmas. Therefore, the corresponding age-long experience has been accumulated in the esoteric schools, known as mystic, cosmic, and transcendental.

This experience is difficult to study and analyze scientifically since meditation states do not generally yield to verbalization. They can only be hinted at, these hints being expressed by symbols and interpreted in terms and concepts of a certain culture, though any mystic experience is by its very nature invariant with respect to the entire manifold of its manifestations through the variety of religious systems and philosophical conceptions of a psychocosmogonic character. Hence follows a very important conclusion that verbal notions of all religious systems are, as a matter of fact, synonymous. And it is exactly for this reason that one is able, having rejected the superstition of possessing the only true belief, to perceive the whole religious experience of humanity. Ecumenism as part of *Weltanschauung* was realized long ago [. . . there cannot be Greek and Jew . . . (The Letter of Paul to the Colossians, 3:11)], but now it has come to the surface as a logical completion of human spiritual evolution.

In the following sections of this chapter we give a sketch of various meditation techniques and the resulting states of consciousness, without claiming in any way to embrace all of the information on the topic known at present. We shall resort both to religious experience and to strictly scientific research.

B. On the Meditation Practice

Meditation practice is extremely diverse. It seems possible to say that every person in the long run elaborates his or her own techniques of interaction with the unconscious, often being quite unaware of doing so.

However, many techniques have become standard and can be learned. Some of them require only a few minutes a day; others presuppose complete immersion in them. Silence and solitude are necessary conditions for some of them, whereas Zen teachers, for example, suggest meditation amid the bustle of everyday business life.

Recently, a number of guidebooks for those who wish to meditate have come out. We indicate only some of the latest editions: Emmons (1978), Allen, Gawain, and Bernoff (1978), Tarthang (1978), Chitrabhanu (1979), Rogers (1976*b*), Ram (1978). The last 170 pages of the book by Ram Dass contain information on meditation centers and places of seclusion in the United States and Canada. There has also appeared a solid, annotated bibliography (Gawain, 1978).

These guidebooks are, indeed, guides in the literal meaning of the word, since they contain detailed descriptions not only of meditation techniques, but also of what a person submerging into his own self may feel at different stages of this submergence. They lead the meditator over the spheres of his consciousness, noting positive and negative aspects of relaxation and liberation from various tensions.

A broad use of relaxation techniques (to which the abundance of literature on the subject testifies) is not accidental. Western culture, with its drive towards the mastery of the world, preaches constant tension and concentration of efforts, and this results in permanent emotional and mental stresses whose compensation is, as a rule, of a chaotic and destructive nature (for example, alcoholism).

There is an acute need for relaxation and meditation in its natural form: it not only removes stresses and thus brings positive psychosomatic results, but it also teaches us to control mind and emotions by acquainting us with our inner Ego.

John Rogers (1976*a*), whose work in this field is well known, has provided very precise instructions for the neophyte practitioner of meditation. These exercises have been widely publicized in the United States and involve isolation, relaxation, use of simple objects of concentration (as in hypnosis), intoning of traditional sounds, controlled breathing, detachment from the sensations induced by meditation.

Now it is time we spoke in somewhat greater detail about the *mantra* without making an attempt to define it in a concrete way. We would rather allude to the "experts" who practice the mantra and are familiar with its esoteric aspect. Such an expert is Lama Anagarika Govinda, a representative of the East, well acquainted with the specific features of the European consciousness. Govinda has mastered not only meditation techniques but also the faculty to "record" meditation in paints: he is a painter as well. His book devoted to creative meditation and multidimensional consciousness is illuminated by pictures whose content is meditation. Below we quote the passages (Govinda, 1976*a*) that reveal the meaning of the mantra and its esoteric content.

> Mantras are neither magic spells whose inherent power can defy the laws of nature, nor are they formulas for psychiatric therapy or self-hypnosis. They do not possess any power of their own, but are ingredients of the human psyche. They are archetypal sound and word symbols that have their origin in the very structure of our consciousness. They are, therefore, not arbitrary creations of individual initiative, but arise from collective or general human experience, modified only by specific cultural or religious traditions.
>
> The mantra thus connects our peripheral consciousness with our depth consciousness, which represents the totality of our past. Our past, however, reaches back to a time before the creation of structural language and fixed word forms or concepts. Thus the earliest mantric expressions or seed-syllables (bija) are prelingual, primordial sounds which express feelings but not concepts, emotions rather than ideas.
>
> As in music we can discern a different vibrational character in all mantric vowels: the O is a rounded, all-inclusive sound, and it is certainly not by chance that in Greek and Roman scripts it has been symbolized by a circle. By superimposing the anusvāra upon this sound, it is converted into the mantric seed-syllable OM. As such it has always been regarded—from the earliest times of Indian history until the present day—as the universal sound. In the words of Rabindranath Tagore, "OM is the symbolic word for the infinite, the perfect, the eternal. The sound as such is already perfect and represents the wholeness of things. All our religious contemplations begin with OM and end with OM. It is meant to fill the mind with the presentiment of eternal perfection and to free it from the world of narrow selfishness."
>
> OM is like the opening of our arms to embrace all that lives. It is like a flower that opens its petals to the light of the sun.
>
> OM is the ascent towards universality, HUM the descent of the state of universality into the depth of the human heart. OM and HUM are like counterpoints in a musical score.
>
> The mantra takes on different dimensions and evokes different

mental images and visualizations, depending on whether the mantra is applied to the universal realm of the Dharmakaya, or to that of the Sambhogayaya, the realm of creative vision and spiritual enjoyment, or to that of the Nirmanakaya, the realm of action and transformation of both body and mind.

Of extreme interest is meditation *with young children*. Reports on this subject can be found in *The Journal of Transpersonal Psychology*. Meditation techniques for children were elaborated and put to use in a comparatively short period of time. The bibliography on the subject is rather vast and was partially listed earlier in this chapter.

We would like to dwell on an article by Maureen H. Murdock (1978) in which she speaks about her experience of meditation with elementary school children practiced for an academic year. She chose a simple beginning meditation from Deborah Rozman's books (Rozman, 1975, 1976) and rehearsed the pace of instructions, since the breathing rate of children is different from that of adults, and this might partly mistune the meditation.

The Murdock experiments indicate clearly that elementary school children, after simple preparation and training, may experience nearly the full range of psychic transformation through meditation. The therapeutic aspects of this experience are also evident.

The author also remarks that the children's concentration span immediately after meditation become longer and more intense as the months progressed. They increased their ability to shut out distractions. Their use of color in their art projects became more intense, free, and alive. Many drew or painted intricate mandalas. They began to treat each other with more concern, interest, and love. Very quiet children (especially boys) who never volunteered information about themselves consistently shared at quiet time their feelings and rich images.

The author emphasizes changes in interpersonal relations. The children became relaxed enough to talk about hurt feelings. Such relations become possible only when the children trust that their feelings will be heard and responded to. This trust stems, perhaps, from the fact that meditation, teaching one to interact with the inner world and promoting balance between the inner and outer life, helps to get rid of self-centered egocentrism.

Meditation also expands creative imagination. The need to train the activities associated with right hemisphere of the brain was emphasized at a conference in Los Angeles on 30 April 1977 entitled "Educating Both Halves of the Brain." According to one participant, meditation is one very strong answer to the question asked at the conference, "When do we teach love?"

The last thing we would like to say in connection with Murdoch's article is as follows. The author reports the parents' response to meditation: some of them were present at quiet time and even participated in it. Some of the parents were led by their kindergarten children in meditation at home; the parents were very pleased and felt that it had added a new dimension to their family life.

Murphy and White (1978) found that the state of meditation can also be achieved in peak moments during competition. It has become clear that what we are dealing with here are not somatic changes but psychological ones. In competitions time is compressed immensely, and so personal time is changed. The sportsman is entirely in the present. He feels only the "here and now"; the past and the present disappear as well as awareness of the external world. Everything is concentrated on a single action, and there is nothing outside it. At these moments the sportsman can enter the altered states of consciousness typical of deep meditation. They include the out-of-body experience, the feeling of immortality, ecstasy, time stopping, extrasensory perception, awareness of the "other" —"a sense of divine presence, a source of strength outside the self." All this results in the release of hidden energies.

These unexpectedly discovered common features in sports and ancient religious practice pose the question of training athletes in a new mode. It becomes evident that training should be not only somatic but also psychological. Meditation in its usual form naturally comes to the fore. This is the simplest and most accessible method of psychological self-education.

The above paragraphs are a brief summary of the book by Murphy and White (1978). It is based on a bibliography including 538 titles, most of which have been published during the past two decades.

Now we would like to move to a scientific study by Kornfield (1979) aimed at deep investigation of meditation, which the author calls insight. His paper is based on five two-week periods and a three-month period of intensive meditation training. The latter is described as follows:

> A typical daily schedule includes seven to nine sessions of sitting meditation for forty-five minutes to an hour; four or five periods of slow, mindful walking for thirty to forty minutes; and regularly scheduled periods for meals, rest and meditation instruction (Goldstein, 1976). In addition, students are instructed to develop a continuous and careful attention to each movement or action which takes place between fixed periods of group sitting and walking. Retreats usually take place in a silent monastic setting and all other such activities are prohibited. This leaves the student outwardly undistracted, providing a simplified environment for assisting in the task of self-observation. (p. 42)

Summarizing the data obtained, Kornfield gives a generalized description of a meditation state. Below we quote the most interesting, to our mind, fragments of this description:

1. *Meditation* itself is not an altered state of consciousness, but can be seen as a series of mental exercises designed to effect certain changes in how a person sees or relates to the world. As such, we cannot study a meditative state, but only examine the kinds of states, experiences and changes produced by various meditative practices . . . *Mindfulness* meditation is much more than a process of simple relaxation . . .

From our data it seems clear that the modern psychiatric dismissal of these so-called "mystical" and altered states as psychopathology —referred to as ego-regression to an infantile state—or labeled as psychic disorder, is simply due to the limitations of the traditional Western psychiatric mental-illness-oriented model of mind. . . . Rather, these experiences are normal perceptual changes happening in predominantly healthy individuals as part of a rigorous and systematic mental training of concentration and mindfulness . . .

The data show a strong positive correlation between student reports of higher levels of concentration (focused and steady mind-states) and reports of "unusual altered states and perceptions" . . . The development of the insight practice appears to have increased the frequency of moments of mindfulness in the retreat environment . . . Likewise, intense emotions and mood swings are a universal part of the practice reported in mindfulness retreats . . . Spontaneous body movement, often described as "unstressing" and "energy release" is commonly reported during mindfulness retreats . . . Body pain is reported as a frequent meditation experience. Many students describe finding new ways to relate to their pain as a result of mindfulness practice . . . Rapture and bliss states are also common at insight retreats and are usually related to reported increases in concentration and tranquility . . . Marked decreases in sleep and eating occurred during the practice at intensive retreats . . . Exceptionally vivid dreams and nightmares are a very common experience during insight retreats. Also reported are general increases of awareness before, during and immediately following sleep times . . . There are few reports of spontaneous psychic phenomena in the sample studied. Experiences described as "out-of-the-body" travel are the kind most commonly noted . . . Meditation does not appear to be a linear learning or developmental process. Instead, the "mindfulness" meditation[4] appears to include periods of regression, restructuring and reintegration as part of the basic growth pattern. (p. 50–53)

---

[4] Mindfulness meditation (in Buddhist terms *vipassana*) includes three stages: Preliminary (or Moral)

This is a purely scientific,[5] statistically supported description of features common for the majority of subjects in systematic and intensive meditation. The article quoted includes several, though very short, fragments of reports.

Summing up, we may say that the aim of meditation is to achieve a state which could be called a controlled waking dream. In a dream we are free from the paradigm of our culture and so it is also possible to say that the aim of meditation is *dehypnotization* (Walsh, 1979), the liberation of consciousness from the induced rubbish of thoughts, images, and fantasies. In other words, meditation proves to be directed at gaining inner freedom through liberation from identifying ourselves with preconceptions imposed on us by the discrete, dualistically oriented vision of the world.

C. Meditation in Eastern Christianity

What we have in mind is the tradition of Byzantine *hesychasm*. Here is what Meyendorf (1974) writes on the point:

> The most ancient and originally the only existing meaning of the term reflects the anchoretic contemplative way of life of Christian monks which appeared in Egypt, Palestine and Asia Minor at the end of the IIId century and especially at the beginning of the IVth century. The word "hesychia" (ἡσυχια) which means "silence," "peace" indicates the ideal of individual anchoritism, very different from the monastic communal life founded by Pakhomy the Great and presupposing strict outward discipline of life and labor. Not excluding external rules, the life of an hesychastic monk was determined by inner prayer, "wise doings," aspiration for personal "deifying" as a start of transforming other people and the whole world. (p. 292)
>
> In the contemporary scientific literature the term "hesychasm" is often applied to a psychosomatic technique for performing "Jesus's prayer" which was noted among Byzantine monks in the XIIIth and XIVth centuries. "Permanent prayer" since Euagrios was one of the principal attributes of contemplative monasticism; "Jesus's prayer" is a constant appeal in various word combinations to Jesus Christ whose name, according to St. John Climacus (VIIth century), should be "joined to breathing." These words were sometimes understood literally; to use breathing as a way to concentrate one's attention and

---

Training, Concentration Training, and Insight Training (on the relation between the two latter stages, see p. 101).

[5] Also note a detailed, despite its briefness, review by Walsh (1979) devoted to experimental research on meditation states, carried out in the traditions of Western psychology.

link the prayer with the unbreaking somatic function and thus to achieve the state of "permanent prayer." As distinct from platonic spiritualism of Euagrios, this psychosomatic "method" ($\mu\varepsilon\theta o\delta o\varsigma$) of prayer presupposes a positive attitude to the bodily, material aspect of human life. It is related to the tradition of scriptures attributed to Macarios the Egyptian and, which is highly probable, was used among Bogomils[6] (in its crude, folk, almost magic form). (p. 293)

There are grounds for believing that the tradition of hesychasm in some semiunderground form has been preserved almost to the present moment in Russian monastic life, especially in such phenomena as *starchestvo*[7] and *skhimnichestvo*[8] which played a very important role in Russian spiritual life opposing the official ritual Orthodoxy going back to Joseph of Volotsk.[9]

Ideologically, *starchestvo* always existed under a cover of mystery, though one could from time to time come across mention of it in literature (recall starets Zosima in Dostoevsky's *Brothers Karamasov*). The esoteric aspect of this trend was broken after the appearance of the book *Candid Narratives of a Pilgrim to His Spiritual Father*. This is a story of a hesychast method of prayer told by a man wandering about Siberia in the 1850's. The history of the book is of interest. Its author is unknown. A copy of the original manuscript came into the hands of a monk on Mount Athos; then it passed to the Abbot St. Michael's monastery at Kazan and was printed at Kazan in 1884. It has, of course, become a bibliographic rarity. We had an opportunity to get acquainted with this book in its English translation, *The Way of a Pilgrim* (1965), from which the following quotations were taken.

The pilgrim learned of Jesus's prayer both from the oral teachings of his spiritual father, a starets of Irkutsk, and from the book *Love for the Good*, an extensive collection of works by the Fathers of the Orthodox Church of the period around the eleventh century.

---

[6] Bogomils were a heretical movement which emerged in the Balkan countries at the beginning of the tenth century. Their teaching proceeds from the idea of the world's duality (incessant struggle between good and evil), rejection of the Old Testament, negative attitude toward the state, and condemnation of wealth. The formation of their teaching seems to have been affected by Manichaeism, a trend of Gnosticism. The Bogomils, in their turn, brought to life certain West-European heresies, namely, Catharic and Albigensian. The Bogomils were connected with Byzantium through Paulicians, a heresy formed there in the seventh century.

[7] Starets means a monk distinguished by his great piety, long experience of the spiritual life, and gift for guiding other souls. Lay folk frequently resort to *startsi* for Spiritual counsel, and in a monastery a new member of the community is attached to a *starets* who trains and teaches him.

[8] Skhimnik means a monk (nun) of the higher grade. The Russian skhimnik is the Greek *megaloschemes*.

[9] The Victory of Joseph of Volotsk over Nil Sorsky, who personified the mystic branch of Orthodoxy, signified the submission of the Church to the Russian state, its loss of spirituality. For details see Fedotov (1959).

It seems relevant to quote here a few teachings of the Starets on the technique of an unending prayer.

> Here is a rosary. Take it, and to start with say the prayer three thousand times a day. Whether you are standing or sitting, walking or lying down, continually repeat "Lord Jesus Christ, have mercy on me." Say it quietly and without hurry, but without fail exactly three thousand times a day without deliberately increasing or diminishing the number. God will help you and by this means you will reach also the unceasing activity of the heart. (p. 12–13)
>
> For two days I found it rather difficult, but after that it became so easy and likeable, that as soon as I stopped, I felt a sort of need to go on saying the Prayer of Jesus, and I did it freely and willingly, not forcing myself to it as before.
>
> I reported to my starets, and he bade me say the Prayer six thousand times a day, saying, "Be calm, just try as faithfully as possible to carry out the set number of prayers. God will vouchsafe you his grace." (p. 13)
>
> Waste no time, therefore, but make up your mind by God's help from today to say the Prayer of Jesus twelve thousand times a day. Remain in your solitude . . .
>
> I did as he bade me . . . The thumb of my left hand, with which I counted my beads, hurt a little. I felt a slight inflammation in the whole of that wrist, and even up to the elbow which was not unpleasant. Moreover, all this aroused me, as it were, and urged me on to frequent saying of the Prayer. (p. 14) . . . I lived as though in another world, and I easily finished my twelve thousand prayers by the early evening. (p. 15) . . . Now I give you my permission to say your Prayer as often as you wish and as often as you can. (p. 15) . . . During sleep I often dreamed that I was saying the Prayer. And during the day if I happened to meet anyone, all men without exception were as dear to me as if they had been my nearest relations. But I did not concern myself with them much. All my ideas were quite calmed of their on accord. (p. 16) . . . Again I started off on my wanderings. But now I did not walk along as before, filled with care. The calling upon the Name of Jesus Christ gladdened my way. Everybody was kind to me, it was as though everyone loved me. (p. 17)
>
> After no great lapse of time I had the feeling that the Prayer had, so to speak, by its own action passed from my lips to my heart. That is to say, it seemed as though my heart in its ordinary beating began to say the words of the Prayer within at each beat. Thus, for example, *one*, "Lord," *two*, "Jesus," *three*, "Christ," and so on. I gave up saying the Prayer with my lips. I simply listened carefully to what my heart was saying. (p. 20)

These last words seem especially noteworthy. They distinctly express the major goal of hesychasm: achieving a specific psychosomatic state through the sensation of Time as Prayer coming from within one's heart of hearts.

The book finishes with the praise to the Power of Prayer said by the Skhimnik. The burden of the praise is as follows:

> . . . Pray, and think what you will . . . Pray, and do what you will . . . Pray, and do not labour much to conquer your passions by your own strength . . . Pray, and fear nothing . . . Pray *without ceasing*. (p. 207–208)

It would also be relevant to go back to the source of hesychasm and quote some other words on the mindful prayer, prayer–meditation, which accustomed "the mind to keep concentrated on one point."

> The quality of a prayer is communication (*merging* into one being) and *communion* of man and God. (John Climacus)[10]

> Jesus's prayer . . . is in its essence a direct, most intimate and live *communion* of our spiritual nature, or of the inner man, with Our Lord Jesus Christ . . . and through him with God–Father and Holy Spirit. (Skhimnik Ilarion, 1910)

> The true prayer is that which comes directly from one's heart and ascends to God. And no other prayer is a prayer if it is not such as this. And all our care in the act of praying should concern this. But our mind is usually encumbered by a lot of non-divine thoughts, our will—by many daily concerns, our heart—by compassions and earthly pleasures and for this reason for us to ascend to God is the same as to climb out of the quagmire. Small prayers are very useful for this purpose. They accustom *the mind to keep concentrated on one point*; little by little they draw the compassion to themselves and distract from the daily concerns. This effect becomes stronger if one prays them not only in the ritual hours but also in some other time. The finite fruit is a formation of the feeling towards God, inseparable from the ceaseless prayer, or is the same. It brings about a live communion with God—the goal of spiritual life. (Episcop Feofan, 1898, Book I, p. 235)

> . . . God is everywhere; act so that your thought should also be always with God. But what are you doing? Thoughts are dancing like gnats in their columns, and over thoughts are feelings of the heart. In order *to join the thought to one point*, startsi used to accustom themselves to the ceaseless pronunciation of a short prayer; because of the

---

[10] The Reverend John Climacus (Lestvichnik Yoann) was born about 525; at the age of 16 he entered Sinai convent and in 554 he became a hermit—first in a cell and then in a cave. He lived thus for 40 years, whereupon the Sinai monks elected him their Superior; his year of death is unknown. The name Lestvichnik Yoann (St. John of the Ladder) is derived from the title of his book *The Ladder to Paradise*.

habit and frequency of its repetition such a prayer was pronounced
as if by the tongue itself.

Through this the thought also joined the prayer, and through the
prayer—the ceaseless contemplation of God. The habit linked the
prayer with the memory of God, and the memory of God with the
prayer, and thus they mutually held each other. So came the life with
God. These short prayers had been various, but later everybody preferred only Jesus's prayer: "My Lord Jesus Christ, Son of God, have
mercy on me." Everybody got accustomed to repeat it and with it
guard the memory of God. So you see now the place of Jesus's
prayer and its significance. As it is, this is not an intellectual prayer,
but a *verbal, external* one, as all other written prayers, but this is a
means towards a mindful prayer when someone is praying to God.
(Episcop Feofan, 1898, Book II, p. 55–56)

The above quotations show that, according to the teachings of Holy
Fathers, the quality of prayer is defined by such words as "merging," or
"communion." We also see that the external part is not the prayer–communion proper, but a preceding part helping *to join the thought to one
point*, to concentrate, to gather one's thoughts, and, moreover, to remain in this state: "to live with God."

We emphasize these words primarily because they express the internal
relations between esoteric schools practicing meditation. The state of
meditation is felt as *merging*, or *communion*.

The states of communion can be witnessed from aside: on this aspect
the text of a dialogue between the priest N. A. Motovilov with the Reverend Serafim Sarovsky,[11] one of the most outstanding representatives of
Russian holiness of the recent past, is of interest:

> You will remember this firmly and forever, though you can't al-
> ways remain in such a state, but if you feel this within yourself at
> least a little, you must know, my heart, that you are in the Divine
> Spirit.

This state of being "in the Divine Spirit" (i.e., of merging) is described
in this dialogue in detail, and sensory impressions and sensations determining the state of acquiring "the Divine Spirit" are indicated.

This state can first of all be noticed visually. We say "first of all" because the first thing to which Motovilov's attention is drawn and which is
confirmed by the Reverend Serafim is the *light*.

> We are now in the completeness of the Divine Spirit. Why aren't
> you looking into my, poor Serafim's, eyes?

[11] Serafim Sarovsky (1759–1833), iheromonakh (one of the grades in Orthodox Monasticism), Desert
Father and hermit, the latest of the canonized (1903) Russian saints. The record of his dialogue with
Motovilov can be found in the book by Denisov (1904).

I can't, because your eyes cast lightnings, and my eyes ache to look at them, and I can't look at you, Father Serafim, because you're brighter than the sun.

The description repeatedly emphasizes the bright and intensive light and the impossibility of perceiving it with the eyes (eyes "cast lightnings," "brighter than the sun," "eyes ache," "the light pricks my eyes," etc.). The next impression is peace "exceeding any mind."

"I feel such peace in my soul," I replied, "that there is no word to express it."

Further, "inexpressible sweetness" is mentioned. Then "such joy as no tongue can tell." Then follows "remarkable warmth."

"But how," he [the Reverend Serafim] went on, "can it be so warm? It is now the end of November, it is winter, there is snow under our feet, and snow on our heads, and it is snowing and the wind is blowing, so how can it be as warm as in the baths?" And he added: "So, the warmth is not in the air, but within ourselves. This is the warmth which we mention in our prayer to God: 'Warm us with the warmth of Your Holy Spirit' . . . So this warmth is not in the atmosphere of the air, but in the atmosphere of our soul and flesh, and it is also in our spirit."

And at last comes smell. Speaking of smell, Motovilov recalls that this smell was sweeter than the fragrance of scent. Supporting this impression, the Reverend Sarafim remarks:

. . . those were the scent extracted from the flowers on the earth, and this is heavenly fragrance of the Divine Holy Spirit; and it must be so that this fragrance is innumerably stronger and sweeter, as if from the breathing of the life of our God, the Creator."

Thus the Reverend Sarafim Sarovsky claims that the perception of the Divine Spirit is accessible to our organs of feeling in the above categories: our eyes see the light, our nose feels the smell, we perceive it "vividly, clearly, distinctly."

However, this is "the most extreme completeness" of the Divine Spirit, and nobody can remain for long in such a state.

For instance, if God had granted us, poor, with such a state at least for a day, we could not have stood this, and our perishable flesh would *have broken*, and we would have died, though joyful and

God-inspired our death would have been; because this our joy would
have led us to a greater spiritual ecstasy, and we could not have taken
any food or water, and *having melted* from the inner sweetness, we
would have lost our temporal life, because our flesh in the present
fallen state cannot endure such a force of inspiration of the Divine
Spirit.''

We have dwelt at length on the texts of Oriental Christianity first of all
so as not to form an erroneous impression that the practice of meditation
was typical exclusively of the spiritual life of the Far East. It would seem
correct to believe that meditation, in its various manifestations, was
common to all developed religions. We are not in a position to quote here
a sufficient number of papers to prove this hypothesis, but the formulation of the problem is essential in itself: if this hypothesis is proved, this
will be an important contribution to our conception of human nature.

From the psychological viewpoint it would also be important to pay attention to the existing differences both in meditation techniques and in
the description of meditation states which are primarily determined by
the general outlook of those experiencing meditation.

From the excerpts quoted above it distinctly follows that in the description of meditation states achieved during mindful prayer, as should
follow from the hesychastic outlook, psychosomatic characteristics come
to the fore: inexpressible joy, warmth, the feeling of light, and smell; the
last two characteristics are also felt by those present. The state itself is
characterized by complete aloofness; it is even death-like; one cannot
come across any mention of the new vision of the world. This may be
compared with the meditations of the Western mystic Eckhart, to be
briefly discussed in the next section. His sermons contained the cardinal
philosophical questions; the obviousness of his answers was determined
only by what the preacher had experienced in the depths of his spirit.
This makes his sermons very attractive but, naturally, only for those who
can experience the same.

It is interesting to draw attention to sharply negative attitudes toward
language in hesychasm. Medieval Russian culture was a culture of silence. It produced no written monuments, and we can judge its spiritual
content only by the images it created: icons, plastic architectural forms
of churches, church decorations, illuminations in holy books. We possess no written interpretations of holy texts which would be clear for us
and enable us, people of a verbal culture, to comprehend the peculiarities
of the medieval Russian outlook. What has remained is not only iconological thinking but also an iconological form of its expression (Pomerants, 1974). The uniqueness of Russian medieval culture lies in its source:
in Byzantine hesychasm.

D. Meditation in Medieval Europe:
The Sermons of Meister Eckhart

> *He brought praise to the great invisible virginal Spirit,*
> *the silence of the Father in a silence of the living silence of*
> *silence, the place where the man rests.*
>
> GOSPEL OF THE EGYPTIANS

For some reason or other, meditation is primarily connected with Oriental spiritual life, but actually the spiritual life of the Medieval West was also submerged in the state of meditation. Of great interest in this respect are the sermons of Meister Eckhart[12] which contain not only descriptions of the states of meditation but also of the new experience he had acquired during these states.

According to Eckhart, meditation is silence in which new consciousness is acquired. Here is what he says on this point in his sermon "This is Meister Eckhart from whom God hid nothing" (Eckhart, 1941).

> This, then, is the saying of the wise man: "While all things were wrapped in peaceful silence . . . a secret word leaped down from heaven, out of the royal throne, to me." This sermon is to be on that word. (p. 95)
>
> Let us take first the text: "Out of the silence, a secret word was spoken to me." Ah, Sir!—what is this silence and where is that word to be spoken? We shall say, as I have heretofore, it is spoken in the purest element of the soul, in the soul's most exalted place, in the core, yes, in the essence of the soul. The central silence is there, where no creature may enter, nor any idea, and there the soul neither thinks, nor acts, nor entertains any idea, either of itself or of anything else. (p. 96).
>
> In Being, however, there is no action and, therefore, there is none in the soul's essence.
>
> The soul's agents, by which it acts, are derived from the core of the soul. In that core is the central silence, the pure peace, and abode of the heavenly birth, the place for this event: this utterance of God's word. By nature the core of the soul is sensitive to nothing but the divine Being, unmediated. Here God enters the soul with all he has and not in part. (p. 97)
>
> Of nothing does the soul know so little as it knows of itself, for lack of means. (p. 97)

---

[12] Meister Eckhart (1260–1327), a German theologian and philosopher, was a Dominican monk of knightly descent. In the last years of his life, the Catholic church accused his sermons of being heretical. Two years after his death, twenty-six of his propositions were proclaimed as such in a papal bull. His sermons were recorded by his listeners from memory.

When all the agents of the soul are withdrawn from action and ideation, then this word is spoken. Thus he said: "Out of the silence, a secret word was spoken to me." The more you can withdraw the agents of your soul and forget things and the ideas you have received hitherto, the nearer you are to [hearing this word] and the more sensitive to it you will be. (p. 99)

This is the way a man should diminish his senses and introvert his faculties until he achieves forgetfulness of things and self. (p. 99)

May God, newly born in human form, eternally help us, that we frail people, being born in him, may be divine. Amen. (p. 102)

And here is a direct description of meditation as relaxation aimed at becoming a "desert":

Above all, claim nothing for yourself. Relax and let God control you and do what he will with you. The deed is his; the word is his; this birth is his; and all you are is his, for you have surrendered self to him, with all your soul's agents and their functions and even your personal nature. Then at once, God comes into your being and faculties, for you are like a desert, despoiled of all that was peculiarly your own. The Scripture speaks of "the voice of one crying in the wilderness." Let this voice cry in you at will. Be like a desert as far as self and the things of this world are concerned. (p. 115)

Eckhart's conception of Time is extremely interesting. Note that he considered Time together with Doing:

. . . I have also said that deeds and time are nothing of themselves. And if they are nothing in themselves, then, the person who loses them loses nothing! It is true. Still I have gone further; neither Time nor deed has any being or place of itself. In fact, they only issue from the spirit out into time. Whatever the spirit does afterwards, it must be in another deed at another time, and neither of these can ever get into the spirit in so far as it is either deed or time. Neither can it penetrate God, for no temporal deed ever got into him, and for this reason alone it becomes as nothing and is lost. (p. 138, from the sermon "The fruits of good deeds live on")

We are also struck by the problem of the *fullness of Time:*

In the fullness of time, grace was born. The fullness of time is when time is no more. Still to be within time and yet to set one's heart on eternity, in which all temporal things are deed, is to reach the fullness of time.

One Scripture says that three things there are, that prevent a person from knowing anything about God at all. The first is time, the second, materiality, the third, multiplicity. As long as these three are in me, God is not mine nor is his work being done. Thus St. Augustine says: "The soul is greedy, to wish to know so much, and to have and hold it, and so, grasping for time, materiality and multiplicity, we lose what is uniquely our own." As long as [the spirit of "Give me"] "More and More!" is in man, God can neither live nor work. All these things must be got rid of before God comes in and you may have them in a higher and better way, namely, that the many are made one in you. Thus, the more multiplicity there is, the more you will require unity in yourself, if one is to be changed into the other. (p. 151–152)

When time was full, the grace was born. That everything in us may be made perfect, that the divine grace, may be born in us, may God help us all! Amen. (p. 155)

However, this view has its dialectical opposition:

Three things there are that hinder one from hearing the eternal Word. The first is corporeality, the second, number, and the third, time. (p. 203, from the sermon "Distinctions are lost in God")

Whereas in these fragments one can hear the appeal to give up any action and thus stop time and obtain Beatitude, in the sermon "God enters free soul" we hear the hymn to action, and in this hymn the words of the preacher sound very chivalrous:

"Wife" is the optimum term that may be applied to the soul. It is even above "virgin." That within himself, a man should receive God is good; and receiving God, the man is still virgin. Nevertheless, it is better that God should be fruitful through him, for fruitfulness alone is real gratitude for God's gift and in fruitfulness the soul is a wife, with newborn gratitude, when it bears Jesus back again into the Father's heart. . . . your soul will bring forth no fruit other than the discipline to which you are so anxiously committed and you will trust neither God nor yourself, until you are finished with it. In other words, you will find no peace, for no one can be fruitful until he is done with his own work. (p. 208)

What I have been saying to you is true, as I call on Truth to bear witness and my soul to be the pledge. That we, too, may be castles into which Jesus may enter and be received and abide eternally with us in the manner I have described, may God help us! Amen. (p. 211, from the sermon "Distinctions are lost in God")

Listening to these amazing words full of deep and sometimes mysterious meaning, we see philosophy turning into poetry. But under the cover of these rather unfamiliar words that have much in common with the apocrypha of early gnostic Christianity, we discover with surprise our own ideas which we are trying to develop in this book.

It seems to us that what we have so verbosely expounded about meditation is contained in Eckhart's words on the silence of the soul. And our conception of individuality as a selective, probabilistically weighted manifestation of a unique integrity seems to have much in common with his ideas that people are linked with integrity through being in non-being. And, finally, our attempt to define personal time through Doing sounds almost like an exposition of Eckhart's thoughts about time. And we see with amazement that the power of meditation had enabled the medieval Catholic preacher to acquire the dialectical comprehension of Doing which is again in harmony with our ideas.

But we constantly feel the desire to look for a new language and to express it. Strange as it may seem, we can actually comprehend what had been said in the old language only after we find that we have managed to say it independently in a new language. We observe then the contact of two different consciousnesses separated in time by many centuries.

E. Dream as a State Close to Meditation

> *Dreams are the voice of the unknown . . .*
> JUNG

The meditational state of consciousness is naturally compared with certain dreaming states. Humanity seems to have been attracted by dreams from time immemorial: people were eager to understand their role, to classify and interpret them. A brief historical account of the interpretation of dreams is given in the book *The Forgotten Language* (Fromm, 1951). Historically, especially interesting is the interpretation of dreams found in the Talmud. Fromm repeats as a refrain the words of Rabbi Chisda: " . . . the dream which is not interpreted is like a letter which is not read."

In European culture it was Freud who first drew people's attention to dreams. We are not going to dwell here on his well-known theory which, though extremely popular in the West, is, to our mind, too one-sided and therefore unavoidably simplifies the entire manifold of human drives and reduces man to an asocial and primitively irrational creature.[13]

We consider the approach of Fromm, who also starts from psychoanalysis but tries to broaden and deepen the conception of dreams, much

---

[13] Jung, who for some time had been Freud's personal friend, subjected the sexually oriented Freudian concepts to a penetrating and at the same time devastating criticism (Jung, 1965). Independently of Freud, Jung came to understand the major role of dreams, but he ascribed to them another meaning, having connected dreams with human spirituality and evolution and participation in the cosmic, collective unconscious.

more interesting. Below we quote several statements from his above-mentioned book (Fromm, 1951):

> . . . all myths and all dreams have one thing in common, they are all "written" in the same language, *symbolic language*. (p. 7)

> The myths of the Babylonians, Indians, Egyptians, Hebrews, Greeks are written in the same language as those of the Ashantis or the Trukese. The dreams of someone living today in New York or in Paris are the same as the dreams reported from people living some thousand years ago in Athens or in Jerusalem. The dreams of ancient and modern man are written in the same language as myths whose authors lived in the dawn of history.

> Symbolic language is a language in which inner experiences, feelings, and thoughts are expressed as if they were sensory experiences, events in the outer world. It is a language which has a different logic from the conventional one we speak in the daytime, a logic in which not time and space are the ruling categories but intensity and association. It is the one universal language the human race has ever developed, the same for all centuries and throughout history. (p. 7)

> . . . I believe that symbolic language is the one foreign language that each of us must learn. (p. 10)

> Indeed, both dreams and myths are important communications from ourselves to ourselves. (p. 10)

> Symbolic language is a language in which we express inner experience as if it were a sensory experience, as if it were something we were doing or something that was done to us in the world of things. Symbolic language is language in which the world outside is a symbol of the world inside, a symbol for our souls and our minds. (p. 12)

> While we sleep we are not concerned with bending the outside world to our purposes. We are helpless, and sleep therefore, has rightly been called the "brother of death." But we are also free, freer than when awake. We are free from burden of work, from the task of attack or defense, from watching and mastering reality. (p. 27)

> Sleep and waking life are the two poles of human existence. Waking life is taken up with the function of action, sleep is freed from it. Sleep is taken up with the function of self-experience. When we wake from our sleep, we move into the realm of action. (p. 28)

> Consciousness is the mental activity in our state of being preoccupied with external reality—with acting. The unconscious is the mental experience in a state of existence in which we have shut off communications with the outer world, are no longer preoccupied with action but with our self-experience. The unconscious is an experience related to a special mode of life—that of nonactivity. (p. 29)

> . . . the paradoxical fact that we are not only less reasonable and less decent in our dreams but that we are also more intelligent, wiser, and

capable of better judgment when we are asleep than when we are awake. (p. 33)

However, despite the broadness of his views, Fromm links dreams only with human personality. A transpersonal, cosmic attitude toward dreams can be found in Jung (quoted from Fromm, 1951):

> Man is never helped by what he thinks for himself but by revelations of wisdom greater than his own. (p. 97)

We would like to quote here the following words of Jung (1962):

> I am doubtful whether we can assume that a dream is something else than it appears to be. I am rather inclined to quote another Jewish authority, the Talmud, which says: "The dream is its own interpretation." In other words, I take the dream for granted. The dream is such a difficult and intricate subject that I do not dare to make any assumption about its possible cunning. (p. 31)

Nevertheless, Freud, Jung, and Fromm, like many other authors of the remote past, all try to *interpret* dreams, i.e., to translate them into the familiar language of everyday reality determined by our culture. Interpretations of dreams by Jung, scattered through his books, are extremely interesting and meaningful. He seems to have had a real talent for this.

But perhaps another approach is possible: direct, unconceptualized comprehension—an attempt to understand without reflection, in the way one understands music or poetry. One does not, probably, exactly understand something, but is carried away without inner opposition to what has been evoked by the dream and what must reveal itself in our waking life. In other words, one must be deeply attentive to one's dreams since it is in dreams, on the unconscious level, that our value concepts are reconstructed. We shall return to discussing this problem in section G of this chapter.

Of interest in this respect are the activities of Rogers (1976a). For him a dream is not a text to be interpreted ("mentalized") but the concrete reality that yields to mastery only through personal experience. But let him say it in his own words:

> The process may vary tremendously from time to time. You may experience night travel for only part of your sleep state; your consciousness may be comparatively dormant during the rest of your sleep. The dreams and travel may take a short amount of time, or all night. Your meaningful experiences may come shortly after you go to sleep, in the early hours of the morning, or just before you get up. Do you get the idea? There is no only way. There are many ways. You have to discover your own. (p. 32)

When you learn the techniques of how to expand your consciousness (and recording your dreams is an important one) you can be aware of all levels of consciousness at the same time with an awareness that is as real as the awareness of the physical that you have right now. This multidimensional awareness comes with a realization and a knowing and a being; it does not come from thinking about or mentalizing this material. (p. 33)

The dream state, the night travel on the other side, is a learning experience. It is a progression of our consciousness into the higher levels of Light. Our freedom lies in the Soul Consciousness. When we reach there, we can go even higher into the Supreme God center and become a co-worker with God. The progression that is open to us is endless and infinite. As we travel above the Soul Realm, we come into total awareness of God-Consciousness and we experience the great Ocean of Love and Mercy. There are no words for these experiences. To have the understanding, *you* have to experience it. You have to do this for yourself. I can't do it for you, let alone tell you. You find the truth within yourself. You move through *all* the levels of consciousness. No matter what, you don't stop; you continue the progression. If you don't stop, you cannot be found by illusion. As soon as you stop and say, "This is it," the illusion will be there to put you in bondage. Keep going—always. The night travel is a training ground in the illusion. Through the dream process you can learn to recognize and bypass the illusions, continually. These are our lessons of spiritual unfoldment. But you must work through these things by yourself; your spiritual development is individual. I can point out the way; I can be a way-shower. I can travel with you and stand by you. I can clarify things for you and support you and guide you, if you'll let me. I am with you always, but I cannot do it for you. You must bring to yourself conscious guidance and direction if you are to move yourself forward on the path of your spiritual inner awareness and the path of your spiritual evolvement through the lower worlds into the realms of pure Spirit where you reside in the freedom of your own Soul Consciousness. (p. 33–34)

These fragments show us that the dream is meditation in its natural form. Later, in section G, we attempt to consider the problem of dreams with respect to human creativity.

Extremely interesting for a scholar studying consciousness is the idea of the prophetic nature of some dreams. Solving dreams like riddles that predict our future seems to have been typical of all cultures except ours, which has to a great extent lost contact with the unconscious. Why was this procedure considered so important? What brought it about? It will never do to reject all of the past as ignorance.

We think that solving prophetic dreams is one of the forms of probabilistic prediction inherent in people. People in their everyday life constantly forecast events both close and remote in time. By leaving their homes, people forecast possible events of the day; by getting married, entering a college, or taking a job, they forecast situations of the remote future. Such forecasting, characterized by a high degree of uncertainty, is always probabilistic (Feigenberg, 1972): a person must always be doubtful as to the predicted events, and he should be aware of these doubts, thus preparing himself for the possibility of a different outcome. Any rigid forecasting would unavoidably bring people in their further activities to blind alleys.

At the same time, if we proceed from the conception developed here, we may assume that forecasting—at least, of significant events—should occur at the unconscious level, in dreaming, when the activities of the unconscious are not blurred by the distractions of the waking hours. Hence, it would be natural to expect forecasting dreams to be of a symbolic nature.

Indeed, prophetic dreams are commonly classified according to the following pattern: symbolic dreams and metaphoric dreams; dreams as images from the anti-world which forecast the future by interpreting the dream as an anti-event (e.g., in the simplest case if one dreams that a lost thing is found, this means it is lost for good); and, finally, dreams interpreted on the basis of verbal homonymy [e.g., if one dreams of a horse (loshad') in Russian, this means he will be lied to ("lie" is "lozh'" in Russian); the pronunciation of the first letters of the words "loshad'" and "lozh'" is almost identical].

It is natural to assume that the interpretation of symbols may only be probabilistic. Therefore, Bayes's theorem is again relevant here. The semantics of an isolated symbol taken outside a concrete situation may be denoted by the prior distribution function $p(\mu)$; in a concrete situation y there emerges a preference function $p(y|\mu)$ by means of which, according to the theorem, the initial, prior concepts are reduced. This explains the important role of dream interpreters—those who are able to choose successfully the preference function. One such famous dream interpreter who went down in history was Joseph the Beautiful. Below we quote the parable of the dream with seven cows (Genesis, 41).

17. Then Pharaoh said to Joseph, "Behold, in my dream I was standing on the banks of the Nile;

18. and seven cows, fat and sleek, came up out of the Nile and fed in the reed grass;

19. and seven other cows came up after them; poor and very gaunt and thin, such as I have never seen in all the land of Egypt.

20. And the thin and gaunt cows ate up the first seven fat cows,

21. but when they have eaten them no one would have known that

they had eaten them, for they were still as gaunt as at the beginning. Then I awoke.

22. I also saw in my dream seven ears growing on one stalk, full and good;

23. and seven ears, withered, thin, and blighted by the east wind, sprouted after them,

24. and the thin ears swallowed up the seven good ears. And I told it to the magicians, but there was no one who could explain it to me."

Joseph was able to guess the meaning of the dream:

29. There will come seven years of great plenty throughout all the land of Egypt,

30. but after them there will arise seven years of famine, and all the plenty will be forgotten in the land of Egypt; the famine will consume the land,

31. and the plenty will be unknown in the land by reason of that famine which will follow, for it will be very grievous.

32. And the doubling of Pharaoh's dream means that the thing is fixed by God, and God will shortly bring it to pass.

The interpretation is obviously situational, for only Pharaoh's dream could be interpreted on such a wide national scale. Of importance is the comprehension of an uncertain nature of the dream; like a contemporary interpreter with a probabilistic disposition, Joseph emphasized that the "doubling" of the dream increased its significance (the probability of dreaming the same dream, if we were able to calculate it, would make us reject the idea that we are dealing with a random phenomenon independent of the situation). Joseph's interpretation produced such a strong impression on Pharaoh, that he "set Joseph over all the land of Egypt," and the latter, by his clever actions, managed to save Egypt from famine, whereas all other lands suffered greatly from it.

It seems superfluous to speak here of metaphorical dreams since metaphorical interpretation is to a certain degree symbolic. We would rather direct attention to dreams interpreted as anti-events. Again, such an interpretation is always uncertain. One can never state unambiguously what the situation will be in our world, which is the anti-world with respect to the dream. We feel that forecasting by means of an anti-situation is a trick of our consciousness which arbitrarily makes the forecasting void of rigid determinism.

As to the interpretation of dreams on the basis of homonymy, this is merely vulgarization. The same is true of dream books: they are only a profanation made by those who did not actually understand that the interpretation of dreams was an art. For us it is important that this art mastered by mankind is one of the manifestations of the richness of human psyches.

We should state at once that not only adult humans have dreams; in some other, uncontrollable form they are inherent in children and even in birds and animals. If this is actually so, then perhaps this is further evidence in favor of the hypothesis that all of us, people and animals, are attuned to the same fields of the semantic universe. In any case, this is what Galvin (1979) wrote:

> . . . William Dement (Stanford Univ.) reported in 1958 that a cat's EEG showed a regular pattern identical to human rapid-eye-movement sleep. This conclusion gave sleep researchers a much-needed model with which to study the mechanism of sleep and what causes it. Virtually every mammal and bird studied since then has been shown to have REM sleep. Earlier, in Chicago, Nathaniel Kleitman and Dement noticed something equally extraordinary: newborn babies, too, have rapid eye movement during most of their sleep. Are cats, dogs, and babies dreaming? If so, about what? If not, what is the meaning of this intense internal activity?

Perhaps animals differ from people in that their unconscious is projected onto psychological subspaces of an essentially smaller dimension. The intriguing mystery of dolphins may have a very simple solution consisting in the fact that their psychological subspace is very close to the human.

We are not able to dwell here upon the numerous studies devoted to the physiological procedures of dream research. Encephalographic methods of studying the brain in the dream state have developed intensively from the beginning of the 1950's. Researchers have discovered the relationship between dreams and certain phases of encephalograms, though the semantics of dreams still remains outside the sphere of their investigations.

Perhaps, the major result of these studies is the recognition that, in contrast to what Pavlov and many other scientists asserted earlier, in dreaming the cortex of the brain is not inhibited but, on the contrary, is in a very active state. Could we assume, proceeding from this fact, that it is in dreams that our basic concepts are formed, and in waking hours they are only comprehended and expressed verbally?

It is relevant to note that in certain situations dreams may acquire more reality than events experienced in a waking state. They can seem real for many years. Below we quote a fragment from the memoirs of Vera Figner (1964), a martyr of Russian revolutionary action:

> The new life began. The life amidst deadly silence, the silence to which you are constantly listening and which you hear; the silence

which, little by little, wraps you up, penetrates into all pores of your body, your mind and your soul. How horrid is it in its wordlessness, how terrible in its soundlessness and in its accidental breaks! By and by you start to feel some mystery close by: everything becomes unusual, enigmatic as in a moonlit night in solitude, in the shadow of the silent wood. Everything is mysterious and incomprehensible. Amidst this silence the real becomes vague and unreal, and what you imagine seems real. A long gray day boring in its idleness, resembles a sleep without dreams. And at night you dream, and your dreams are so vivid and poignant that you must persuade yourself you are only dreaming. And so you live, and your dream seems to be life, and your life—only a dream. (p. 10).

In this way reality is turned upside down: the complete switching off from Doing proves to be an entrance into the world of another existence. The ceaseless forcible silence opens up another reality of existence. The versatility and adaptivity of our psyches consist in its faculty to discover facets of existence even where a man is forcibly switched off from it.

F. Knowledge as an Experience

It is not possible for any to see anything of those that are established unless he becomes like them. Not as with man when he is in the world: he sees the sun, but is not a sun; and he sees the heaven and the earth and all other things, but he is not these—so it is with the truth. But thou didst see something of that place and thou didst become these: Thou didst see the spirit, thou didst become spirit. Thou didst see Christ, thou didst become Christ. Thou didst see the Father, thou shalt become Father. Because of this, [here] thou seest everything and [dost not see] thyself. But thou seest thyself [in that place]. For what thou seest thou shalt [become].

THE APOCRYPHAL GOSPEL OF PHILIP

The common Western concept of what *knowledge* is is determined by a fuzzy system of criteria of what is scientific in science. This system of criteria could be called a paradigm of positivism. Positivism as a philosophical teaching is but an attempt to view this paradigm through a system of distinct structures. Not many scientists would agree to such a view on the paradigm though they exist and work within its boundaries.

The Marxist view of logic and the methodology of science is, when all is said and done, nothing more than another attempt to comprehend and justify the same paradigm. The main attribute of this paradigm is the rejection of a psychological approach in gaining and applying knowledge. This fundamental premise leads to many others, rather of a methodological nature, which prove to be common to both trends of thought indicated above. Among these premises are acknowledgment of the omnipotence of logic, belief in the objectivity of knowledge, a tendency to reduce all phenomena to elementary mechanistic processes, rejection of the consideration of metaphysical problems, and a scornful attitude toward human inner experience.

But there could be a different approach to what *knowledge* is. It might be regarded as a result of an immediate experience. Below we try to clarify the nature of such knowledge by three illustrations. We begin with a simple one.

1. They say there are people who can easily recognize a brand of brandy by tasting it. The mark of brandy is a symbol, a unit of semiotics, and the taste of brandy is the semantics underlying this symbol. A taster can easily put the semantics in correspondence with a respective symbol but cannot pass the information of semantics he gains while tasting brandy to another person lacking a similar experience. Communication carried out on the semiotic level yields no semantic information about a symbol to a person who has never experienced such semantics.

2. No writer or poet seems to have ever succeeded in conveying by the words of our language the experience which may accompany the state of intimacy. Only a hint is possible here. And we can hardly hope to have a computer stirred by such a hint, no matter how sophisticated computers may become in the future. Perhaps this is a manifestation of the sixth sense. Its intensity may vary as the intensity of the other five senses varies in different people: far from every person who can hear has an ear for music. In the various cultures this sense was developed differently, one making it delicate and fine, another reducing it to an obscenity. The Tantrism mentioned earlier managed to use this sense as a means of entering the state of meditation.

3. Imagine for a moment that people deserted the disfigured Earth but left behind certain working devices. When a person from another planet arrives on the Earth, he starts to study a working television set and records a number of data sets characterizing the changes in electric fields, light fields, and heat fields. Further, he would naturally subject the data to spectral analysis and try to interpret them. Would he be able by such an instrumental method to grasp the semantics underlying the data?

In all the above illustrations we dealt with a reality which can be seen only through man. Here we involuntarily come close to the viewpoint of the existentialists. In order to obtain knowledge, one simply has to be in the world (être au monde, according to Merleau-Ponty; in der Welt sein, according to Heidegger).

At the beginning of our era, European culture had had two alternative ways of obtaining knowledge: Aristotelian, which was completed by a scientific–positivistic, instrumental vision of the world, and Gnostic–Christian, which opened up the road to the depths of the world by knowledge as an experience. Gnosis is the knowledge of the world in its universal meaning, knowledge gained by merging with it through Love. Knowledge became Joy, and World became God. One of the astonishing koans of Christianity sounds as follows:

> These things I have spoken to you, that my joy may be in you, and that your joy may be full. (John, 15:11)

The mystics of Medieval Christianity tried to gain this joy through prayer and *meditation*, eliciting the love for Christ in their hearts.

Existentialism, or to be more correct its branch called religious,[14] tried to restore the idea of a de-personalized God as an existential integrity, an idea completely lost during ages of dogmatic discords. Below we quote Burtt (1965), who sets the rather gnostic Gospel according to St. John apart from the rest of them, i.e., the synoptic Gospels.

> The Synoptic Gospels, in their conception of God and His relation to man, belong with the prophetic writings of the Old Testament. God, besides being the creator of all things, is for them essentially the moral governor of the universe and the good Father in relation to men as His children. John's insight was that this conception is far from adequate; rather, what Jesus had disclosed at the Last Supper is the clue to the true nature of God. And Jesus himself must have caught the essence of that vision, although its verbal expression, with him, probably remained in the form of parable and practical counsel. God is really a redeeming power, radiating everywhere in the universe and through all time the transforming love and sustaining hope that Jesus radiated in the limited temporal and geographical setting of his career. When this new insight was fully developed in the form of Christian doctrine it was no longer enough to think of Jesus as the promised Messiah. He must be the incarnation in human form of the infinite spirit of God, who has chosen to share the limitations and sufferings of men in order to awaken in them a responsive union with His boundless love. The celestial majesty and absolute self-suffi-

---

[14] Kierkegaard (1813–1855), a predecessor of contemporary religious existentialism, attempted to oppose to Hegelian dialectics another one, subjective and *qualitative*, regarding it as the basis for a human personality which "cannot be thought." Intimate, personal experience was regarded by Kierkegaard as unspeakable, inexpressible, indefinite, non-objectifiable, incalculable. Perhaps we, in this book, are trying to elaborate the problem formulated by Kierkegaard but not solved by him.

ciency that were essential in the earlier idea of God are now implicitly
renounced; God becomes one with man in order that man may become one with God. . . . love and expanding awareness intrinsically
belong together. . . . The central insight of religious existentialism is
the search for authentic selfhood in a search for love and that this
search provides the inclusive setting in which all experience and every
way of thinking can be wisely understood. (p. 85–87)

From these words it follows quite obviously that, if knowledge is regarded as *an expansion of personality*, in the system of religious concepts
love becomes a symbol of knowledge. This is true not only of Christianity, but also of Buddhism, in which meditation may be directed at the
feeling of love for all that exists.

We are often told that knowledge received through this form of experience cannot be passed to others. According to many, the noncommuni-
cability of this form of knowledge has shifted it to the background as
compared to the communicable knowledge of positivist science.

Recently, I became acquainted with a very interesting paper by Negley
(1954) discussing the lack of a basis for communication in ethics. But
where does the main difficulty lie: in the absence of an adequate language or of common experience of the problem?

In this area an article called "The Secret Language of Identical Twins"
(Corney, 1979) is illuminating:

> . . . By the time they were six years old, Grace and Virginia Kennedy,
> apparently healthy and energetic identical twins, spoke to each other
> in a rapid-fire language that nobody else understood . . . Somehow,
> in the extended privacy of a world without regular visitors, the sisters
> had made a language of their own—a "twin language," which oc-
> curs fairly often in very young twins, but rarely in children so old and
> almost never to the exclusion of any other tongue. After two years of
> speech therapy at the San Diego Children's Hospital's Speech, Hear-
> ing and Neurosensory Center, the twins retain a few words of the pri-
> vate language. Pathologists haven't yet broken their entire secret
> code. The most maddening part of the Kennedy twins' story is that
> they may never be able to explain it either. There is no way to tell
> whether Ginny and Grace (now 8½) will ever remember the sound or
> the secrets of the private language—or whether they have any idea,
> right now, about why these large people fell over themselves just to
> hear twins converse. (p. 16)

Many examples could be cited when an unusual intimacy gives rise to a
simple language comprehensible only for people who are intimate with
each other. Recall, for example, the declaration of love between Levin
and Kitty in *Anna Karenina*. Perhaps when we speak of important things
in our everyday language, we understand each other to the degree that we

are inner "twins" to each other. The perpetual urge toward creating new languages is probably a ceaseless attempt to establish communication where a sufficient amount of common experience is lacking.

Above we considered manifestations of *experience* on a very large scale, from the elementary taste sensations to the state of Christian love. We feel that all such manifestations basically have a common human nature which would be alien to a computer.

Now let us consider science—specifically, mathematics, its extreme and the most interesting manifestation. Can we assert that mathematical knowledge is completely contained in the system of symbols and in logic which links them? Perhaps for the Great initiates of mathematics, for those who exist there as creative workers, mathematics is a state of experience.

For the rest, mathematics is represented only by mathematical texts, and their only concern is to make them look correct. However, a mathematician cannot remain satisfied with only this one concern: this became obvious after the appearance of Gödel's theorem on incompleteness from which it follows that no strictly formalized concept of what a faultless mathematical proof is can be elaborated (Kleene, 1952). The history of mathematics demonstrates that many major discoveries entered mathematics on rather shaky grounds: e.g., this was true of mathematical analysis at the moment of its discovery. But there seem to exist people absolutely unable to experience mathematical texts—hence their sometimes aggressive rejection of such texts. How else can antimathematism be explained? The language of mathematics and its formal logical operations should be clear to anybody who is able to make use of our everyday language, maintaining the same logic.

From the above standpoint, the prospect of creating the bionic brain seems very attractive. On this point Stine (1979) said:

> . . . To date, the computer's power has been applied only to complex calculations or to simple, repetitive chores. That will not always be so. We will eventually build the first intelligence amplifier, a blend of computer and brain, optimizing both. We will link the brain and nervous system directly to the electronic computer, without the cumbersome keyboards, printers, and TV displays we use today. The computer will become not an antagonist but the ultimate extension of our reasoning, memory, and computational ability. We are closer to building an intelligence amplifier than most people realize. (p. 16)

We could add here that this attempt seems realistic and attractive. Humans will keep the faculty of knowledge as an experience, and the computer will be handling the tiresome and exhausting work of logically ordering our experience and storing in its "mind" the information to be memorized. The culture of today has made us concentrate the major part of our energy on this computer-like activity.

If this hope is realized, this will, perhaps, bring us back to the completeness of meditation.

G. Creative Scientific Activity as Unconscious Meditation

In this chapter we have tried to describe meditation in the entire manifold of its manifestations. However, it seems impossible to describe this manifold very exhaustively. All of us in our everyday life constantly resort to the unconscious constituent of our consciousness by using various techniques, often of a deeply private nature, determined by our individual peculiarities: genotype, upbringing, or spiritual maturity. As we have indicated above, by meditation proper we understand the techniques of resorting to the unconscious which have been specially elaborated and have become rather popular.

Creative scientific activity, even in its everyday manifestation, has features of unconscious meditation. Imagine a researcher who has failed to solve a problem. He stops experimentation and goes to the library. If he is lucky, the library is cosy and compact and readers themselves can choose any book on the shelves. Here he can rest from his usual environment, from the determined trend of thoughts, and from the forced dialogues with his colleagues. In the library the researcher may start looking through books which have nothing to do with his unsolved problem: this is a peculiar way to look into oneself. But this activity, which would seem absurd to an observer, is deeply meaningful: the problem leaves the waking, logically structured consciousness and the researcher begins to feel its unconscious aspects and its fuzziness. The familiar point of view disappears, and so the familiar phenomenon can be viewed now from a new angle. And then a sudden piece of luck: not quite knowing how, the researcher picks up a journal containing an article whose title allows him to see the problem from a new, fruitful angle. The following is an example borrowed from everyday experimentation.

Almost 50 years ago one of the authors of this chapter participated in work aimed at elaborating a photocathode sensitive to infrared light by sensitizing it with a complex dye. The formulation of the problem had been quite substantial: there had been a basic foreign publication, and it was known that the given dye increases the sensitivity of photoplates to infrared light; there also existed a theory based on complicated quantum-mechanical concepts. However, the official period for completion of the work was near its end, and no positive results had been obtained. With each new experiment we seemed to be coming closer to the expected result, but failed again and again. Intensive experiments were going on every day, and our entire team stayed in the laboratory until late at night. Then somebody managed to make the problem "fuzzy" and look at it from a new angle: the unstable effect we were observing could be explained not by the dye but by water of crystallization which entered it as a component. After another experiment it became clear that no other effect was observed if the dye was sublimated in high vacuum. But why had none of us foreseen this beforehand? All the hypnotizing theoretical structures related to the complex molecule of the dye proved absolutely superfluous. Work on the problem was stopped immediately, and the research project was terminated.

At present, immense efforts are spent to elaborate systems of information retrieval to facilitate scientific and technological research. But every scientist who actually participates in research knows that the publications one needs, sometimes quite unexpected and stimulating, are come across as if by chance. One only has to tune one's consciousness to their search. There is no rational explanation of this phenomenon within the existing scientific paradigm, and therefore systems of information retrieval have to be elaborated. One hears about the pertinence and relevance of a document, and so on. But what is the use of making a retrieval system void of a fuzzy viewpoint?

We are not going here to analyze from all aspects the process of scientific creativity. Note only the book by Hadamard (1949) in which the author emphasizes the fact that, in the creative work of mathematicians, in the process of insight, neither words of our everyday life nor mathematical symbols occur. The process takes place on the subconscious level, and on the conscious level its results are expressed by a system of symbols that enables us to communicate both with ourselves and with others.

An illustration of this phenomenon is provided by the words on creativity written by Sir William Rowan Hamilton:

> An *undercurrent* of thought was going on in my mind. . . . An *electric* circuit seemed to close; and a spark flashed forth, the herald (as *I foresaw, immediately*) of many long years to come of definitely directed thought. . . . (Hankins, 1980, p. 293)

And elsewhere:

> I then and there felt the galvanic circuit of thought *close*. . . . I felt a *problem* to have been at that moment solved—an intellectual want relieved—which had *haunted* me for at least *fifteen years before*. (Hankins, 1980, p. 293)

It is by Hamilton's readiness to receive the impulses from the semantic cosmos that we explain both his adherence to triads and quaternions mentioned above (p. 85) and the striking fact that his ideas on the optical–mechanical analogy were so much ahead of his time.[15]

It seems relevant to say here a few words concerning the fact that scientific–technological forecasts are of a mythological rather than a scientific nature. Moreover, in such situations science has often taken a negative, foreboding attitude. This is expressed in a compact and highly readable article by Eugene Garfield (1980). Garfield states that the first controlled, man-carrying, mechanical flight in history was made by Orville Wright on 17 December 1903, at 10:35 a.m., but almost five years went by before it was generally accepted that the Wright brothers had flown in their machine. And how could it be otherwise, remarks Garfield, when the most learned professors, including Simon Newcomb, had scientifically proved that powered flight was impossible?

The first negative article by Newcomb had appeared several weeks before the famous flight took place (22 October 1903). The name of Professor Newcomb was widely known: he was professor of mathematics and astronomy at Johns Hopkins University, founder and first president of the American Astronomical Society, vice president of the National Academy of Sciences, and director of the American Nautical Almanac Office. As a scientist, he still has not lost his significance: according to *Science Citation Index*, in the 16-year period from 1961 to 1976, he was cited 183 times.

Garfield also indicates that as early as in the thirteenth century Roger Bacon, hardly proceeding from vague scientific ideas, foresaw the possibility of a man-carrying mechanical flight:

> It is possible to make engines for flying, a man sitting in the midst thereof, by turning only about an instrument, which moves artificial wings made to beat the air, much after the fashion of a bird's flight. (Gibbs-Smith, 1974) [we quote from Garfield (1980)]

It is of interest that Bosch, a fifteenth century artist, saw by his inner sight and painted an almost modern plane, a tank, and a submarine (see Figures 11.1, 11.2, and 11.3). In Figure 11.1 the spectator is struck by an antenna going between the head and the tail of the flying bird and smoke as if from an engine inside the bird. In Figure 11.2 one can clearly see a tank turret on the back of an animal moving with the help of wheels, and in Figure 11.3 there appears something that looks like a submarine. All these are only visions, but how could they appear so many centuries

---

[15] One of the founders of quantum mechanics, E. Schrödinger, in 1926 emphasized the significance, for the new comprehension of the microworld, of Hamilton's discovery that the laws of geometrical optics and those governing the motion of particles could be expressed in the same mathematical form (Hankins, 1980). It is noteworthy that Hamilton was also a poet (though his style was abstract and ideal); he "insisted that science and poetry were the two clearest expressions of truth" (Hankins, 1980, p. 386).

FIGURE 11.1

FIGURE 11.2

FIGURE 11.3

before their time, before technology enabled their appearance? Perhaps fantasy not so much goes before actual scientific–technological progress as directs it.

It would be naive to present a creative researcher as a receptor tuned to receive what we call insight. The unconscious is not in any way a warehouse which stores the ready-made pre-conceptions of scientific theories. What has been scooped from the unconscious must be comprehended, i.e., presented in a form acceptable to the contemporary culture. The new must be prepared by the old; at the same time *it should not logically follow from the old, or it will not be new.* But if we look carefully into the new, we shall always see the old within it. It has often been indicated that all the new significant philosophical theories always converge to something known and comprehended long ago. The same is true of science: in its seemingly most unexpected manifestations we always recognize ancient ideas. Of great interest in this respect are the works published by the American physicist Capra (1975, 1976), who tried to trace the origin of some contemporary physical ideas in the philosophy of the Ancient East. In one of our papers (Nalimov and Barinova, 1974), we attempted to trace the links between cybernetic ideas and Ancient Indian philosophy. But the new is always created anew: it is related to the old only through the unconscious, which stores what had been eternally inherent in humans.

In the process of creativity, the major part seems to be played by the formulation of the problem. By saying that a problem is formulated, we mean that the region of the semantic space is chosen where the answer is to be sought. The problem should be essentially new, sudden, but we look for its answer in the past which exists within ourselves in a hidden, unrevealed state.

Again it would seem relevant to resort here to Bayes's theorem. The prior distribution function of probabilities $p(\mu)$ determines the value concepts coming from the past of the culture. The preference function $p(y|\mu)$ is a *question* posed with respect to the problem y related to the semantics m. Reducing the past along the preference function, we receive the new system of value concepts in which creativity is actualized. In this model insight will be represented by the *choice of the preference function*. It is possible to assume that the choice is made by way of emergence of an image coming from the semantic space. Here the unconscious reveals itself. We may also believe, as we already said, that as the idea of air flights matured it was affected by images of the type depicted by Bosch. Probably all the facts in the prehistory of air flights so vividly described by Garfield (1980) had been thus stimulated. The images of the unconscious are far from always imprinted and memorized by human consciousness. We are prone to believe this to be similar to dreams. When we wake up, we can instantly forget our dream without having time to transfer it through our consciousness, but we still have the feeling that we have had a very significant dream, and we behave and make decisions prompted by our dream. Recall the proverb "An hour in the morning is worth two in the evening."

Proceeding from our model, this proverb can be interpreted as follows: we dream an image which allows us to *reconstruct the distribution function of probabilities for the value concepts* so that we are now able to make a decision which earlier we could not make. The reconstruction of the distribution function takes place at the unconscious level: the conscious activities start after this reconstruction is completed. It may be that the unconscious image turns out to be connected with our conscious activities through a new *preference* function $p(y|\mu)$, determining the new vision of the problem m or perhaps giving rise to a new outlook. The interpretation of dreams generally takes place at the unconscious level.

It was understood long ago that the essentially new features of our outlook also require a new language:

> And no one puts new wine into old wineskins; if he does, the wine will burst the skins, and the wine is lost, and so are the skins; but new wine is for fresh skins. (Mark, 2:22)

The radical reconstruction of the value orientation in the semantic space can probably give an impetus toward the evolution of a new language.

It is natural to ask to what extent directed meditation can increase the creative potential of a scientist. The answer to this question is not easy to give. Each creative scientist is sure to have discovered his or her own deeply personal and usually not consciously realized ways of entering the state of meditation. We would like to believe that regular and methodologically elaborated procedures may increase spontaneous creativity.

This is based on our own experience: the part of this section on the model of creativity, as well as what was written about Time in Chapter 7, has emerged as a result of participating in intensive sessions of collective meditation on Time. But what is written here is not in any way a decoding of the images accompanying the meditation sessions. To our mind, the images affected us otherwise: through the mechanism of revelation of the unconscious which we tried to describe through a system of Bayesian concepts.

The above question may be reformulated as follows: Will directed and systematic meditation increase the creative potential only of those who are preparing themselves for scientific research? We have no answer to this and cannot obtain one without serious and extended research. We emphasize here that a creative researcher is not only a man receptive to the symbols of the semantic fields but also a personality with a powerful intellect.

At this point we would like to pose a question: What is knowledge? Imagine that you enter a big library with long shelves of books in it. Imagine also that by special training you have achieved the skill that allows you to pump everything written there into your memory. Will you actually possess scientific knowledge about such pumping?

If we have to convey our scientific knowledge to the inhabitants of other worlds, what is it better to send: the encyclopedia or the entire lot of books and journals? And if we do the latter, shall we actually convey scientific knowledge? Can scientific knowledge be handed over to a computer even if the memory restriction is removed?

We are inclined to believe that our scientific knowledge is not contained in our books. Rather, they are means of making it possible. Certainly, not all scientists are the carriers of scientific knowledge. One of the present authors for a dozen years worked side by side with a mathematician to whom the entire range of mathematics was transparent. It was amazing to watch him at seminars when he effortlessly understood reports often presented in a most incomprehensible form. Sometimes he had failures and got irritated over some paper, but a few days later he would come and say: "What an interesting problem! I have already started to elaborate it." He is a mathematician by nature, and the totality of mathematics, not merely a single branch of it, is open for him. I had an impression that I was watching the Great Adept of mathematics. He was surrounded by the Initiated of another, lower rank. The majority of scientists do not contribute to innovations in science; scientific knowledge is closed for them. [Recall that according to Wiener 95% of mathematicians are of this type (see Nalimov, 1981b).] Their knowledge is to a great extent only that which is contained in books. But without them, as well as without books, science cannot exist.

Here, of course, we cannot answer the question of how the process of scientific creativity goes on. The only thing we have managed to do is to dissect it into subproblems and to emphasize the role of spontaneously occurring meditation (i.e., meditation of which the person is unaware). We would like to believe that this opens up the way to experimental research.

H. Meditation as a Journey Inside Oneself

So, what is *meditation*? In the broadest meaning of the term, this is a directed journey into the depths of one's consciousness, the discovery of oneself. Like any other journey, it is sure to enrich a person and expand his personality. But on this road, as on any other, one may lose the way and encounter fatal dangers.

If we proceed from the conception of human individuality developed in Chapter 1, then the journey inside oneself will be interpreted as a reconstruction of the distribution function of probabilities determining the person's individuality. Above we said that the field of attributes on which this function is constructed contained the entire human ethnogenetic and phylogenetic past, as well as the entire potential future, but the personal consciousness held all this in an attenuated form, with small probabilities of realization. During a journey inside oneself, a person may so radically reconstruct the distribution function determining his personality that he will feel as if he is either in the remote past or in the distant future of mankind. The journey begins on returning to the past, and so a person finds himself in the astral world.[16] Interaction with this world is experienced as a reality. Voluminous literature is devoted to the description of astral–demoniac visions, including here the experience of Christian ascetics.

When in the process of the inner journey the distribution functions of

---

[16] The concept of the astral world widely used in the literature remains extremely ambiguous. It is usually related to lower manifestations of the self. In *our* terms, such manifestations are linked with the remote phylogenetic past of human consciousness. They are easily projected outside, taking the shape of surrealistic creatures as, for example, in the paintings by Bosch. It is also common in the literature to speak of an astral body as a certain, clearly *singled out* part of consciousness. In contemporary culture this singling out seems to occur only in certain situations of specific psychic functioning. Such a situation may, for example, take place in a monastic solitude. Leaving the society, severe asceticism and the tendency to reconstruct one's Ego in accordance with an ideal pattern may lead to the splitting of a personality. The part of consciousness not fitting to the ideal image is reflected outside. The praying ascetic identifies himself, on the one hand, with the powers of light; he may even feel he is conversing with Christ. On the other hand, he may be tempted by the demonic power. The word itself "temptation" testifies to the irrepressible urge to identify oneself with the singled-out double which we call the astral body. (We speak in detail about psychological doubles in Chapters 16 and 18, where we introduce the concept of multidimensional psychological space).

probabilities that determine human personality are reconstructed, a person may identify himself with other, higher essences. What is actually happening is, perhaps, the person's encounter with himself in his other potentially possible incarnation.[17] The person does not recognize himself and projects the unrecognized onto the external world; he identifies the projected with another, higher essence and obeys it, or at least unconditionally believes it. This gives rise to many delusions. We would like here to quote Rogers's *Inner Worlds of Meditation* (1976b).

> The process of meditation can be a useful tool in discovering yourself. (p. 13)
>
> It's not unusual for people to meditate twenty or thirty years and never get further than the astral consciousness. They may develop a communication with their own inner guide, which could be part of a past incarnation process. They may think that they have reached an inner Master, but the Master forms do not work on the astral realm of Light. For the most part, what you experience in the astral realm is *you* working in those areas—*you* working through many of your own illusions, hallucinations, and fantasies. (p. 16–17)
>
> When you go into the emotional realm, because earth is a planet of negativity, you may experience some turmoil. (p. 19)
>
> There is another level within you, even beyond the fantastic state of intellect, and that is the soul. In Soul, you are the It of Itself. You are eternal. You are light everlasting. You become and are and recognize that you are the Alpha and the Omega, the Sarmad, the God of creation. But also in that realization, you only know that you are these things on the realms *within yourself*. Many people who have traversed this have said that they were God, not realizing that they were only within the realms of their own consciousness. When you are in your inner universe, you are working through patterns by yourself. (p. 24)

In our terms, all said above may be reinterpreted as a ceaseless reconstruction of the distribution function of probabilities determining a person's individuality. During a journey inside himself, a person carries out an intensive experiment over himself: he recognizes himself in the entire potential manifold, and in the karmic or even generally human, phylogenetic past. The keen interest of modern Western man in meditation is easily understandable: the culture of our time has squeezed human individuality, and the distribution function determining personality is becoming needle-shaped. Meditation is a technique that allows people to loosen this unbearably narrow structure, to make it fuzzy. Its attractiveness lies in its property of enabling the traveller easily and painlessly to return to his former Ego, and at the same time to retain the newly gained

[17] We discuss in detail the idea of reincarnation existing from ancient times in Chapter 16.

experience which can also be comprehended at the familiar level of waking consciousness. It opens up the possibility of conscious reconstruction of oneself. This has much in common with the ideas of German existentialism on the dynamics of human nature; a man is viewed as Dasein—existing where he chooses to exist.

However, everything said above is true only of the reconstruction of the distribution function over the part of the space of psychological attributes which is familiar to the person: experienced either in this life, or in his past, or in the human past. In Chapter 1, we said that the distribution function embraced the whole limitless potential future of the person, inherent in our Ego with negligibly small probabilities. Description of the journey to this area of the semantic space becomes extremely difficult, as does the journey itself. In this journey it is as if a person leaves his own boundaries, though in fact there are no boundaries: human Ego contains the entire reality of existence with some very small weights (probabilities). The ancient author Hermes Trismegistes expressed this in the following words: "The whole macrocosm is reflected in the man as a microcosm." The journey into one's yet unexperienced future requires help. Here is how Rogers (1976*b*) tries to describe this:

> You can go back into these realms by yourself whenever you want. You can do this sometimes by using a mantra or through a form of initiation. But if you are going to traverse the high realms of Light—the outer realms of Light—and go into the ocean of love and mercy (which is reflected in the inner consciousness), you have to know the keys to get away from the body and into those outer realms.
>
> When you do this, you may find yourself traveling with lots of people. And that is one way to know whether you are traveling in your own inner realms or in the outer realms. When you're in the outer realms, the Mystical Traveler will be with you, and there will be other people present, also. When you're on your own inner realms, you're there by yourself, for the most part. (p. 25)
>
> The work of the Mystical Traveler usually is not to work in your inner worlds. His work is to work with you in the outer worlds, the invisible worlds of Spirit, and to get you into a oneness with God. To reach that oneness with God, you must get beyond the mind which says, "Oh, it's all a bunch of baloney . . . and it's just not for me." You must get beyond the emotions that say, "That hurts too much; I can't stand that." You must get beyond the imagination that throws up images that distract and delay. As long as those things work for you, that's fine. But when you come to the point where they're not doing it for you, then—and this is a plea as well as a challenge—sit down with yourself and maybe for the first time in your existence of all these lifetimes, find out what is going on with you. Get down to the basics. (p. 26–27)

The last lines have much in common with the gnostic idea that a man is part of the world's wholeness. In our terms, the entrance into another reality is but a shift of the center of the distribution function toward the yet unexperienced state of consciousness. The degree of shifting may differ: perhaps the psychologists of ancient times, introducing the celestial hierarchy—angels, archangels, seraphim, cherubs, etc.—wished to convey a similar idea, but expressed it in a mythological language.

We would also like to remind the reader that the European religious–mythological consciousness has a legend of Atlantis as a superhuman race. This is probably a concept of the potential future of humanity projected in the past. European mysticism up to recent times preserved a dream of the future superhuman race (see, e.g., the novel by Lytton, 1972). In the Nazi madness this dream turned into a horrible grimace. The Oriental concept of *nirvana* also seems to reflect a dream of the complete merging with the world's wholeness, when the distribution function becomes equiprobable over the entire field of the semantic universe. Entrance to nirvana signifies the erasure of the personality, its death. However, the state of nirvana may not be perceived as dying if it is viewed as merging with *the fullness of existence*, as an entrance to the *ultimate* reality for which a man proves to have been prepared during numerous journeys in the worlds of his soul. Then it is not death, but recognition of one's own self in the fullness of existence.

Thus, we can express the ancient knowledge of man in a new language, that of the number which reveals the probabilistically weighted vision of the world. Does a new attempt to describe things known from time immemorial sound more attractive?

I. About Those Lost in the Depths of Their Consciousness

From the viewpoint of our conception of a probabilistically fuzzy nature of human individuality, no distinct demarcation line can be drawn between mentally sane and insane people. We do not have in mind only the so-called cases of borderline patients whose mode of the probability distribution function determining human individuality has shifted not very far from the region containing the modes of people considered sane, but also those whose distribution function is such that the bulk of the probability density is shifted very far from this region. In this case patients are characterized by a sharp display of the part of consciousness which, in its weak and hidden form, is inherent in all people. People can get into these states in deep meditation or in dreams; they identify themselves with these states, but the way back, to a common state of consciousness, is always open for them. In other words, insane people are those lost in the depths of their soul. Some of them turn out to be carriers of another consciousness whose manifestations are impossible within our culture, and this accounts for their tragedy and its ugliness. Here is what Elsa First (1975), a British psychotherapist, wrote on this point:

> The more we can look at madness—as people did in Shakespeare's time—as a sign that something is wrong in the state of Denmark, the more we will be able to respect the mad. (p. 61)

To support this idea, First quotes Laing (1967):

> There are an infinite number of worlds the mind can construct . . . some are scary, some little understood, some might actually be incomprehensible. Some of them are certainly maladaptive and dysfunctional in our society . . . The cluster of acceptable forms of symbolization, meaning-assignment varies through history, in different social circumstances. What is outside the acceptable cluster may, under special conditions of role allocation, be accepted as genius. (p. 62)

And further she writes:

> Laing's obstinate elusiveness about "madness," his refusal to define it, comes down to this: We should not look at any mental expression as "sick" in itself. We can only say that person had had certain experiences, valid for himself, that he was unable to interpret and make coherent in a way that communicated itself acceptably to his fellows. (p. 62)

No wonder many foreign psychiatrists view madness as a social disease rather than a medical disease.

From time to time one comes across Western psychological papers in which certain mental diseases are interpreted as an awkward wandering through the depths of one's consciousness. For example, Bregman (1979) drew attention to the book by Hennell (1967), first published in 1938, who described his psychosis, stay at a hospital, and recovery. Retrospectively, after his recovery, he said that his illness related to the sensations of cosmogonic fantasies, including the feeling of a contact with another reality, and this had a flavor of the Truth. Some of the authors who have commented on Hennell's book (Laing, 1967; Assagioli, 1971) are ready to acknowledge that another reality he felt has an ontological status; they also say that in his traveling through the depths of his consciousness Hennell needed a guide rather than a physician; otherwise, he would not have mixed up the transpersonal and the personal and would not have described literally what had to be described mythologically. We would like to add here that nobody seems to regard "The Revelation to John" (Apocalypse) as exactly madness because of its mythological nature, though the question of including it in the Canon, where, by the way, it looks rather exotic, had once been long disputed. It would also be relevant to draw the reader's attention to the interest many psychiatrists show in Swedenborg (see Dusen, 1974). Emanuel Swedenborg (1688–1772) was a uniquely versatile and gifted person: a scholar who published works in seventeen branches of knowledge, a musician, a member of Parliament, a polyglot who spoke nine languages fluently, and at the same time a mystic who regularly traveled in the depths of his consciousness. His spiritual research is presented in many-volumed editions, often hardly comprehensible. In that period, these works of his gave rise to unfavorable criticism, including the accusation of heresy. Dusen (1974), a clinical psychologist, was surprised by the similarity between his own observations and those of Swedenborg:

> It seems remarkable to me that, over two centuries of time, men of very different cultures working under entirely different circumstances on quite different people could come to such similar findings. (p. 87)

Dusen finishes his article with the following words:

> It is curious to reflect that, as Swedenborg has indicated, our lives may be the little free space at the confluence of giant higher and lower spiritual hierarchies. It may well be that this confluence is normal and only seems abnormal, as in hallucinations, when we become aware of being met by these forces. There is some kind of lesson in this—man freely poised between good and evil, under the influence of cosmic forces he usually doesn't know exist. Man, thinking he chooses, may be the resultant of other forces. (p. 87)

What is said above may be interpreted in a much softer form. To our mind, it is even more elegant to say that what had once been referred to higher and lower hierarchies is actually inherent in any person and in a normal state is merely unrevealed or revealed only weakly.

This helps us to understand the roots of the recently emerged movement in the West directed at protecting mentally insane people. It is also natural that psychiatrists, enriched by the experience of the extreme manifestations of human psychology, start to publish philosophical works. The most vivid examples are Jung and Jaspers. Although we know the latter primarily as an existential philosopher, we must not forget that he was also a founder of a new psychotherapeutic trend, the so-called existentialist psychotherapy whose burden is the certainty that a physician must first of all himself enter the unusual state of mind of his patient. Certain papers of the Russian psychiatrist Gannushkin[18] are also of a

---

[18] P. B. Gannushkin (1875–1932) was the founder of "minor psychiatry," the teaching of borderline states between sane and insane people.

philosophical flavor, though it would be correct to agree with Appel (1959) that it was existentialism which linked together psychiatry, religion, and philosophy.

We would also like to emphasize here the following phenomenon. The work of a psychiatrist seems sometimes to open up for him an entrance to the unconscious. This was much dwelt on by Jung. Below we quote an episode from the case of a patient who committed suicide (Jung, 1965).

> At about two o'clock—I must have just fallen asleep—I awoke with a start, and had the feeling that someone had come into the room; I even had the impression that the door had been hastily opened. I instantly turned on the light, but there was nothing. Someone might have mistaken the door, I thought, and I looked into the corridor. But it was still as death. "Odd," I thought, "someone did come into the room!" Then I tried to recall exactly what had happened, and it occurred to me that I had been awakened by a feeling of dull pain, as though something had struck my forehead and then the back of my skull. The following day I received a telegram saying that my patient had committed suicide. He had shot himself. Later, I learned that the bullet had come to rest in the back wall of the skull.
> (p. 137–138)

Jung himself interprets this event as an entrance into the collective unconscious for which time and space are relative.

We cannot here analyze in detail all the problems mentioned earlier despite their significance for the basic theme of our book: they can be considered seriously only by a professional psychiatrist.

We are going to confine ourselves to a single remark. There was once a keen interest in the correlation between genius and psychic disturbances (e.g., recall the famous Italian psychiatrist Lombroso,[19] who was very popular at the end of the nineteenth century and the beginning of the twentieth), but now it seems that this interest has vanished. However, we feel it to be essential to note that certain manifestations of psychic diseases can be interpreted as a result of the entrance to the semantic fields of the unconscious becoming wider than is allowed by the existing culture. What is received through this entrance turns out to be too heavy a burden for the person involved. His obsessive and at the same time awkward attempts to express what he has learned by his inadequate linguistic means look morbid. Psychiatrists believe the most dangerous symptom of schizophrenia to be not image-bearing delirium but paranoidal conceptualization.

All of us who work in science constantly come across schizoid conceptualizers. Their modes of behavior vary greatly: some are persistent, even

---

[19] Cesare Lombroso (1835–1909) was an Italian forensic psychiatrist and anthropologist who founded the sociological theory of criminality in which an essential role is attached to heredity.

bold, and others are modest and humble. But all of them have one common feature: they ardently want *to be heard*, but nobody hears them. Moreover, they cannot be heard, for their structures are dull and look like a parody of science. But can one actually be sure they have nothing to say? Perhaps the reason for their tragedy is their inability to express themselves, their lack of sufficient intellectual power to create a language in which a new idea could be presented convincingly. Is it not this acutely felt impotence which makes them madly persistent?

Science has no criterion which would allow us to separate scientific conceptions proper from schizoid constructions. If the new looks elegant, if it strikes us, it may on that ground acquire creative power and, therefore, a scientific status. The inner progress of science seems to depend on the fact that, during a scientific evolution, new possibilities are revealed for the emergence of hypotheses which could be called mad since they move farther and farther from the familiar ideas we are prone to call common sense. One of the distinctive features of a true scientist is that he not only can be heard, but also can hear others. A schizoid conceptualizer not only cannot be heard, but cannot hear others either.

Schizoid structures are especially often observed in conceptualizers professionally unprepared for this kind of activity. Their initial knowledge is usually at the level of popular journals, but they do not seem to be in the least embarrassed by the fact that they do not actually comprehend scientific concepts whose sense is fully revealed only through a process of profound study. By the way, this constitutes also the negative side of popularization which can easily turn into profanation. Sometimes one cannot help thinking it would be better if science were kept more esoteric.

Of special interest are conceptualizations of a borderline nature—those which can be heard by only a small circle of people. Here attention is drawn to an outstanding personality, Helena Blavatsky (1831–1891), the founder of the Theosophical Order. As far as we can judge now, she was an unusually gifted woman, very attractive for her versatility. Her consciousness was open for direct contact with the Semantic Universe. However, her basic voluminous work, *The Secret Doctrine* (for its shortened version, see Blavatsky, 1966), produces a rather odd impression. This is a specific revelation claiming to expose the truth lying at the base of all the great religions of the world. This new wisdom is presented in the guise of a scientific language. It looks like a re-exposition of scientific cosmogony, geology, and anthropology based on knowledge alien to science. This impression becomes especially vivid when, as in geology and palaeontology, we come across accurate indications of time intervals for the periods of past history. Blavatsky seems to have followed very carefully the writings of nineteenth-century scientists: Faraday, Maxwell,

Crookes, Tyndall, Huxley, Darwin, and many lesser figures. She directed her sharpest polemics against positivism and the Jesuits, but remained imprisoned by the then omnipotent scientific outlook. Knowledge obtained as pure insight had to be presented in the mode of scientific theories. This is the tragedy of such "theories": everything would have been perceived otherwise if what Blavatsky had learned had been presented by symbols—images arbitrarily polysemantic and void of unjustified concreteness—in the form which ancient thinkers preferred to all others. At the same time a considerable portion of her theories about the Gnostics[20] (of an esoteric flavor) seem to have been supported by the recent discovery of the Dead Sea Scrolls and other archaeological items. The structures of Blavatsky are less mythological than those of modern physics and cosmogony. We feel that such pseudoscientific work must have antagonized both positivist scientists and spiritually disposed people. However, we know that Blavatsky had many followers; they exist even now. It is noteworthy that there has been formed on the basis of her work a peculiar sect among intellectuals. It is also of interest that people like Blavatsky, though lacking her power, appear today as well. To our mind, the phenomenon of Blavatsky must be of great interest to a psychologist. A new microreligion has sprung into being in front of our eyes, a religion based on deep conceptualization, which meets some of the demands of our time when the belief in scientific positivism is reaching its summit. It is also significant that Blavatsky, in her versatile and enormously intensive activities, in an exaggerated form made use of those specific traits of human consciousness which open up the possibility for scientific creativity.

Almost everything said about Blavatsky is true of Rudolf Steiner, the founder of anthroposophy. Being an ardent believer in the existence of spiritual laws, he made an attempt to create a science of the spiritual World. In his all-embracing works one feels the paradigm of positivism even more than in Blavatsky's, though at the same time Steiner thought that everything he said was nothing more than an interpretation of what he had heard from the archangel Michael, the leader of humanity (he believed that, being initiated, he had acquired a special right to such an interpretation). Here we again come across the same phenomenon: projecting oneself outside and the perception of oneself as a hierarchically higher creature.

Two other works can be mentioned here. Eliade (1976) remarks that the erudite and devastating critique of quasi-religious and occult teach-

---

[20] We draw the reader's attention to Blavatsky's first book (Blavatsky, 1877), which seems to be of greatest interest to contemporary readers since it deals with the origin of Christianity, including the teaching of the Gnostics.

ings of late has come not from scienticism but from the depths of spiritual thought itself; the works by Guènon, including his critical book (Guènon, 1921), acquired broad popularity after his death (Guènon was close to both Western and Eastern esoterism).

We would also like to say a few words on the phenomenon of sectarianism, which is extremely interesting not only for a sociologist but also for a psychologist. It may be regarded as a spontaneous experiment that enables us to observe the unusual aspects of human consciousness. Sects unite people who, because of certain peculiarities of their psychological constitution, find themselves outside modern culture. They may deviate from the axis of culture to both sides: to all-embracing theorizing, on the one hand, and to a specifically stimulated entrance to the unconscious, on the other hand. The latter trend may be interpreted as a regression to the phylogenetic past [Pentecostals (for details, see Samarin, 1972), Khlysts, Stundists, etc.], and must be of special interest for a psychologist studying the unconscious. But the former trend is also interesting. Once I had a chance to speak with a sectarian, a molokanin (one of the Russian sects), who, though an uneducated man, was a brilliant interpreter of the Bible. He started the conversation with a request that he be asked a question, and the question was immediately answered by a key phrase from the Bible. Then he began to interpret the phrase. It was done with great elegance: for each word from the key phrase, he would find all other phrases in which the same word occurred. (This can be easily done since the Bible is often provided with an index for word occurrences throughout the whole Bible.) As a result the listener would be presented with the semantic field of the phrase, which embraced the entire manifold of the texts of such a heterogeneous source as the Bible. This allowed one to conceptually comprehend the Bible, a profoundly mythological source. This technique seemed to me very instructive, and I thought it would be nice if we used it while studying the system of ideas of a thinker.

If we acknowledge as legitimate the assertion that society is heterogeneous by nature, then the protection of such sectarianism will mean the protection of the health of society.

J. Taxonomy of Consciousness

> *The part becomes no less than the whole, and the whole—*
> *no bigger than the part.*
>
> RICHARD DE ST.-VICTOR

Now we would like to make a few remarks of a metalinguistic character on the use of the language of probabilistic concepts. The traditional way of describing the integral, holistic vision of the world in the language of discrete notions always looks awkward. For example, Smuts (1936) says that what we see in nature is an integrity presented hierarchically: each integral piece is a part of a larger integral piece. In the language of probabilistic notions, the consciousness of each person includes the entire semantic universe in all its boundlessness: human personality, its alienation from the world, is partly realized as determined by the selective distribution function constructed over the whole field of the semantic universe. The indistinct features obviously coexist in the darkened state of consciousness, and no clear-cut boundaries can be observed here. *All* that exists is not part of the whole, but *the whole itself*, each of its manifestations being organized by measure expressed through *number*.

In Chapter 1 we spoke of the difficulties in biology stemming from the discreteness of taxonomy. We come across the same difficulties when we start to classify the levels of human consciousness, though these difficulties have been partly overcome by the arbitrary fuzziness of the taxon boundaries which is absent in traditional biology in the explicit form.

Above we spoke of the "celestial hierarchy" as a kind of classification of potential states of consciousness yet unachieved by people: its mythological character testifies to its fuzziness. The gnostics in their epoch suggested classifying people according to the triple system of consciousness: according to spiritual type, *pneumatics*—the possessors of gnosis; according to psychic type, in which the soul of man void of truly spiritual gnosis remains submerged in the illusions of everyday life, with its adherence to emotions and forms of behavior forced by society; and according to flesh–sensual type, *hylics*. Such a classification can hardly claim to be rigorous. The well-known Jungian classification of psychological types[21] (Jung, 1971), an interesting classification by Holland (1973) with a pragmatic tendency, and the classification of levels of the unconscious by Wilber (1977) in no way resemble taxonomy in biology, though the latter, as was mentioned in Chapter 1, is implicitly fuzzy and probabilistic. However, Wilber's classification is of interest. He selects the following four forms of the dynamic manifestations of the unconscious:

Archetypic unconscious determined phylogenetically.

The *Submergent* Unconscious which was once conscious, in the lifetime of the individual, but is now screened out of awareness.

The *Embedded* Unconscious: the part of the unconscious superego embedded into consciousness.

---

[21] Note that from the point of view of a psychologist the taxonomy of horoscopes might also present a certain interest. Horoscopes elegantly delineate types of people classified according to their spontaneous behavior, which manifests itself independently of the goal set and actual circumstances. Strange as it may seem, spontaneous behavior may often be related to animal behavior: that of a tiger or a dog. Perhaps this accounts for the concept of the astral aspects of the human self connecting man with his phylogenetic past.

The *Emergent* Unconscious—the subtle structures of the unconscious emerging as sudden explosions.

Also noteworthy is a broader classification suggested by Wilber and Meadow (1979):

1. The gross realm: The physical body and all lower levels of consciousness including the psychoanalytic Ego and simple sensations and perceptions.
2. The astral realm: Out-of-the-body experiences and certain occult knowledge.
3. The psychic realm: psi phenomena such as ESP, clairvoyance, and precognition.
4. The subtle realm: Higher symbolic visions, light, higher presences, and intense but soothing vibrations and bliss.
5. The lower causal realm: Beginning of true transcendence and the undermining of subject-object dualism.
6. The higher causal realm: Transcendence of all manifest realms.
7. The ultimate: Absolute identity with the Many and the One. (p. 68)

This classification, attractive for its resorting to human depths, strikes the reader by the fact that the way to the *Absolute Integrity* passes through six distinctly delineated spheres separated from one another. In terms of a probabilistic vision of the world, this rhetorical awkwardness disappears immediately: each of the spheres proves to be a selective facet of the Integral. Passage to the Ultimate state signifies merely the removal of selectivity in the distribution function of probabilities given on the semantic continuum.

One should keep in mind that the taxonomic division of the continuum is, strictly speaking, impossible even if its occurrence is not related to selectivity given by the distribution function. This assertion follows from purely mathematical reasoning. It would be relevant here to recall the Dedekind axiom of continuity. Roughly speaking, its corollary is that dividing the segment AB into two classes, we have to deal with the limit point C (the point of Dedekind section) which may belong both to the first class and to the second one. Here lies the principal difficulty of taxonomy: a limit point situated between the two simplest, semantically one-dimensional taxons may belong to both of them. This gives rise to endless discussions. Wishing to avoid them, we shall have to change slightly the algorithm of division, but we shall still obtain new limit points. The precision of our judgments will unavoidably be permanently eroded.

It would seem more rational to exploit the models given by a fuzzy set, i.e., by a set over which a weighting function is constructed that determines the degree to which the segments of the set belong to the problem under study. What in the traditional language we are inclined to perceive as a dichotomous pair, in the language of probabilistic notions can be described as an attempt to divide unambiguously into two parts a set of elementary events over which a more or less distinct bimodal distribution function is constructed. This problem, insoluble in such a formulation, is further aggravated by the increasing informational entropy of concepts and therefore by smoothed bimodality. In other words, the bimodal (double-apexed) function will tend to turn into a smooth rectangular distribution, and therefore the possibility of representing two subsets of a fuzzy set as opposed dichotomously will disappear.

If we are ready to acknowledge (at least metaphorically) the nature of consciousness as continuous, we shall have to reject the language of taxonomic description.

Within our system of concepts, constructing the hierarchical classification which must always be based on a distinct taxonomy is no longer necessary. The hierarchically arranged vision of the world is replaced within our system by its vision through the metric arrangement of the semantic space over which the probabilistic distribution function is constructed. The advantage of such an approach lies in the possibility of using as a base concepts with weakened distinctness; perhaps this is the only system of concepts which would enable us to speak of human consciousness without irritating the interlocutor by the arbitrary taxonomic division of the Whole.

An urge to see the integrity of the world through its hierarchical structuring seems always to have suppressed the human idea of freedom and humiliated human dignity. It is relevant to quote Eckhart (1941) once more:

> The soul cannot bear to have anything above it. I believe that it cannot bear to have even God above it. If he is not in the soul, and the soul is not as good as he, it can never be at ease. (p. 163)

K. Can the Unconsious Be Socially Controlled?

The real and the unreal are amazingly intertwined in our life. Whereas there exist numerous institutions that control the real, i.e., the conscious (namely, education, law, social structures, etc.), we can hardly name any institutions formed to control or, perhaps more accurately, to harmonize the unreal, i.e., the unconscious.

Historically, the harmonizing of the unreal in its interaction with the real was achieved through religion. Religious rites, no matter how diverse they were, were always aimed at relaxation and concentration which allowed one to tear himself away from everyday concerns and go deep inside his own Self. Then symbols started to act, and the reality of the non-real was revealed through them; and this made possible the contact between the non-real and the reality of everyday life. We do not know whether it was done well or badly, and such an estimation can hardly be made. Another thing is important: it would be of interest to consider the historical process, as well as the contemporary state of things, from a new angle which is revealed through the wish to see what is happening in the interaction of the real and the unreal. But who can do this?

Jung seems to be the first scholar who attempted to view things from such an angle. Note that a psychiatrist was the first. We cannot help asking: Is it possible to present history from the viewpoint of a psychiatrist? History as madness or, to say it more gently, as the real (i.e., that comprehended at the level of reasoning) affected by the unreal. Gumilev's (1979) concept of *passionaries* as the motive power of history is, perhaps, an attempt to describe events from a psychiatric viewpont.[22]

Here we shall confine ourselves to several quotations from Jung (1953) on the role of Christianity in forming West European consciousness:

> Christian civilization has proved hollow to a terrifying degree: it is all veneer, but the inner man has remained untouched and therefore unchanged. His soul is out of key with his external beliefs; in his soul the Christian has not kept pace with external developments. Yes, everything is to be found outside—in image and in word, in Church and Bible—but never inside. Inside reign the archaic gods, supreme as of old; that is to say the inner correspondence with the outer God-image is undeveloped for lack of psychological culture and has therefore got stuck in heathenism. Christian education has done all that is humanly possible, but it has not been enough. Too few people have experienced the divine image as the innermost possession of their own souls. Christ only meets them from without, never from within the soul; that is why dark paganism still reigns there, a paganism which, now in a form so blatant that it can no longer be denied and now in all too threadbare disguise, is swamping the world of the so-called Christian culture. (p. 12)
>
> It is high time we realized that it is pointless to praise the light and preach it if nobody can see it. It is much more needful to teach people the art of seeing. For it is obvious that far too many people are incapable of establishing a connection between the sacred figures and their own psyche: that is to say they cannot see to what extent the equivalent images are lying dormant in their own unconscious. In order to facilitate this inner vision we must first clear the way for the faculty of seeing. How this is to be done without psychology, that is,

---

[22] The contemporary Russian historian L. N. Gumilev introduced the new term "passionary" to denote people who possess inborn, irrational, passionate temperament that enables them to become a motive force of history.

without making contact with the psyche, is frankly beyond my comprehension. . . . Psychology is concerned with the act of seeing and
not with the construction of new religious truths, when even the existing teachings have not yet been perceived and understood. (p. 13)

Of great interest are Jung's views, developed through the whole of his
book *Psychology and Alchemy* (Jung, 1953) on the role of alchemy in
Medieval Christian Europe:

> Whereas in the Church the increasing differentiation of ritual and
> dogma alienated consciousness from its natural roots in the uncon-
> scious, alchemy and astrology were ceaselessly engaged in preserving
> the bridge to nature, i.e., to the unconscious psyche, from decay. (p.
> 34)

In Medieval Western Christianity, alchemy supplemented the latter
with its thoroughly developed and sophisticated symbolism. A double
belief generated by two logically incompatible conceptions proved necessary to harmonize the life of Medieval Christians. Double belief gave rise
to a life in two worlds. The second world of the Western Middle Ages
was the world of carnivals during which Christian Europe returned to its
pagan state. According to Bakhtin (1965), carnivals occupied about
thirty percent of the year. Now we understand that this was a supplement
to Christianity which was unable to liberate the unconscious.

We could add that the underground of Western Christianity also preserved the heritage of gnosticism, the branch of Christianity which had
been turned toward the ecumenical depths of the human spirit. As long
ago as the second century A.D., gnosticism gave way to the branch of
Christianity which later became official and which submerged belief in
metaphors and gave it a severe, rationalistic flavor (St. Augustine,
Thomas Aquinas). Gnosticism had gone underground, having preserved
the romanticism of the mystery of a contact with the incomprehensible
(see, for example, Jonas, 1958; Rudolph, 1977). It lurked in certain orders, both monastic and secular, and sometimes came to the surface at
crucial moments: during religious wars or revolutions. Quite recently,
many authors grieved over the almost complete loss of all primary
sources. And then suddenly the discovery in Nag-Hammadi.[23] This is almost unbelievable.

The Russian Middle Ages also knew double belief: Christianity was
stimulated and supported by paganism, which remained the shadowy
side of orthodoxy. Double belief was unavoidable for ethnic non-Sla-

[23] In the middle of our century in Upper Egypt, fellahs digging earth in Nag-Hammadi region found a
hiding place which turned out to contain a vessel with 13 codices which contained about 50 gnostic texts.
Those are revelations of a cosmic flavor, philosophical speculations, talks, dialogues, and, especially important, gospels, acts, letters, and revelations which had been previously considered irretrievably lost.

vonic minorities—and there were many of them—since they did not know either the Russian or the Church-Slavic belief. For them, Christianity existed only through rites which, though powerful, were underlain by consciousness structured by pagan ideas. As to the Russians themselves, they also lived their everyday lives according to pagan rites: even now this can be distinctly seen in not so remote regions of the USSR. It is noteworthy that the old Russian clergy did not oppose the accompanying paganism (if it was not too defiant); moreover, sometimes the clergy even took an active part in pagan festivities. Many sacral ceremonies in the country obviously simulated ancient rites. Recall also the Shrovetide, one of the brightest and most important holidays of pagan pantheism, which entered the Christian calendar as a supplement to Lent. This holiday of the reviving Spring helped to make understandable the holiday of Christ's resurrection, and Easter, prepared by Shrovetide, became more significant in Orthodoxy than in Catholicism. The clergy was afraid not so much of paganism as of sectarianism, of different versions of Christianity. It was sects, not the pagan relics, which were driven underground. And maybe hesychasm, retained in the semi-underground of the Russian monastic asceticism, performed the same role as gnosticism had in the West.

The historical process, i.e., the progress of science and its popularization, started to destroy not so much Christianity itself as the supplementing constitutents, such as alchemy or pagan relics, which opened up the way to the unconscious.[24] And Christianity, having lost its connection with the unconscious, also lost its power. This accounts for the explosion of destructive forces in the two world wars and for Nazism as an attempt to come back into contact with the unconscious through the artificially implanted archaic symbolism.

It is of interest to analyze the state of matters in the United States from this viewpoint. The impression we get is that there is going on a spontaneous search for new ways to harmonize the manifestations of the unconscious.

First of all, what we observe is a multitude of beliefs. Here again, we think it relevant to quote the same book by Jung (1953):

> Now if my psychological researches have demonstrated the existence of certain psychic types and their correspondence with well-known religious ideas, then we have opened up a possible approach to those contents which can be experienced and which manifestly and

---

[24] Christianity, due to its deeply mythological character, is sufficiently stable toward scientific criticism. Christian myths in their potential content are incomparably richer than the primitive pagan myths of the European past. They may be easily re-interpreted according to the changing conditions. Note that one of the forms of re-interpretation became its de-mythologization, which in the USSR was represented by Leo Tolstoy and in the West, by Bultman (see Jaspers and Bultman, 1958).

undeniably form the empirical foundations of all religious experience. (p. 14)

If mosaic elements of society are indeed divided into certain clusters, each of which is organically capable of only one religious manifestation, then the right and the ability to choose freely among the multitude of religious systems for those who have chosen successfully opens up the way to harmonizing the unconscious.

One can also observe in the United States the emergence of numerous quasi-religious systems directed at interaction with the unconscious. One of them was the movement of hippies; at its height it resembled the revival of ancient mysteries (Reich, 1970). Another such system is psychoanalysis clad in scientific terms and for this reason not contraindicated for a scientifically disposed society; it exploits the therapeutic confession performed under the survey of physicians and accompanied by the analysis of symbols seen in dreams. The third form which also seems to be quasi-religious is mantra-like painting, i.e., surrealism and abstract painting. The fourth is an almost mass resorting (in certain circles) to meditation with a purely therapeutic goal. The widespread interest in religious-philosophical Oriental teachings represents another attempt to discover a means of direct contact with the unconscious, in a more efficient form than can be achieved in traditional Christian ceremonies.

However, all these trends are largely the possession of certain circles of intellectuals. And what about the rest? Black holes are always filled sooner or later: either by sex, drugs, and alcohol, or by a drive to mindless (from the point of view of others) violence.

And now a few words about Western Europe. We have to acknowledge Nazism to have been an explosion of the unconscious. It was a tragic and ugly response to the scientism and other modern aspects of European culture, Judeo-Christian in its source. Scientism, with its nihilistic attitude toward the unconscious, broke the integrity of consciousness. And the unconscious, in its inferior forms, got out of control.

At present, a few facts have become known concerning the occult basis of Nazism both in a generally methodological aspect and in the concrete activities of the higher officials [see Ravenscroft (1973) and Pauwels and Bergier (1977)]. Even certain seemingly rational scientists were affected by the power of mad ideas. For example, there exists a quite technically serious description of experiments directed at spotting submarines, based on the occult conception of the Earth's concavity. Another example is the German physicists who attacked Einstein's relativity theory as Jewish abstract physics in contrast to true Aryan experimental physics.

However, nobody has so far made a historico-psychological analysis of this phenomenon. Psychologically, Nazism can be regarded as a case of an astral epidemic, where the medium for the infection is represented by the lower part of the human Self rooted in the ethnogenetic or even phylogenetic past of mankind. Such epidemics can be characterized by the same periods as common epidemics. Both have a latent period, a period of exponential spreading, and then a decline to almost the zero level, immunity, etc. We already considered this similarity (Nalimov, 1981*b*). Perhaps what is happening now in the Moslem countries is also an astral epidemic.

The world is constantly changing. The tragedy of today consists in the fact that the old is being destroyed more rapidly than the new is being created. This brings forth the feeling of being lost. But what is actually lost are the forms of harmonizing life in its combination of the real and unreal. We constantly come across a passionate desire to cope with the sequences of this de-harmonization. One of the manifestations of this tendency is the atavistic urge to restore the lost Protestant morality; another manifestation is social criticism (E. Fromm, H. Marcuse, A. Etzioni, R. Blauner, B. Murckland, etc.) giving birth to a number of positive programs often resembling a social Utopia. But is it possible that a trend deriving from a stock of contemporary culture will eventually acquire real significance?

Our modern culture is generated by science. However, science itself has also undergone a striking stratification: a part has broken out far in advance; other branches still belong to the remote past.

The idea of the world as an empty space void of medium and filled with isolated particles doomed to long-range interaction was introduced by Newton. Contemporary physics rejected the idea of the discrete vision of the World. (We have said much on this point elsewhere). For us it is important to emphasize here that the general scientific outlook has preserved what was built into it at the very beginning. The concepts which left physics remained and took roots in other branches of knowledge. In biology this is represented by the idea that the potential of all life on the Earth is contained in the gene-molecular code which is independent and self-sufficient. In sociobiology there emerged the concept of the selfish gene (Dawkins, 1976): and so we saw a man as a genetic machine. In psychology, at least in its major trends, man is considered as a discrete creature doomed to the same long-range interaction as Newton's atoms. Culture, with its informational super-saturation, turned out to be a medium of *dwelling*, not that of *existence*. Man turned out to be closed within his inner world—he existed like an isolated particle in Newton's void.

Alienation. This idea was already quite poignant in the teaching of the Gnostics. The entire process of development of the modern phase of Western culture has been accompanied by assertions concerning alienation: Hobbes, Rousseau, Fichte, Schiller, Marx, existentialists, contemporary social criticism. The reasons were quite numerous: the absorption of personal rights by the state in Rousseau's theory of the *Contrat social* (social contract); the effect of the irrepressible progress of technology; private property and labor distribution; and even merely existence under social conditions. Now alienation has acquired the force of an alarm-bell —and a new meaning: man is *alienated from himself.* The transpersonal semantic continuum in which man is embedded was proclaimed non-real. Imagine that a particle existing in the endless interaction with the physical field would have consciousness alienating it from the idea of the field! Then the existence of such a particle would have been as uneasy as that of the contemporary man. The cosmos would have been filled with the sound of the electronic alarm-bell. The electronic particles would have to borrow from people the cult of demons and demiurges, as well as the vogue for astrology.

The search for the ways of harmonizing the real and nonreal is, as a matter of fact, the urge toward creating a new culture. It is in this sense that we can say we live through the second Mediterranean.

L. Indivisible Integrity of Consciousness

Above we have constantly contrasted consciousness and the unconscious. But this dichotomous opposition so typical of our culture is nothing more than a rhetorical figure. Without contrasting, we cannot speak. But, in fact, we always deal with an indivisible integrity.

The indivisible integrity of consciousness may well be seen through the semantic analysis of related words given bilingually.

The reader can see in Figure 11.4 the French words describing the vari-

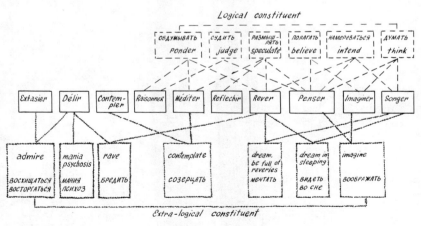

FIGURE 11.4

ety of manifestations both of our consciousness and of its unconscious component. The Russian equivalents for these words were found in the large French-Russian dictionary. We see with a certain amazement that all the French words reflect one and the same semantic field, namely, different combinations of its parts. All the French words prove to be synonymous: they join one another through their Russian equivalents. The same is true of the Russian words. For example, such words as sozertsat' (contemplate), videt vo sne (dream), bredit' (rave), etc., which obviously relate to the extralogical aspects of consciousness, join through French words the words which seem to relate to purely logical aspects, such as dumat' (think), razmishlyat' (reason), sudit' (judge), etc.

We would like to emphasize here that it is easier and more pleasant to make such an analysis on the basis of bilingual dictionaries rather than explanatory ones. This can probably be explained by the fact that the paradigmatic pressure of today is not so strong in bilingual dictionaries.

And now, one last remark: the bilingual dictionary reveals the difference between the two French words _Contémplation_ and _Méditation_. If the first one has only one Russian equivalent, sozertsanie (contemplation), the other one is translated by three words: razmishlenie (reasoning), obdumivanie (pondering), sozertsanie (contemplation). The semantic field is much broader in the second case. Perhaps the new translation loan word _méditation_ from French was introduced into the Russian language for this reason.

Chapter 12

Symbols

A. Symbols in the Variety of Their Manifestations

A symbol is a specific sign greatly different in its effect upon us from the familiar signs of the semiotic world, though outwardly it looks like all the other signs. A symbol *directly* links our active life realized in *Doing* with the semantic world of our unconscious. We might say that a symbol is a *synonym* for meditation; it opens up the entrance into the unconscious the way meditation does. Watching how a symbol affects people, we are enabled to see the manifestations of the unconscious. History carries out its experiments with nations through symbols.

In recent decades symbolism became an object of thorough studies: books and theses have been written about it. Here we indicate just a few of them: Goldsmith (1976), Symbolisme (1971), Bryson et al. (1954), Alleau (1976), Govinda (1976b), Jung (1953), Jaspers and Bultman (1958),[1] Dolgin et al. (1977), Cooper, (1978). Perhaps it would be relevant to emphasize the fact that one of the first substantial books on symbolism was by a Russian author, namely, Andrey Belyi (1910), writer and symbolist-poet, though it has almost lost its significance by now. Looking through this seemingly thorough study, one notices with amazement how far people have gone since then on the road of studying this ancient phenomenon. Naturally, we are not able to review here the entire range of assertions on the nature of symbols. We are going to confine ourselves only to certain aspects of this phenomenon.

First of all, we would like to consider the relations between symbols and familiar linguistic forms. Many scholars, including Fromm (1951), whom we profusely quoted above, think it possible to speak of dreams as

---

[1] This book contains an account of the discussion between Jaspers and Bultman on the possibility of de-mythologizing Christianity. The standpoint of Jaspers is naturally extremely negative.

an instance of a symbolic language. Fromm does not find impossible the idea of the existence of a language whose semantic elements are symbols. LaFarge (1954) wrote on this point:

> Symbols are a *language*, the most universal and powerful language known to men. Language itself, after all, is a set of symbols. (p. 121)

However, I do not agree with the concept of symbols as semantic elements of the language. In my earlier book (Nalimov, 1981*a*) I formulated the idea that one of the most important characteristics of language is its hierarchical structure: a phoneme, a morpheme, a word, a phrase, a text. The last can also be structured into chapters, sections, and paragraphs. But the same is not true of symbols. A symbol contains the complete text within itself. A word is underlain by a semantic field revealing itself through other words of the context. A symbol has a unique manifestation. I would like to quote here Toporov (1979).

> There also exist symbol texts which it is more rational to refer to as a special class of "supertexts" both due to their exclusive semantic depth and meaningfulness, their ability to function as a symbol of higher sacral values, the specific attitude towards them on the part of those who use them, and due to their peculiar status as a text in a broad taxon space. (p. 116–117)

Also of interest are the words of Gallagher (1954):

> Symbols are not only necessary in religion, they are often a psychologically more effective medium for the communication of ideas and values. When one cannot deal directly with things and actions in themselves, symbols have a greater psychological impact than words, because symbols are themselves things or actions; and as such are closer to things than words, serving as reproductions of things or re-enactments of actions. They impress the most vivid sense—the eye—as well as the ear, and the other senses. Because of their concreteness they have a greater impact on the imagination, the memory, the feelings. They give an analogical knowledge of inner realities, meanings, values; and if the symbols are in good taste, they present ideas and ideals not merely as something to be known, but as something to be loved. (p. 117–118)

And now I quote the words of McKeon (1954):

> In its more general use, "symbol" includes any token which serves as proof of identity and any like guarantee in the relations and affairs of man. The particularity and universality of the symbol are inseparably conjoined: it is the mark, immediately and unmistakably recognizable, of a relation which requires, without question or argument, actions of a particular kind. So far as particularity is concerned, the symbol is more concrete and evocative than myth or argument . . .

the symbol is richer and more relevant than myth or argument, and although it is an inexhaustible source of interpretation in narrative and in proof, it provides a ground of action and cooperation at once more reliable and more direct than the continuities of history or the consequences of demonstration, for it can move men who are ignorant of history and insensitive to argument. (p. 21-22)

Symbols cannot be destroyed either by criticism or by inconsistent facts. They can only come to an end in a certain concrete manifestation, and then they go down into the underground of the collective unconscious.

However, a symbol is not easily differentiated from other signs. Outwardly, one and the same sign may have various facets. For example, the word *freedom* may at one time be perceived as a usual and rather neutral word of our language, whereas at another time it may represent a concept: there seems to have existed not a single philosopher who managed to avoid the temptation to interpret this concept. Finally, *freedom* is a symbol which may directly affect not only an individual but, at crucial moments, whole nations.

Above I mentioned that symbols are not elements of the usual logically arranged linguistic contexts. At the same time, they may strengthen and support one another. In this case it is as if they complete one another and create a specific image, a *mandala* (in Oriental terms) in which parts are endowed with the totality. The Christian *Trinity* proved to be such a symbol united through its complexity.

Symbols seem to acquire their most vivid manifestation in historical evolution. This assertion can be illustrated by the following examples, considered only briefly and schematically.

The Great French Revolution (1789) represents the social realization of the symbol of *Freedom*. Another symbol, *Equality*, emerged side by side with the previous one, and later, perhaps during the revolution of 1848, reflecting the romanticism of the period, the third member of the triad came to the fore: *Fraternity*. [This idea is developed by Ligou (1969).]

Thus, there appeared a new, masonic interpretation of the *Trinity*, one of the major Christian symbols. It became the slogan of Masonry (Nys, 1908). The intensive preparation for a new understanding of the symbol *Freedom* had begun long before the Great French Revolution broke out. Here is what Nys, a Belgian scholar, wrote on this point:

> . . . in 1787 there were 636 lodges controlled by the two masonic rulers of France: the Great East and the Great French Lodge; they were in general very numerous. The historian Georg Kloss notes that the masons recruited their members in all the classes of French society; Augustin Barrnell, the enemy of masonry, says that the suburbs Saint-Antoine and Saint-Marceau were completely "masonized."

> Barrnell estimates the number of French masons during the revolution as 600 thousand. "At least 500 thousand," he writes, "were ready to revolt at first sign." This is an obvious exaggeration; but history allows us to state the intervention of the lodges and make a conclusion concerning the great number of their members . . . the majority of revolutionaries belonged to secret masonic societies. (p. 101)

Our task does not include any detailed description of the related facts. On the role of Masonry in the Great French Revolution, see also Kropotkin (1909). Alluding to Nys, Kropotkin wrote:

> Nearly all revolutionists of renown were freemasons—Mirabeau, Bailly, Danton, Robespierre, Marat, Condorcet, Brissot, Lalande, and many others were masonic brothers, and the Duke of Orléans (Philippe-Egalité) remained its national Grand Master down to May 13, 1793. On the other side, it is also known that Robespierre, Mirabeau, Lavoisier, and probably many more belonged to the lodges of the Illuminates, founded by Weishaupt, whose aim was "to free the nations from the tyranny of princes and priests, and as a first step, to free the peasants and the working men from serfdom, forced labour and guilds" (p. 540)

The study of the role of Masonry in the Great French Revolution has been continued up to now [see, for example, Annales (1969) and Palou (1964)], and it is difficult to come here to any clear conclusions since only meager documentation is at our disposal. Besides, the whole thing is veiled by a romantic mystery. This question is important for us only because the entire masonic movement is permeated by Symbols. Internally, this is a teaching expressed through Symbols with complex rites; intellectually, this is a ceaseless reinterpretation of ancient Symbols in the images of everyday contemporary life; externally, this is an attempt at their social realization. Masonic iconography is remarkably rich.[2] During the three recent centuries Masonry presented itself as an antithesis, opposing in the dynamic interpretation of ancient symbolism both scientific positivism and the rigid conservatism of the churches. Reinterpretation of the Trinity as Freedom, Equality, and Fraternity was preserved almost to our time: it sounded as a tocsin in the days of my own youth. It is not for nothing that the great Russian poet Alexander Blok saw Christ through the blizzard of the Russian Revolution. But later, on the roadless roads,

---

[2] It seems here relevant to compare it with one of the Buddhist sects, namely, the Shingon school. It asserted the esoterism of Buddhism to be so deep as to exclude any possibility of a written expression: it could only be given as an insight through images. This school possesses the richest and brightest iconography among the rest of Buddhist sects, though it basically contains only two images: The Diamond Mandala and the Feminine Mandala (for details, see Rambach 1979).

the third segment of the Trinity was lost by some people and rejected by others.

Perhaps it will not seem too absurd if I say that the formation of the United States was linked to a new interpretation of the symbol of Freedom. Many founders of the American republic are known to have been Masons: Benjamin Franklin, Thomas Jefferson, John Adams, George Washington; the last was a grand master of the Pennsylvania lodges. It is only natural to ask whether Franklin deliberately introduced the masonic principles into the law of his country. By the way, note the Trinity in the structure of Power: President, Congress, Supreme Court[3] (the last, as opposed to the European tradition, enjoys equal rights with the two other members of the Trinity and can interfere with the official life in its most important manifestations). Franklin put on the banner of the United States five-pointed stars on an azure field, as on the arches of masonic temples.

Now let us make a short excursion into the remote past. The pyramids of Ancient Egypt always amazed Europeans by the measureless labor spent to build them without a visible functional goal. It became clear long ago that the pyramids were not merely pharoah's tombs (Barbarin, 1969; Tompkins, 1971) but the constantly created symbols drawing the whole life in Egypt to themselves. Perhaps these incomprehensible monuments conceal the mystery of an amazing length of existence of this ancient culture which had managed to avoid degeneration and ecological problems while developing on a negligibly small area. The medieval Gothic temples might also have been such symbols. Both pyramids and Gothic temples were based on sacral geometry through the number expressed in curves, vertical lines, and volumes (Charpentier, 1972). We see here the numeric symbolism elaborated in Ancient Egypt. We heard its echo through Pythagoras, Cabbala, and Alchemy. And since we have raised the subject of numerical symbols, I wish to remind the reader about the tragedy of the Russian church schism.[4] People had to choose

[3] The desire to see the ideal power as threefold so deeply inherent in human consciousness was more than once reflected in philosophical speculations. In Aristotle's treatise on politics we find the triple division of the state authority. It was revived and advocated by the French philosopher Montesquieu in his great book *L'Esprit des Lois*.

[4] The Russian church schism is in itself an extremely interesting phenomenon. Its first wave emerged in the fifteenth and sixteenth centuries when Nil Sorsky, a Russian church and public figure and the well-known head of the *non-acquisitive* trend, who developed mystic and ascetic ideas similar to Byzantine hesychasm, resisted another church figure, Joseph of Volotsk, the supporter of the *ritual* trend which advocated the militant interests of the Church. At the Synod in 1504, the supporters of Joseph achieved the condemnation of the non-acquisitive heresy: its echo survived in *starchestvo*, mentioned above. The supporters of Joseph gave birth to the concept that "Moscow is the third Rome," which played an important role in the ideology of the Russian state. The second wave, the schism proper, emerged in the seventeenth century, provoked by the reform of Church's ritual whose true meaning was centralization of the Church and the strengthening of the power of the Patriarch. For some period (the end of the seventeenth

one of the two radically different ways of religious life, and this choice
was brought down to the opposition of a two-finger cross to a three-fin-
ger cross. People burned themselves for the two-finger cross, but their
sacrifice was not accepted.

But let us come closer to our days. On 1 March 1881, the Russian tsar
Alexander II was assassinated. The details of the assassination were horrible, but nothing followed: no revolt, no plunders, no riot, no earth-
quake—nothing. According to memoirs, revolutionaries were shocked
by this "nothing." But in fact, it was a significant phenomenon, and its
significance consisted exactly in that nothing happened. The Symbol of
the Russian Empire, for which and around which the yet unseen luxury
of Peterburg had been created, proved empty. The symbol was destroyed
by a bloody onslaught, but nothing happened. However, it took dozens
of years to comprehend it. Meanwhile, a new symbolism started to be
created, through readiness to accept death: Sofia Perovskaya met her
death calmly and proudly; Vera Figner spent 20 years in solitary confinement, and she only had to repent to be pardoned.

Communism is not merely a concept, but first of all a Symbol. Historically, it can be traced back through the history of Europe up to Christ's
Annunciation, Qumran communities,[5] and Therapeutae.[6] Marx was a
genius to catch the breathing of this Symbol which he expressed in the
words: A spectre is haunting Europe, a spectre of Communism.

The Communist Manifesto beginning with these words proved to be
the most powerful statement of Marxism: in Russia alone, before 1917 it
was reissued 60 times.

It is of interest to quote here McKeon (1954):

> . . . The failure to consider the symbolic uses to which the writings of
> Marx have been put has led us into the error of supposing that their
> effectiveness in the development of communism and in the promo-
> tion of the ideological conflict can be countered by proving that they
> expound false history and state unsound philosophy. (p. 29)

> The first should be concerned with the operation of Communism
> itself as symbol, not only in attaching different men—farmers, work-
> ers, artists, scientists—to Communism by different appeals, but also

century), the important part of the Schism was the exposure and condemnation of the social vices. The
schismatics were suppressed savagely, though their less important followers, old-believers (starovery), remained until our time.

[5] The Qumran community seems to have entered the Essenes, the social-religious trend in Judea in the
second half of the second century B.C. through the first century A.D. Certain features of the Essenes resembled the early Christian church. They practiced property sharing and distributed money to each according to his need.

[6] The Therapeutae was a Judean religious community similar to the Essenes, situated in the vicinity of
Alexandria. It is known primarily as a result of its description by the philosopher Philo of Alexandria. A
simple life and disdain for wealth were among its characteristics.

in providing motivation for common action strong enough to run counter to the claims of all other symbols. The second should be concerned with the use of a philosophy or a body of doctrine as a symbol and with its effect on action and on response to facts and arguments. (p. 35)

And for a few words about Nazism. The mad ideas were remarkably supported by the ancient symbols. Meetings and marches acquired the nature of mysteries. The swastika,[7] one of the most ancient symbols of the collective unconscious, could be seen everywhere: on banners, military uniforms, books, etc. This symbol is found among the archeological remains of ancient Baltic peoples.

The following quotation is also relevant here (Boas, 1954):

> Symbols are used by human beings, not merely to communicate ideas and feelings to other people, but also for lyric expression and for the clarification of one's own ideas and feelings to oneself. (p. 215)

> If then a revolutionary group sets up a new economic order without providing for the satisfactions which people find in the old symbols, it may discover that its action has been futile. (p. 226)

These peculiarities of human behavior, concealed from the external observer, seem to have been known to Nazi leaders. How else can all this be explained?

As far as the role of Symbols in various aspects of human activities is concerned, we should primarily mention art. However, this subject is boundless, and we are going to confine ourselves to a quotation from Gallagher (1954):

> To describe all the types and uses of symbols in the arts would be to write a history of human ideas and beliefs; as sooner or later these find symbolic expression in the arts. (p. 209)

I would like to emphasize here an idea which seems important to me: everything that has ever existed on Earth is sooner or later, and perhaps not only once, reflected in art through Symbols which are the signs that preserve the unbreakable integrity of time. What has once existed does not go away: it affects us, lives within us, reminds us of itself, and determines our behavior.

Matters are much more complicated when we start to analyze the role of symbols in science. Modern science was historically preceded by al-

---

[7] I can give another illustration of an arbitrary use of the same symbol: on a bank note of the value of 250 rubles issued in 1917 by the Provisional Government of Kerensky, one sees in the center a double eagle, the old symbol of the Empire, but now crossed by a swastika. What an odd and meaningful combination of symbols!

chemy, which was founded entirely on symbols and remained free from any theoretical elements. It is noteworthy that ancient symbols, as we now distinctly see, possessed creative power. Everything man had learned in the pre-scientific world—metallurgy, production of glass, construction of grandiose building, treatment of many diseases—had been discovered through the use of Symbol and Myths. Alchemy made many important discoveries, including the invention of gunpowder and some laboratory equipment which is partially used even nowadays; progress, however, was extremely slow. It is to be remembered that even Isaac Newton spent a great deal of his time brooding over problems of alchemy, astrology, and the proper chronology of the Bible.

Science chose the way of constructing theories. Scientific terms became comprehensible. People were enabled to pose *questions* to nature. Recall that logically each question has two constituents: the question proper and the assertive part that makes the question legitimate. The assertive part of the question is a laconic, very compact formulation of our knowledge about the nature of the phenomenon to which the given question relates. Compactness of knowledge lies in conceptualization. In these terms, a *mathematical model* is a question posed to nature by man (Nalimov, 1981*b*). By the way, this may explain why the psychology of thinking lacks mathematical models: psychologists cannot ask a meaningful question since they cannot formulate their knowledge of the nature of human consciousness in a compact form.

However, despite the fact that science is conceptual, symbols have hidden themselves within it and affect our reasoning. This is primarily true of the manifestations of scientific paradigms.

Such words as Matter, Law, Chance, Evolution, when used paradigmatically, cease being concepts and become symbols. In this case they are not based on any scientific conceptual contents. They are filled with certain integral meaning, this integrity being the result of the historical evolution of science and its struggle to strengthen the scientific vision of the world, provoking emotional explosion, protest, sharp rejection of anything new. Symbols seem to be created constantly, but some of them turn out to be ephemeral whereas others have a long life. And they are created in such a purely intellectual sphere as science.

I could give a more serious example of the turning of a scientific concept into a symbol. This transformation is especially distinct in contemporary physics, where many concepts acquire such a high degree of abstraction that they can no longer be interpreted in terms of the external world unambiguously and in a form comprehensible for a layman. Modern physics, as well as modern mathematics, being afraid of the vulgarization that unavoidably accompanies popularization, started to shrink into its esoteric shell. This has produced a religious attitude toward science. The difficult journey toward obtaining Universal knowledge has begun to recall the preparation for initiation into sacred mysteries. In my earlier book (Nalimov, 1981a) I quoted a collection of statements made by physicists on the physical meaning of the ψ function compiled by the American philosopher Abel (1969). These statements are various and mutually inconsistent. Abel asks: Can we say we know something if we cannot express our knowledge in words? The answer seems obvious: We can express our knowledge not only through verbal concepts but also through words which become symbols. The abstract symbols of physics, as well as other scientific symbols, allow a scientist, if he is initiated, to enter the semantic universe through his unconscious and find there the explanation of the phenomena under study. When he wishes to transmit his knowledge, the scientist uses a symbol as a common linguistic sign—this is how the ψ function entered the Schrödinger equation. So, after all, science turned out to be arranged exactly like any other human activities.

As a matter of fact, the legitimacy of symbolism in science was acknowledged not long ago. At the beginning of our century, it was said that matter had disappeared in the abstractions of the new physics. I remember as a youth seeing books, obsolete already by that time, in which Maxwell's equations were interpreted in the mechanistic mode, the only one conceivable for an unsophisticated man: they were illustrated by pictures of men rowing boats which crossed waves and other things of the kind.

B. Simple Geometric Symbols

I am going to confine myself to considering only the simplest symbols, i.e., geometric ones, which we shall encounter in the subsequent experimental chapters. A complete description of religious symbols would take up too much space. A detailed description of symbols can be found in the illustrated encyclopedia compiled by Cooper (1978), which contains almost 1,500 entries.

As a matter of fact, we can say very little about symbols. One can trace their emergence long ago in the historical past, their broad geographical spreading, the changes in their form. One can at last describe some of the numerous interpretations ascribed to symbols in various culture. It is true, however, that such interpretations never reveal the whole meaning of a symbol. Any attempt to penetrate into the depth of a symbol can only be based on meditation.

What I am going to say is largely borrowed from a book by Goldsmith (1976).

Let us begin with the symbol of Trinity.

The Triangle, the geometrical emblem of three things, one above two, the two lower uniting to produce the higher, or the union of the positive and negative forces to produce the third, is the most complex and mystical, as it is the most uncompromising of all symbols. (p. 144)

From earliest times primitive man appears to have grasped the idea of the three-fold nature of the universe—the divine, the human, the natural world—and that he himself was the image or mirror of the macrocosm, composed of three things—body, mind, soul or spirit. The idea of "three in one" seems to have been a part of man's consciousness as far back as tradition takes us. (p. 144)

Three Pillars typifying Wisdom, Strength, Beauty, or Wisdom, Power, Goodness were used to symbolize their triune gods by the very early Egyptians, Hindus, Druids, Mayas and Incas. (p. 146)

There were innumerable triads in Egypt that personified the chief forces of nature under different groupings. In time, however, Osiris, Isis and Horus absorbed the functions and attributes of all the other gods and became the mightiest gods of Egypt. (p. 147)

The Triangle is one of the symbols of the Buddhist triad. (p. 152)

A triangle with its apex up is a symbol of fire, an architectural sign of the fire prayer directed to heaven.

If we now turn to the quite recent past, we shall see that the famous Hegelian triad is also an exposition of the same symbol of trinity. Perhaps all this is a reflection of the original trinity of the world: three-dimensional space, triune time (past–present–future), three dimensional perception of light.[8] Our thinking is triple: three constituents form a syllogism. In the works of Plotinus (1956), a non-Christian philosopher completing the evolution of pre-Christian thought, the supreme Being has three facets. Perhaps, quite unconsciously, all of us prefer the trinity: trilogy, triptych . . .

The subsequent constructive developments of a triangle are five-pointed and six-pointed stars. This can be easily seen from Figure 12.1. I am going to dwell on these symbols below.

A triangle repeated four times, which ascends to the sky, is a pyramid. The solar (fire) connection between a triangle and a pyramid was noted by the well-known Russian poet Bal'mont (1914):

> I would like to remind you of the words I once said speaking of Mexican symbolism: the solar and highly awesome origin of the Pyramid seems to be indubitable. When the evening Sun, especially after

---

[8] This follows from the empirically discovered law of color addition: if any four intensive color stimuli are given, it is always possible to write a color equation between the multiples of these stimuli:

$$wW = xX + yY + zZ$$

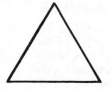  

FIG. 12.1. Construction of a pentacle and Solomon's Seal from an equilateral triangle (from Goldsmith, 1976).

> a storm, pierces the mass of clouds with its rays, one can clearly and distinctly see in the sky a design of a pyramid crowned by the solar disk. The fire and storm pyramid made of rays and clouds takes thoughts from the Earth up to the sky and to what is there the brightest and most powerful, to the Sun. That is why in the countries of sun-worshippers, of Mexicans, Egyptians, or Mayas, the pyramid built on the Earth and ascending to the sky in its prayer is an architectural psalm petrified forever in its reverence. (p. 128–129)
>
> A pyramid is a triangle repeated four times which ascends to the Sky. (p. 127)

Plinius the naturalist connected the etymology of the word "pyramid" with the Greek word pur ("pyr"), which means fire. In esoteric interpretations, a triangle is the symbol of fire. So it may be that Plinius, as well as many other ancient authors, actually was right because the pyramid, being a ritual edifice, served as a place of initiation where the initiated with the fire of his spirit lifted the veil of Isis, which could be lifted by no other means, to see the Rose of Isis.

It becomes obvious that the Trinity, one of the principal Christian symbols, goes back to the beginnings not of one people but of the whole of mankind. The same is true of other simple symbols, e.g., of the Cross. Here is what Goldsmith (1976) writes on this point:

> *The Cross* is found among the most sacred hieroglyphics of Egypt. It appears thus × (still used as a sign of multiplication), and thus + (the plus sign) and again thus T—the *Sacred Tau*. And constantly repeated on all the old Egyptian remains, one sees . . . the *Crux Ansata*, the Egyptian Ankh, the Key of the Nile, the Key of Life or the Cross of Egypt. Peculiarly identified with Egypt, yet it is found as a religious emblem among all the other races of antiquity. (p. 39)
>
> The meaning attached to the *crux ansata*—also implied by the simpler cross—is "Life to Come." (p. 40)
>
> The *Tau Cross* was considered a divine symbol by the ancient Mex-

icans, who called it the Tree of Life, Tree of our Flesh, Tree of Nutriment. (p. 40–41)

The *Cross* has been associated with the *crossed fire stick* of the Chinese, it has been likened to a bird with outstretched wings, to two human figures crossed, and to man himself standing with outstretched arms. Interpreted in the latter sense as symbolizing the divine potential Man—we can understand why criminals were nailed to the cross, the symbol which they had profaned; and why a man who cannot write still signs his name with a cross. (p. 41–42)

The *Cross* with a wheel in the centre is one of the oldest symbols of majesty and power in India and was given to Vishnu. (p. 42–43)

The swastika is a variety of the cross. Again I quote Goldsmith (1976):

The *Swastika* is a Sanskrit word composed of *su* good and *asti* being, with the suffix *ka*, and is the equivalent of "It is well," or "So be it."

It was revered in India three thousand years before the Christian era, and is stamped on archaic vases and pottery found in India, Persia, China, Italy, Greece, Cyprus; on ancient bronze ornaments in England, France, Etruria; on weapons and various ornaments in Germany and Scandinavia; on Celtic crosses in Ireland and Scotland; and in prehistoric burial grounds in Scandinavia, Mexico, Peru, Yucatan, Paraguay and the United States.

Apparently it was never adopted by the Phoenicians, Babylonians, Assyrians or Egyptians, although it has been found in Egypt, the inference being that it was brought there by the Greeks.

It was used before the Aryans commenced their migrations, and has been called the oldest Aryan symbol. (p. 95)

The Swastika was the cross of the Manicheans and was their sole symbol. During the second and third centuries the swastika was the only form of cross used by the Christians. (p. 97)

It seems that the appearance of the well-known cross in Christianity

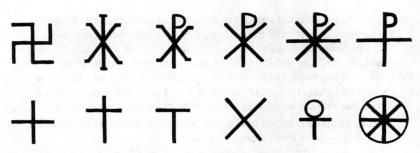

FIG. 12.2. Various forms of the Labarum (from Goldsmith, 1976).

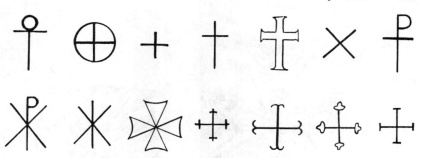

FIG. 12.3. Schematic representation of various forms of the Nubian cross (from Dinkler, 1975).

must be referred to the post-Constantinian epoch (Dinkler, 1975). The famous *Labarum*, the national banner of Imperial Rome (beginning with Constantine I) bears various images of the Cross, which is simultaneously the monogram of Christ. In Figure 12.2 the reader can see the striking variety of forms of the Labarum. It can be compared with the principal types of Nubian crosses shown in Figure 12.3.

We notice with amazement that crosses become many-pointed, like stars. They may be three-, four-, six-, and eight-pointed; they may also be combined with a circle. The only type lacking is a five-pointed cross, but then we never come across four- or seven-pointed stars: they are difficult to construct [five- and six-pointed stars can be elegantly constructed of triangles (see Fig. 12.1), and an eight-pointed cross–star can be constructed of two rectilinear quadrangles]. We sometimes came across more complicated compositional symbolics: a four-pointed cross within a five-pointed star. Crosses and stars express the numerical symbolism that was distinctly formulated as long ago as by Pythagoras and has its roots in Egypt.

Here I am going to say a few words about the numerical symbol *eight*. The gnostics and Pythagoreans ascribed to this number a deep mystic meaning: it signified the Great Ogdoad,[9] the fullness of divine potentialities. In Christian culture this symbol was retained in the architecture of temples (Catholic and Gregorian) in which the rectilinear octahedron is repeated in the base of the temple, in its dome, etc. Besides, the structure itself of the most widely used four-pointed cross may represent the image–pattern of figures resembling eights. Vertical and horizontal components of the cross are represented by twisted lines whose windings form eights. In mathematics the figure eight placed horizontally represents infinity.

---

[9] Ogdoad is a term derived from the Greek ὀγδοάδος.

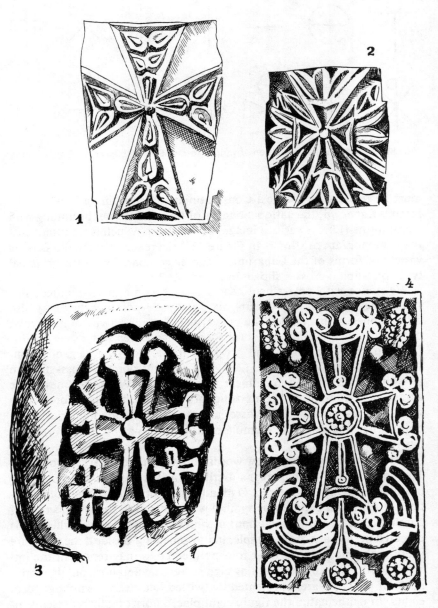

FIG. 12.4. Nubian crosses (1 and 2) (from Dinkler, 1975) and Armenian Khachkars (3 and 4) (from Stepanyan and Chakmakchyan, 1971).

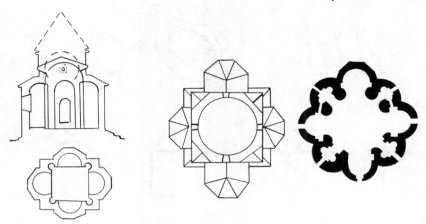

FIG. 12.5. Schematic representation of the plans of Armenian temples (from Marutyan, 1976).

When traveling in Armenia, one cannot help but be amazed by the abundance of *khachkars*, eight-pointed crosses decorated with ornaments. Some of them are shown in Figure 12.4. [See the book by Stepanyan and Chakmakchyan (1971)], where they are compared with eight-pointed Nubian crosses. The number eight turned out to be the burden of medieval Armenian architecture [see Fig. 12.5, composed on the basis of the book by Marutyan (1976)]; however, I failed to find in the literature a meaningful explanation of this phenomenon from the general culturological viewpoint. Historically, this may perhaps be explained by the fact that Armenian spiritual culture was frozen at a level when it was still close to the sources of Christianity, or it may reflect the influence of the Order of the Templars who had their residence in Armenia and whose symbol was an eight-pointed cross.

The semantics of the Cross are considered in detail by Toporov (1979). I shall quote here a short fragment which has a direct bearing on our subject:

> The presence of the center as a *crossing* to which everything comes defines the role of the centering effect of the Cross. It is exactly this feature which explains the specific urge towards the center of the subject, the tendency to connect with it the most intensive and personal drives (the feeling of a special awareness of the center and most intimate relation to it). The center becomes a spot which enables the subject to move vertically into the depths of mytho-poetic and religious space with mysteries. The center and the Cross as its bearer, as an indication to it, become the starting and finishing points of meditation and prayer, the means providing the maximum psychophysio-

FIG. 12.6. Children's drawings and phosphenes (below) (from Oster, 1970).

logical effect on the depth of the unconscious and turning these processes of ascension (deepening) and spiritual sublimation into an efficient psychotherapeutic procedure (cf. the use of the Cross in folk and mystic meditation, in various cases of hypnosis, etc.). (p. 118–119)

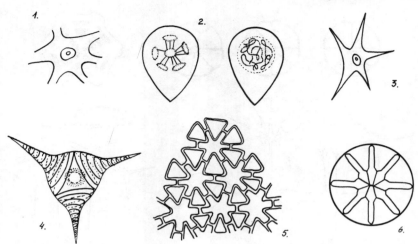

Fig. 12.7. Simple symbol-like geometrical forms occurring in nature (from Thompson, 1943): (1) a gangliose cell of a horse; (2) circular shapes of chromosomes formed in spermatogenesis of a mole cricket; (3) spermocell of Inachus in the form it takes in a 5% solution of HNO₃; (4) spermocell of Dromia; (5) star-shaped cells in the core of Jeneus; (6) diatom *Asterolampra marylandica.*

I would like to emphasize here the following rather obscure phenomenon: simple geometric symbols are so much inherent in our consciousness that they immediately appear in our field of vision when our eyes are mechanically affected [this is called a *phosphene*; see, for example, Oster, 1970]. Phosphenes can be met in children's drawings and folk ornamentations. The reader can see this in Figure 12.6, which is compiled on the basis of the above-mentioned paper by Oster.

Note that both phosphenes and many simple geometric symbols repeat the forms constantly occurring in nature. Figures 12.7 and 12.8 show several such symbol-like geometric forms of animate nature [according to the book by Thompson (1943)]. We see here three-, five-, six-, and eight-pointed stars, a cross, and a cross-like shape that resembles a crucifix; some of these forms are encircled; in one case chromosomes make a figure resembling an eight. Thompson also emphasizes the fact that ancient artisans reproduced the forms occurring in nature. He illustrates this observation by comparing flask-shaped corrugated shells with Roman ceramics (see Figure 12.9.). The essential thing is that the shells have almost microscopic size: to see them, one needs a magnifying glass. Therefore, it is hardly possible to claim that a direct borrowing had taken place. Perhaps, the Holy Grail, one of the most vivid and romantic symbols of the European Middle Ages, as well as the Bowl of Buddha, the cup of Jamishi in Islam, and a cup of Heracles may turn out to be the archetypic symbols whose prototypes are forms of animate nature. It seems relevant

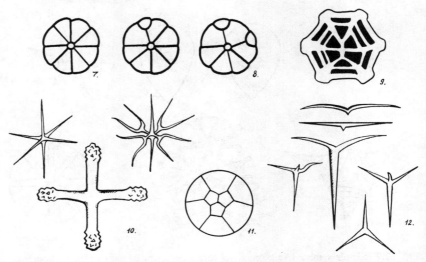

FIG. 12.8. Simple symbol-like geometric forms occurring in nature (continuation): (7–8)
several versions of the canal system of the medusoid (Eleutheria); (9) partitions
within the coral Heterophylla; (10) skeleton needles of hecsaactinide sponges;
(11) polyhedrons on a leaf of the weed Goniodoma of the Peridinium genus;
(12) skeleton needles of calcareous sponges.

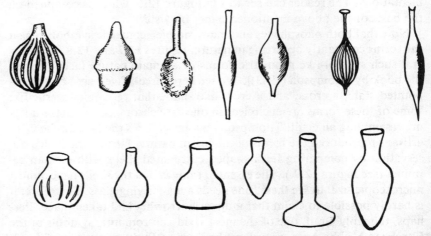

FIG. 12.9. Various kinds of microscopic shells of the Lagen genus and Roman ceramic
vessel (below) (from Thompson, 1943).

1.

2.

FIG. 12.10. Crimean tamgas (1); Kalmyk tamgas (2) (from Lavrov, 1978).

to remind the reader that certain biologists believe many geometrical forms observed in the animate world to be determined not by the optimality of their functioning but by a certain pattern indifferent toward the process of adaptation. This suggests that the same forms once were read from the semantic universe immediately by Nature, and another time, by the depths of our unconscious.

Note that *tamgas*, the property signs used to mark horses, can also be the material for studying the archetypic origin of symbols. The amazing fact is that they are common for peoples of very different regions. These signs perceived now as identifying marks seem to have played a very significant part in the life of tribal society. Now it is only the variety of their use which hints at this fact. Below we quote Lavrov (1978), who studied Caucasian tamgas.

> Such stamps were sometimes used to mark the cattle, they were also cut on door-posts and door-folds, on the house pillars, on the wooden dishes, on rattles whose sound accompanied dances, were written on the stone tombs, on road posts or walls of buildings, were painted on banners and rocks as well as placed on documents instead of signatures and stamps. (p. 91)

Hence it becomes quite obvious these symbols are not only property marks but also signs of its magic protection. In Figures 12.10 and 12.11, the reader can see several Crimean and Kalmyk tamgas as well as signs from Western Europe, America, and the Canary Islands borrowed from the above-mentioned book by Lavrov. Try to compare them with the Roman labarums in Figure 12.1.

And now a few concluding remarks. Sometimes it is said that *meaning* in its most compact form is manifested through *Symbol* (see, for example, Scholem, 1976). However, it is clear that the Symbol is not a common code sign. The semantics underlying it is so vague it cannot be decoded through our common everyday texts. The only thing we can do is to say something about Symbols that embraces their history. Symbols have a startling property: they can acquire new meanings without losing the old ones, despite their seemingly complete incompatibility.

I already mentioned that the swastika symbol had been attributed a new meaning. The same is true of Solomon's seal. The history of this symbol is illuminated in detail by Scholem (1976). It turns out that it became a symbol of Judaism only in the nineteenth century, when the Jews started on the road of national renaissance and consolidation.

Earlier it had not been opposed to other symbols and occurred not only in Judaism but also in Arab and Christian cultures. Sometimes it served as a symbol and sometimes merely as part of an ornamentation, combined with a five-pointed star and a swastika. The six-pointed star can be seen on the title pages of occult and mystic books edited in the

FIG. 12.11. Tamgas from: Western Europe (3); America (4); Canaries (5) (from Lavrov, 1978).

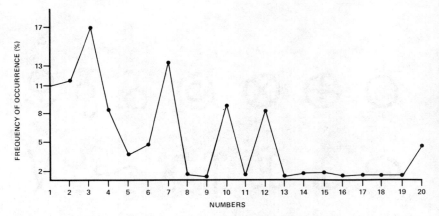

F<small>IG</small>. 12.12. Frequency of occurrence of words denoting numbers (from unity to twenty) in the Bible. The figure is composed on the basis of "Symphony," an index edition indicating the places of occurrence for all the words in the Bible. For each word denoting a number, all its derivatives were taken; e.g., the word "three" unites such words as "third," "thrice," "trinity," etc. The total number of words in the Bible denoting numbers from 1 to 20 is 1,471.

nineteenth and twentieth centuries, when it already seemed to be associated with Judaism.

The pentacle has acquired even greater significance: it became the symbol of the Masonic Order and of the Soviet Union and its army; it also entered the national banner of the United States. In the remote past, both of these stars had been the magic symbols of power and could act as talismans, though the corresponding numbers had been charged with rather specific notions which, as a curiosity, have been preserved to the present. Here is one of the typical occult descriptions of the number five (Papus, 1910):

> But 5, which is the number of the fall, is also *the number of will,* and will is an instrument of restoration.
>
> The initiated know why the replacement of four by five is only temporally pernicious; how man, split in his integrity and lying in the mud after the fall, learns to win a personality, truly free and conscious. He returns after his fall stronger and greater; thus *evil* follows the *good* only temporally, in order to make true what is better.
>
> This number 5 contains deep mysteries; but we have to stop here so as not to start ceaseless digressions. (p. 128)

I should emphasize here that the Symbol plays a specific role: a new conceptualization attributed to it acquires a new status; it enters human consciousness organically and becomes part of it. At some deep levels of consciousness, the new becomes inseparable from the old determined by the entire past of the culture. Moreover, the new strengthens the old. Acting in a new way in a new situation, a person preserves *integrity* in his succession to the old. And hence comes the emotional force of the Symbol.

The Symbol is a key unlocking our consciousness for an extralogical perception of the new. The possession of Symbols is, perhaps, the most remarkable distinction between human consciousness and computer intelligence. Despite all the differences between human consciousness and computer intelligence, we must acknowledge with amazement that the *number* itself may act as a symbol, i.e., again as a key unlocking consciousness. The role of numerical symbolics can be traced quantitatively by making a frequency analysis of words denoting numbers in the texts of ancient cultures. As an illustration, Figure 12.12 represents the frequency of occurrence of such words in the Bible. Obviously predominant are the numbers *three, seven, ten,* and *twelve.* This seems to have no other explanation than the sacral nature of these numbers. However, the text under study lacks even a mythological explanation of this sacral nature. It is likely to go back to some very deep levels of consciousness. It is relevant to ask here: Is it possible that statistical analysis of the frequency of occurrence of words denoting numbers can become an instrument for comparing the unconscious in cultures with different historical pasts? This may lead us to one of the fundamental problems: What is the invariant of the unconscious?

The study of the role of symbols in human history is a study of the unconscious in an experiment which has been going on for dozens of centuries.

C. Mandalas[10]

In this chapter I must at least briefly touch upon *mandala*, one of the principal concepts of Eastern spiritual life. In a somewhat schematic manner we might say that mandala is a further development of a simple geometric symbol: its transformation into a complex image, a pattern reflecting the state of consciousness achieved in the process of meditation.

I quote here the book by Govinda (1976a):

[10] Mandala is a Sanskrit word. Its literal meaning is: round, a (solar) disc, a circle, a wheel, a group, a circle of people, quantity, manifold, a way, an orbit, a halo (around the sun), a ball, the retinue of the tsar, a region, a country, the name of chapters in "Rigveda." The circle is a symbol widely used in the East, and it has numerous interpretations. On the one hand, this is the symbol of the world curvature—of space, time, and life in its endless cyclic repetitions; it may be said to oppose the Western linearity of the World perception giving rise to the naive ideas of evolution and involution. On the other hand, a circle containing a point inside encircled by concentric circles is a projection of the cone whose apex a person strives to achieve in meditation, passing through many worlds.

> The mandala is like a map of the inner world, which we want to explore and realize in the great venture of meditation. (p. 60)

At the same time the author of the above-mentioned book emphasizes that "a mandala can have no meaning for people who have no idea of the underlying tradition and symbology" (p. 60).

Mandala may be given by the symbolism of Buddha's postures:

> The Buddha—like all Enlightened Ones—is represented as sitting on a lotus throne. The lotus is the prototype of all mandalas, all centralized systems of a spiritual universe of intricate relationships. It is the prototype of all Cakras or psychic centers, in which the chaos of unconscious forces is transformed into a meaningful cosmos, and in which individual existence finds its fulfillment in the final realization of Enlightenment, the state of completeness (the state of being entirely "whole," which we call "holy"). (p. 102)

It is also emphasized that the emergence of the mandala in consciousness should be preceded by certain preparedness:

> The structure of the mandala itself, which precedes the visualization of the divine figures, must have been thoroughly fixed in the mind before the actual meditation begins. The mandala is built in the form of a universal temple on top of the sacred mountain, representing the axis of the universe (and corresponding to the spinal column of the meditator). This temple is open to the four directions of space, and in each of the four entrances stands one of the guardians of the threshold. The temple is surrounded by three protective circles: first a circle of lotus petals symbolizing the purity of heart, as basis for the ten transcendental virtues; second, a circle of diamond scepters (vajras), symbolizing the strength and determination of the concentrated mind; and third, a circle of flames, representing the purifying force of higher knowledge, in the fire of which all dross and impurities are burned away, and in which everything that had coagulated is liquefied and integrated into one great upsurging experience. (p. 95)

The last words of this quotation can be compared with our conception of the continuous nature of the deep layers of our consciousness where discrete (coagulated) notions determined by words, discrete signs of our language, are interpreted (Nalimov, 1981a).

If we turn now to Western culture, we may claim Orthodox icons (the true ones, not used for the sake of decoration), as well as Catholic sculptures, also to be mandalas. The tradition of Christian monastic meditation–prayer included the visualization of Christ's image; this is again a mandala whose emergence was preceded by a specific tuning. Many scholars are prone to believe that the cardinal difference between the Oriental religious outlook and the Western one is revealed through the difference between mandalas. I believe, however, that the principal difference concerns the traditions determining the prior disposition. On a very deep level we are dealing with the manifestation of one and the same property inherent in human consciousness and remaining invariant in the entire variety of its manifestation. In contrast to simple geometric symbols, a concrete mandala is not invariant toward several cultures.

Of great interest is the spontaneous appearance of mandalas in the work of the artists not specially prepared for this. The image of Demon by the Russian poet M. Yu. Lermontov (1814–1841) and especially that by the Russian painter M. A. Brubel (1856–1910) are naturally perceived as spontaneous mandalas. The pictures by M. K. Čiurlionis (1875–1911), a remarkable Lithuanian artist and composer, are undoubtedly mandalas though they are hardly predetermined by the traditions of Catholicism in which he was brought up. This brings forth the following question: To what degree was Čiurlionis himself prepared to comprehend his own works? Perhaps the cause of his mental disease was his unpreparedness for what descended on him, while his soul was yet unprotected and open?

I have noticed with a certain amazement the mantra-like nature of the pictures by the contemporary Lithuanian painter Grushas Bronus. His pictures in the technique of glass-plastics are mostly of the same kind. Roughly speaking, they may be called abstract, though they generally contain an image of an object, which as a rule can be perceived as the feminine essence becoming a symbol of the universal cosmic essence. To understand these pictures, one has to resort to the book by Grof (1975), who in his experiments with LSD demonstrated that his experimental records were full of experiences of the intrauterine life. Such an experience helps the patients to open up an extremely rich semantic matrix in their consciousness. Perhaps an artist during his creative work also tries to re-experience the intrauterine life so as to enter an altered state of consciousness and, probably, push the viewers of his work toward it. Besides, one of Bronus's favorite images is a vortex, and this reminds us of the Hindu cosmic concepts in which not only space was curved but time as well, and the universe could be represented as a gigantic mandala composed of symbols situated or moving circularly and illustrating the interaction or overlapping of spiritual and cosmic forces [for details see Govinda (1976*a*), p. 258–259]. A picture by Grushas Bronus is presented in Figure 12.13.

In a broad sense a mandala is an image that directly affects our unconscious, beyond any conceptualization and, moreover, not yielding to any conceptualization. At the same time it is void of any directly felt emotional charge such as that which is usually inherent in landscapes or other objective paintings. If this is actually so, then such new trends in art as abstract painting represent stubborn attempts to find new mandalas. And instead of absurdly resisting these trends, our art critics had better

"Женщина с голубем"

FIG. 12.13 A picture by Grushas Bronus: Woman with Dove.

become acquainted with the psychology of the unconscious. As a matter of fact, these trends made use of certain deep states of human consciousness, organically inherent in us. Of interest is the rejection of these forms of art by broad circles of intellectuals: I believe this to be a manifestation of the protective agressiveness of modern culture which demands that consciousness be locked in a conceptualized outlook.

From my viewpoint, a still life is also a mandala, since the objectivity of a still life is objectless. What meaning, for example, does an image of a tomato have for a spectator? Why should it have any emotional or conceptual charge? I remember how at the exhibition of Morandi's still lifes I was struck by the fact the museum was far from crowded: there were only a few people in its halls. Indeed, the paintings seemed to be endless versions of the same clay jars and other vessels. But a person who remained in front of one painting for some time started to feel the waves coming from the depth of the painter's consciousness and filling the hall. You could almost hear them.

In the fourth part of this book, we are going to speak of our own experimental results and describe the mandalas obtained by painters while meditating over word semantics.

D. Concluding Remarks

Why do symbols so powerfully affect us? The question does not seem too difficult to answer if we turn again to the probabilistic model of consciousness. We have to acknowledge that one of the remarkable peculiarities of our consciousness which distinguishes it from a computer consists in the fact that its unconscious component can be revealed through symbols that provoke the spontaneous emergence of new and unexpected preference functions $p(y|\mu)$ which generate new value concepts $p(\mu|y)$ while solving a new problem y. The essential thing is that the symbol which has provoked the reconstruction of value concepts does not relate to the new problem y in a way noticeable for our reflective consciousness. The new value orientation opens up a new vision of the situation, gives rise to a new Doing, and makes possible a new conceptualization that justifies Doing on the conscious level. The suddenness of the value re-evaluation is fraught with an emotional shock. The possibility of a new Doing liberates the sleeping potential of a person and sometimes of society.

What is said above is nothing more than an attempt at a phenomenological description of consciousness. Its mechanism, if any, remains hidden. As follows from the term itself, the unconscious should not have any mechanism. And if this is actually so, consciousness as a whole remains spontaneous, i.e., void of mechanism. Perhaps the only thing we can do is to give phenomenological descriptions without trying to conceptualize.

The reader may be surprised that I have not said a single word about the Freudian interpretation of symbols. The reason is that I believe Freudianism to be too deterministic. It absorbed the rigid scientific positivism of the second half of the nineteenth century and the beginning of the twentieth century. It is senseless to criticize Freudianism, which is merely boring in its Pandeterminism.

Chapter 13

Experimental Study of the Unconscious

Revelation of Semantic Fields Underlying Words of Everyday Language[1]

A. Introduction

One of the means for the direct experimental study of the unconscious is the revelation of semantic fields underlying words of our everyday language. Earlier (Nalimov, 1981a), I elaborated the conception of a probabilistic semantics based on the idea of probabilistically weighted fields that make the meaning of words, discrete linguistic carriers, explicit. However, I did not manage to discover these fields by common tests. As has now become clear, my failure was caused by the fact that I had not taken into account an almost obvious situation, i.e., that the comprehension of verbal meaning is determined by the interaction of two constituents: consciousness and the unconscious. In the former case we deal with logical structures, and in the latter, with images and symbols.

Thus, semantic fields underlying words prove to be the manifestation of the unconscious. To avoid possible terminological misunderstanding, I emphasize that the term *unconscious* in this book is used in a broad meaning.

B. Experimental Procedure

The experiment was aimed at revealing semantic fields underlying the following words: *freedom, slavery, dignity*. Its method was a directed

---

[1] Written in cooperation with J. A. Drogalina.

group meditation realized with the help of auto-training (AT).[2] AT is the simplest procedure known to me for expanding the scale of Doing *S*, leading to a slowing down of personal, psychological time. AT was conducted for 20 to 25 minutes; its text, accompanied by music and read by a professional hypnotist, was tape-recorded.

The aim of the AT stage was maximal relaxation. At the next step subjects in a state of relaxation were given the goal word, and the experimenter suggested that they should interact with it, meditate over it. The instruction was as follows: "Freedom . . . don't think, don't reason . . . experience it. I am entering it, I'm becoming it, I'm experiencing it."

At the last stage the subjects, still partially in a state of relaxation, recorded their impressions related to the experiencing of the goal word.

Each experiment included three sessions carried out on different days; at each session only one word of the triad was given: *freedom*, *slavery*, or *dignity*. We had four experimental series, each of which included the three words.

Subjects were fairly diverse: engineers, pilots, professional painters (they recorded their experience in paintings and drawings), and mentally ill people who retained a faculty for contacts.

The age range was also diverse; it had no upper bound. This, however, did not affect experimental results in any way, nor did the place where the experiments were conducted: Armenian mountains, the center of Moscow, a hospital for the mentally ill. The total number of subjects was 190; the number of texts–records, 172; and the number of drawings and paintings, 18.

C. Choice of the Key Words

The experimental results and, moreover, the likelihood of success are naturally determined first of all by the choice of words for meditation. We chose a text consisting of the verbal triad that imply the basic notions of the collective unconscious. The task of our experiment was to make their hidden content explicit.

The concept itself of the *triad* as a triunity acts as an ancient symbol with implicitly rich semantics (for details, see section B of Chapter 12). Recall that Dante's *Divine Comedy* is triune: *Paradise-Heaven*, *Purgatory-Earth*, *Inferno-Underworld*. These are not merely three separate parts, but unity in three facets that answer our original ideas of the unconscious concerning the ontological meaning of the trinity. Purgatory is

---

[2] The application of AT is commonly connected with the names of Schulz (Germany, France) and Jacobson (in English-speaking countries). A description of the contemporary use of AT in psychology, medicine, and education can be found in Boon, Davrou, and Macquet (1976).

here an intermediate link. It is essential that from the apocryphal sources[3] (which, however, were reflected in the official iconography) it follows that Christ after his death (after leaving the Earth) had to descend into the Inferno before he could return to the Heavenly sphere through his resurrection. The *fullness* given by trinity should be completed. Descending into the infernal spheres is a theme constantly repeated in the myths of various cultures. Greeks had Ulysses traveling to the Cimmerian country and Orpheus descending to the Inferno. Guénon (1957), alluding to the study by Miguel (1919), speaks of the predecessors of the *Divine Comedy* in the works of Moslem culture: the architecture of Dante's Inferno turns out to be a copy of the Moslem Inferno.

Guénon analyzes in detail Dante's numerical symbolism, revealing the esoteric quality of his works, which goes back into the remote past.[4] Recall the above-mentioned ideas of the gnostics on the triple human nature corresponding to the triple structure of Dante's world. Hence, it is clear that the theme of descending into the Inferno signifies the journey inside oneself. In other words, it means descending into one's phylogenetic past: overcoming it through transfiguration via the triune integrity of existence.

But now let us return to our key words. They reflect the same triad used by Dante, but in contemporary language comprehensible to us. Freedom is Heaven versus Slavery, the infernal essence. The intermediate state is Dignity. It signifies human behavior in Purgatory, where a person has to acquire, according to Paul Tillich, the Courage to Be, a phrase he used as the title of his book (Tillich, 1952). However, we must confess that we became aware of these links only at the stage of evaluation of the results from the viewpoint of their culturological comprehension. At the beginning, when we chose the key words, we proceeded from our unconscious, not being aware of our motives for the choice.

D. Experimental Results[5]

> *Flight is the property of Gods.*
> K. BAL'MONT

The specific feature of our experiment and its radical difference from all publications on the subject that we are familiar with consists in its be-

---

[3] See, e.g. the second part of the apocryphal Gospel of Nicodemus (Scheidweiler, 1963).

[4] Guènon tries to prove that Dante's esoterica is borrowed from the tradition of the Templars to whom he seems to have secretly belonged. Dante's attitude toward the suppression of the Order by Philip the Fair is expressed in Purgatory XX, 91–96.

[5] The analysis of the first experimental series (experiment 1) was published as an article (Nalimov, Kuz-

ing of a systematic character. Grof (1975), who experimented with LSD, indicated the absence of invariants when altered states of consciousness are entered, and we can say our experimental results were highly similar; moreover, we can even speak of the possibility of constructing matrices of semantic fields that act as invariants of the collective unconscious and are revealed by means of a key word which seems to be the center of crystallization of the semantics experienced.

Words controlling meditation not only act as concepts reflecting the paradigm of the existing culture but also are symbols (as we already emphasized above) going back to the remote past. Therefore, the depth of penetration into the unconscious was determined not so much by the degree of relaxation as by the choice of a symbol that touched upon the basis of human spiritual existence and thus was heavily charged psychologically. Symbols belonging to the language of the unconscious are the keys to the unconscious. Relaxation is only a condition that provides the possibility for using the key.

The texts–records of experimental results can be divided into four categories:

1. Records containing new experience. By new experience we mean interaction with the reality beyond the boundaries of common activities, concepts, associations, or reasoning; new experience is accompanied by corresponding psychosomatic phenomena.
2. Associative experience proceeding from past experience (in contrast to new experience which represents an unprecedented state).
3. Texts–reasonings representing a chain of speculations conditioned by the key word.
4. Texts–clichés containing stereotyped associations and speculations.

Naturally, we were primarily interested in the texts belonging to the first category, which will be considered below in a generalized form. This concerns records obtained in experiments with sane people (experiments 1, 2, and 4). Texts obtained in experiments in a hospital for the mentally ill (experiments 3 and 5) will be considered separately.

Three experiments were carried out with the key word *freedom*; the total number of records was 72: 66.6% contained new experience; 12.5%, associations; 8.4%, reasoning; and 12.5%, cliché. The semantic matrix of *freedom* can be represented by the words: flight (soaring)—boundless space—joy—light.

In experiment 1 the dominant words were "space" and "light"; in experiment 2, "flight"; and in experiment 4, "flight" and "space." The

---

netsov, and Drogalina, 1978). O. A. Kuznetsov participated in organizing and carrying out several experiments to be described later.

sensation experienced as joy is a typical positive emotion sometimes expressed emphatically as *boundless joy*. The texts are abundant in epithets testifying to the reality of the experience.

To illustrate our description, we quote below several very typical texts:

> I felt weightless, soaring in a vast boundless space. It had neither boundaries, nor color. The striking thing was that I was so light and could control my position in space. The entire space was filled with very far away worlds with fuzzy outlines close to spheric. I could reach any of these worlds in an instant, with light's speed or, perhaps, just in an instant. But when I got into this selected world, I did not feel anything. It disintegrated into lots of far away separate worlds. I did not feel colors or shapes. And I was not in the least disappointed not to be able to examine these worlds.

> To the word "freedom": I saw wind blowing in space. I had a feeling of joy, flight, the sun, absence of any necessity. I also felt weightless.

> Far below I see the beautiful, peaceful Earth, and I am flying above it in the waves of light.

> There appeared something impetuous which whirled around in a vortex and dashed upwards from the Earth. Darkness remained behind. This vortex was accompanied by energetic music. Then everything calms down, and now only blue sparkling sky is spreading around. Complete freedom of actions. The music becomes more flowing and majestic. But suddenly my glance turns downwards. There, below, other people try to take off from the Earth and fly upward. Many succeed. The air, the blue sky is overcrowded. And again everything dashes upwards, in space. First only the black sky and far-away star can be seen. Then everything disappears and you see golden glitter which you try to reach. Suddenly you feel that you are free from this light as well and you begin somersaulting and whirling around in this medium.

> Below there is a dark cellar. A man is ascending through the open doorway. His hair, face, and shoulders are lit by rays of light. But he returns into the darkness. There is someone else in there. They both are walking along the cobblestone road of an ancient town. The streets are empty. Nobody can be seen. Their steps become faster in a joyful motion. They take a running start and now both of them are flying. They are sailing in the air. They are side by side with free people. The music is light and happy, some people descend and sit down on the rays of the sun . . .

There were also texts which recorded the state of freedom as an out-of-body experience. The essential feature of these records is passing through a tunnel with the subsequent soaring in the air, momentary transference in boundless space, and identification with the sound going upwards:

I began to leave the Earth, to fly away. The Earth remained far below, and everything on its surface was turning small, miniature, and absolutely alien. My flight was odd—I was turning into the sound of an organ pipe. Then above me there appeared a dome of a temple and I went through the dome, being the organ sound . . .

These records have much in common with the contents of the book by Moody (1975) describing the experience of clinical death as reported by reanimated people. In this comparison again, death becomes the synonym for freedom: death signifies the passage into another, free-from-body state. In the records for the word "slavery," this state is described as leaving darkness, entering light, and soaring in it:

When the word "slavery" was uttered, I had a vision of sharply condensing darkness with a spot of light in the middle. The spot is very bright, but I can't make a movement towards it. Then I had an image of being imprisoned by a plant with greenish-red leaves. I seem to have been entangled by seaweed which was by and by entangling me still more. The bright light of the spot is gradually fading out. My movements are feeble and I can do nothing to liberate myself. But at a certain moment my strength returns, I manage to break the fetters with a sharp movement, and then I am swimming towards light.

Note that the records of our experiment describe images, impressions, and experiences not directly related to the experience of paradigmatic consciousness of our culture, the collective consciousness. This is another kind of experience reflected in the records of the majority of subjects, the experience of the collective unconscious. We are dealing here with the consciousness of the far-away past which is not explicit in the consciousness of our culture. We may select texts with a gnostic flavor that contain the notion of multitudes of worlds, or texts with a hermetic tendency that reminds us of ancient initiations.

For the word *slavery*, three experiments were conducted. The total number of records was 44: 68.2% contained new experience; 6.8%, associations; 9.1%, reasoning; and 15.9%, cliché.

The semantic matrix of *slavery* can be represented by the words: darkness—heaviness (depression)—light (as liberation).

Darkness is a general image, including dark cellars, gloomy vaults, black caves, everything black, dark, suppressing, and paralyzing. Negative emotions prevail, namely, feelings of depression, heaviness, desperation, and oppression.

Light acts as a saving force that liberates the participant from this state. The urge toward Light and interaction with it again bring about the sensation of flight, either impetuous or smooth, accompanied by detailed description of changing landscapes and techniques of the flight.

Below we quote the most typical records of meditation over the word *slavery*:

> Blackness of a cave, oppressive vaults with a tendency to close over you; a very faint gleam from the entrance, and everything is slowly falling down in an abyss.
> In front, near the faint gleam of light, the ceiling of the cave threatens to collapse.
>
> Huge gray cubic stones covered with scabs; I am also covered by the same scabs all over; I watched them appear on my body, especially on my legs, some of them were festering.
> Then I felt them appear on my face; black and dark-green lizards were scurrying between my legs.
> Far away I saw black birds with necks like those of griffins but without white feathers around them.
> I thought they were coming to peck at my scabs. I felt repulsion and got out of the state of meditation.

This text is borrowed from the records of the second experiment, whose participants emphasized negative emotional states aggravated by the hostility of the environment (sharp stones of another planet, faceless figures, etc.).

Thus, *slavery* is existence in the darkness, submission to darkness, suppression of feelings, and depression.

From the three experiments on the word *dignity*, the total number of records was 39: 66.6% contained new experience; 12.8%, associations; 10.3%, reasoning; and 10.3%, cliché.

The semantic matrix of *dignity* can be represented by the words: light —joy—darkness (exit from darkness) where "light" is an active force defeating darkness.

Interaction with various manifestations of light brings about positive emotions and, primarily, the feeling of joy (again, as was the case with *freedom*, it is sometimes expressed emphatically as *unbearable joy*), and of peace.

Light fights against darkness and is opposed to it as a positive force, the experiencing of which causes positive emotional states. In experiment 1 darkness acts as a background on which light is dominant, as well as positive emotions produced by it. Experiment 2 adds to the pattern an upward vertical motion linked by the transformations of the symbols: cross, triangle, stars. In experiment 3 the semantic matrix is not distinctly expressed; nevertheless, its main components are words related to the two previous experiments: man—joy—flight (space)—light. The sequence of the constituents is determined by their meaningful charge in the records.

These are the most typical texts on the word *dignity*:

> Above I see a sharply curved steep arched bridge over an abyss formed by a shining four-petaled shape . . .
> Below flowers sparkling in space.
> A flood of light directed from above into a dark gap of a stone vault.
> In the fiery space (of heatless fire) there sparkle cross-shaped stars, lots of them . . .
> From below light is ascending in a broad wave through the space; it is transformed into two rays (as in a tuning indicator); light over-floods the space, trying to push out something dark which is resisting it . . .
> The whole fiery space is traversed by elongated edges of a sparkling cross-shaped star, and, as if growing from its live, pulsating core, a flower grows, looking like a heart ablaze, as if sent by the star.
> And the feeling of unbearable joy . . .

> A battlefield after a fight in the far-away past. Everything is dug up, maimed, and wounded. I am leaving the battlefield. It is dark, twilight. I am wandering in a gloomy lifeless country. It looks like after a drought. The ground is cracked. I stop at a large wooden cross, half-demolished and corroded with age. I am standing in front of It. And It becomes alive, regains new power and strength. It starts to shine with quiet light. The light goes upwards and downwards. To the right and to the left of the cross I see two figures in white gleaming clothes. They are turned to me. They pass a message very important for me. I feel power within myself. There appears the gleam of the sun rising somewhere behind the mountains. The cross disappears and I see a road in front of me, winding up into the mountains with snow tops. My clothes start glittering in the first rays of the rising sun.

It should be emphasized that texts–records are of a mythological character and include symbolic images and symbols which represent signs of the archetype, going back into ancient times. The symbolism is especially vivid in paintings of our artist subjects[6] (see Color Plates 1–3). These symbols include first of all a cross, a triangle, a square, and a circle (which in the texts is most often linked to the words the sun, a sphere, a ball), as well as symbolically charged images: fire, water, light, a temple, a priest, hands, a bird, a bee, a rainbow, a road, a key, a staircase, etc. Above (see section B, Chapter 12) we already said that the symbolism

---

[6] In the descriptions accompanying the color plates, we give our interpretation of the paintings. These are naturally only some of the possible interpretations: each reader can find his own interpretation of the paintings. The meaning of mandala-like paintings is always broader than any of their possible interpretations. We give our interpretation only in the hope that it will provoke the readers.

of the cross, which plays such an important role in Christian consciousness, historically goes back to Egypt, where the cross with the upper part representing a loop is a symbol of life and a key to the purport of life. It is a sign of initiation and an amulet worn at the belt. Most probably this symbol, as we already indicated earlier, goes back to a time more ancient than the Egyptian: it is organically embedded in our consciousness, which is manifested even by the fact that it appears in our field of vision as a result of mechanical pressure on the eyeball; this phenomenon is called a "phosphene."

In several experimental records and paintings we see the symbol of a cross both fixed and undergoing different transformations, e.g., the horizontal part of the cross is transformed into a circle in a horizontal projection or into an eight, also in a horizontal projection. Eights occur as well as elements of an eight-edged cross. This symbolism is also very interesting and meaningful. Recall that in gnostic and Pythagorean teachings it had a deeply mystical meaning denoting the Great Ogdoad—the fullness of divine potencies. In the Christian culture it was retained in the architecture of temples (for details see above, section B, Chapter 12).

Elsewhere we also dwelt in detail on the symbolic polysemy of a triangle, a circle, and a square.

A triangle repeated four times and ascending to the sky is a pyramid. This image also occurs in our records, alternating with a glittering and iridescent prism.

These symbols come close to other images found in the records, also symbolically charged, e.g., the image of hands, which frequently occurs in descriptions. The polysemy of *hands* is obvious: they signify catching, possession, property, and also curing—touching sore spots with hands. It is also a hearth with its warmth and kindness; it is a prayer; and the hands of a person crossing his eyebrows form a cross. Here hands and the cross merge, which resembles the transformation of the linear (horizontal) part of the cross into a circle; another image represents a snake biting its tail (again a horizontal line transformed into a circle). Another example is a key in the lock. One of the interpretations of this image is erotic. But other interpretations are also possible: it signifies entrance of one essence into another, the dichotomy of the world disappearing in merging, the life-giving force of the world; again, a key resembles the cross of Egyptians, or, to be more precise, a cross in the shape of a key unlocking the meaning of the world. The symbol is polysemantic because its semantics are given in the space of a greater dimension. Each of its interpretations is a projection onto the subspace of a lesser dimension. However, despite the seeming variety of their manifestations, symbols are signs expressing one and the same thing: human participation in the semantic cosmos (in the extra-temporal form of cosmic consciousness as manifested in symbols).

Symbols, in contrast to words, do not receive their meaning through the probabilistically weighted fuzziness of the semantic field, through its reduction conditioned by the filtering character of the context (Nalimov, 1981*a*). Symbols are semantically full and are revealed not through logical structures, but through meditation that removes the opposition of the cognizer and the cognized, through entering the essence of the object and complete merging with it. Symbols do not have a conceptual status but an ontological one. Symbols are the keys unlocking what is potentially contained in human consciousness. We would like to quote here Tillich (1966):

> Religious symbols say something to us about the way in which men have understood themselves in their very nature.

However, for us, representatives of Western (logically structured) culture, any record represented by symbols seems foreign (as do mystic states of consciousness). We perceive as comprehensible only that which is expressed by concepts—alienated structures separated from the direct ontology of the world.

And now a few words about the experiments in a hospital for mental diseases with a group of schizophrenic patients (experiment 3) who retained the faculty for contacts (meaningful communication). All the patients who participated in our experiment were intellectuals.

The characteristic feature of all these records (excluding one, whose author, as we learned later, was a "borderline" case) is the absence of metaphors, images, symbols; they are a-mythological. They represent a chain of stereotyped speculations operating with paradigmatic concepts of our culture and, moreover, with ready-made cliché. They are inert from the viewpoint of creativity. They produce the impression that the entrance into creatively loaded spheres of the unconscious is closed for their authors. These patients act as automata with a set program, though they possess certain individual features. Here are several examples:

> When I heard the word "freedom," I imagined the Island of Freedom—Cuba, as well as songs connected with this word. Then I remembered the song: "Oh, how broad is our native country . . . where a man can so freely breathe."[7] I also imagined myself riding a motorcycle and singing. At last I imagined that I am discharged from the hospital. I am at home playing with my children and in the evening I am going to the theatre with my spouse.

> 1. Boys writing on a wall with a piece of charcoal: "Peace to the World" and "Freedom."
> 2. The windows of our hospital are barred.

---

[7] A very popular official song praising the free life in the USSR. Its melody has been taken as the call sign for Soviet radio broadcasts abroad.

I had only one concept in connection with the word "freedom":
"Freedom is the realized necessity." No other associations emerged
worth remembering.

Compare these with a record by the patient diagnosed as a "borderline
case":

> Soaring in the boundless sky. The feeling of peace, joy, blueness,
> limitless horizon.

This text differs from those cited above (as well as from the rest belonging to this group); at the same time, it has much in common with the texts of mentally sane subjects; this allowed us to express our doubts as to the degree of illness of this patient. These doubts were supported by the psychiatrist treating him, who informed us that the patient had been diagnosed as a "borderline case." He is a man of principles, and this feature of his makes his behavior non-normative, aggravated by the positive feedback,[8] which interferes with his realization in society.

We would also like to quote another, quite typical, stereotyped text ("as far as I see")—a response to the word *slavery*:

> This word is, naturally, very familiar and belonging to the past. As
> far as I see, slavery is a word reflecting the extreme degree of a person's dependence on another person or society as a whole. This was
> an immediate association. It also occurred to me that slavery is an extreme form of exploiting people . . .

We would like to emphasize once more that the authors of the texts in experiment 3 are not able to cross the boundaries of conceptual structures within which they have been trained. They remain within the boundaries of rational consciousness and are deprived of the possibility of gaining new experience. The entrance into a state of meditation is denied to them.

It would be premature to claim that we can suggest a new diagnostic attribute, but we would like to draw the reader's attention to the fact that, in our experiments with sane people, at every session about 10% of the subjects were unable to enter into the unconscious. Their records look very similar to those obtained in experiment 3, as the reader can see for himself. Below are quoted two such texts pertaining to the words *freedom* and *dignity*.

> Freedom: impossibility of freedom when a person oppresses another, exploitation of one person by another. True freedom is possible only in a classless communist society. Then it is associated with flight, a free flight of a bird; free creativity for the common good;

---

[8] In the cybernetic sense a positive feedback, in contrast to a negative one, strengthens the abnormality of behavior rather than corrects it.

> self-sacrifice and the feeling it is mutual. The beautiful future. The role of the future generation, upbringing of children on a new level, both psychological and scientific.
>
> Dignity: an ability, having freedom of actions and thoughts, to behave with dignity among people, one's friends. To treat people with dignity, without humiliating them, and respecting the dignity of others.
> Freedom and dignity must be one, and worthy behavior must be a natural need.
> One must preserve dignity in slavery, fight for one's rights, and all deeds and actions must be dignified.
> In the fight for freedom, all actions should be dignified, worthy of the attitude of people around you and of their respect.

Note that in some records of this type the key word is repeated many times, becoming a kind of magic incantation, its meaning remaining unrevealed. Such texts are characterized by the lack of synonyms, inclusion of imperative modalities ("should be," "must be"), and many words beginning with the same letter (primitiveness of associations).

What we are dealing with here is the magic consciousness that attaches extremely great importance to rituals, which for people of contemporary culture is, perhaps, a weak form of schizophrenia.

In the hospital for mental diseases, we also carried out an experiment with neurotic patients. These are the so-called "borderline" patients, some of whom have weakly manifested symptoms of schizophrenia. We are not going to analyze in detail their records—they are short and inexpressive. One can't help feeling in them depression and constraint. Consider only one of them:

> I quickly felt warmth, relaxation in my arms, but when I felt it in my legs, I got afraid: I got the feeling of weightlessness which frightens me. A bit later I calmed down but the thought that had frightened me did not completely disappear.
> I saw a grove, but Freedom—no, I did not feel it.

According to the psychiatrist treating her, this patient has an obvious syndrome of depersonalization and loss of contact with reality. The feeling of weightlessness was one of her chief complaints.

When in a collective meditation normal subjects had a sensation of weightlessness or flight, and even felt out of body, this was accompanied by emotional enthusiasm and the feeling of joy; in the above case similar sensations were a source of depression and fright. We believe this striking difference in evaluations of similar states can be explained as follows: for normal subjects their new experience is a short and inspiring journey into a new and inwardly agreeable state of consciousness but one that is inconvenient for everyday life; for the neurotic patient this state that is

Color Plates

Plate 1. Artist V. S. Gribkov

Freedom. Among the pillars without any walls, under a chandelier without a ceiling, on a round ground painted with black and terra-cotta rhombs, in the countryside a circle of women in white clothes. Conic capitals of the pillars are repeated by the symbols of infinity in the chandelier; the circle of the pillars unlocked into the reverse perspective is repeated by the circle of women; the circle of the chandelier, by the circle of the floor; the flame of the candles, by the figures of priestesses. The whole composition depicts the mystery of the feminine Attic Temple merging in Nature, the feminine essence of the World.

Slavery. A big gray boulder of a cubic shape covered with scabs (it was thus seen by the artist) in the empty gray space. Black griffins flying to "peck at the scabs" and to cleanse the boulder with which, according to the verbal record, the artist identified himself. The act of cleansing is that of suffering, but also of liberation. Perhaps, that is why in the center of the boulder, in its heart, we see another space, another perspective (reverse), another color—the green one, the color of hopes, another mood in the opening.

Dignity. Three hierarchically arranged spaces of light colors; on the foreground dark and light symbols of simple geometric shapes. In the light harmony of the hues they look somewhat disharmonious. The symbols are clearly discrete, though they do not break the composition of the light spaces.

Freedom

Slavery

Dignity

PLATE 1

Plate 2. Artist A. N. Dyachkov

Freedom. Through the thin grille (perhaps, the balcony railings) I see fields, a river, a man-of-war with masts resembling Catholic crosses. Over this grilled landscape there is a round yellow sun crossed by a black diagonal cross, dark sky with stars crossed by black eight-pointed crosses. The symbols of crossing the sun and the stars, incomprehensible at first sight, are actually the same railing, its projection onto the images of light and life. The railing is a symbol of the obstacle between the World and man who exists in order to interact with this world. Therefore, *freedom* is a state without any railings, interaction without interference. The semantics of "freedom" is given here through the apophantic transcendence.

Slavery. A blue cross is spread in the dark space. Near its base a human face distorted by emotions over a heap of yellow objects resembling coins.

Dignity. The picture fixes the moment observed by the artist when a pearly cloud is torn. Inside the cloud there appeared symbols of regular geometric shapes—crosses, circles, triangles. A diagonal ray of light dissects the cloud.

Freedom

Slavery

Dignity

PLATE 2

Plate 3. Artist B. P. Safronov

Freedom. Dark cosmos and white light compose a dichotomous pair; near its base on the foreground there is burning (or even growing) a bush of fire. The fire is represented not as an element but as something live, growing naturally and participating in the process of life.

The live fire destroying the dichotomy—the division and splitting of the integrity—becomes a symbol of freedom. It destroys the splitting and therefore restores the integrity.

> This is a plot against the age:
> Weight, count, time, and fraction
> This is a torn curtain.
> (M. Tsvetayeva "The Trees")

The merging of the creative and destructive functions in one act is a state of dialectical fullness, preserving the properties of both essences. In the history of Western culture, we observe division as a dichotomous opposition, splitting which set fire to the auto-da-fé of the Inquisition to burn heretics—to kill, instead of burning dichotomy and thus restoring.

Slavery. On the dark background with the outline vaguely resembling a human torso, a black dense round spot smashes the light splashing it. A stream of light is directed to the light from above, forming a composition resembling an exclamation mark which, in the context of the given composition and colors is perceived as a symbol of danger.

Dignity. A soaring winged cross with a distinct center marked by a bright white-golden circle inside of which can be seen a triangle, also white-golden, with an edge downwards. The space around the cross is shining with iridiscent pearly hues with emerald and crimson flashes, illuminating white spirals.

Freedom

Slavery

Dignity

PLATE 3

Plate 4. (top) The drawing made by the imbecile patient at the session of musical psychotherapy ("Sirens" by Debussy). (bottom) The drawing made by the same patient to the accompaniment of ritual Japanese music of the twelfth century.

PLATE 4

Plate 5. Artist: V. Gribkov

The Break-up of the Universe. Theme: *The Nature of Time*. The painting shows the frame of the universe unlocked by the feminine hand, the hand of the world's mother. In the palm of her hand there is a diamond shining like a star. The ray from the star goes to the sun; below the red Earth in a black vortex; the sun and the Earth are surrounded by the yellow space. Time is again revealed through the myth of the creation of the world in its ancient version. Here are the comments of the artist:

> The palm with the rays emitted by a diamond?—it lies on my forehead. The palm supports a white wedge of light coming from the sun.

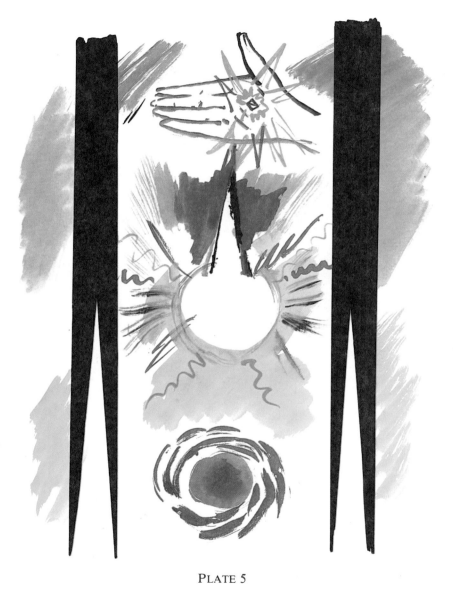

PLATE 5

Plate 6. Artist: A. Dyachkov

The Labyrinth. Theme: *Time as merging of the past, present, and future* (the first session). Artist's comments:

> Listening to the text about the past I saw in the gigantic yellow desert an immense labyrinth resembling that of Knossos, a labyrinth going out of sight under the rays of a huge sun. Then I saw the plan of the labyrinth; it resembled an Oriental mandala. At the word "mandala" on the background of the ornament emerged a black symbol with a yellow glow in the center. The ornament of the labyrinth-mandala was reddish-ochre.

PLATE 6

Plate 7. Artist: N. Obukhov

The Crown. Theme: *Time as merging of the past, present, and future* (the second session; it was suggested that the participants name the color of the past, present, and future). Artist's text:

> At first, when the dot emerged, it was light and the circle dark; the dot increased shining and became light orange-yellow, but it gradually changed color, and this was also true of the circle, which changed its color from black through the shining bright to orange-yellow. Then a dark circle appeared pulsating from the center. The past; I am little. Dark space with the emerging shining cross which was small at first, then increased to a definite size, but did not fill all the space.
>
> In the dark space of the present a body appeared emitting light in the direction of its motion. Then there also appeared space, somewhat shifted to the side and divided into dark and white.
>
> Eternity had a more pleasant shape and was silvery-yellow against a dark space.
>
> "Ego" had a shape of two different apertures, or circles, or balls. One ball was dark against the light space, the other was golden-light against the dark space.

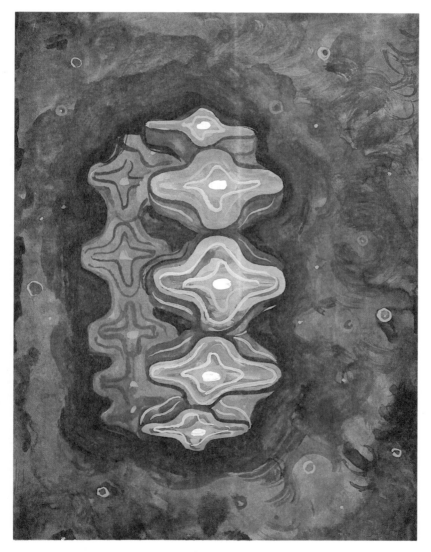

PLATE 7

Plate 8.   Artist: B. Safronov

Sequential Images. Theme: *Time–Name*. Text: the apocryphal Gospel of Philip. Artist's comments:

> A shining black-violet butterfly, with the silvery-white aura and golden stars on its wings. In the center a glowing road (bluish-silvery) going away from me upwards.
> There emerged an eye (dimly), and the right ear started to vibrate. A flower with four petals.
> The text of the Gospel of Philip is recited: through the radiant space I begin to discern a fluorescent sphere and below a cross of bones against the dark background. The cross is projected onto the sun, everything is in motion . . . At the sound of the word "name" a shining vibrating eye emerges from the empty space in the middle . . . A burning cross shaped like a vertical line with a diagonal cross-beam, flame and fire on its edges . . . Incomprehensible symbols appear: the space is several times overturned and turned inside out; there are wings either of a butterfly or of an angel somewhere, and I feel these wings behind my back. A lotus flower; it turns into the sun pouring light on me; everything dissolves in light.

PLATE 8

alien to our culture and that makes existence within it impossible is constant and oppressing. She is a sick person lost in the depths of her consciousness. We think a metaphor could be of help here: imagine that you are walking in the mountains, through an unknown thicket; you admire the landscape, but the moment you begin to see yourself as lost, lost hopelessly and forever, your attitude will change immediately: what previously enraptured you now only depresses you.

Summing up the results obtained in the experiments of directed group meditation, we could say that the text triad *freedom—slavery—dignity* is not only an encoded record of certain concepts within our culture but also the name of a myth which has concrete existential reality: this myth becomes a concrete experience, obtained under definite conditions and proper stimulation. The majority of the subjects proved capable of transcendence—crossing the boundaries of conventional structures of the culture: the words of the triad become not concepts but concrete states, a real existential experience. Human beings, despite their submergence in the stereotypes of conceptual structures, proved to be *ready* for this state. We consider this of the utmost significance. These states are inherent to human nature, but as a rule they remain closed under the paradigmatic deposition. However, the entrance there is not barred. A person (especially in modern culture) may get there under the influence of many circumstances. In addition to resulting from meditation, these states can arise spontaneously as a result of metabolic disorders, disorders of sensory perception, intensive emotional excitement, or in sport at the moment of peak experience (Murphy and White, 1978). They may also be brought about by forced (compulsory) relaxation. All of this was discussed in detail in Chapter 8. They can be induced by acute psychosis, hypnotic trance, anesthesia, and convulsive fits, as well as by psychedelic drugs such as LSD. These states also accompany the death experience, as has been reported by reanimated people (Moody, 1975; Noyes, 1974).

Altered states of consciousness often take a form defined as mystic, transcendent–cosmic, or religious, and no wonder, since they are characterized by experience alien to rational consciousness: this new experience consists in interaction with spheres entitled Ultimate Reality. According to Paul Tillich, religious perception is embedded in human consciousness, and this is true if we consider religious experience as a proof of such states when a person is not separated from the environment but merges with it—when he is not alienated from it by conceptions and reflections of his ideas but perceives it without intellectual "noise," directly.

It is the experience of such states of merging and communion that people called God. Ultimate Reality is immanent in human consciousness. Fichte called this immanence "the feeling of truth in man," and Jung believed consciousness to be "religious by its nature." Experimental records testify to this statement: our subjects belong to the category of people who have never been taught a perception of reality which could be called mystic experience, but under specific conditions they discover it by themselves.

Here lies the peculiarity of our experiment. Its results are distorted neither by special selection of subjects nor by their preliminary preparation in an esoteric system.

We are dealing with consciousness in its spontaneous manifestation. To emphasize this idea, we would like to draw the reader's attention to the fact that meditation has been practiced for ages, and there undoubtedly has been accumulated impressive experience, but all these records are distorted ("biased"), either by special selection (joining monasteries, brotherhoods, and orders) or by special esoteric training. Therefore, these data were not general, but had a nature of initiation, which made them exclusive and often unachievable.

The semantic[9] analysis is supported by semiotic analysis, the results of which are given in Figure 13.1; the latter analysis was accomplished by a procedure of multidimensional mathematical statistics (cluster analysis) on the basis of the total frequency of vocabulary of experimental records, about 10,000 words. The words *freedom* and *slavery* each had a

---

[9] *Semantics* is the science about meaning, whereas *semiotics* is the science of the symbolic aspect of the text.

---→

FIG. 13.1.   Dendrogram showing clusters of words according to their frequency of occurrence in the records of the four experiments. The vocabulary of the records (containing 641 words) was compiled of words occurring more than once. The objects (variables) of the classification were represented by 12 experimental sessions (the triad of words in the four experiments), and attributes by the frequency of occurrence of the above-mentioned words. The distances plotted horizontally are arbitrary; vertically they are $1 - \varrho$, where ϱ is the correlation coefficient. On the dendrogram the first cluster is made by the variables "freedom 1-I" and "freedom 4-II." These variables proved to be statistically correlated, their correlation coefficient being .66. This cluster (after the variables were pooled together) was joined by the variable "freedom 10-IV"; the correlation coefficient here equals .49. This cluster of the second hierarchical level is joined by the variable "dignity 3-I" which frames it; thus a cluster of the third hierarchical level is formed. Analogously, the second branch of the dendrid is formed: the first cluster is made by the variables "slavery 2-I" and "slavery 5-II" ($\varrho = .57$), they are joined by "slavery 11-IV" ($\varrho = .51$) and all this is framed by the variable "slavery 8-III" ($\varrho = .41$). The third branch of the dendrite begins with the union of the two variables "dignity 6-II" and "dignity 9-III" ($\varrho = .44$), they are joined by the variable "freedom 7-III" ($\varrho = .25$), and then the third branch joins the two former branches ($\varrho = .23$), forming a cluster of the fifth level. Note that for our number of observations, assuming we deal with a normal distribution, for the 1% level of significance even the correlation coefficient $\varrho = .15$ would have been significant.

experiment	I	II	III	IV
FREEDOM /СВОБОДА/	1	4	7	10
SLAVERY /РАБСТВО/	2	5	8	11
DIGNITY /ДОСТОИНСТВО/	3	6	9	12

clear-cut cluster. The word *dignity* had no cluster of its own. It acts as a link between the two other clusters. And this is quite natural: above, in section C of this chapter, discussing semantics of our *triad* in an historical, cultural aspect, we noted that the word *dignity* occupied the intermediary, dividing position between the words *freedom* and *slavery*, similarly to *purgatory* in Dante's *Divine Comedy*.

Words from the records of experiment 3 occupy peripheral positions in the clusters (words of experiment 3 had not been included in the analysis, since this experiment was carried out later).

In contrast to the tradition of scientific research, the authors of this book were not only experimenters, but also acted as subjects, taking part in all meditation sessions. This circumstance is important, on the one hand, because we as authors received the direct experience of what we were studying. On the other hand, this allowed us to establish relations of certain symbols occurring in records to the current state of our own consciousness: with anxiety which had remained as a burden in the unconscious. Of interest in this respect is the record, quoted below, as a meditation response to the word *freedom*:

> I felt relaxation immediately—after the first few words of the AT text. I felt I was standing on the sandy beach at the edge of quiet, light, bluish water. It looked like the shore of the lake Issyk-kul [a large, extremely beautiful mountain lake situated in North Tien-Shan].
>
> Suddenly ball-shaped clots of dark-violet fog scudded swirling above the ground. These were small clouds of irregular ball shape with broken edges. They started whirling around me, then flew away and were replaced by others. It was alarming, like in the mountains before a storm.
>
> At the sound of the word "freedom" a light green ray fell to the ground from above. And it has become clear the way is open: I may go.
>
> I felt myself above, in a cave-like hall. It was a fairy-tale cave—it was not limited spatially: I saw above the starlit night sky, and below the storm of violet wreathing balls. There were no limits from the sides either—it resembled a cosmic belt, a layer of the Universe. But it looked like a cave: gigantic stalactites resembled candles. They were shining from inside with soft light. I felt joy, light, and freedom. The feeling of myself disappeared, though I was there.
>
> Then the vision disappeared as suddenly as it had appeared.
>
> The feeling of relief remained. But the dark violet balls are not forgotten—they fade away, but do not disappear altogether.
>
> Later I strained my memory to recall where I had earlier seen this heavenly cave. Perhaps on some painting—but which one?"

This meditation record is of interest in two aspects. The ball-shaped clots of violet fog are the reflection of the anxiety which, by an effort of will, was pushed deep into the unconscious. In a meditation this anxiety came to the surface but now in a symbolic form, and it did not leave the field of vision of the participant even when he was in a state of freedom. This meditation resembled a dream, in which we go through our anxieties clad in a symbolic form, though we are not always aware of them. In this sense meditation is *akin to a dream*. It is a piece of self-analysis carried out by means of a conscious and directed entrance into a state of dreaming.

At the same time meditation is something more than a common dream. In the above meditation the subject had an unusual, i.e. not typical of his imagination, image of a cosmic belt. This new image could have been induced by the book by Guénon, *L'ésoterism de Dante*, which the subject had finished reading on the eve of the meditation session. Moreover, about a fortnight after the meditation it became obvious for the participant that the *triad* of words selected for the collective meditation was synonymous to Dante's *triad*. This idea, to our mind, proved to be the new image of a cosmic belt which had appeared during the meditation session. Thus, the observation of meditation images helps one to carry out a kind of self-analysis: it enables one to watch the process of one's own creative work in the dynamics of its manifestation at the unconscious level.

E. Certain Considerations on the Validity of our Experimental Results

We feel it necessary to emphasize once more the experimental task and the criteria for estimating the states achieved. The ideology of our experiment proceeded from two approaches. On the one hand, we relied on the concepts of the mathematical theory of experiment; on the other hand, on the idea of the continuous nature of our consciousness.

The necessity of emphasizing each of these approaches stems from the numerous rebukes from psychologists because we did not carry out a control experiment. We feel these rebukes to be based on a misunderstanding. The idea itself of a control experiment is rather old fashioned. Modern mathematical theory of experiment does not make use of this technique in its traditional form. The control is made directly on the basis of *the data of the same experiment* in which all the independent variables included in the model are varied.

The experiment starts with a certain model: $\eta = \varphi(\mathbf{x}, \Theta)$. For this model an optimal experimental design is constructed. From the experimental results, parameter estimates $\hat{\theta}_1$, $\hat{\theta}_2$, . . ., $\hat{\theta}_k$ are obtained, as well as the variance for these estimates, which allow us to test the hypothesis that these estimates are statistically significant. Then the model's adequacy is evaluated in a similar way. The reduction in variance which represents the model's accuracy—its closeness to the experimental data—is again estimated on the basis of the same principal experiment. No additional control experiment is carried out. However, the total number N of observations in the experiment must always exceed the number K of parameters estimated. There is naturally another method: the entire set of possible observations is divided into two subsets N_1 and N_2. One of them ($N_1 = K$) will serve to obtain parameter estimates and the other will be used as a control. But it can be easily shown mathematically that such a method will be significantly less efficient (see Nalimov and Golikova, 1981).

In a psychological experiment whose results are, as a rule, unquantifiable, the above procedure cannot be reproduced completely, but it can be kept in mind as a reference point. This is exactly what we did. Our initial premise (model) was that the records must break up into clusters (groups of semantically close texts), and among them we hoped to spot a cluster reflecting the verbal semantics imprinted in our unconscious or, in other words, the semantics undistorted by the impact of the contemporary culture that forms our present-day consciousness. This expectation came true (for details see section D of this chapter).

However, we feel the necessity of additional explanations.

From our probabilistic model of language (Nalimov, 1981a), it follows that the manifested part of the word field is determined by the cultural dominants fixed in dictionaries and encyclopedias. The semantics out of use in the given culture is found in the tail part of the distribution function of probabilities given over the semantic field; i.e., it is suppressed and exists with a low weight.

Our task was to reveal the fragments of the semantic field from the tail part of the distribution function, i.e., those which are suppressed in our culture and pushed into the unconscious from the present-day consciousness.

The experimental task predetermined the choice of the experimental procedure. Common tests did not yield records which would be in any interesting way different from an article of an explanatory dictionary, i.e., from the manifested part of the distribution function. It was necessary to get free from the paradigmatically given pattern, the familiar form of logical structuring.

Therefore, we decided on using AT relaxation, achieved by slowing down the personal, psychological time, and emotionally charged words-symbols inherent in human consciousness. All this taken together allowed us to cross the boundaries of the existing paradigm and thus broaden our interaction with the semantic field.

Experimental results are reflected in written records and paintings, whose major part contained images and symbols typical of mythology.

Can these results be trusted? We are inclined to answer this question positively. We carried out a series of experiments and obtained about 300 records. Each experiment is a random sample from a general population.

If the semantic field of the word *freedom* is regarded as a single general population, random samples should be lexically and semantically comparable.

On the dendrogram shown in Figure 13.1, the reader can see the distribution of our experimental records among clusters. As we already mentioned above, the records for the word *freedom* fell in one cluster, and those for the word *slavery* fell into another. These two are joined by the records for the word *dignity*.

Hence, it follows that we are dealing with semantics that is stable and, therefore, *non-random* in terms of mathematical statistics. Note that this conclusion is made on the basis of the entire material we have at our disposal, without a special control experiment which certain psychologists are prone to consider crucial.

It is also relevant to note that in the records the *myth* itself stood out as a criterion. This is a psychological, purely human criterion since it contains images and symbols. The abundance of epithets in the records testifies to the fact that the interaction with these images, their experiencing, did take place.

Special attention should be paid to the experience of flight: it is undoubtedly organically embedded in our consciousness. This is proved by: (1) the great number of people flying in their dreams, (2) the obsessive feeling of flight in many patients in hospitals for mental diseases, and (3) the abundance of flying creatures in myths, these creatures being hierarchically higher than people: e.g., in Christianity such winged creatures capable of flying were angels, archangels, seraphim, and cherubs.

The experience of the state of flight seems to be a sign of penetration into the depths of consciousness hidden from us in a waking state.

It is relevant to recall here the therapeutic Cathartic dances, imitating flight by leaps which seem not to touch the ground (Eliade, 1976). Perhaps here lies the remote origin of contemporary ballet.

The state of relaxation can also be somatically controlled, since it is accompanied by the sensation of warmth, tingling in the finger tips, pulsation in arms and legs, a feeling of peace and inner balance, if the key word has positive semantics. Such a state can continue for several days.

Also essential for the state of relaxation are changes in spatial–tem-

poral interactions, which are often recorded in the texts as a free and instantaneous transference in the boundless space (up to "here" and
"now," which signifies the momentary transference into any spatial
point).

All this coincides with the criteria selected for the altered states of consciousness mentioned in section A of Chapter 11.

Therefore, the content itself of the records is a control for us. Note
that the group of subjects from the Institute of Psychology (experiment
4) all yielded results which, without exception, represented highly similar, semantically myth-like texts; this seems to be accounted for by the
fact that the subjects had earlier undergone auto-training (AT) and the
state of relaxation was familiar for them.

We ascribe a special significance to the emergence of myths in our
texts, not only because myth-like texts recurred from one experiment to
another, but also because they constituted the major part of the records.
Symbols and images are the language of the unconscious (this was discussed in detail in Chapters 11 and 12). Myth is an immanent component
of the unconscious, its manifestation. The fact that, though our subjects
were not experts in the history of cultures and symbols, the records they
wrote were full of images and symbols proves that in our experiments we
managed to get into direct contact with the unconscious.

In our present-day consciousness, myth is pushed down into its underground. The culture of our days has lost contact with myth (Jung, 1962).
It gave place to logical structures constructed over a system of concepts.
Interaction of the two levels of our consciousness, mythological and logical (the latter being reflected in explanatory dictionaries), will be considered below, in section H of this chapter. The very possibility of a meaningful consideration of this interaction also testifies to the validity of the
semantics reflected in the records.

There emerges one more question: In what way should we evaluate
subjects whose records remained on the level of associations or standard
cliché? Could they be brought into a state of relaxation by means of
stronger techniques than the one we used? We do not know how to answer this question. It could be that a stronger technique would increase
the number of people getting into the first cluster. For schizophrenic patients such a technique should be a strong therapeutic procedure.

We feel that our experience shows that AT combined with adequate,
emotionally charged key words is a good basis for dividing people into
clusters. Perhaps in everyday life people also act in accordance with their
clustering with respect to their readiness to resort to their unconscious.
However, it is clear that further research in this field is desirable.

In concluding this section we would like to say that in a psychological
research project it is not common manifestations of psychic phenomena,

averaged and statistically evaluated, which are important, but rather unusual, rarely occurring phenomena which as a rule remain concealed from us under the cover of the contemporary cultural paradigm.

F. Comparison of Our Experiment with the Results Obtained by Grof

Here we would like to emphasize the fact that our results have much in common with those described in the book by Grof (1975), mentioned above. His method of research consisted of applying LSD, which is a much more powerful instrument than AT and also is convenient because its doses can be gradually increased to provide the entrance into the unconscious at a deeper and deeper level. His book was based on experiments carried out in clinics for 17 years with a therapeutic purpose. Psychologically interesting results appeared at the final stage of the therapy. Our experiments are to a certain extent comparable with Grof's results only because in our case the weak degree of relaxation achieved by AT was strengthened by the interaction with the key words–symbols.

It should first of all be noted that Grof directly observed the expansion of dimensions of the psychological spaces which are responsible for the comprehension of sensual experience:

> Not infrequently, LSD subjects discover dimensions in music that they were unable to perceive before. In the sessions, it appears to be possible to listen to music with one's whole being and with a completely new approach. Frequently, music seems to resonate in different parts of the body and to trigger powerful emotions. One of the most common statements one reads in subjects' reports about LSD sessions refers to the feeling that on the session day they *really* heard music for the first time in their life. (p. 40)

The author speaks of *synaesthesia* when an impulse coming through one sensory area evokes responses of the other senses: e.g., a person can "see music" or "taste colors." We would like to remind the reader that the Russian composer Alexander Scriabin saw the color of music in his usual state of consciousness. A broad interest in color-music which has recently arisen testifies to the fact that human consciousness is ready for synaesthetic perception, but it has not yet opened up.

The most important thing is that Grof has obtained experimental proof of the fact that the unconscious is holistic in its transpersonality. According to Grof, this presents a mystery for contemporary science. Discussing the nature of psychotraumatic factors, Grof remarks:

> Psychoanalysts have usually thought in this connection about con-

stitutional and hereditary factors of an unknown nature. LSD research seems to indicate that this specific sensitivity can have important determinants in deeper levels of the unconscious, in functional dynamic matrices that are inborn and transpersonal in nature. Some of these factors, when brought to consciousness in LSD psychotherapy, have the form of ancestral, racial, or phylogenetic memories, archetypal structures, or even past-incarnation experiences. (p. 72)

This is supported by many verified examples. One such was a patient who had never been interested in Egypt who suddenly recollects his past Egyptian incarnation as an embalmer and is able to describe in detail all the relevant procedures. Other patients could describe the functions of various Egyptian deities, the symbolism related to them, and the esoteric significance of the pyramids and the sphinx. Information of this kind can easily be verified by consulting archaeologists and anthropologists. Even more amazing are the cases of phylogenetic memory: patients identify themselves with animals, birds, or various species of fish or insects and report details pertaining to behavior or perception which often seem to transcend the scope and limits of human fantasy and imagination but which, according to the experts in these fields of biology, are quite accurate. Much less frequent were the instances of experiencing the consciousness of a plant or a germinating seed. Again, these identifications were accompanied by amazing details:

> Subjects have also reported that they witnessed botanical processes on a molecular level; they were aware of the biochemical synthesis underlying the production of auxins, vegetable pigments, oils and sugars, aromatic substances, and various alkaloids. (p. 182)

We would like to quote here the complete outline of a very interesting description of a past incarnation:

> The session started with a feeling of "pure tension" that was building up to higher and higher levels. When the tension was transcended, Michael had an experience of overwhelming cosmic ecstasy; the universe seemed to be illuminated by radiant light emanating from an unidentifiable supernatural source. The entire world was filled with serenity, love, and peace; the atmosphere was that of "absolute victory, final liberation, and freedom in the soul." The scene then changed into an endless bluish-green ocean, the primordial cradle of all life. Michael felt that he had returned to the source; he was floating gently in this nourishing and soothing fluid, and his body and soul seemed to be dissolving and melting into it. The experience had a distinct Indian undertone; he asked the therapist whether this state of unity of the individual self with the universe was described in Indian religious scriptures. He saw numerous visions of Hindu worship, mourning ceremonies on the Ganges River, and Indian yogis

practicing in the monumental setting of the Himalayas. Without having had any previous knowledge of Hatha Yoga, Michael intuitively assumed several of the classical body postures (asanas) because they seemed best suited to his present state of mind.

This ecstatic condition was suddenly interrupted and the sense of harmony deeply disturbed. The water in the ocean became amniotic fluid, and Michael experienced himself as a fetus in the womb. Some adverse influences were endangering his existence; he had a strange, unpleasant taste in his mouth, was aware of poison streaming through his body, felt profoundly tense and anxious, and various groups of muscles in his body were trembling and twitching. These symptoms were accompanied by many terrifying visions of demons and other evil appearances; they resembled those on religious paintings and sculptures of various cultures. After this episode of distress passed, Michael re-experienced his own embryological development, from the fusion of the sperm and egg through millions of cell divisions and processes of differentiation to a whole individual. This was accompanied by an enormous release of energy and radiant light. The sequences of embryonic development were intermingled with phylogenetic flashbacks showing the transformation of animal species during the historical evolution of life.

Toward the end of the session, Michael returned to the feelings of fusion and melting in the ocean alternating with identification with the entire universe. On this general background, he had numerous visions of ancient Egypt, with pyramids, royal tombs, majestic granite sculptures, and various deities and mythological figures. These ecstatic visions continued until late at night; the last vision in the session was a triumphant cruise of an Egyptian princess with her elaborate retinue on the Nile River.

The following day, Michael was in the calmest, most joyful, and most balanced emotional condition he had experienced in his entire life. After this session, his psychotic symptoms never reappeared. Several years later, he got married and left Czechoslovakia. He has been able to take full responsibility for himself and his family and to cope with all the hardships associated with the life of an emigrant. (p. 235–236)

If up to the recent past the technique of recollecting past incarnations entered the secret, esoteric part of some religious teachings, now, after the discovery of LSD, it has become an object of clinical studies. This is noteworthy in itself: science begins to acquaint itself with the facts known in certain religious experience from time immemorial. Another thing is also of importance: the teaching of reincarnation which was known not only in the Far East but also in early gnostic Christianity, in the teachings of the Orphics and of Pythagoras, was formed on the basis of real experience. At the same time we are far from thinking that this experience immediately generates the naive conception of *karma* as a rigid law of cause and effect. Trying to be cautious, we assume that the reincarnation identifications are a sufficiently significant basis for elaborating the idea of a transpersonal and transtemporal (extra-historical) nature of the unconscious.

The book by Grof contains the facts that allow us to formulate the following conception of the transtemporal nature of the unconscious: ontologically, the unconscious in its integrity comprises everything which, in its historical manifestation, seems to us to occur at various points of the same scale. Grof's patients reported semantic revelations of the unconscious which, to our mind, could also have occurred in the past, sometimes in the remote past. We know of instances of creativity in the past that could be produced by highly similar insights. Here are several illustrations (Grof, 1975):

> Patients often visualize fields dominated by abstract geometric designs or architectural patterns that underlie all the dynamic color changes. These elements are often described as interiors of gigantic temples, naves of incredibly beautiful Gothic cathedrals, or decorations in Moorish palaces ("arabesques"). Sometimes these visions are compared with paintings of abstract artists such as Mondrian and Kandinsky; a very characteristic perceptual change is geometrization of human faces and bodies as on cubist paintings. Some individuals report they achieved the state that helped to gain insight into the world of Seurat and Van Gogh.
>
> Oneness with life and with all creation. In rare instances, an LSD subject can have the feeling that his consciousness has expanded to encompass the totality of life on this planet, including all humankind and the entirety of flora and fauna, from unicellular organisms to highly differentiated species. . . . The experiential extensions of consciousness in LSD sessions are not limited to the world of biology; they can include macroscopic and microscopic phenomena of inorganic nature. (p. 183–184)

We believe that it is these and similar manifestations of semantics that gave rise to all the instances of a holistic vision of the world, including here Whitehead, Smuts, and St. Francis of Assisi as well as the gnostic Christians, especially Manichaeans, who had asserted the omnipresence of Christ—under the roadside stone, in the road dust, and in the air. Incidentally, some of the texts recorded during our experiments, e.g., those which describe freedom as a passage through innumerable worlds, are of an obviously gnostic nature. The unconscious seems to preserve the semantics which long ago gave birth to a gnostic interpretation of Christianity.

Planetary consciousness. From this point of view, the earth appears to be a complicated cosmic organism with the different aspects of geological, biological, cultural, and technological evolution on this planet seen as manifestations of an attempt to reach a higher level of integration and self-realization. (p. 185)

Coming across such manifestations of the semantics of the unconscious, one cannot but recall the monuments of Russian cosmogonic thought. Perhaps the book by the Russian geochemist V. I. Vernadsky (1977), *Scientific Idea as a Planetary Phenomenon*, quite unusual today, was a response to meditation.

People with a solid background in physics and mathematics sometimes, under the effect of LSD, leave the boundaries of rational comprehension of the complicated modern physical and cosmogonic theories and highly abstract mathematical structures. In an altered state of consciousness, these latter become subjectively tangible. But perhaps this is what happened in the past to the authors of these structures at the moments of insight. Abstract structures are a form of transferring knowledge accessible for all the people adequately prepared for this. But the comprehension of what is presented in an abstract form may be double—on one occasion formal, purely external, and at another time non-formal, opening up the vistas of further creative evolution.

Grof attaches a special significance to the first trauma a person encounters, the trauma of birth. Of interest is the parallel between birth and death:

We entered this world helpless, naked, and without personal possessions, and so we will leave it. (p. 118)

Indeed, inwardly we are ready to agree that we had already experienced death when we came to this alien world from another reality. Therefore, the fact that LSD enables us to recall the process of birth and the preceding intrauterine states acquires a special importance. According to Grof, patients prove to be ready for recollections of the intrauterine life at the end of the therapeutic course, after the traumas of the conscious life are resolved. The memory matrix developed in the process of recollection of the intrauterine life and biological birth turns out to be extremely rich: it comprises what had been overtly expressed in the entire manifold of mythological, religious, and even philosophical conceptions. For example, the traditional representation of the Christian hell or of the underworld of the Ancient Greeks turns out to be a reinterpretation of the memory of that phase of delivery when the uterine contractions encroach on the fetus, but the cervix is closed—another world. The world of another reality is felt to be unachievable as by a sinner in hell. For sophisticated individuals, this experience usually results in a fresh understanding of existentialism. We cannot dwell here on the description of how the matrix of memory is revealed when a person recalls his or her birth. Note only that the study of a state of "non-existence" has also become possible, so to speak, from the other end, i.e., in reanimation (Moody, 1975), which again was provided by the progress of technology. Strange as it may seem, it is the progress of technology that has enabled us to study the unconscious not esoterically. We would like once more to emphasize the fact that everything said above has much in common with the Oriental idea of the illusory nature of the dichotomous opposition of life and death.

Extremely interesting are the manifestations of the semantics of the unconscious which can be compared to mythology, occultism, mysticism of religious teaching, and science fiction. Among them are the following: meetings with astral bodies; revelation of new communication channels with the universe; the faculty of speaking unfamiliar foreign languages (compare with the Christian Pentecost when the apostles "began to speak in other tongues" and the phenomenon of glossolalia); detailed description of seeing Gods and demons and their relation to corresponding cultures; stories minutely corresponding to the myths of Mesopotamia, India, Egypt, Greece, Central America, and other countries; startlingly detailed accounts of the sequence of experiences and purely theoretical basis of Kundalini Yoga; discovery of other strange and alienated worlds, existence of other dimensions in the worlds co-existent with our world, the feeling of the Universal Consciousness and metacosmic Void which turn out to be the same.

And, finally, of great interest is the vision of universal symbols and the revelation of their esoteric meaning. Among them are complicated geometrical compositions that closely resemble Oriental mandalas. However,

> The most frequent symbols observed in the sessions were the cross, the six-pointed star of David, the Indo-iranian swastika, the ancient Egyptian ankh (Nile cross or crux ansata), the lotus flower, the Taoist yin-yang, the Hindu sacred phallus (Shiva lingam), the diamond and other jewels, the Buddhist wheel of death and rebirth, and the circle (frequently appearing as the archetypal gigantic snake Ouroboros devouring its tail). (p. 201)

We see with amazement and admiration that Grof managed during a very short period, only 17 years, to lift the veil over the creative laboratory of culture of the whole of mankind. In ancient times the mystery was guarded by the requirements of esoterism; nowadays it is protected by the rigid logical structure of Western consciousness. For some reason or other, the time has come to show people the sources of their creativity which link them to the Universe. Everything began with LSD,[10] a compound synthesized by chance. But was it really by chance?

The corollary significance of this discovery remains hard to evaluate. We believe it to be a turning point in the history of Western culture, but it will require many years to comprehend and master what is discovered.

We are very glad that the results of our much more modest experiments have much in common with what was obtained by Grof (we had carried out our experiments and discussed their results before we became acquainted with Grof's work). It is important that our results were obtained by means of much simpler and more natural procedures. Also, it is especially significant that our experiment had a specific semantic goal. If Grof managed to discover in semantically non-directed experiments what had earlier been revealed in the evolution of culture, a directed experiment will, it seems, open up the possibility of true creativity. But is that really so? In any case, we see quite plainly that the dynamism of Western culture, from the moment it became scientific, was determined by the fact that we had discovered how to ask meaningful questions burdened with a multitude of possible answers. Can this tradition be continued if we consciously and directly address the unconscious?

In an attempt to comprehend the results obtained by Grof, we can make an important step toward the construction of a model of the unconscious: ontologically, the unconscious has an extra-temporal nature. We see that the unconscious is always ready to manifest the semantics which had already been manifested some time long ago. Nothing disappears in the irrevocable past. Strange as it may seem, we return here to ancient gnostic conceptions, according to which God as a fundamental principle existed outside of time. It is noteworthy that the problem of time is a stumbling block in the conceptions of the origin of the Universe after the explosion. According to some scientists, there had been no time before the explosion; according to others, time, though it had existed, had been of a different nature.

The ability to consciously enter the unconscious by means of slowing down personal, psychological time is also a manifestation of a special status of the unconscious in this respect.

Now a few words on the reliability of Grof's results. His book, in contrast to ours, does not contain experimental data. All verbal texts are given as retold by Grof; the original material is represented only by the patients' drawings. This absence of the documentary texts arouses sharp

---

[10] In the USSR experiments with LSD are carried out only on the cell level—all the rest are prohibited. Again, we are about 20 years behind.

distrust in psychologists, but we believe these attacks to be unjust. Grof seems to have chosen retelling in a desire to present his material in a concise and clear form. According to Grof, he had at his disposal vast amounts of material, often obtained from non-intellectual patients. If this is actually so, word-for-word records, often touching on rather delicate points, would look awkward and rude.

The reliability of Grof's results is supported by their similarity to our experimental results. The possibility of a random or erroneous coincidence of some very important results and texts obtained by different researchers and in different countries who worked, besides, with essentially different subjects and used essentially different techniques has a very low probability.

Grof's results are also comparable with the experience of analyzing one's internal world as described by Jung (1965). The dreams he describes often go back into the distant past of European culture and are thus of a reincarnation nature. By inducing a chemical effect, Grof managed to extract from the patients' unconscious what Jung was able to feel within himself as spontaneous and unprovoked experiences.

G. Comparison of Our Results with the Experience of Musical Therapy

Both from our experimental results and from those obtained by Grof, there follows the necessity of recognizing the validity of the concept of the collective unconscious introduced by Jung. However, now Jung's ideas also need to be made more abstract and profound.

We find much more attractive the concepts of extra-personal or transpersonal psychological spaces. Within this system of concepts, personality may be given by the selective manifestation of these spaces. The probability distribution function given on this psychological or semantic space may serve as a measure of selectivity. We spoke of this in detail in Chapter 1.

Within this system of concepts, the unconscious is represented by the part of psychological space which is in a suppressed, weakly manifested state. Both our experiments and those of Grof were aimed at revealing this part of psychological space which is suppressed for our present-day consciousness. The possibility of revealing the suppressed part of consciousness can be especially vividly illustrated by the experiment with mentally ill people who, as a consequence of the gravity of their disease, have been isolated from real life from early childhood. It turns out that images which could not be borrowed from life can be induced to appear in their consciousness. Thus, an unbiased experiment can be carried out.

FIG. 13.2. "Flowers"—a typical drawing by the imbecile girl.

What we have in mind is the experiments carried out by the psycho-therapist–musician J. G. Shoshina in Tbilisi hospital for the mentally ill. Of special interest in her research are the experiments with a group of three children fifteen years of age who had lived in the hospital all their life. Their diagnoses were schizophrenia, intellectual debility, and imbecility. The case of imbecility was of medium severity, i.e., almost total weak mindedness, a meager vocabulary (about fifteen words), the absence of concepts, etc. This imbecile subject (a girl) could only draw cross-like flowers that never formed a composition (see Figure 13.2), one drawing being an exact copy of another one. It seemed quite impossible to teach her to draw anything else, even after twenty-five trials.

The experimenter carried out a session of musical therapy. The piece of music was "Sirens" by Debussy. The listening was preceded by the suggestion that the patients draw while the music was playing. Subjects were seated at different tables.

All three subjects drew the sea (one of these pictures can be seen in Color Plate 4). The drawings were strikingly different. The girl with intellectual debility drew seaweeds and fishes in the sea. On the drawing of the imbecile patient (Color Plate 4), one can see the sun over the sea and fir trees reflected in the water (they are turned upside down). The sea is painted blue with a green shade. The patient has never seen the sea: she has been living in the hospital since she was 18 months old. She entitled her drawing "Big Water": the experimenter managed to elicit the answer from her after prolonged questioning. Two weeks later, the girl was asked to draw the sea. Her further drawings resembled the first one but were less emotional and expressive, without any color shades.

The experiments with the imbecile patient were continued. Each time her drawings made while listening to music were sharply different in their subject, technique, and the paints used from her usual stereotype colors. Color Plate 4 shows her picture drawn while she was listening to ritual Japanese music of the twelfth century. This picture is again strikingly complicated in its composition: the gigantic sun in the sky, a rock with a tree on it, and water below. The rock and the water are green. After long, tiresome questioning she managed to explain that the water under the rock was green because the rock was green.

Does not all this testify to the fact that music—its rhythm changing the personal time—reveals the submerged part of the patient's consciousness? Her vision is filled with images which could not be borrowed from her real life since she has spent it in a hospital. The only possible explanation seems to be that the individual consciousness, even that of a gravely and hopelessly sick girl, is still to a certain degree connected to the collective consciousness, to its experience, and this latter can be unveiled at least a little.

H. Comparison of the Semantic Fields of Our Experiment with the Semantics of the Explanatory Dictionary[11]

Simultaneously with the experiment of collective meditation, the description of the word "svoboda" ("freedom") in the Russian explanatory dictionary (Ozhegov, 1972) was analyzed.

The procedure was as follows. First, all the words contained in the explanatory article for the word "svoboda" were written out (except the auxiliaries and link words). This resulted in a list of twenty words. The procedure was repeated for each of these twenty words, and so on. We decided to end the procedure the moment we came across a word not listed in the dictionary.

After the completion of this procedure, we had a list of 1,084 words belonging to the semantic field of the word "freedom." Comparison of this list with a set of words obtained in the psychological experiment (916 words) showed that their area of intersection was 338 words.

Then we started to consider the distribution function of frequencies for the set of words obtained in the psychological experiment as a sample estimate of the probabilistic weight of the semantics of the word "freedom" inherent to our unconscious and the distribution function of fre-

---

[11] This section is based on analysis carried out by L. R. Moshinskaya.

FIG. 13.3.   Bayesian reading of the experimental records to the word "freedom." On the abscissa are plotted the words of the record according to decreasing frequency of occurrence. On the ordinate are plotted: (1) frequencies of occurrence of the words in the records (crosses); (2) normalized values obtained after multiplying these frequencies by the frequencies of the words in the text of a dictionary (Ozhegov, 1972) explaining the meaning of the word "freedom" (dots). The Ozhegov dictionary is considered as a filter given by our culture. The figure contains only the three first pages of the graph (A, B, and C).

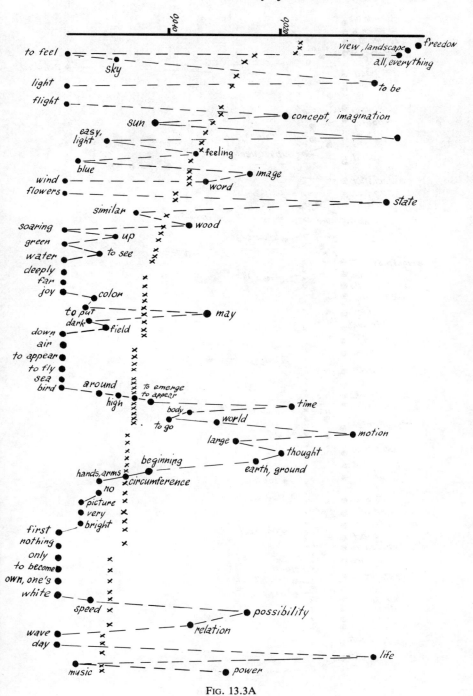

FIG. 13.3A

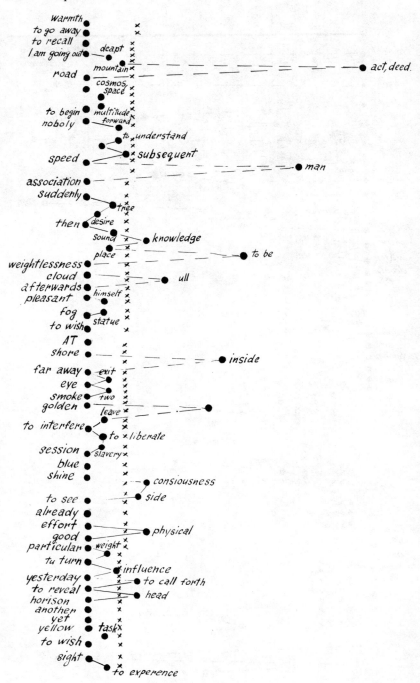

FIG. 13.3B

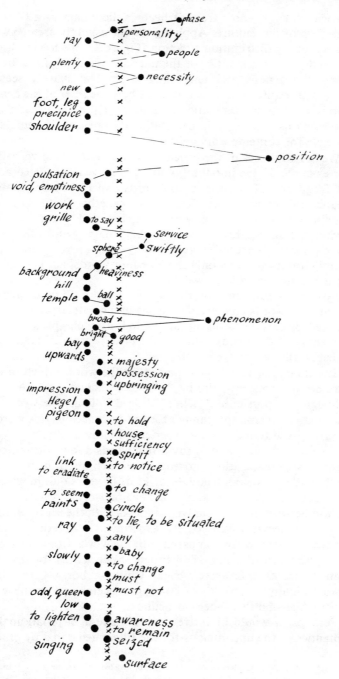

quencies for the words from Ozhegov's dictionary as a filter set by the paradigm of our culture. Applying the Bayesian theorem,[12] we obtained the frequency distribution function (Figure 13.3) showing how our culture reduces the semantics of the unconscious determined by our entire past—ethnogenesis and anthropogenesis. The sharply seesaw-shaped curve that resulted is an illustration of how the filter of the contemporary culture dissects the semantic continuum of the unconscious, turning it into a set of separate marks delineating the areas of the semantic field acceptable for contemporary culture.

We are witnesses of the process of making the field verbally discrete. For example, in the initial set whose points were arranged according to the frequency of occurrence of words, we clearly see a semantically meaningful chain: to feel—light—sky—quietly—flight. On the new diagram it is given by only two words: "to be" and "light," the latter word having a low weight. Another verbal chain, wind—flowers—state—wood—soaring—green—water—deeply—far—joy, also semantically meaningful, is given by only three or four words, among which only the word "state" has a large weight.

In the environment for the word "freedom" taken from the dictionary, all words connected with the immediate experience of the state induced by this word disappear, as well as such epithets as "blue" or "green" and the words "the sea," "bird," "road," etc., by means of which mythologems are constructed.

The dominant role is now played by the words which in our culture have become concepts: "to be," "space," "state," "time," "motion," "thought," "possibility," "life," "deed." Thus, the word "freedom" also becomes a concept, though for our unconscious this word denotes a specific psychosomatic state experienced individually.

It seems relevant here to say a few words about a traditional experiment of free association carried out with children in the sixth through ninth grades of school (children of 13 to 16 years old) in which our triad of words was taken as a stimulus. The noteworthy result is a small intersection between the associative responses with the set of words obtained in our principal psychological experiment. Moreover, semantically, many responses, when compared with the words from our records, seem to be the result of a noise constituent. Such words for the word "freedom" were as follows: cabbage—Chile—a bore—Corvalan. For the word "dignity": tank—TV set—bag—vegetable. For the word "slavery": Chile—bottle—cider—pencilbox.

Perhaps, it would be interesting to make a Bayesian analysis of the semantics of the unconscious for the filters generated by other cultures,

---

[12] To be able to deal in both cases with functions constructed on the same set, we introduced into each of the two sets the missing words, ascribing to them frequencies two orders lower than the lowest one among the observed frequencies.

despite the formality of such an analysis stemming from the difficulty of constructing the initial ordered semantic set on the basis of limited sample data.

I. Concluding Remarks

The well-known American psychologist Tart, reporting on his studies of altered states of consciousness at the symposium "Spiritual and Transpersonal Aspects of Altered States of Consciousness" in Toronto in 1978, addressed the audience with the following concluding words (Tart, 1979):

> Many people interested in transpersonal psychology would reject the orthodox scientific position as simply ignorant and arrogant, but we cannot ignore the enormous power and authority of orthodox science in our times. When I started these comments I said that I wanted to be provocative, and I hope I have been so: how do you, transpersonal psychologists, feel about being considered studiers of illusions by the more prestigious in the establishment? And what can be done about it? (p. 73)

We are ready to meet this challenge and answer it. From the material quoted above, it follows that only records of mentally ill people (schizophrenics) and texts of a comparatively small group of people with a sharp dominance of rigid logical reasoning lack a mythological or illusory interpretation of the meaning of words–symbols. Therefore, an illusion is an important constituent (aspect) of the creative consciousness. But what do we call an illusion?

If computer programs for an artificial intelligence are given an arbitrary semantic background, this will never give rise to creative activity by a computer. Consequently, an illusion is semantically meaningful. We call this semantics illusory only because we are ignorant of the mechanism of interaction of the unconscious myth-like images with the manifestations of consciousness.

From the meaning of the concept itself of the unconscious, it seems to follow that from the viewpoint of the logically structured consciousness it should look like an illusory consciousness. The refusal to consider the illusory constituent of our consciousness is equal to the assertion that it is *computer-like*.

But if we are going to treat the *unconscious* in its transpersonal manifestation in earnest, the variety of the accumulated data makes us acknowledge the insufficiency of this helpless, apophantical-sounding term. We consider it possible to assert that what we are witnessing now could be called the *semantic universe*, or *semantic cosmos*, coexistent with our *temporal cosmos* and, moreover, manifested within it.

Chapter 14

An Experience of
Meditation Hermeneutics[1]

And why are we bending helplessly,
We feel that somebody has forgotten us,
The horror of ancient temptation becomes clear
When just by chance
Two poles, two blades of grass, or two shafts
Instantaneously form a cross,
moved by someone's hand.
          "DESCENDANTS OF CAIN" BY N. GUMILYOV

Hermeneutics is an art of comprehending the meaning underlying signs–symbols or texts. Broadly speaking, *ontology* is also a task of hermeneutics: the decoding of the meaning of the world clad in objectivized symbols.

In its narrow meaning, *hermeneutics* deals with decoding the semantics of ancient texts. When this task is fulfilled by means of common and familiar methods of logical comprehension, this unavoidably leads to distortions produced by the paradigm of our culture. The semantics of ancient texts is filtered through probabilistically weighted contemporary ideas. We describe the mechanism of this filtration by the Bayesian model frequently mentioned above.

In the experiment to be described in this chapter, we made an attempt to contact the unconscious directly, omitting all the strata laid over it by our culture. In sessions of collective meditation achieved by means of auto-training-induced relaxation, we tried to read an ancient text, pro-

[1] Written in cooperation with J. A. Drogalina.

ceeding from the experience of ethnogenesis stored in the depths of our consciousness.

The object of meditation was a graphic text. It was a composition of one symbol, the cross, varying in both its shape and details (see Figure 14.1).

This is a *pattern*, a mandala of medieval Armenian Christianity. It was carved on the inner pillar of the temple in the Kecharis monastery (eleventh to thirteenth centuries) in Tsakhkadzori (the Caucasus). Armenia is a kind of museum of ancient Christian architecture, having become Christian as long ago as the fourth century. (Christianity was proclaimed the official religion of Great Armenia in 301 A.D.) One might say that Christianity came there directly from its source. The vicissitudes of Armenian history made possible the preservation of ancient symbolism which was, perhaps, strengthened by the influence of the Templar order,[2] whose esoteric teaching was externally expressed by the symbols decorating the interiors of buildings, including temples.

The dating of this text (the cross) is unimportant for us. It could be the latest copy made by a person who did not comprehend the built-in meaning, or it might be the creation of a person reproducing in the familiar symbolism what had been stored in the depths of his unconscious.

We were struck by the unusual form of the text, by its significance supported by the surrounding scenery of a half-ruined temple, and we decided to try to revive the semantics of the text through ethnogenetic memory.

Above (see Section B, Chapter 12) we dwelt in detail on the symbolism of the cross. Now we would like to emphasize the numerical character of the symbol. The number itself is an original sign, the archetype of our unconscious [this idea is brilliantly developed by Meschkowski (1979)]. The cross proves to be a natural symbol not only of graphic images but also of a three-dimensional, sculptural representation of the numbers *three* (the Tau cross), *four* (a common four-edged cross), and *eight* (Armenian khachkars, Nubian crosses, the Maltese cross). By means of small contrivances, the cross may be transformed into other numerical shapes. We shall consider here only the opposition of the symbolism of the numbers *three* and *four*.

Jung (1962) stresses that the number *four* constantly occurs in dreams in various material shapes (four persons in a boat, a four-cornered room or garden, four chairs, four colors, etc.). He further emphasizes the role of the number *four* in alchemy, medieval mysticism, and earlier religions. The *quadrature of the circle* had not only a mathematical mean-

---

[2] We have already indicated above that Armenia had been the place of residence of this order (see the appendix to Lizerand, 1964).

FIG. 14.1. The initial mandala—a symbolic text recorded by symmetrical crosses discovered by the authors in a temple of the Kecharis monastery in Tsakhkadzori, Armenia. The image was carved on a stone pillar. Reproduced on a scale of 1:2.5.

ing, but also a mystical meaning: it contained the mystery of the trans-formation of the Universe symbolized by the circle, sphere, or concentric circumferences. Jung (1962) wrote:

> The application of the comparative method indubitably shows the quaternity as being a more or less direct representation of the God manifested in his creation. (p. 72)

At the same time he noted that the quaternity was rejected by the later Christian dogmas:

> I cannot omit calling attention to the interesting fact that whereas the central Christian symbolism is a Trinity, the formula of the un-conscious mind is a quarternity. As a matter of fact even the ortho-dox Christian formula is not quite complete, because the dogmatic aspect of the evil principle is absent from the Trinity, the former leading a more or less awkward existence as devil. Since a God identi-cal with man is a heretical assumption, the "God within" is also dog-matically difficult. But the quaternity as understood by the modern mind directly suggests not only the God within, but also the identity of God and man. Contrary to the dogma there are not three but four aspects. (p. 73–74)

> The quaternity in modern dreams is a product of the unconscious. (p. 77)

Let us now come back to our mandala (Figure 14.1). This is a pattern composed by four-pointed crosses. But almost every point has a triple completion. The big central cross is formed by spiral lines that impart dy-namics to it. These lines compose recurrent eights[3]—the number divisible by four. The crosses are arranged in two trinities: one of them consists of the big central cross and two that are smaller but similarly decorated; the other one is composed of the three small, simple (not decorated) crosses and a group of four crosses framed by triangles. Two trinities and a qua-ternity again form a trinity, but the whole composition is completed by a small quaternal cross: this is the cross that is crowned by a framed dome. In short, the whole mandala is a compositionally framed unity of the numbers *three* and *four*.

If we take into account everything said by Jung on the opposition of

---

[3] A few words about the number *eight*, in addition to what was said above (see Chapter 12, Section B). We are quoting here the *Encyclopedia of Traditional Symbolism* (Cooper, 1978): "*Buddhist*: Comple-tion; all possibilities . . . *Chinese*: The whole; . . . *Christian*: Regeneration; rebirth . . . *Egyptian*: The number of Thot. *Hebrew*: Perfect intelligence: splendour; . . . *Hermetic*: The magic number of Hermes . . . *Hindus*: 8×8 is the order of the celestial world established on earth. *Islamic*: The throne which en-compasses the world, supported by eight angels, . . . *Japanese*: Eight is the "many"; there are eight gods in the heavens . . . *Sumero-Semitic*: The magic number of Nebo. *Taoist*: All possibilities in manifestation with the Pa Kua representing the forces in the phenomenal world. (p. 118)

the numbers *three* and *four* and the dogmatic rejection of the latter number in its broad meaning, then our supposition of the ancient nature of the mandala becomes very plausible.

We carried out two meditation sessions over the mandala. The group of participants was small, consisting of seven people of whom two were professional artists. Four people had had a previous meditation experience.

After two sessions we had at our disposal thirteen texts, two paintings (later reproduced on canvas in the standard size 70×70 cm), and five drawings.

The general impression obtained from both the experimental material and talks with the participants in the experiment was as follows: these experiments led to stronger inner tension than those in which the triad of words had been used (see Chapter 13); visions occurring in the experiment were more difficult to describe, both verbally and graphically. This observation is supported by the fact that some participants (not professional artists) tried to draw, and one of the artists accompanied his drawing by a lengthy verbal description: the image he observed was displayed dynamically and could not be adequately depicted in the static drawing. The same image kept occurring in the visions: the cross appeared, but it was surrounded by less abstract, very expressive patterns. It was as if the highly abstract image of the initial mandala became more concrete. Perhaps the perception of contemporary abstract painting goes along the same lines, and this might have given rise to unfavorable criticism just because its perception required the faculty to pass into the state of meditation.

It is quite obvious that the mandala from the temple in Tsakhkadzori made the participants achieve states bordering on the familiar reality. The texts and drawings are often of an explicitly reincarnation character.

Figure 14.2 represents a cross pattern explained in detail by its author–artist:

> The most noteworthy feature seems to be the metamorphosis of the thickening edges of the cross: whirls of energies, opening buds of light; if the cross is personified, these are the pulsating receivers of energies: fingers, toes, head, and hair.
>
> The big cross turned into a figure with spread out arms; then it began to rotate around its vertical axis, again resembling a figure in a quick rotation or a dance. Two lesser crosses also turned into figures once repeating the same dance, another time bending to the big cross.
>
> The main cross with its winding contour seems to be spreading into a multidimensional space, and the others are coming hierarchically lower and lower into simpler words.

FIG. 14.2.   Drawing by the artist V. G. Kazmin. His detailed explanation of the drawing is
given in the text.

In Figure 14.3 the initial mandala turns into a road (a blue road to the temple, as the explanatory text elucidates).

In Figure 14.4 one can see above a radiant cross soaring up; below on the right is a contour of a large, bent feminine figure: this is the yet unspread, uncreated, intra-uterine world. Inside the world's bend is its life

FIG. 14.3.   Drawing of a non-professional artist. Explained in the text.

essence, like the chaos, composed of shifted and fuzzy projections of tri-angles. The author of the drawing explained it as follows:

> All emerged from a bright shining pulsating point and has gone into it. First a dark cross, as if its silhouette. Then, what is pictured here.

Below are cited several of the most interesting verbal records:

FIG. 14.4.   Drawing of another non-professional artist. Explained in the text.

A large book is sailing up from the darkness below. It is closed, and on its cover I see golden patches of light and flashes. Then a blueness starts rising from the book. The blue space is spreading, broadening and deepening; everything is blue and light. The book is no more; there is the blueness, very deep, it draws me in, I don't feel like coming back from it. I wish to enter it more deeply.

The cross was crossed with a radiant onslaught, was multiplied in spheres of intersected rhythms, was carved by the glittering; each glittering multiplied again and broke out with glitter. This was growing, was splintered; its parts suddenly expanded as if from the inside and spread out in the intermittent radiance. The rays were crosses inside the cross and seemed boundless abysses of intensity . . . Crosses from the cross were cascades of light and were wrapping and filling the space of empty, but luminous volumes with beauty.

I saw a very large forest, high trees; I saw the light-blue sky and then it suddenly got dark, and windy, and something big, huge, and black was flying through the forest; I saw a hole in the darkness—yellow, with the violet light above; I saw a cross, and a huge man beside the cross . . . somebody caught the cross and was readily carrying it in the sky, and it grew bigger and bigger, then everything was gone, only something blue and round as a hoop remained.

The pulsating space.

Grapes of firey lines.

Streams . . . Currents or phosphorescent streams in different directions.

A whirling of these currents trying to move . . . This motion could not evolve into the Motion of Energies in the space—the large cross of the composition (the Universe) . . .—solar plexus (man).

Cross-like patches of light on the water.

Cross-like flowers.

Everything is mixed. No currents, no whirling.

Phantoms flash out on the creatures with spread out limbs.

A shaggy-haired creature with spread out arms likening itself to the cross, shakes small streams off its arms. Very funny.

Black round spots are slapping into the space. Awfully funny. There is nothing more any longer.

At first lights, flames . . .—calmness, the cross, planar and eight-edged.

Plenty of symbols of the Solar Wheel.

They compose an ornament framing the rhomboid with the cross inside it (I cannot reproduce it but I see rays) . . .

And, at last, the most obvious and finding the verbal expression (and which makes me feel blissfully happy, no words can express this sensation; and I think I experience this not to a full extent, otherwise one would not wish to come back after such an experience.)

The sphere of light or energy, the cross is born out of it and fills the space with its pulsation, its rhythm.

I saw a procession: monks, knights carrying candles and torches were ascending the mountain and entering the stony enormous bulk of a dark temple. The mystery began: the temple became lighter, crosses flashed out on the walls. The crosses were shining, glittering, sounding. The rhythm of their radiance carried me away. The temple was transfigured . . . I recollected what had been forgotten long ago . . . distant forgotten past . . . or maybe it was not the past.

The same procession moving to the temple on the mountain. I am walking together with monks and knights . . . They are carrying crosses, candles, and torches . . . We enter the temple, and the crosses grow very large, they are placed now inside the temple in a certain order forming the structure given by the planar drawing we are meditating over . . . The drawing becomes three dimensional . . . The crosses start to shimmer . . . The people are gone, and I am gone together with them . . . We experience death and ascend upwards, into the spheres of light . . . The Light meets us with drops of light . . . The Light like the rain of luminous drops falls down in shining streams to meet us . . . I am covered with drops of Light, wet with Light . . . Then everything comes abruptly to an end . . . I feel distinctly that the cross is the symbol binding Life and Death into a unity. The text composed of the crosses is a dance of the mysteries, a music notation of what is happening in the cosmic union of Life and earthly Death.

The drops of Light, the drops from Light.

The author of the last two records gave a general account of the episode in meditation which he had omitted in the verbal records as a result of its deeply intimate nature. According to him, this episode related to the experience of a boundary state between life and death. Outwardly, it looked like this: a road winding among the rocks of the foothills. It is twilight. He is walking along the road with a feeling of the deep inner seriousness of what is happening. The road seems to follow the way covered in his lifetime, and somebody is evaluating the direction of the way . . .

This involuntarily brings to mind the image of a *Balance*. Such images can often be seen in church frescoes. Often good and evil deeds are weighed on the balance. This is a bit irritating with its naturalistic primitiveness, though the image of the *Balance* seems to be underlain by the idea borrowed from the inner experience that in a boundary case a person actually evaluates his own life. Perhaps, this is why the *Balance* is one of the zodiacal symbols. Recall the last moments of life of Prince Andrey as described in Tolstoy's *War and Peace*.

After two sessions we stopped the meditation over the cross mandala, having understood the significance and depth of the contacts with the unconscious that it brought about.

Chapter 15

On the Roads of Time[1]

It's troublesome that I'm with minutes,
They have confused me immensely.
                                   A. VVEDENSKY

This chapter deals with meditation directed at expanding our concept of Time. Going along various roads of Time, we tried to learn more about ourselves and the world into which we are submerged.

A. Experimental Procedure

We had twenty-five meditation sessions. They differed radically from those described earlier both in the meditation technique and in the characteristics of the participants.

The sessions were thematically divided into the following categories:

1. *Time—the nature of Time.* It was suggested that the subjects inwardly experience Time, enter it, become it. Six sessions were devoted to this task.
2. *Fullness of Time.* The suggested experience was the stopping of Time. Two sessions.
3. *Time—Who am I?* It was suggested that the participants try to become aware of themselves by listening to personal Time. Three sessions.
4. *Time—Name.* The suggested experience was the concept of Name[2] as a cosmic, extratemporal essence of personality. One session.

[1] Written in cooperation with J. A. Drogalina.

[2] The concept of the *Name* is one of the most ancient ideas in religious philosophy. A whole chapter was devoted to the problem of the Name in an earlier book (Nalimov, 1981a). The Christian conception of the Name is elaborated by Bulgakov (1953); as a matter of fact, the *glorification of name* was officially condemned by the Orthodox Church at the beginning of the twentieth century.

5. *Time—Cross.* Here we return to the topic touched upon in Chapter 14 but give it another interpretation by suggesting the revelation of the most ancient symbol of our unconscious through Time unlocking the circle of great Silence. Note that the only session was carried out on Easter day.[3]

6. *Time—Bell.* The suggested experience was Time as entering the Bell —a symbol of Time that had often occurred during the preceding sessions. It was our first attempt at a cyclic meditation in which we returned to what had been seen earlier. One session.

7. *Time in the Gospels.* The image of Time was evoked by fragments from the four canonical Gospels containing the word *Time*. Four sessions.

8. *Time*—its revelation through concentration on the *expanding point*. One session.

9. *Time as merging of the past, present, and future.* Three sessions.

10. *Time*—as reexperience of the meditation experience of Time by Alexander Vvedensky.[4] The poem by Vvedensky quoted below, in section E, was read. One session.

And now a few words on the techniques of our meditation sessions. The first four sessions on theme 1 were free flame meditations (for details on flame meditation see Rogers, 1976*b*). The rest of the sessions (two of which also related to theme 1) were carried out with the help of auto-training (AT), but from session to session the AT text and the accompanying music essentially changed: when evaluating the response of the participants, we tried to strengthen the verbal and musical effect, being quite aware of the fact that the AT text should be chosen in accordance with the peculiarities both of the theme and of the group of participants (we can hardly hope to compose an optimal text invariant with respect to the group structure). At the end of the AT text were included words pertaining to the meditation theme. For example, to prepare the participants for theme 2, we included the words of Eckhart on the fullness of Time quoted above (see Chapter 11, section D). For themes 3 through 5 we used excerpts from the apocryphal Gospels of Thomas and Philip; in the last session devoted to theme 5 we made use of several poems by Gumilyov of a reincarnation character; these are partly quoted in Chapter 16. Music accompanying AT was always of a religious nature: fragments from Gregorian chants and from the works of the Polish com-

---

[3] Another technique of meditation over Time, proceeding from a different problem formulation, is given by Tarthang (1977).

[4] A. Vvedensky (1904–1941) is known mainly as an author of nursery rhymes. Actually, he was a poet-philosopher. In the 1920's he belonged to the union Oberiu (Union of Real Art), a group greatly concerned with the problem of Time.

poser Penderecki, music of *paneurhythmy*,[5] Japanese temple music of the twelfth century (Gaku), Częstochowa monastery music, Russian choir music of the sixteenth through eighteenth centuries (performed by the Yurlov choir), etc. The room was always darkened; on the table in the middle of the room, a large candle was burning; later it was put out. For us AT was always a procedure that facilitated entrance into the state of meditation.

Now a few words about the participants. They were mostly professional artists. The first session was carried out in Vilnius with a group of young painters. Beginning with the fifth session, a kernel group of four artists was always present. As before, immediately after the session the artists made small sketches, usually in color, and later reproduced them as paintings. Here we faced a sudden difficulty: the artists' visualizations became very dynamic, apparently as a result of the meditation theme. What we received from them was only a most vivid fragment of their visions. This fragment was accompanied by an expanded verbal text and sketches. One of the artists drew a succession of small pictures surrounding the principal image on two of his paintings: a display of the sequentially changing images, though fragmentarily given. All in all we had at our disposal about one hundred paintings, to say nothing of the sketches.

The dynamism of visualization is a good thing in itself, for it enriches the experimental results; at the same time it was the cause of many troubles both in the presentation of material and in its evaluation. Its variety cannot be reduced to a compact record convenient for publication.

To avoid making this chapter inadmissibly cumbersome,[6] we are limiting ourselves to presenting the verbal records of a single participant who participated in all the sessions. We also include only one painting by each of the four artists in our kernel group. Verbal records accompanying the paintings contain not so much our own explanations as those of the painters themselves.

B. Verbal Records

Theme: *The Nature of Time*. Flame meditation, in silence (four sessions).

> Suddenly in the flame of the candle there appears a cross, a shining cross. It is transformed into a star. The candle has converged into a

---

[5] Modern mysteries revived in Bulgaria and, it is said, continuing the tradition of Bogomils (see footnote on p. 109).

[6] We have also prepared an expanded version of this chapter including almost all the material we obtained. This version is intended for readers who wish to undertake an independent analysis of the experimental results.

shining point. It started to emit broad rays forming an eight-pointed star. Then around the central point appeared many shorter rays forming a dense shining halo.

At the sound of the word TIME in empty half-dim space without depth there appears a big black bell. It occupies almost the entire space. The bell begins to shine like a candle. It emits rays—yellow, golden, and bright. The shining bell starts diminishing and by and by sinks into the depth, into a deep space which was not there before. The bell becomes a receding star. The star moves farther and farther away, leaving behind space filled with soft light . . . No fog—there is now soft space; no bell—there is instead a shining yellow point, a star, in a far away, deep, and soft space. (Record 1)

A spiral has burst out; its spires are shining with bright, iridescent colors. Inside the spiral there is a dark core. The spiral starts rotating on a revolving core. It is rotating like a top, more and more rapidly, and then suddenly bursts out, disintegrating into sparkling drops. The space is filled with the rain of multicolored, needle-shaped, sparkling little cores. They are shining with pure iridescent colors . . . Then everything is gone. (Record 2)

For a long time my consciousness was quiet and peacefully empty. Suddenly I saw myself in the black clothes of a monk standing in front of a burning candle in a huge dark stone temple. Then it was as if I entered the candle, which became a shining temple itself. (Record 3)

Deep inside there burst out the idea that Time is the fire of the World. The World is burning out in the fire of Time. This seemed very important. Together with this preserving image I saw a big black bell. It was slightly tilted, and in it a big clapper sounded the alarm. Silence inside, the time of the quietly burning candle, while outside— the sound of alarm provoking disarray. (Record 4)

Theme: *The Nature of Time.* Meditation prepared by AT (two sessions). In the first session relaxation was achieved by means of AT accompanied by fragments of *Paneurhythmic* music; in the second session we reproduced the instructions for *energy meditation* (see Rogers, 1976*b*). The formulation of the meditation task included Eckhart's words about Time (see Chapter 11, section D).

I heard the measured sound of a church bell. Dark night; it is snowing heavily. The snow starts whirling around. It forms a large dense torus. The torus becomes colored: on the dark blue background red and blue stripes are winding around it. Everything is whirling and rotating, and I am standing in the center, immobile. The torus is elongated into a huge gray crater whose apex is lost in the boundless perspective, and in its apex there is a shining point, as a goal. But it is not clear where I am. Perhaps I turned into the crater converging to the point. (Record 5)

At the sound of the word TIME the light in which the guide called me to dissolve started to darken to twilight. Deserted highlands in twilight. The landscape is almost black, though far away one can see white mountain tops. A temple. It is invisible, as if immaterial. Within the temple it is dark. I enter the Temple and feel there the presence of a gigantic but invisible figure—the Demiurge of the World. He makes a sound and this sound counts off the Time—different Times: the principal Time and many other Times. There is something somber and majestic about Him. He does not create the World, nor does He govern it—He only changes Times, and then everything goes by itself, as it can or will in these Times. Long do I stand listening to the principal, universal course of Time. Then I leave the Temple, or, to be more correct, the Temple of Time goes away through me. And I again become myself. (Record 6).

Theme: *Fullness of Time* (two sessions). In the first session relaxation was achieved by a modified version of AT accompanied by the medieval Japanese music Gaku. In the second session breathing and energy meditations were used, preceded by Polish medieval religious hymns. In both sessions task formulations included the words of Meister Eckhart on the Fullness of Time (see Chapter 11, section D).

It is dark. In the darkness of twilight lies the Earth, immobile in the funeral procession. The darkness is condensing and there appears the figure of the huge winged angel, dark but friendly. He is the guard at the exit from the darkness and silence. He does not block the way, though he suggests that one should return back, into Time. (Record 7)

In an Egyptian temple I am sinking into ritual sleep. Somebody light and invisible takes me by the hand and firmly holding it leads the way.

In semidarkness I am passing through a somber mountainous landscape. Again the road is blocked, as before, by the huge black Angel. But now his wings are unfolded and lifted; he turns into his wings, and now there is a passage opening through him: the passage to a gigantic black bell. The big clapper is slowly and regularly beating against the inner edge of the bell. I enter it and become the bell, Time . . . I am Time, and this is agreeable and easy. I feel I can change time and if I do this, then certain silhouettes emerge in the mist, they even seem familiar, though I do not recognize them. But I do not feel like changing anything. It is very nice, pleasant, and easy to be one's own time.

At this moment I hear the voice of the guide: "Fullness of Time" and I feel I must go farther, to the cone formed by the bell. I reach the edge point of the cone and feel again the warmth of the leading hand. I must go through this point and enter another, diverging cone. From this latter cone I see the space filled with shining mist. It is Silence, the Void. The hand holds me firmly. I understand I am standing at the exit from life. This is a new and powerful sensation. It seems necessary to cease completely being myself and enter this Nothing. Then something will be opened. This must be the end of life. But the guarding hand holds me firmly and allows me only for an instant to glance at the abyss which I must become. Then the way back. Passage through the point. The way in the cone of the bell— but now with my lateral vision I see some people. They got stuck here, and are glued to the walls of the cone.

The exit from the bell. The heavy black wings are lifted again; I am treading on rocky mountain ground. The sun is rising behind the mountain. But the most important thing is that I have the feeling of my contact with Nothing. And this seems to be very significant. (Record 8)

Here we believe some comments are desirable: *The Fullness of Time* is distinctly perceived as the entrance into another reality. This entrance is blocked before us and is guarded by the guard of life. Another reality may be terrifying, though it is perceived not as the end but as the transcendence of the familiar reality. In this way we perceive leaving life in the depth of our consciousness.

What is described above can be compared with the books by Moody (1975, 1977), *The Egyptian Book of the Dead* (Budge, 1967), and *The Tibetan Book of the Dead* (Bardo thödol, 1960).

Theme: *Who Am I* (three sessions): energy meditation, Eckhart's text on silence. The third session was carried out half a year later than the first two: breathing exercise to Penderecki's Stabat Mater; Gumilyov's poems of reincarnation character: "In Those Days," "The Gray Indian," "Stockholm."

Again, as in the previous session, I am approaching a large Bell; but there is no guard any longer—the entrance to the Bell is now opened for me.

The Black Bell begins to get lighter, everything around is woven of light. Its sound becomes the emanation of light. I easily enter the Bell and become it. But now I am tracing with my eye not the diverging cone of the Bell (as before) but the spiral of its body. There, inside the spiral, semidarkness. Again I see the mountainous landscape in twilight. On the top of the mountain there is a Castle. I am in the chapel of the Castle. A few candles are flickering. The service is going on. All of us are dressed in gray. I feel light, strikingly clear, and solemn. Suddenly other, bigger candles blaze out. It becomes clear: we must go outside where huge red fires are alarmingly burning in the night. Our clothes become white. The Bell's light is mingled with the dawn slightly glimmering behind the mountains. (Record 9)

It seems I have again easily entered the Bell of Time. But this time it was so familiar that I do not concentrate on this.

I entered the point, the apex of the Bell. In front of me there is a mountain in twilight covered with snow. On the top of the mountain I see a Gothic temple, immaterial, woven of slightly glimmering threads of green. It is in the white mountain snows.

I enter the temple, and the guide says, "Out of the silence a word will be spoken to you . . ." Silence. I am the silence of the green temple. Either I am within it, or it is within myself. I understand: different Times and different Ego come to this temple.

I come up to a blue cone of light and try to enter its crater. I enter: the shore of the blue sea, marble columns on the shore. It had been my temple, and I had been its priestess. Then I had been penetrated with love and gentleness. This is the lost part of my soul. I strive to recall it. But the guide says, "It is time to come back." (Record 10)

I saw myself as an elder (mentioned by the guide reciting the poem by Gumilyov) in white linen clothes. He was drawing ornamental lines on sand. Suddenly the bell began to sound (as a response to a sharp change of tone), and the ornament turned into a road through ages. It was twilight, and I was a wanderer walking along this stony road winding across gray highlands.

I was walking for a long time—I don't know where. Suddenly everything shuddered and was lit by the bright sunlight. I saw the shore of a Southern sea. Very familiar marble columns (I often see them in my recollections) and a group of people in light white clothes. I knew that I, then a woman, was to be among them. For an instant I saw her image. The sound of the bell was slow and melodious, rather like a harp. We were listening to the Teacher.

Then the bell started to sound the alarm. The sea, the storm, an ancient ship. And a long way in the darkness, in the mist, in storms. Nothing can be discerned. The bell has calmed down—now it sounds as in a church. A Northern medieval town. I, now a man, a common man, am going along narrow streets and enter a Catholic cathedral. Its interior is common and very familiar. (Record 11)

We are again going to comment on these records. We see that the mechanism of formation of religious myths giving rise to the idea of reincarnation is reproduced fairly easily and is provoked by quite simple means. Perhaps this is to say that the preparedness for reincarnation recollection is not hidden by many layers of the unconscious but is situated somewhere rather close to its surface. We are ready to open up our ethnogenetic memory and perhaps also our phylogenetic memory. This should be emphasized not only for culturologists but also for those who study the psychology of scientific creativity.

Theme: *Name* (one session). Breathing meditation; music, Częstochowa liturgies; text, fragments 10, 11, 12, 49, and 59 from the apocryphal Gospel of Philip (Till, 1963). These texts revive the ancient, by now lost concept of the transcendental nature of the Name. Below we quote three fragments from the Gospel, typical of its style:

12. One name alone is never uttered in the world—the name the Father gave to the Son.

49. O, if I could /receive/ a symbol which /archonts/ could not have stood, —this name!

59. . . . But if someone has received the Holy Spirit, he has the name as a gift.

And here is how these bewitching words were reflected in meditation:

Black Southern night. Sandy seashore. Somebody is preaching near the marble columns. I hear his words—they are the words pronounced by the guide. The Name is a ray of light emitted by the star; it is revealed when the word is uttered. We all are within this ray; it is so bright that nothing can be seen except this cone of light. The light becomes blue and soft. My Name is the name of this star. I feel it within myself or myself within it. For a moment everything becomes incomprehensible, quite different, in the incomprehensibility of this other world in an instantaneous contact with it. But then I am again on the sandy shore. I am walking in the starlit Southern night filled with my Name. My burden is lucid, no matter whether it is light or heavy. (Record 12)

In this way are experienced Texts which lay at the source of our culture and are separated from us by almost twenty centuries. How easily and joyfully do we return to our past!

Theme: *Time—Cross*. The session took place on Easter day (one session). Breathing meditation; music, Gregorian chants, Christmas carols (Polish choir music of the sixteenth through eighteenth centuries). The meditation task was determined by the day of the session. The stimulating text: fragment 67 from the apocryphal Gospel of Philip. The text from the Gospel begins with the following words (Till, 1963):

67. The truth did not come naked into the world, but it came in images in symbols. It (the world) does not receive it (the truth) otherwise. There is resurrection and the image of resurrection. They should be truly revived through the image. What is resurrection? And an image through an image—it also should be revived . . .

And here is the meditation response to these words:

In a deserted mountainous landscape there appears the Cross. It starts to sound and glimmer with blue light. The ray from the Cross goes upwards to a blue star.

It is possible to enter the ray, and so I enter it. There is no deserted land any longer: I see the blue glimmering silvery space. In it there is a hardly discernible ornament of a shining web. On the web I see a small spider, or a scarab; it shines like a diamond. It is engaged in something—very business-like and efficient.

This is a friendly spider, it is mending holes in my web. It is myself, the web is also myself or my destiny. I can't go any farther until the holes are mended—they go down into a dark, frightening depth. I hate to part with the spider-scarab. Then the sensation of lightness and complete liberation. As in childhood, after the Easter matins. (Record 13)

Theme: *Time in the Gospel of Matthew.* Relaxation: flame meditation in silence; breathing meditation accompanied by Polish music of the fifteenth and sixteenth centuries; text, fragments from the Gospel of Matthew containing the word TIME accompanied by Penderecki's "Passions According to Luke."

Christ came down to the Earth as the silver, shining, transparent rain. The rain is accumulating on the ground as silver dust. The wind of time started to disperse the dust, scattering it over the ground, over its fields and roads, mixing it with the road dust and choking up the road ruts with it. The storm now stopped, now swept up the silver rain mixed with the ground dust with a new force.

And in the dusty mist, every now and then appeared a fuzzily outlined figure in a long white cloak. It seemed that somebody invisible, indiscernible, was trying to gather the silver of the rain and compose the ornament. But the wind was dispersing it. The wind growing more and more furious is dispersing it. (Record 14)

Theme: *Time—Past, Present, Future.* We give here only the record of the first session (all in all there were three of them). Relaxation: flame meditation in silence; breathing meditation accompanied by Polish Christmas carols and a Haydn string quartet.

An angel flying in the sky—he is not seen but only felt with a striking clarity. His large silver wings, flapping, scatter a silver path across the sky. Silver snowflakes glimmer with flickering iridescent sparks.

I see myself as a boy and later, too, in the future—see vaguely, in the mist of silver dust. I recognize myself in those standing behind the silver dust. But they do not interest me, they are alien.

The wings close up the path, there is now a ring in the shining sky. Then they unlock it in a sphere. The sphere goes upwards into the sky, expanding, and now only the iridescent sparks remind me of it and signify it. It was easy and good to feel oneself the dust of the silver path—it was carefree. There was only freedom. (Record 15)

Theme: *Time—meditation over the poem by Alexander Vvedensky*. Relaxation: flame meditation in silence; breathing meditation accompanied by Polish music of the Middle Ages and Renaissance. Text, the poem by Vvedensky (partially reproduced in section E of this chapter) without musical accompaniment. The session was finished with music by Bach.

> The candle is burning on the table.
> The candle becomes Time. Pure Time. I also become Pure Time, a vessel for Time. My breathing, my consciousness are now the flickering flame of the candle.
> The candle moves away. I am moving away from myself. The candle is moving away into the sky. Into the dark nocturnal sky. It becomes smaller and smaller, brighter and brighter in the blackness of the empty sky. The candle becomes a star. It glitters with changing lights—yellow, blue, and green. The glittering star begins to dissolve in the sky. Everything around lightens and becomes silvery. All is filled with the drops of shimmering light.
> This is the Time of the Universe, the bosom of the World. (Record 16)

C. Paintings

As we already said above, we reproduce here only four paintings (see Color Plates 5–8). The verbal records for these four paintings are presented with the paintings (following p. 196). Verbal records for fifteen additional paintings follow. The first two records are for paintings by Lithuanian artists; the remainder are for paintings by the four artists in our kernel group.

Artist: Grushas Bronus. Title: *The Bell*. Theme: *The Nature of Time*.
The painting shows a multicolored spiral-shaped bell with the predominance of yellow in a complex color space. The chime of the bell is spreading like white drops of light. The correspondence to the above records is striking: in record 1 the bell is first black, and then it begins to shine; in record 2 a spiral disintegrates into drops; record 4 also describes the bell but now sounding the alarm, and the disarray injected by the space around the bell in this painting also resembles the alarm.

Artist: R. Dubonis. Title: *Rhythm of Space*. Theme: *The Nature of Time*.

The painting has restless rhythm accompanied by the birth of the material world (represented by black boulders) and of life: an eight-pointed cross inscribed in a double circle. The intensive rhythm can also be seen in paintings of other artists who participated in the same session (these paintings are not described in this book). In one of these paintings the rhythm quiets down, having produced a capsule-like world. We have an impression that the nature of Time could also be revealed through the myth of the origin of the world. The painting can be perceived as the alarm announcing the birth of the world.

Artist: V. S. Gribkov. Title: *The Break-up of the Universe*. Theme: *The Nature of Time*.

Two pictures were produced. On the first one, break-up in the black frame of the universe; a big yellow bell is swinging; rhythm of yet empty but already split colorful space; behind the space, perhaps born from it, is a small yellow sun; the earth is yet in the darkness behind the frame of the universe. The artist describes what he has seen as follows:

> Black gates which I was going to enter are torn overhead by a white (sparkling) disk, and in it a glittering yellow bell (bronze, not gold). Blurred sun in the upper right corner.

The second painting appears as Color Plate 5.

Title: *The Scarab*. Theme: *The Nature of Time*.

The myth of the origin of the world is completed by a picture representing a multi-membered scarab against a yellow background (again the color yellow). The scarab goes forward (to the right and downwards); at the same time it is dominated by a rotation symbolized by the circle. Each member of the scarab sets its own rhythm. Below are two crossed hands—peaceful and serene. On each hand there is a ruby: "My hands are crossed with two rubies," the artist wrote on the picture. Crosses that appear under the scarab also seem ruby. The world in its two facets: rebellious and quiet. The image of the scarab from this picture echoes with that of the spider-scarab (record 13) which emerged in the session devoted to the theme *Time—Cross*.

Title: *The Star*. Theme: *Time—Cross*.

The artist gives the following comments on his picture:

> The horizon distinctly divides the space into white (above) and dark—black and blue (below). In the center there emerges a star with eight points. The bottom point is a clear-cut white triangle crossed

with black lines. The top point is a yellow triangle, the light. *The black bottom seems to interfere with my urge* to move into the depth, and this feeling is preserved to the end of meditation. At the end of the meditation I saw a white cross that seemed to be a road on which people were moving one by one.

Title: *Heraldry*. Theme: *Time as merging of the past, present, and future* (the third session).

This painting proves to be a symbolic reflection of an expanded field of images provoked by the poems of Gumilyov: "We are not in the world . . .," "You remember the palace of giants," "Descendants of Cain," "On the Way." These poems were recited during the session to the accompaniment of Penderecki's Psalms of David. Here is what the artist writes about the evolution of his fantasies:

> I relaxed slowly and gradually, and enjoyed it. The music created the feeling of harmony and peace.
>
> Images started appearing, first vague, but plenty of them. Fragments of indefinite symbols and unsteady, but concrete, objects. I am sailing in a black gondola along a blue canal; the blue sky. A blue key appears in the sky; then its outline becomes red and shining. New features are added to it; it seems to be mobile. It is transformed into a cross and begins to shine on a white triangle (one angle downwards); then a red triangle is wedged into it from above. The space around is shining blue. The white triangle is crossed with brown lines. A new melody. I have a feeling of some trouble. But it is nice to let my imagination run free. In general I have a feeling not so much of great revelation, but of *extreme* easiness of *fantasies*. I am sailing in the gondola into a cave. The gondola is now edged with red, and there is a red bow on the stern. Then I cut the canvas I am working at with my nose and sail farther. A small black dot surrounded by the shining pink. Suddenly this circle bursts out, and I am inside the glittering blue. I feel very light. All troubles have remained behind, but I am not flying or soaring; I simply am. Again, an unpleasant sky in front of me—pink, yellow, violet. But I overturn it with my palms, tear it through. Behind this shimmering sky I see a soft green meadow (the past). Silvery sky. Girls in white clothes with silvery sparkles and long silvery hair are whirling around. I am also whirling without touching them or paying any attention to them. I am going past them, and farther!
>
> The consciousness has gone.
>
> I am swimming, it is very pleasant to swim . . . The distance is agreeable, but I am not willing to go far away; I am afraid to swim from my shore. In the distance there is white sand and soft-blue sky. Suddenly the sand is covered with a white smooth canvas, with unstable gray letters quivering on it. Suddenly I am near this distant

shore. It is pleasant to throw part of the canvas over myself. The canvas is unexpectedly light. The letters turn into wavy lines, like the threads of a tissue. A very tender rosy sun is rising—one can look at it easily. I am wearing a rosy cloak. The sun is a rose with closed petals. The shore is not sandy any longer; it is covered with soft green grass. Candlesticks with burning candles are standing on the palms of hands; then the fire is burning on the palms. But perhaps these are the flowers of a lotus. I am walking. The sunrise is behind my back. A blue cloak is fluttering on me, as if blown by the wind. I feel I am imagining all this, but it feels nice and it is easy to imagine things.

Now the radiance has gone. I see a blue tulip in front of me. I pick it up. I smell it, but there is no smell. Then I grind the flower with pleasure between my palms. The moisture repealing the dryness of the bright light feels pleasant to my palms.

Artist: A. Dyachkov. Title: *The Lightning*. Theme: *The Nature of Time*.

Artist's comments:

Meditation as oblivion. The image is constantly changing. The lightning (hard) either white against a black background, or black against a white background. Suddenly I broke out of meditation—came to my senses. First I felt my heart aching; then the sensation was gone, forgotten.

Title: *The Spindle*. Theme: *Fullness of Time* (the first session).

As follows from the artist's comments, the picture reflects the concluding moments of the meditation:

Pyramids in the shape of marquees against the red glow; phosphorescence behind the pyramids. Red clouds look very real. Then I was transferred (I grasped this immediately) to the ancient East. To the right on the foreground the Assyrian figure of a winged lion. Further a long wall against the greenish-blue sky. Behind the wall the radiance of the white glow. Then I seemed to be transferred to Egypt. I was inside the closed circle of a wall. Dark sky. In the middle of the stone wall was a fluorescence shaped like a huge spindle.

Title: *The Angel*. Theme: *Time in the Gospels* (the first session—the Gospel of Matthew).

The meditation images are broken. I am ascending above the Earth. I see radiance in the distance. Under myself there is a road going far away, to the radiance. In front of me in the space I see a large three-dimensional flying cross (a carved Orthodox kind). The cross is shining with a golden glow. Then it turns into the figure of a golden angel who is also shining. I see wings on his back. Then the angel turns into a glowing disk (UFO). The disk flies rotating over the radiance, over the Earth. The disk turns into a gigantic shining dagger of a cross-like shape and hangs over the radiance on the Earth. Now I discern this radiance to be the lights of the night city.

Dyachkov's third painting, *The Labyrinth*, is shown in Color Plate 6.

Artist: N. Obukhov. Title: *The Phallic Temple*. Three paintings all relating to one session. Theme: *Fullness of Time* (the second session). Artist's comments:

> When the introductory words were pronounced, I saw images of a beautiful organ ascending upwards. Then the organ started to transform into a many-arched Gothic construction rapidly growing upwards. I saw the wings of a black angel (black wings) against a red stripe; then suddenly the middle of the wings was lined by a narrow pointed white stripe.
>
> There appeared a diminishing door with a black rectangular hole, but I was afraid to enter it. Then somewhere from the left a luminous body began to appear insistently; it filled the whole space. By and by it moved to the left upper corner, and from the right emerged a cross with crucified Christ. This image remained for a long time; then the space started to fold up along the axis of the cross, and the sun became black.
>
> Now there was a completely black space in front of me. Terrifying. Some time later a white shining dot emerged, which moved, rotating with an enormous speed. I speeded along with it, more and more quickly. I had a horrible feeling that in a moment I would be smashed into smithereens. I was deadly frightened. In this fright my body suddenly unfolded like a fan representing the spectrum of color converging to one point. I see the white top of a cliff; on it is a white horse head with a flying mane. The mane fills up the whole space and turns into the white space.

The next painting by Obukhov, *The Crown*, is shown in Color Plate 7.

Title: *The Flower*. Theme: *Time as merging of the past, present, and future* (the third session; text, poems by Gumilyov mentioned when describing the painting *Heraldry*).

This painting shows a mandala: the female womb in the middle of a flower. The artist did not write an explanation but told us that when his son, a boy of five, had seen the picture, he had said: "This is the place from which babies are born."

Artist: B. Safronov. Safronov's first painting, *Sequential Images*, is shown in Color Plate 8.

Title: *The Winged Serpent*. Theme: *Time in the Gospels* (the Gospel of Matthew).
Artist's comments:

> Something is flying, either wings or luminous flows and a strange fuzzy spot in which one can discern once an eye, another time an ear emitting light . . . now there is a town . . . a building is transformed into a bushy branchy tree; like an explosion, the crown of the tree is spreading upwards . . . A bright ray is coming from above, from the ray there shows a wing, then a tree again with fluorescent fruits, and the ray of light is winding round it . . . Then all turns into a big glowing bird or an angel.

Title: *The Crystal*. Theme: *Time as merging of the past, present, and future*.
Artist's comments:

> The dot was at first black against a black space, but later, when I entered the dot, I became lilac or violet, and the space around me was shining blue. Everything started to merge and became iridescent. The opalescent greenish circular glow appeared and melted away . . . At the moment of "birth" everything was illuminated by a bluish-golden radiance and it was shining up to the moment when the awareness of "today" came. When my "sight" went to the future, there appeared bright, intensive radiance from above—this golden-blue radiance emanated from the top of my head. First there emerged a shining triangle without distinct boundaries, with fuzzy edges, filled with a blue glow . . . A striking sensation of merging with light: of weightlessness and a feeling of being directed (by myself)—all this is merged again in a bluish-silvery mist. It resembles the plasm producing stars.

Title: *The Ring of Power*. Theme: *Time—Meditation over the poem by Vvendensky*.
Artist's comments:

> I did not perceive the words of the text and now have no idea of what was read, but at the same time I completely lost myself and did not feel myself any longer—I was dissolved. Only at each shift of "extra-temporal" and "extra-spatial" layers, I felt the newly emerged sensation and the new merging and dissolution in these cosmic spatial layers to be a new birth, a "turning inside out" of myself and the space . . . At some moment, I don't now remember exactly when, there appeared a black winged monster that flew into me and swallowed me . . . I got into the rotation of the black space in which the rays of "light" were also black. Black threads plaited this black space into an intricate ornament. They formed a strikingly beautiful

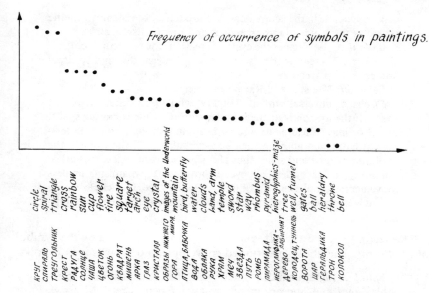

FIG. 15.1.   Frequency dendrogram of symbols composed on the basis of the paintings.

crater, a flower which seemed to have been calculated with a mathematical thoroughness . . . I broke through these spaces into new worlds flying to meet me—or was it myself who was flying to meet them?

To complete this section, we give (see Figure 15.1) the frequencies of occurrence of the most simple symbols in the paintings which can be selected easily and unambiguously. These are either geometric symbols or those easily derived from them, e.g., the sun, an eye, a tree, etc. We did not consider complex mythological symbols or symbolic representation of dynamics. For the construction of the diagram, the entire manifold of the paintings at our disposal was used.

We shall confine ourselves to a few comments. The first place on the frequency diagram is occupied by the *circle*.[7] In the broadest interpretation this is a mandala, whose semantics was dwelt on in detail in Chapter 12 (section C). In an effort to deepen our comprehension of the semantics of this word, we quote the pertinent fragments about it from the encyclopedia of symbols (Cooper, 1978):

> *Disk*: The sun; renewal of life; perfection; divinity; power . . . The

---

[7] We considered the two words disk and circle synonymous. In our diagram the circle with a hole in the center represents an independent symbol—a *target*. The sun is also separated by us as an independent symbol.

disk with a hole in the centre denotes the circle of the cosmos with the centre as the Void, the transcendent and unique Essence . . .

Buddhist: The circle is the cycle of creation, the centre of Void . . .

Chinese: The sun is the "sacred disk"; heaven; divinity; spiritual and celestial perfection . . .

Egyptian: The sun god Ra; power; renown . . .

Circle: A universal symbol. Totality; wholeness; simultaneity . . . the Self; the unmanifest; the infinite; eternity; time enclosing space, but also timelessness as having no beginning or end, and spacelessness as having no above or below; as circular and spherical it is the abolition of time and space, but also signifies recurrence. It is celestial unity; solar cycles; all cyclic movement; dynamism; endless movement; completion; fulfillment; God: "God is a circle whose centre is everywhere and circumference is nowhere" (Hermes Trismegistus).

The second place on the frequency diagram is occupied by the symbol of the *Spiral*. The above-mentioned encyclopedia describes it as follows:

Spiral. A highly complex symbol which has been used since paleolithic times and appears in pre-dynastic Egypt, Crete, Mycenae, Mesopotamia, India, China, Japan, pre-Columbian America, Europe, Scandinavia and Britain . . . It variously represents both solar and lunar powers; the air; the waters; rolling thunder and lightning; it is also a vortex; the great creative force; emanation . . . It can also signify continuity . . . The spiral also shares the symbolism of the labyrinth and the danced, or walked, "maze" . . . Spirals, or whorls, are associated with the spinning and weaving . . .[8]

We are not going to continue here the semantic analysis of the symbols discovered in the paintings. The inquisitive reader can go on with it with the help of the encyclopedia (Cooper, 1978).

From our material described above, it becomes fairly evident that the first two symbols of our frequency diagram are directly related to the concept of Time. But in order to demonstrate the relation of the remaining symbols to this concept, we had to make a thorough analysis of their semantics from which we are going to deviate here. It is important to emphasize that our symbols represent a selective sample of their entire existing variety. In particular, our sample almost completely lacks symbols personified by animals—a fish, a tiger, a lion—though their semantics is rich and their frequency of occurrence in the cultural monuments of the past is fairly great. We also have but a few symbols denoting parts of a human body. Such a widely used Oriental symbol as lotus is also absent in our sample.

---

[8] This fragment includes as explanatory the words which we select as independent symbols: *water, hieroglyphics, labyrinth, the sun*.

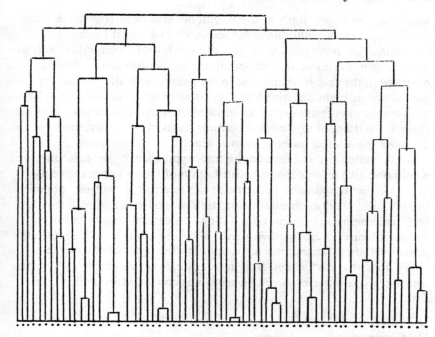

FIG. 15.2. Dendrogram of distributing 64 paintings among clusters in a 15-dimensional
space (for each object-painting were determined 15 values of the nominal variables characterizing absence or presence of the color attribute and its intensity
on a 4-level scale). The points on the abscissa correspond to the paintings. On
the ordinate χ^2 distances between clusters are plotted in an arbitrary scale. The
dendrogram characterizes the structure of color interrelations in the group of
paintings under study.

And now a few words concerning the way the ideas of Potentiality, in-
separably linked (as was many times said above) with our perception of
Time, are reflected in the paintings. Above (in Chapter 9) we emphasized
the revelation of Potentiality in the myth about the omnipresence of
Light in Matter. Light thrown in the dark (inert) Matter proves to be the
initial creative force: this motif can be found in India, Iran, and Egypt,
and in gnostic texts. The personification of Light thrown in Matter is the
symbol of semen, or the sperm[9]; a ritual attitude to sperm can be found
in many ancient mysteries. In this case the symbols of Potentiality are
phallus and vagina. The Judeo-Christian culture has made these symbols
sound obscene, but in the depth of consciousness they are preserved in
their spiritually sanctified purity. Thus, phallus and vagina turn out to be

[9] We proceed here from the last chapter of the learned and brilliantly written book by Eliade (1976).

synonyms for Light. Both of these symbols kept occurring in the paintings of our artists, either unambiguously or in a veiled form.

The internal perception of Light, the symbol of Potentiality, and its color display are constantly present in the meditation states. This can be observed in the verbal records and in the paintings of all the three experimental series. Light and also flight (or its attributes, for instance, wings, etc.) are the manifestations of the meditation states, and this makes them close to the states of mysteries. These attributes, we dare say, can serve to diagnose the altered states of consciousness.

Being unable to dwell here on the color symbolism of the paintings, we would only like to note that the distribution of the paintings into clusters in a 15-dimensional color space (with the selected χ^2 metrics), obtained by statistical analysis, is essential in itself as evidence that in the experiment embracing more than 60 paintings[10] a certain color structure was formed (Figure 15.2). In other words, a picture is not merely a set of objects: they are arranged into a structure by the unity of the theme.

We hope that further research in this direction will enable us to penetrate deeply into the levels of consciousness concealed from direct observation.

D. Comments

The vast experimental material obtained in our research and only partly presented here needs thorough analysis which could turn into a substantial independent study of an interdisciplinary nature requiring the participation of anthropologists, culturologists, art critics, psychologists, and psychiatrists. Here we shall confine ourselves to brief comments.

First of all, we would like to underline the community of symbols occurring in the records describing the experiencing of Time. In the entire material obtained in our experiments, the following constantly recurrent images can be selected.

Time as rhythm: intensive rhythm—the alarm; pulsating circles; a flying drop-like spot; waterfalls of stones.

Time as dynamism of space: boundless space; rotating space; breaking-up space; a slit; a black hole.

Time as a bell: a black bell; a spiral-shaped bell; a bell sounding the alarm; a crater; a diverging cone.

Time as a spiral: a spiral disintegrating into sparkles of light; a red-hot

[10] We included in the cluster analysis only the paintings presented in the standard form (no sketches were taken into account).

spiral; a spiral—the fire of the world; spiral-shaped sparkling roads; lightnings.

Time as a temple: the temple of Time; an Egyptian temple; a phallic temple; a pyramid; a castle; an organ; a staircase boundlessly going upwards; an arch; a tunnel.

Time as expansion of the myth: an angel; a black angel; a winged lion; large black wings; a guard, a feeling of his hand; a triangle; a rocket-like soaring up cross; a fire pillar in the shape of a woman; a diamond; an eye; a shining star; a sword; a scarab—the rhythm of its members; a spider mending a web; crossed hands; the hands of the woman—the mother of the World; feminine womb in the middle of a flower; a crown; a snake; a peacock with its tail spread; soaring spindles.

Time as light: vibration of light; color and colored light; colors smoothly turning into one another; glaring combinations of colors; the dominance of yellow; the dominance of black.

It would be extremely interesting to make a detailed historico-culturological analysis of the entire variety of the symbols that occurred in our experiment. It also seems tempting to carry out similar experiments with representatives of other cultures, e.g. Moslem or Buddhist. Will these experimental results essentially differ from ours?

Verbal records, paintings, and explanatory texts to them may serve as the basis for composing psychological portraits of the participants. Here we shall touch on this subject only cursorily. It seems that our small group of participants can be strictly divided into the three types of consciousness.

The first type is characterized by mythological patterns of the unconscious which are most distinctly manifested by the participant whose verbal records have been given above. His texts represent a sequentially developing myth with the recurrent images of a knight, angel, temple, and castle. This myth pertains to the Medieval or Hellenic past. Mythological patterns can also be found in the paintings and explanatory texts of the artists A. S. Dyachkov and N. V. Obukhov, and sometimes in those of B. P. Safronov. But these myths pertain to another past—Egyptian or Mongolian. We see that those experiencing the meditation feel their participation in the ethnogenetic past in a different way. Psychologically, this helps them to discover features of the personality previously unnoticed.

The second type of patterns could be called poetic–symbolic. This is especially typical of the artist V. S. Gribkov. His vision is full of graceful poetic images that resemble the poetry of Aleksander Blok. His images are refined, soft, and romantic. But this is true only of his meditation experience. The artist's professional style is quite different.

The third type of patterns is astral. This is the well-known world of surrealistic (sometimes threatening) dreams, reflecting the unconscious anxiety and discontent imprinted in the lower levels of consciousness. It is obviously characteristic of the artist B. P. Safronov. His meditation consists of the sequential astral visions: a severed head, a scanning ear, a vibrating eye, the space turned inside out. This also reminds us of the pictures by Dali though, in contrast to the latter, in Safronov's professional paintings astral moments are far from being dominant. The contact with the astral world can also be observed in the paintings of other artists, though to a lesser degree. For instance, one of the paintings by V. S. Gribkov (not included in the book) has the image of a grayish-green frog in a rhomb, with a tadpole inside (does this not resemble Bosch?). However, for Gribkov these are but unpleasant episodes. Only the participant whose verbal records were given above seems to lack the astral images completely.

Of interest also are the motifs of suppression. A participant whose records are not given here has a constant motif of being sealed by the cross. Dyachkov's paintings are full of tense colors: the dominance of black and gray; black is combined with blue. Overcoming of tension: in one of Gribkov's paintings he cuts the tops of waves with a sword, and feels good. Accessibility or inaccessibility of the entrance into Nothing are the indices of the depth of personalization, alienation from the whole, participation in the ultimate reality.

We are not going here to develop the theme of psychoidentification: it could be the object of a thorough and profound study. We believe it could open up much broader prospects than those of psychoanalysis. What we are dealing with is not the analysis of personality but its *revelation* in its deep self-awareness.

For us, the authors of this book, it is essential that, on the one hand, we have succeeded in seeing the variety of symbols of Time—a bell, a spiral, a shell, lightning; on the other hand, and this is especially important, we have experienced the contact with Nothing and learned how other people experienced their contact with it.

The chapters about Time, Nothing, and Reincarnation within this book represent the conceptual completion of this series of meditations. We were writing these chapters while taking part in meditation sessions devoted to the problems. The content of these chapters—their main ideas —were maturing gradually.

Our interest in the problem of creativity made us watch ourselves closely as the book was being written. However, the results of these observations cannot be distinctly formulated. Only one thing is certain: we had an impression that meditations prepared our consciousness; they seemed to prepare it for the spontaneous emergence of new concepts of

Time. The inner work was constantly going on, even in sleep. The evidence for this assertion is a dream which can be described as follows:

> Perhaps this was a dream. When one dreams, one always wakes up, but not into here, but into there, into another reality. The dream can also turn into a spontaneous meditation. This is what happened today.
>
> The *clock* has always been one of the most significant symbols of my dreams. It is through its appearance, in good repair or damaged, that I used to foresee coming events, sometimes threatening, sometimes favorable.
>
> And so I saw the clock again . . . a familiar clock . . . an alarm clock, on the shelf. But the clock hand was moving very fast, counting off hours like minutes. This troubled me. I got up and checked all the other clocks—the same thing everywhere. *Hours pass like minutes*. I checked the time by the telephone—again the same. Then I saw that the minute hand was moving very slowly: *minutes pass like hours*. So it has become clear: Time is splitting.
>
> One must now live in two *Times*: one time is passing faster than usual; the other, more slowly. If this is so, it signifies that one Time is going *forward* and the other *backward*. But the clock, being a mechanical device, cannot show time going backward. It is only a human being who can live both forward and backward, in a psychological aspect. Man seems to do exactly this, but he is unaware of these two directions: he submits his consciousness to the mechanical manifestations of life. The absurdity of the way the clock was going turned out to be a symbol, a koan to be solved in meditation following the dream.
>
> Time is a loop coming from one point. This point is the beginning of life and its end. At any segment of the loop, a person moves to the node in both directions at once: forward and backward. This motion in different directions naturally has different speeds: at first the forward motion has a greater speed, then vice versa. The break of the natural correlation of the speeds is one of the manifestations of deeply disharmonious life.
>
> When a person gets in the node simultaneously from both ends, this is the end of life: he passes onto another spire of the spiral of the cone situated in a three-dimensional spatial concept of Time. The Time of one life is two-dimensional (a loop in the two-dimensional geometry of Time), while the reincarnational sequences of lives represent realization of life in a three-dimensional geometry of Time.
>
> They say that very old people recall their childhood easily and in great detail: they are coming to the node of life in their backward motion. The exit from life is difficult if a person has come to the node from one direction, but has not yet reached it from the other.
>
> Perhaps a person following an intensively spiritual path can within one lifetime psychologically pass from one spire to another. If this is

really so, the three-dimensional character of Time becomes a tangible and controllable reality for him. Reincarnational recollections also represent the faculty to enter consciously the third dimension of Time.

Sleep itself, a deep sleep with meaningful dreams, enables us to control the speed of motion in both directions. This accounts for the ability to foresee the future and experience the remotest past as the present.

Perhaps this is what happens, in the psychological aspect, with culture: it also moves backward and forward. This can probably explain the infantile features of youths and even of adults in a highly developed scientific-technological society. Again the motion to the node in both directions. Outwardly this splitting is perceived as schizoid culture.

We have cited the above dream with the subsequent spontaneous meditation only to show how we can sometimes watch our own course of thinking. We call the interpretation of the dream spontaneous meditation—it immediately followed the dream, occurring at the moment of awakening. The beginning of the interpretation is still mythological. But gradually it starts to include familiar phrases. It ends with reasoning of a waking rational character.

The dream and meditation can be regarded as the interpretation of the words from the Gospel of Thomas quoted as an epigraph to Chapter 6, which constantly came to mind during the waking-hour ponderings over the problem of Time: "For where the beginning is, there shall be the end."

This dream can also be viewed as the revelation of the recurrent images from the series of meditations: Time as a spiral, a spiral shell, or a bell whose crater one could enter. But perhaps the ancient symbols–archetypes—the wheel of life, the snake biting its tail, the swastika in its original meaning as a symbol of the Sun Wheel—also convey a similar content.

It seems relevant to consider here to what degree human consciousness is prepared to accept the idea of the closed Time which was lately formulated in cosmogony (Davies, 1977; Misner, Thorne, and Wheeler, 1973). What we have in mind is the conception of the cyclic Universe which allows its reversion, i.e., backward motion in time. But the idea of a Universe symmetrical in time requires an exclusively coordinated conduct of its innumerable atoms. This accounts for the temptation to regard Time as reversible, i.e., to believe it possesses the topology of a circumference. Then, according to Davies (1977):

> To regard one big bang as "the beginning" and the other as "the end" is mistaken. They are both in a sense "beginning" consistent with each other. (p. 197)

To our mind, this resembles the words from the Gospel of Thomas quoted above. Further Davies wrote:

> The idea of a cyclic world is at least as old as Aristotle. In more recent years the general theory of relativity has yielded a number of situations in which the future histories of objects apparently join up with their pasts. It has never been clear just how physically meaningful such situations really are, but the implications of such possibilities for philosophy are profoundly disturbing. Free will in a closed-time universe could not exist. The condition of a system could not be changed at will because its future would also be its past. So its present condition would depend on its *future* behaviour, which is what we seek to change! (p. 198)

We can, of course, say nothing about the reality of the idea of closed Time. For us it is important to emphasize that somewhere in its depths the human consciousness is prepared for such a perception of the grammar of Time. This fact makes us ponder over the reason that we prove to be prepared (on the level of our unconscious) for the ideas that cosmogony only now starts to consider scientifically. The answer to this question is the concept of the present as the conversion of the past according to the future (see Chapter 8). In this multiplicative model the present is *symmetrical*[11] to the past and future: these two differ only on a level of interpretation which is arbitrary. In a psychological aspect, the existence of the present in the grammar of Time serves to reconcile us with the symmetrical nature of Time. By the way, it is noteworthy that seventy percent of the paintings of one of our participants (the artist A. Dyachkov), produced after meditation over the theme Time, contain a spiral as a symbol of cyclicity.

E. Concluding Remarks

We are often asked whether the records cited adequately reflect reality. It seems to us that such a formulation of the question is not valid. Here, as in physics, the world is revealed through its interaction with the receiver. The participant fixes what he has seen on the screen of his mental vision—he acts as a selective receiver. His interaction with the semantic field is primarily determined by his preparedness for the interaction.

However, we would like to emphasize the two following circumstances

---

[11] A psychiatrist participating in the discussion of the paintings drew our attention to the fact that the painting shown in Color Plate 6 could be interpreted as a horizontal hourglass whose two symmetrical parts symbolizing *the past* and *the future* are connected with a shining yellow spot symbolizing *the present*. In other words, this picture testifies to the fact that the artist's consciousness acknowledges the symmetry of *the past* and *the future* broken by the shining *present*.

which make us treat the results obtained in earnest. The first is that on the frequency diagram (Figure 15.1) all the upper places are occupied by symbols directly pertaining to the concept of Time. The second thing is that the records of the participant whose verbal records were quoted strikingly resemble those of the participant Jim quoted in the book edited by Milner (1978). The similarity of records obtained in experiments carried out in different countries and by use of utterly different procedures testifies to the fact that we contact here certain invariants of the deep levels of consciousness.

Meditational study of Time can in no way be regarded as finished. Many interesting problems may yet be formulated. For instance, will artists be capable of learning to see and depict the world without it being wrapped in Time? Will they find new expressive means to depict human contact with Nothing? How will Time be perceived in meditational experiments by physicists–theoreticians professionally studying the problems which require the search for a new vision of Time and Space?

When we discussed these problems with the theoretical physicist A. A. Grib, it also seemed desirable to introduce meditation as an exercise for students attending a course of lectures on contemporary theoretical physics. Few students are prepared independently to transfer highly abstract knowledge of contemporary physics to the level of their unconscious and thus open up for themselves a new angle for viewing reality. Yet, only people who manage to do this have a chance to become scientifically active researchers.

It also seems attractive, while studying the nature of Time, to enter more deeply into the semantic field of the Universe than has been done in our experiments. However, it is not clear whether we shall succeed in penetrating into the nature of Time, though in science this question continues to emerge. Recall that Gödel (1949*a*) found a solution with closed time for Einstein's gravitation equation: the world line of existence crossed its own past.[12] Perhaps the poem by Alexander Vvedensky quoted below is the result of meditation over Time.

Conclusion to "The Bells"

It's unbearable. For whom? For me. How? Unbearable. I am alone like a candle. I am seven past four, eight past four, like nine minutes past four a candle ten minutes past four. Not a trace of the moment. Neither four o'clock. Nor a window. But all is the same . . . Then the night comes for. Time rises above us like a star. Look, it has become visible. It rises above us like the night. Christ has risen from the dead—the last hope.

---

[12] The model with closed time caused a heated discussion in both its ontological and mathematical aspects. While for Gödel (1949*b*) the idea itself of time proves illusory rather than not. Einstein, in his turn, suggested that this solution by Gödel be removed from consideration as not having a physical sense.

Introduction

All that I am trying to write here about Time is strictly speaking incorrect. There are two reasons for that.

1. Any person who did not comprehend Time at least a bit, and only he who did not comprehend it, comprehends it at least a bit, must also cease to comprehend all existing things.

2. Our human logic and our language slide over the surface of Time.

Nevertheless it is possible to assert some principles of our superficial feeling of Time and they will make clear the way into death, into twilight, into broad incomprehension.

If we feel the wild incomprehension we shall know that nobody can oppose it with anything lucid. Woe is us, who started to think about Time. But then, with the increase of this incomprehension it will become obvious for you and me that there is no woe, no us, no thinking, no Time.

Objects

Our house has no Time, our everything has no Time. Even the present, the present time, of which it has long been known that it does not exist, the man did not give to the object. So it turns out that the house, and the sky, and the forest do not exist even more than the present.

When a person lived in his own nail, he was upset, he was crying and moaning. But once he noticed there was no yesterday, no tomorrow, that there is only today. And having lived through today, he said: so what? Neither do I have this today, nor does he who lives in the man that hops like mad, that drinks and eats, who sails in a box, who sleeps on the grave of his friend. We are in a similar position. So what?

And he started to contemplate peaceful neighborhood, and in the wallsides of the vessel of time God showed himself to him.

The words by Vvedensky quoted above seem to be the most absurd ones ever said about Time. But the nature of Time is such that meditations on absurd ideas about Time perhaps offer a better chance than any other text to break through the familiar web of naiveté and to perceive Time in all its incomprehensibility.

*   *   *   *   *

We have traveled along the roads of Time in this experiment and experienced the windings of this way:

It's troublesome that I'm with minutes,
They have confused me immensely.

PART V

REMARKS ON THE WORLD HOLISTICITY

On the Threshold of Part V

I see the World in its holisticity.[1]

The holisticity of the world is one of the major premises of this book.

In this part of the book, I return once more to the aspects of the holistic vision of the world which have not been sufficiently elucidated in the previous chapters.

The first two chapters of this part deal with the problem of reincarnation and of the prospects of interaction between science and religion. No matter how dim the first of these problems is, one thing is clear: the idea of reincarnation originated from the inherent human desire to see the world as holistic and to explain within this frame of vision the manifestations of the human psyche observed in reality which have up to now simply been ignored by our culture as not serious enough to be discussed scientifically. The idea of reincarnation was used to try to answer the poignant question of what death is. Not only was death frightening by itself, but also it broke the human urge inherent to consciousness to perceive the Universe in its indivisible integrity. In such a formulation the problem of death became limited to religious outlooks. At present our desire to deepen our knowledge of human nature has forced us to reconsider the ancient problem anew, using the possibilities which have opened up recently.

---

[1] The term holism (Greek ὅλος—whole, integral) is broadly used in contemporary philosophy. It was introduced in 1926 by Smuts (a philosopher, South African public figure, and English field marshall) to denote integral unity (Smuts, 1936).

The second problem is far from having its origin in the urge to bring together two different essences. What I have in mind is making use of their complementary opposition as a reflection of the complexity of man comprehending the world.

The last chapter of this part represents another, summing-up view of the world given in its wholeness.

Chapter 16

Belief in Reincarnation as a Projection of the Idea of Human Participation in the Indivisible Integrity of the World

We are only a sign, but its meaning is dim . . .
"MNEMOSYNE" BY I. K. HÖLDERLIN

An individual person is a sign, but what is its semantics? If we are prone to regard the sign of a *Word* as having no time and being underlain by more or less static semantic fields continuous by their nature and participating in the entire Semantic Universe, then it would seem natural to regard Man, a sign with personal time, as underlain by the same semantic continuum unbroken by time. As I said above (in Chapter 6), Death is the cessation of Doing, the stopping of personal time, but not a destruction of the semantic continuum whose selective manifestation is an individual in this concrete realization. In other words, death is only the cessation of the given concrete manifestation of the Semantic Universe. But how do these manifestations of the universe personified in human individualities emerge? Are they linked by the chain of reincarnations on a large Time scale? These questions have been tormenting mankind from time immemorial.

The idea of reincarnation—the repeated births of one personality—goes back to ancient time. It seems to have been typical of all the great religions of the World, including earlier Christianity. Now we have no doubts that this conception was based on inner mystic experience. We came into contact with it immediately at our first sessions of collective meditation, as did Grof in his experiments with LSD; we dwelt on this in detail earlier.

Science, in its urge to reduce all the psychic phenomena to physical ones, refused to notice the everyday occurrences of our life which had to

259

be explained by reincarnation. The unconditional credo was that an individuality begins with the birth of the body and stops with its death. Jung was the first to make a breach in science. Jungian psychology is represented by the idea of the continuity of consciousness unbroken by births. But now Jungian psychology seems to have become an inseparable part of officially accepted psychological science.

At present, separate, outstanding reincarnational phenomena are being studied scientifically enough both in a documentary aspect and in a methodological one by the American psychologist Ian Stevenson. But, paradigmatically, his research again remains outside contemporary psychological science, though it is not rejected by the latter altogether. Stevenson is Carlson Professor of Psychiatry and Director of the Division of Parapsychology, Department of Behavioral Medicine and Psychiatry at the University of Virginia School of Medicine.

Above (in Chapter 6) we already considered an instance borrowed from a paper by Stevenson. The first volume[1] of his interesting study (Stevenson, 1975), containing the description of ten extraordinary reported cases of reincarnation in India, came out in 1975.

Here I limit myself to considering certain everyday manifestations of a reincarnation character which have been ignored.

First of all, we should turn to poetry. It is among poets that we find people who especially deeply feel their participation in past cultures.

The first one to mention is I. K. Hölderlin (1770–1843), a German poet, who emphasized his attachment to the Hellenic world. Below we quote the beginning of his poem "The Only One."

> What force
> Has chained me to the ancient, blessed
> Shores so that
> I love them more than my native land?
> As if I am sold into
> Celestial slavery,
> Where Apollo was marching
> In his regal image

Recall that Goethe was also an ardent adherent of Hellenism. It is sufficient to indicate the second part of "Faust."

The vision of Plato is clearly carried in this stanza from Wordsworth's "Intimations of Immortality from Recollections of Early Childhood."

---

[1] The second volume of this work is devoted to the description of ten cases of reincarnation in Sri Lanka, and the third and fourth describe cases in Thailand, Lebanon, and Turkey (the author has at his disposal the description of 1,300 cases related to various countries and various cultures). The first volume contains a detailed description of the author's method, with a thorough analysis of the sources of possible errors. In the fourth volume the author is going to publish a chapter devoted to general discussion, including his interpretation of all the cases considered.

Our birth is but a sleep and a forgetting:
The Soul that rises with us, our life's Star,
 Hath had elsewhere its setting,
  And cometh from afar:
 Not in entire forgetfulness,
 And not in utter nakedness,
But trailing clouds of glory do we come
 From God, who is our home:
Heaven lies about us in our infancy!
Shades of the prison-house begin to close
 Upon the growing Boy,
  But he
Beholds the light, and whence it flows,
 He sees it in his joy;
The Youth, who daily farther from the east
 Must travel, still is Nature's Priest,
 And by the vision splendid
 Is on his way attended;
At length the Man perceives it die away,
And fade into the light of common day.

And when we read the verse of the Russian poet Aleksander Blok (1880–1921), we discern behind the external appearance of a poet-aesthete the medieval knight with his cult of the Beautiful Lady, especially in his cycle of poems "The Strange Lady," partly in the cycles "Faina" and "The Snow Mask," and in the direct appeal of the fairies to the knight in the songs of the trouvère Gaetan ("The Rose and the Cross"):

"The immutable law to the heart"
That is what she said,
And repeated in tears;
"Your future way is wandering!
What is awaiting you?
Mark your strong cuirasse
By the sign of the cross on the chest!"
I marked my chest with a cross
And entered this misty world . . .

Elsewhere Gaetan sings:

Misfortunes and losses everywhere,
What is awaiting you?
Set your shaggy sail,
Mark your strong cuirasse
By the sign of the cross on the chest!
The storm is roaring,
The ocean is chanting,
The snow is whirling,

> The momentous age is dashing forward,
> The blessed shore enters my dreams.

The knight–crusader, in this image, to the surprise and indignation of his many friends, accepted the revolution: he saw Christ "in a chaplet of white roses" in front of "the twelve." His admirers could not understand the genuineness of his poetry.

The Russian poet Nikolai Gumilyov (1890–1921) in many of his poems also managed to convey an amazingly acute feeling of the remote historical past. Below I quote two fragments from his collection of verse *The Fire* (1918):

> And I saw that I was lost forever
> In the solitary passages of spaces and times,
> And somewhere my native rivers are streaming,
> But my road to them is blocked forever.
>
> ("Stockholm")

> When, at last, awakening
> From my dream, I'll be again myself—
> A common Indian dozing off
> Near the spring on the holy evening
>
> ("Ancestor Memory")

The Russian poet Maximilian Voloshin (1877–1937) also had an acute faculty of feeling the events of the historical past. In his verse he experienced them again, and in the journeys over Europe in his young years he trod in the tracks made many centuries earlier by others:

> My spirit was casting off at yellow sunsets
> On a tarred fishing-boat
> With Paul from the pier of Antiócheia
> And from Monserrate to Rome with Loyola
> ("The Quarter of a Century (1900–1925)," 1927)

In the past he was seeking Her, the eternal feminine essence of life:

> In my vain search for her
> I have trampled every earthly path
> From the Himalayan steppes
> To the ancient piers of Europe.
> She is the forgotten dream of the ages,
> She is the unrealized hopes.
>
> ("She," 1909)

In his poem addressed to Marina Tsvetayeva, he writes:

> I am yearning for all the earthly roads,
> For all the ways . . . and I had them . . . lots of them!
> ("To Marina Tsvetayeva," 1910)

And in another poem:

> The tremble and thrill of all the ages and races
> Is living within you. Always. Now.
> ("The House of the Poet," 1920)

He perceived contemporary events not personally, but historically.

> We saw the madness of the whole races . . .
> We have lived through the Iliads of wars
> And Apocalypses of revolutions
> ("To the Descendants," 1921)

But the descendants happened to see even more.

The little-known poet Daniil Andreyev (1906–1959; the son of the Russian writer Leonid Andreyev, very popular at the beginning of our century) asserted that he had very distinct memories of his earlier births. Here is one of his poems from the cycle "Ancient Memory":

> India! —The mysterious name,
> Ancient as my way in the universe!
> The rainbow of the yearning heart,
> Images persistent like memory . . .
>
> Shall I talk about it? —People won't believe me.
> Shall I hint? —They won't understand a single word.
> They'll rebuke me for the dark predilection,
> For the invincible vision.
>
> Shall I ever touch with my beggarly hand
> The light dust of the holy roads,
> Shall I bend my knees where for the first time
> I was born out of darkness by Mother-Earth?

Here is a fragment of another poem from the same cycle:

> But I died. I changed images,
> The days of being, not being itself.
> And, like the quiet snow of the North,
> My face has paled.
>
> Ages were passing. In the lone shabby mist
> I was born and faded away
> On the mute snow of Russia,
> On the Finnish granite of the rocks.
>
> But the image of my first native land
> I cannot burn out from my heart
> Here, to the accompaniment of the sad chimes,
> In this twilight country.

In a private conversation Daniil Andreyev said that once a chink opened up in his consciousness and he learned that in his past life he had been an Indian, a Brahman, but had been expelled from the caste because of his marriage with an untouchable.

The last verse we are going to quote here is a fragment from the poem "Childhood" by A. V. Kovalensky, a Russian writer and poet. The lines quoted relate to the period of his childhood spent on the Rhine.

> And the boy often dreamed
> That in the same stone tower
> With a difficult manuscript in front of him
> He once sat long, long ago, —
>
> And the poplar branches were also bending,
> And the twilight was blue,
> And the dim crimson sunset
> Was looking into the narrow window.
>
> And horsemen were dashing outdoors,
> Monks were jogging on donkeys,
> Merchants were delivering silk and spices,
> And a pilgrim was wandering along the road, —
>
> He was dreaming so distinctly
> The sketches of life lived somewhere,
> Events of the distant past
> And long-forgotten years.

Now let us turn to writers. Recall *The Idiot* by Dostoevsky. Prince Myshkin in an instant recognizes Nastasya Filippovna on the picture, then he recognizes her in Aglaia: "Almost as Nastasya Filippovna, though her face is quite different." Though the author does not say this directly, we have an impression that the relations between Myshkin and these two women are a drama commenced in a very distant past. Both women feel that Myshkin is their hero, both understand and love him, and only they actually understand him. Note the variety of Dostoevsky's characters—Stavrogin Svidrigailov, Rogozhin, Myshkin, the Karamazov brothers—but no matter how different they are, we always recognize one person behind them: their author. However, the same is true of Leo Tolstoy—Prince Andrey, Bezukhov, Levin, Anna Karenina, Khadzhi Murat—again there is one person recognizable behind them all. Perhaps only people with a flexible personality can become really interesting writers. It looks as if in the multidimensional semantic field the weighting function has selected a pattern; but the weights for the fragments of the pattern can easily change. A writer by force of his imagination creates a lot of his possible *doubles*.[2] We can naturally assume these doubles to be

---

[2] Doubles are not identical personalities, but correlated ones. The rank correlation coefficient for the attributes determining these personalities may be either positive or negative, or, in other words, the doubles can be synonymous and antonymous. The idea of the illusiveness of a personality consists in the fac-

the writer's memories of his previous births or presentiments of his future births. But should it be so widely separated in time? Dostoevsky's Nastasya Filippovna and Aglaia are the simultaneously existing doubles for Myshkin; other people lacking his refinement and keenness of his sight do not notice this.

It is noteworthy that many esoteric teachings contain the concept of doubles and their potential materialization, but the information about it is meager.

Now I would like to draw the reader's attention of the odd behavior of certain people in everyday life. For example, you are told that an acquaintance of yours has radically changed: a cultured and educated person, a successful scientific worker, has suddenly accepted Orthodoxy or Judaism with all their out-dated ideas, narrow-mindedness, and intolerance. But after a close scrutiny you see that nothing special has actually happened: the person in question was exactly like this in his scientific activities. His pattern remained unchanged. Only the weights of the pattern constituents have changed, or, in other words, the person has created his double and joined him. We can also give another interpretation, saying that the person has recalled one of his previous births and returned there, but is such an interpretation actually relevant?

One of the most significant manifestations of reincarnation memories is, perhaps, the awareness that they may crucially affect important decision-making. We would like once more to make use of Jung's book (1965). One of the most important events of his life was the liberation from Freud's influence. It happened under the effect of the following striking dream:

> A crowd came streaming toward me, and I knew that the shops were closing and people were on their way home to dinner. In the midst of this stream of people walked a knight in full armor. He mounted the steps toward me. He wore a helmet of the kind that is called a basinet, with eye slits, and chain armor. Over this was a white tunic into which was woven, front and back, a large red cross.
>
> One can easily imagine how I felt: suddenly to see in a modern city, during the noonday rush hour, a crusader coming toward me. What struck me as particularly odd was that none of the many persons walking about seemed to notice him.
>
> In the period following these dreams I did a great deal of thinking about the mysterious figure of the knight. But it was only much later, after I had been meditating on the dream for a long time, that I was

---

ulty to view oneself as a set of doubles. If the doubles become statistically uncorrelated (the rank correlation coefficient does not significantly differ from zero), the case becomes catastrophic, as in schizophrenia, alienation of the two entities within the personality.

able to get some idea of its meaning. Even in the dream, I knew that the knight belonged to the twelfth century. That was the period when alchemy was beginning and also the quest for the Holy Grail. The stories of the Grail had been of the greatest importance to me ever since I read them, at the age of fifteen, for the first time. I had an inkling that a great secret lay hidden behind those stories. Therefore it seemed quite natural to me that the dream should conjure up the world of the Knights of the Grail and their quest—for that was, in the deepest sense, my own world, which had scarcely anything to do with Freud's. My whole being was seeking for something still unknown which might confer meaning upon the banality of life. (p. 164–165)

Thus in a reincarnation dream Jung felt the depth of the abyss separating him from the primitiveness of Freudian materialism.

Some mental diseases often resemble living in one's remotest past. This can be distinctly observed in the drawings of schizophrenic children. Boldyreva (1969, 1974), reviewing the pertinent literature, remarks that certain psychotherapists compare the art production of insane people, including schizophrenics, with archaic art and the art of primitive peoples. However, there are cases which can be regarded as a much deeper reminiscence. One such case mentioned by Boldyreva is a schizophrenic patient identifying himself (in the paraphrene state) with fish and mainly drawing fishes. Boldyreva also describes a case from her own practice:

> Vova B. (a boy), aged 6 (schizophrenia, slow progress). At the age of 2 he began imagining things, often mentioned a country invented by him which he called "Uniform-land." He used to say everything in this country was better than in life: animals, berries, and plants. He said there was built a huge fish-bowl in this country, made of pine-trees, where a giant octopus was living. This octopus was his best friend. The boy "went to meet him," "went to the French war" and "put" on each of the octopus's limbs a wheel to enable him to move faster. At the age of 2 he drew (remarkably well for his age) an octopus with eyes, a nose, and eight legs. Beside the boy drew a man with his major parts of the body; then he also drew a monkey and a cat. All the drawings are expressive and produce a favorable impression, but the octopus is prevalent. At the age of 3 Vova B. started to go to the kindergarten, invented names for himself and for his mother. He called himself "Long-heeled Philippine" and his mother "Common Nose."
>
> The subject of his drawings is unusual for children: schemes, towns, plans, roads to Mars. The patient lived in his fantasies and only with difficulty switched on to other subjects. At the age of 4 he posed odd questions: "Where does the rain, the sea come from?" "What is the weight of a drop when it falls on the ground?" etc. Having listened to the answer, he would say that in "Uniform-land"

everything was different. He said it was situated near the North pole and he "flied" there in a rocket. Next time he would say his country replaced the planet Mars. He thought he was the most important person in "Uniform-land." There is an ocean in his country, larger than the Pacific; it was called "Alandeya." All these fantasies were reflected in drawings and their titles.

At the age of five the boy started using neologisms in his speech, pronouncing a set of incomprehensible incoherent words and calling it the language of "Uniform-land." The inhabitants of the invented country were divided by him into servicemen and various dragons: "submarine" dragons, "rain" dragons, "rock" dragons, "cave" dragons, etc. He drew lots of dragons and other monsters. He was switched onto other subjects with difficulty. If we somehow managed to do this, he drew pictures of the proposed subject very unwillingly. (p. 61–62)

Unfortunately nothing is said as to what happened to the boy later on. Perhaps the recovery of such a patient consists in the possibility of discovering a double fit to live in contemporary society. And if such a patient is really gifted, he could probably become a talented artist or poet. Gauguin's madness, his incomprehensible behavior in the Western world —its rejection and intensive urge towards the world of earlier, more naive culture—has a strong reincarnational flavor. Tahiti turns out to be his ancestral native land where his artistic talent starts to blossom.

The world of the insane child was real for him; it was fantastic only for the psychiatrist treating him. But the poets whose verse we quoted above seem also to have lived in a world of fantasies treated by them as reality. They say this quite openly. But we, as readers, grant them the right to exist in non-reality only because they are poets: Quod licet jovi, non licet bovi.

Another reality is also allowed for artists and prophets. Recall Blavatsky, the founder of modern quasireligion (we spoke about her a little in Chapter 11, section I). Does her *Secret Doctrine* (for a brief version see Blavatsky, 1966) differ much from the fantasies of the young patient? The works of Swift and Dante are also full of strange visions. Our culture, contemporary and past, is penetrated by fantasies from the worlds of other realities, more often than not of reincarnational character. Why do psychologists and culturologists pretend not to notice that? Non-reality, entering a culture, becomes the reality of this culture. And if the extreme forms of submergence in non-reality signify schizophrenia, then perhaps the entire culture is schizophrenic. However, such a train of thought does not explain much, nor does it reconcile us with what we observe in our everyday life.

There are other types of odd behavior which, however, are considered normal. For example, you are walking along the embankment in a late autumnal town and see robust fellows with fishing rods standing for hours up to their waists in the cold, muddy water. What constituent in the pattern of their personality makes them stay in the cold water? Is it again an obsessive memory of the past?

Such examples can be multiplied almost endlessly. In our everyday life we constantly come across manifestations which are easily explained if one accepts the idea of reincarnation. Nevertheless, we believe that the conception of karma which came from the East and the teaching of sequential reincarnations accompanying it is fairly naive. As a matter of fact, in Buddhism, the most mature manifestation of Oriental thought, the idea of reincarnation and everything related to it looked serious enough. The following excerpt from Sangharakshita (1980) is relevant:

> What is reborn? To say that the "being" reborn is identical with the being lately dead would be the extreme of eternalism. To say that he was not identical would be nihilism. Avoiding these two extremes, the Buddha teaches the Middle Way, namely, just this doctrine of Conditioned Co-production, "This being, that becomes; from the arising of this, that arises, etc." Rebirth takes place, but in reality no "being" is reborn. Going as it does so much against the grain of our deep-rooted attachment to the delusion of permanent individuality, this application of the Pratitya Samutpada to the rebirth process is one of the hardest ideas to grasp in the whole range of Buddhist teaching. It is not to be understood even intellectually without careful and *impartial* study and a certain amount of meditation. (p. 96)

The European intellectual tradition, striving for precision and definiteness of assertions, simplified and vulgarized the idea. The widespread Western concept of reincarnation looks cheerless. The initial premises of this model, selected after its logical analysis, prove to be rather shabby. There are at least three of them:

1. The certainty that the human Ego is stable during an almost endless series of births, as well as—unavoidably—in the intervals between births. This is a challenge to the idea of the illusoriness of the discrete Ego which is also a key idea in the East. If the Ego does not remain stable during one lifetime, then what is passed to the karmic chain? Karma, in its evolutionary presentation, seems strikingly egocentric; outside the social and historical context one may and must try to overcome it in a purely personal aspect.
2. Belief that there exists an absolute Time, homogeneous and linear. This naive theory is produced by the noncritical perception of our everyday experience.
3. The certainty that there exists an unconditional, unambiguous law resembling the mechanistic concept of a physical law in the time of La-

place[3] though all the power of our imagination is not enough to see in what way the Law of Karma can be recorded; and if a process cannot be compactly recorded, the idea of the law loses any sense.

If now the teaching of Karma is analyzed by a logically conceivable statistical analysis, it will be fraught with certain difficulties. On the one hand, it is easy to discover instances when quite different persons perceive themselves as reincarnationally related to the same person, e.g., Napoleon. On the other hand, the population of the Earth is growing steadily, and if all the people living now are reincarnationally reduced to the distant past, when the population was very small, what will result? We are quite aware of a certain irrelevance of this argumentation, but it cannot be merely waved aside.

Now, when our vision of the World is so much expanded, we should treat the conception of karma with great caution.

It seems reasonable to limit ourselves to the assertion that the world is double-faceted: continuous and discrete. One of the discrete manifestations of the world is a human personality existing in personal Time. It would seem absurd to try to trace the destiny of the human Ego outside its personal Time, as it would also be senseless to pose a question about the destiny, or, better, about the history of a physical particle outside the boundaries of its manifestation. Now we seem to have seen unmistakably that all our attempts to comprehend the nature of Time, no matter how various they are, are nothing more than the search for a suitable language to describe the unmanifested. What is not manifested in time cannot exist, for we are unable to conceive of an extra-temporal existence. This seems to be not so much a property of the World as of our comprehension of the World. But we can speak about the World only to the degree we are able to comprehend it; to do otherwise would be self-deception. The naive conception of reincarnation is shattered by the above reasoning based only on the analysis of our faculty to comprehend things. It is noteworthy that in Buddhism the description of reincarnation seems to proceed from the idea of closed Time. I again quote Sangharakshita (1980):

> Between the cessation of the last moment of consciousness belonging
> to the last birth, and the arising of the first moment of consciousness
> of the present birth there is, according to the modern Theravada,[4] no
> interval. (p. 95–96)

[3] It is well known that Laplace believed the past, present, and future of the world could be described by differential equations.

[4] Theravada (literally, the teaching of the eldest) is a trend of modern Buddhism, the only surviving Hinayana school which strictly observes traditions (Hinayana, "the small chariot," or "the narrow way," is opposed to the second trend, Mahayana, "the big chariot" or "the great way").

It seems that, according to this conception, what happens in the personal aspect corresponds to the crossing by the world line of its past. We cannot help recalling the concept of Gödel, which was mentioned in Chapter 15. We are certainly far from using the concepts of contemporary cosmogony as a basis for the idea of reincarnation. Another thing is important: the attempt to comprehend the seemingly different and remote problems gives rise to similar ideas of Time. We again face the fact that the traditional concept of time proves insufficient, and the attempt to broaden it is perhaps another evidence of its illusory nature.

Above we often said that human individuality is a specific state of the semantic field; i.e., the selective manifestation of the semantic universe is realized through man. Again, as said above, the selective manifestation may vary, creating doubles (the nature of doubles was discussed above; see footnote on p. 264). The creation of doubles submerged in the cultures of the past seems to give rise to many of the phenomena which we are inclined to regard as reincarnational manifestations.

This assumption may be strengthened by an almost obvious assertion that the entire human past—not only the distant past, the source of Jungian archetypes—continues to live within us in a subtle form. The cultures of the past never die out completely because their manifestation is extremely fuzzy, indubitably much fuzzier than the manifestation of an individual. A culture has no distinct body whose destruction would break off the possibility of Doing. The dying out of a culture signifies the expansion of the scale S of its Doing (for details on the scale of Doing see Chapter 6), but the scale expansion coefficient k, though it can increase almost without limit, never tends to infinity. In other words, the rate of personal time of the culture, no matter how small it is, never tends to zero.

All this argumentation is but a model for sharpening our reasoning. If we turn now to real life, we see that it is densely interspersed by the past: Hellenism in philosophy, Roman law in jurisprudence, Byzantine heritage in the Orthodox Church and also, perhaps, in the state arrangement. And these features are not merely a dead trace of the past but the live essence slightly varying in its temporal occurrences. We constantly observe that in the historical arena the new turns out to be nothing more than a parody of the seemingly distant past. For example, it has been noted more than once that the Nazi idea of the superiority of the Aryan race was nothing more than a parody of the key of the Old Testament: that the Jewish people were God-chosen (see, for example, Gerson, 1969). The same is true of science—even in its most recent structures one can sometimes hear the echo of long-forgotten ideas [see, for example, the book by the American physicist Capra (1975) concerning the similarity between the ideas of contemporary physics and Tao, as well as our paper

(Nalimov and Barinova, 1974) about the predecessors of cybernetics in Ancient India]. Actually, we are living within the vortex of all the previous cultures. And people who feel this acutely may experience themselves through their doubles as a Hellene or a medieval knight. Meditation, dreams, or even psychedelic drugs reveal the things inherent usually only in poets; so why should we be amazed by what we encountered in meditations or what Grof had heard from his patients if we are not surprised by what the poet Voloshin wrote (see p. 262) and, consequently, experienced? There are evidences of the World *holisticity*, of the *preservation* of the past in the depths of our unconscious.

What is said above can be regarded as the second approximation to the model of Karma stripped of its personalistic elements. In this model the idea of the Karmic role of culture[5] comes to the fore, and this is a much fuzzier and more temporally indefinite structure than a human personality. Such a personal approach to Karma is necessary at least because at present, side by side with Freudian and Jungian therapy, there appeared the so-called transpersonal therapy with a philosophical basis aimed at disidentification, the entrance into transpersonal dimensions of existence (see Vaughan, 1979; White, 1979; Boorstein, 1979; Welwood, 1979).[6]

A rigidly fixed Ego, with a lack of flexibility and dynamics, is a state difficult both for the individual and for his environment. Such a person turns out to exist outside society while at the same time remaining within it. Communication with other people, except in its most primitive forms, becomes a burden: why does he need other people if he ought to remain always the same, always himself. Perhaps our contemporary culture tends to increase the egocentric features. One of the indices that this is really so is the growing number of divorces and other signs of social anarchy. People find living together unbearable. What is now called the infantility of youth is probably also the manifestation of egocentrism. An individual loses interest in everything and, therefore, loses the ability to do anything only because he is constantly closed within himself, engaged in his own person, caring only for his pampered inviolability. However, this is a serious topic requiring a special study. But we already feel that the transpersonal constituent looks like the beginning of a counterculture and is, probably, more significant than such outbursts as the hippy movement.

The isolation of the Ego can be overcome through interaction. Recall

---

[5] The idea of Karma here emphasizes the process of overcoming what has not been overcome in the heyday of culture, in its subsequent latent state. The vortex of cultures in our days embraces broader and broader circles of nations. Bellah (1976) notes that nowadays the nations of Asia and Africa are involved in overcoming the culture of the Western World which is not able to cope with this task alone.

[6] Note that the problem of psychological health in its broad comprehension enters the list of subjects covered by the *Journal of Humanistic Psychology*. There is also a new term: holistic health.

that one of the aspects of belief in reincarnation is the certainty that individuals who during their earthly life once entered a significantly deep interaction—loved each other or inflicted great evil on a person—are linked forever. It is noteworthy that this certainty, often treated as a naive superstition, has something in common with the $\overline{K^0}K^0$ paradox in the physics of high energies. This paradox is a specific instance of the well-known paradox of Einstein, Podolsky, and Rosen. Here is what Lestienne (1973) writes on the point:

> In this case, the paradox consists in the fact that a pair of sub-nuclear particles that are formed in a given nuclear interaction, but separated spatially by several tens of centimetres at the time of decay can not decay independently of each other. Roughly speaking, if the first decays within a short interval of time, the second must do so within a long interval of time, and *vice-versa*.
>
> It is pointless to wonder whether a signal is propagated from particle A to particle B to say: "I have decayed; now you must wait before also decaying in your turn." Such a signal would have to be propagated at an infinite velocity . . .
>
> It therefore seems necessary, if we wish to avoid the paradox, to abandon absolutely the idea of the separability of quantum systems even if they have only once interacted in the course of their history."
> (p. 94)

Here a single interaction gives birth to the connection. This elucidates the meaning of Doing: it reveals mutual interconnections of everything, observable even in the world of elementary particles. And while in quantum mechanics we had to reject the concept of isolation between quantum systems, we have even more grounds for rejecting the concept of the isolated human Ego. Note that the paradox by Einstein, Podolsky, and Rosen is one of the greatest challenges made to quantum mechanics. It forms part of the argument between Bohr and Einstein concerning the *completeness* of quantum mechanics; it is not yet clear whether the problem of completeness can be solved by introducing a so-called *hidden* parameter which would possess some outstanding properties. The idea of hidden parameters for some time seemed groundless, but now it has acquired a new significance (Bohm, 1980). We cannot help asking whether the *paradox of reincarnation* (whose discussion we cannot avoid) testifies to the deep incompleteness in the contemporary initial premises of the scientific conception of human nature.

The model of the second approximation also makes prominent the problems of *potentiality*. If the world has two facets, then what is the potentiality which causes the world to be manifested in all its ceaselessly changing variety? If human personality is but the selective manifestations of the Semantic Universe, who determines this selectivity; why and how is the context selected for the psychological reality with which we identify ourselves. Here we are again considering the problem we attempted to analyze above, in Chapter 9.

There is no answer to this question. Humanity used all the power of its collective imagination to find an image for reflecting *potentiality*. But no single image could be created. In Tao it is represented by spontaneity generating harmony outside any law; in Hinduism, by the dancing Siva and the World emerging in the process of a Game; in Judaism, by the severe God Yahweh who possesses the law and has chosen only Jewish people out of everything he created; in gnosticism—for the higher spheres of existence by the spontaneity of birth and for the material world by its creation by the Demiurge who is outside God and is even opposed to him; in the scientific tradition, by the Judaic version of the world creation through the original laws of nature which themselves had never been created. Even if we narrow the problem and try to find an image for *potentiality* giving birth to human personality, a satisfying image still cannot be discovered.

One such image had been that of *fate*. Fate (or at least this was so in the Hellenic Greece) is a potentiality, in no way personal but of a general historical character. It inserts man into the historical vortex, prepares him for it, and expects certain Doing on his part as a response to the historical context into which it has put him. Thanks to an odd coincidence, I am now reading the historical novel by Mary Renault, *The King Must Die*. It looks like a reincarnational meditation about the hero Theseus, the son of Aegeus, the ruler of Athens. The entire book is penetrated by the powerful breathing of fate. Western thought in its literature and art constantly returns to the image of fate. Recall *The Blue Bird* by Maeterlinck: Chronos—time identified with fate and abiding in the Azure kingdom—compulsively pushes the soul into the incarnation. The earth needs a hero, justice should be restored. The alarm sound of fate strikes the reader of the novel *Doctor Zhivago* by Boris Pasternak. The alarm bell of the revolution raises the snow storm whirling far and wide, and, as in meditation, a candle is burning in the teeth of the wind:

> It was snowing and storming all over the earth,
> To all the bounds.
> A candle was burning on the table,
> A candle was burning.

Perhaps, at the cradle of our culture there was another image of *potentiality*, the *Name*. In ancient time Names were ascribed great significance. The Gospel of John says that Christ revealed the Name of God to his disciples. Meister Eckhart wrote that nobody had yet pronounced the Name of God in his time. Bulgakov (1953) made an attempt to restore the lost meaning of this symbol. Below we quote excerpts from his book:

> Ideas are *verbal images* of existence, names are their *realization*. (p. 60)
>
> In the *word*, as in the completing formula, a cosmic force is acting which is felt by means of the word; therefore this force is in a definite sense transcendental with respect to the phenomenal world and to the word in its common meaning. (p. 148)

Still, we have to acknowledge that the idea of *potentiality* is beyond our imagination. We cannot imagine what we cannot experience. Any image, as well as any model, will be empty. So it turns out that in science, too (even in its theoretical constructions), man can suggest only what he was able to experience in his inner psychological world. *Potentiality* is a mystery that we are facing. Its solution can be found through the expansion of our consciousness. And we must acknowledge that the attempt to solve this mystery within the traditional teaching of karma seems rather clumsy.

Nevertheless, how happy we are to meet a person existing within the manifold of cultures. Only such a person can exist outside rigid identification with the paradigm of our time. Only for him is a broad vision of the world possible, filled with the rich content revealed to humanity during its entire history.

The vortex of cultures becomes especially evident at crucial moments. It was so in the epoch of the Mediterranean, long before the Christian era, when the entire spiritual treasury of the world started to contract into a single point: contacts of pre-socrateans with the Persian empire, the journey (according to legend) of Plato and Pythagoras to Egypt and even perhaps to the valleys of India, the victories of Alexander the Great which made the Hellenic World face Indian culture. Alexandria became the spiritual center, and all this formed the ambiance richly satiated with ideas and myths in which Christianity revealed itself and was enriched. The symbiosis of ideas which emerged in Christianity is well described by Blavatsky (1877).

A similar phenomenon is occurring now, when Western ideas came into contact with Eastern spiritual experience, science encountered religion, and the supposed gnostic past of Christianity becomes revealed, having lain hidden for almost twenty centuries. Many forgotten and concealed things have been discovered and are coming to the surface.

In such an epoch our mutual misunderstanding is deepened. The more some people see, the more difficult it is for others to comprehend it. To comprehend another person is to discover within oneself a double who will be the twin to the other person. To comprehend is to become twins. But comprehension means knowledge. So it turns out that Knowledge and Love are synonymous because in Love, more than anything else, a person restructures himself and discovers within himself a double carrying the new Knowledge. In Tantrism mentioned above (see Chapter 10) lovers for a long time prepare their doubles within themselves. In the last act of culmination, the doubles recognize each other and are identified. The boundaries of the personality are lost. Recognizing himself in another person, man recognizes himself in everything. The miracle on the Cross: in the crucial moment the robber gives birth to his double in whom he recognizes Christ, and Christ recognizes himself in the robber. Thus, the miracle is done through Love which is also Knowledge revealed in itself. Gnostic Christianity proves to be a complementation to the Christianity of Love. We come to see that a person reveals himself and crosses his own boundaries through his faculty of imagination so much discussed above. Love, and especially its manifestation called compassion, becomes the synonym for imagination (Thurman, 1961). Synonymy: all our fundamental concepts are synonyms since they reflect the Same. However, "We are only a sign, but its meaning is dim."

Chapter 17

Science and Religion: Is There Room for the Complementarity Principle?[1]

A. Formulation of the Problem

The complementarity principle changes our scientific vision of the world: it gradually becomes more and more polymorphous. We are ready to perceive one and the same phenomenon from different angles, describing it by non-rival models. Even mathematical statistics, traditionally directed at selecting the best and therefore the only true model, is now ready to acknowledge the legitimacy of a multitude of models. However, so far the entire manifold of possible models has remained within one paradigm and was always expressed in the same language, that of contemporary science. Here it seems relevant to pose a question: can the complementarity principle be broadened to the extent of preparing our culture to perceive the world by a manifold of models generated by essentially different paradigms. And if so, will this perhaps lead to the fuzziness and intersection of mutually opposed paradigms.

The divergence between science and religion seems to have started as long ago as in the epoch of Galileo. Both systems aimed at the utmost mutual separation, perhaps as a consequence of the inherited tendency in European culture for a dichotomous vision of the world. This had found its symbolic expression in the myth of original sin, which lay at the source of our epoch. There was a time when science and religion seemed to be mutually orthogonal.

However, from time to time there were attempts to glance at the world in its inseparable integrity. Of interest in this respect are two books which are fairly close both in contents and in foundations. The latter contains

[1] Published in *4S—Society for Social Studies of Science*, 5:9–13, 1980.

the notion of noosphere central for both books, which brings scientific and religious concepts close together. One of the books is written by Teilhard de Chardin (1965), a paleoanthropologist and a Jesuit monk; the other one, by Vernadsky (1977), an outstanding geochemist who occupied a fairly high position in the Soviet scientific hierarchy.[2] It is noteworthy that both books could be published only posthumously. However, such protuberance-like flashes, though they aroused interest, did not affect the contemporary culture in a serious way.

Recently, there appeared papers which trace the parallels between the ideas of modern science and Oriental religious concepts. I mention the book by Capra (1975), though it was criticized by Restivo (1978), who emphasized the traps lying in wait for the studies of this kind. In our paper (Nalimov and Barinova, 1974) we attempted to trace the ideas of cybernetics back to Ancient Indian philosophy. We proceeded from the idea that a priori (before reading the text) we ascribe to the notion a meaning quite different from that ascribed to it in Ancient India. But, ascribing to words the broad meaning of our culture (and thus introducing distortions in the meaning, since the texts are translated into modern languages by using words borrowed from the philosophical vocabulary of the twentieth-century culture), we constantly reduce it as compared with the meaning of the ancient texts.[3] This is what makes hermeneutics so difficult and so attractive simultaneously. However, reading philosophical works of the nineteenth century, we come across the same difficulty: the prior meaning of philosophical terms has changed considerably from that time. Moreover, in science we also face the difficulty of understanding texts. Lysenko was still a Darwinist, though an absurd one, and it was senseless to argue with him since he proceeded from different prior meanings of words. Be it as it may, the possibility of discovering contemporary ideas in ancient texts is fascinating. It may well be an illusion, but comprehension of any contemporary text is no less an illusion.

But no matter how fascinating the parallels between modern science and ancient religions are, they are not enough to bring the two different visions of the world close together.

[2] V. I. Vernadsky (1863–1945), professor and academician, was well known in the USSR not only as a scholar but also as a philosopher and public figure. He is a representative of Russian Cosmism, a natural philosophical trend at the beginning of the twentieth century which tried to comprehend all the phenomena of our earthly life, including human spiritual life, in their inseparable connection with the evolution of the entire Cosmos. Vernadsky paid great attention to the attempt to develop a biological understanding of time. In the tsarist period, being a public figure, he acted as an active opponent of reactionary policy. At the beginning of 1917 he entered the so-called Provisional Government formed immediately after the fall of the tsarist autocracy. After his death there remained a huge archive which has only recently begun to be published.

[3] I considered the mechanism of perceiving verbal semantics in my earlier book (Nalimov, 1981*a*) where I proceeded from the assumption that semantic fuzziness could be probabilistic. The Bayesian theorem that served as the basis for probabilistic semantics was already mentioned in Chapters 2, 3, 5, and 8.

The true contiguity of the two forms of world perception will become possible only after each of them feels the acute need for a new approach to the evaluation of their reality. This is to say that both paradigms must be extended and softened so as to make possible the emergence of a new, unified paradigm. Only in this way will our culture be able to absorb both forms as complementary. *Complementarity*[4] is possible only *under the cover of one paradigm*. But so far this question has not been discussed in the literature. Why?

Today both sides seem to be beginning to feel their paradigmatic insufficiency. Western science has come to feel that the paradigm fostered by it has closed the possibility of studying man. And the problem of man has unexpectedly come to the fore in our culture.

Quite recently, when cybernetics was only in the bud, the majority of scientists believed the problem of *control* to be linked, on the one hand, with the progress of computers, and, on the other hand, with the development of applied mathematics. Now it is clear that the solution of the problem is hampered by our ignorance of man.

It is becoming evident that salvation from the ecological crisis, if any, can only be achieved by creating a new culture (Nalimov, 1981*b*), but, again, this problem is connected with the knowledge of man, and we still cannot estimate his hidden desires and faculties.

B. A Possible Solution

If modern science is willing to cope with the problem of man, it will have to revise at least the following three basic paradigmatic requirements:

1. The requirement of reproducibility. In studies of man, it is not so much recurrence of his states and behavior that is important as their rare and exclusive manifestations which reveal the hidden part of the spectrum of consciousness.

2. The requirement of separating the subject and the object of the research. It is impossible to take a detached view of the parts of the spectrum of consciousness concealed from the direct observation. They must be entered, lived through consciously; they must be discovered within oneself. An illustration is the brilliant descriptions of pupillage by Carlos Castañeda (1968, 1972, 1974)—no matter whether

---

[4] According to the complementarity principle introduced into physics by Bohr, in the process of world description it is necessary to apply mutually exclusive "complementary" classes of concepts, each of which generates its own logically consistent line of reasoning but proves logically incompatible with the others. Bohr was sure the complementarity principle should be used to describe the integrity of live organisms, human consciousness, and human cultures (for more detail, see Chapter 6 in Nalimov, 1981*b*).

these books are actual sketches of an anthropologist or merely a literary device.

3. The requirement to acknowledge as ontological reality only what can be perceived by means of technical devices. This requirement may be opposed by stating that man, too, is a special receptor who is able, under specific conditions and after special training, to discover a reality concealed from physical instruments.

The last requirement is especially hard to fulfill. The essence of science is aimed at the mastery of the world (Nalimov, 1981*b*), and it agrees to accept as scientific only what can be made by human hands and mind; man cannot be regarded as a scientific instrument since he cannot be made in this manner.

It seems impossible to discover a single demarcation line between science and religion. Popper's (1962, 1965) concept of falsification has not provided such a separation either.

Undoubtedly, however, one such division includes the attitude towards *questions*. Any question contains a hidden assertion that makes the answer possible. Science has been developing answers to the question which in a compact form formulated the entire knowledge accumulated up to that moment. Any scientific theory is primarily a question posed to nature. A theory disappears when it stops being a question calling forth answers. The early forms of mastering nature, e.g., alchemy, knew no such questions. Western religion, at least in its traditional form, did not know them either. As to Eastern religions, they permitted questions to some extent (certainly, not to the extent science does), and this may explain the interest in them in the contemporary West.

Religion of today, at least to my mind, has faced the necessity to acknowledge the right to ask questions: many-sided modern questions whose assertive component contains all the novel knowledge of the world. This is the only way for religion to acquire the dynamism it needs.

It is now also necessary for religion to acknowledge the right of experimentation in its domain.[5] Strictly speaking, religion has never been alien to experimentation. Its experiments were personal experience, meditation, or prayer. But what we now have in mind is a directed experiment carried out as the answer to a question.

Contemporary religion and science have a point of contiguity. This is the search for a new culture as the answer to the challenge made by the ecological crisis. I believe the new culture cannot be found without acknowledging a different ontological reality which one could enter to leave the consumers' reality.

---

[5] Our experiment described in Chapters 13–15 of this book is an example of a scientific experiment bordering on religious experience.

Chapter 18

Dialectics of the Open End

Comments on What Has Been Said Above

> *1. The Bhagwan said — The body is called the Field, oh Kountaiya. He who knows this, is called the Knower of the Field by those who know it.*
> *2. Know me also oh Bharat, to be the Knower of the Field in all the fields. The knowledge of the Field and its Knower is, in my opinion "Knowledge."*
> *15. Without and within all beings, unmoving as well as moving, unknowable on account of its subtlety; It is far and near.*
> *16. Undivided, It yet remains as if divided in beings. It should be known as the upholder of beings; the destroyer as well as their generator.*
> *27. He alone sees, who sees the Supreme God, sitting equally in all beings as imperishable in the perishables.*
>
> BHAGAVAD-GITA

Now, when we have said so much, it remains to make comments on all this; naturally, some things will have to be repeated.

A. Vision of the World Through a Number of Complementary Essences

1. In Western culture developed on the basis of bimodal Aristotelian logic, the insufficiency of logic has been discussed more than once and from many sides.

I discussed the linguistic–semantic aspect of the problem in an earlier book (Nalimov, 1981*a*). Other types of logic have also been suggested: dialectical, probabilistic, quantum, three-modal, multi-modal etc.1 But Aristotelian bimodal logic cannot be replaced by another one. It is a natural constituent of our language; it codifies and classifies certain techniques of our verbal behavior. The insufficiency of logic in everyday language is made up for by the use of metaphors. The logic of the text and its metaphorical side are two mutually complementary phenomena. And, to my mind, further evolution of linguistic means should proceed by deepening *language complementarity* rather than by searching for another kind of logic. One of the constituents of the mutually complementary pair, its metaphorical component, has always remained a pariah in science, whose presence science tried not to notice.

2. In the present book I have proceeded from the assumption that we view the world as having two mutually complementary facets: one consisting of points, manifested discretely, and one holistic, continuous in nature, and, therefore, irreducible to a discrete-point concept. One can give a point on the continuum constructively, but cannot indicate the point nearest to the previous one. For example, if we fix the point "zero," then what will be the nearest neighboring points to the right and left? In other words, we cannot imagine the semantic universe as composed of discrete atoms of meaning arranged according to their significance without finding for any pair of arranged pairs responding to the inequality $a < b$ at least a single number c for which $a < c < b$.

It is natural to describe the semantic world perceived as divided within the system of logical structures, but it seems equally natural to describe the same world viewed as continous within the system of fuzzy, probabilistically weighted concepts. Two opposing descriptions which cannot be synthesized into one represent the dialectics of the *open ended universe*.

3. The familiar dialectics of the triad has a closed end, being completed by the synthesis of the two oppositions. As a matter of fact, we are ignorant of the mechanism of the synthesis; it is also unclear what a synthesis in dialectics signifies: does it again mean the only possible conception given discretely, through a concept, or is another representation of it also possible? The dialectics of the open end does not close when it arrives at a new structure or idea. It has another meaning: it sharpens our internal vision-experience, leaving it in a state beyond language. Our argumenta-

---

[1] There was also the logic of "general semantics" proposed by the Polish scholar Korzybski. Its interest for us lies in its sharp criticism of Aristotelian logic, which Korzybski started as long ago as in the 1930's. Speaking of the Aristotelian vision of the world, he introduced the term "elementalism" characterizing the distortion emerging from splitting in the language what was not split in nature. The scientific theory of Korzybski, as well as his behavior, were on the whole very confused, but his criticism was strikingly shrewd. Without being acquainted with his work, we have proceeded from a very similar criticism (for details about Korzybski's semantics, see Rapoport, 1975).

tion about Time, Semantic vacuum, Potentiality, or Karma remains conceptually incomplete, and so they must be. The dialectics of the open end is aimed at provoking consciousness, not at quieting it, and here it resembles the Zen tradition. It is not a cone converging to one point but an opening bell of our world vision.

4. The logic of the open end has much in common with the *reverse perspective* in icon painting discovered by Paul Florensky, an original Russian religious thinker with a mathematical background. The point of convergence in both techniques is not placed outside, beyond the context (as is the case in the European painting) but is turned inside, to a man who thus becomes part of the context and its culmination.

5. The complementarity principle formulated by Bohr, first in physics and then as a general scientific principle, also represents the dialectics of the open end. Its idea is that in order to reproduce an object in its integrity it is necessary to apply for its description complementary, mutually exclusive classes of concepts. An instance of such a description is the concept of the corpuscular wave bi-unity in the behavior of microobjects. In the quantum field theory, it is shown (proceeding from the axiomatics by A. S. Whiteman) that the characteristics of particles can be constructed on the basis of field theory, not of particle theory. This opens up the possibility of corpuscular interpretation of the field theory. We try, proceeding from the field theory of consciousness, to give characteristics of such semantic particles as symbol, word, man. The concept itself of a field turns out to contain the bi-unity through which it can be manifested. The field theory is the point in the reverse perspective of the World vision from which its bi-unity diverges.

6. It seems possible to assert that the structure of theoretical constructions in contemporary physics is gradually becoming open ended. Above (see Chapter 7) we quoted papers dealing with the conception of Time in the physics of the microworld. They are inconsistent. No single adequate reality can be selected from them by using a discriminating experiment. They cannot be reduced to a single general theory by deductive methods. Their value lies only in the fact that their irreducible variety helps physicists to sharpen their vision of the world. Something of the kind is taking place in the physics of elementary particles. There exist more than 200 models within it, many of which are conceptually contradictory. None of them can be rejected or applied as a single model explaining all the observed phenomena. The same is true of nuclear models. And one more thing seems to me especially important: it has become obvious by now that formal methods of constructing mathematical models themselves contain the necessity of presenting experimental results from several models, not from one (Nalimov, 1981*b*). The manifold of models to describe the same phenomenon again represents the propositions of the

open end. But it is far from being clear whether people are prepared for this intentionally incomplete vision of the world.

7. Historically, it was Kant (1929) who closely approached the dialectics of the open end in his *Critique of Pure Reason*, having formulated the antinomy of the cosmological idea based (though, to his mind, only in an imaginary way) on the principle of pure reason. In the *Prolegomenae* (1979) Kant says the following words on the nature of their antinomy:

> Diese nicht etwa beliebig erdachte, sondern in der Natur der menschlichen Vernunft gegründete, mithin unvermeidliche und niemals ein Ende nehmende Antinomie enthält nun folgende vier Sätze samt ihren Gegensätzen. (p. 95)
>
> (This antinomy, not invented, but based on the nature of human reason, and, therefore, endless and eternal, contains . . . four theses and their antitheses).

Below we quote these four antinomies in the exposed form they are given in the *Critique of Pure Reason* (Kant, 1929):

I

Thesis. The world has a beginning in time, and is also limited in regard to space.

Antithesis. The world has no beginning, and no limits in space, but is, in relation both to time and space, infinite.

II

Thesis. Every composite substance in the world consists of simple parts; and there exists nothing that is not either itself simple, or composed of simple parts.

Antithesis. No composite thing in the world consists of simple parts; and there does not exist in the world any simple substance.

III

Thesis. Casuality according to the laws of nature, is not the only casuality operating to originate the phenomena of the world. A casuality of freedom is also necessary to account fully for these phenomena.

Antithesis. There is no such thing as freedom, but everything in the world happens solely according to the laws of nature.

IV

Thesis. There exists either in, or in connection with the world—either as a part of it, or as the cause of it—an absolutely necessary being.

Antithesis. An absolutely necessary being does not exist, either in the world, or out of it—as its cause. (p. 266-284)

And now, 200 years later, we return to perceiving the world through these antinomies without attempting any longer to solve them. The vision of the world through mutually complementary principles, continuity and discreteness, means resorting to antinomy II. Recognizing two principles in human behavior, fated and free (see Chapter 2), is antinomy III clad in a Bayesian model. Acknowledgment of incompleteness, or conventionality, underlying our space-time ideas is an echo of antinomy I. And, at last, the vision of the world in its spontaneous harmony is, perhaps, a specific representation of antinomy IV.

If it is typical of human reason to perceive the world through antinomies, why not try to find a language in which these antinomies (formulated in this or that way) would act as mutually complementary principles. We seem to have developed a more flippant thinking: in contrast to Kant (*see Prolegomenae*, 1979, p. 104), we do not think any longer that cosmogonic antinomy confuses the reason.

8. The new language is constructed in probabilistic logic. Note that the Bayesian formula meets the basic requirements for syllogistics: from the two assertions *necessarily* follows the third one with the same structure. It now becomes possible to speak of the *Bayesian syllogism*. It may be regarded as a generalization of Aristotle's syllogism:[2] the initial premise loses the status of categorical judgments not only by force of its fuzziness but also by force of the fact that the second assertion proves conditional [$p(y|\mu)$ is the conditional function of the probability distribution responding to a particular situation y]. If in the Aristotelian syllogism the two initial assertions are linked by the common middle term, in the Bayesian syllogism all three assertions are linked by the same sematic field μ on which they are constructed. Whereas in the Aristotelian syllogism the inference is a logically clear assertion, in the Bayesian syllogism the inference is the redistribution of weights in the system of initial value concepts, determining the trend of thought on the logically structured level. Thus, it seems that the Bayesian syllogism, in contrast to the Aristotelian one, describes the processes taking place in the deep levels of consciousness and if it is possible to speak of thinking on the unconscious level, then its mechanism is nothing more than redistribution of the probability distribution function on the field of value concepts. Introduction of weights removes the requirement of consistency within the system of initial premises. The concept itself of antinomy proves to be void of its ordinary meaning.

---

[2] The term "syllogisms" (Greek Συλ-λογισμος) is more often than not applied to the categorical syllogism in which two initial categoric assertions linked by the common middle term yield the third judgment called an inference. Categorical judgment is an assertion of the absolute value independent of any conditions.

B. The World's Integrity and Human Participation in It

Proceeding from the language of dialectics of the open end, I have attempted to present the variety of world perceptions accumulated from ancient time in a single key, through the awareness of the unconscious. Trying to comprehend this experience, I, together with my colleagues, experienced it anew in the experiments of directed meditation. Thus we are trying to bind together the broken chain of succession: to speak about the old, long ago comprehended and forgotten things through the new.

1. Numerous terms have been proposed so far to denote the same phenomenon which we are now calling the *unconscious*, but various verbal clothes indicate that the authors of the terms ascribed preferential significance to the separate constituents of this boundlessly broad concept. Freud called it the *subconscious*; Jung, *collective unconscious*, James, *streams of consciousness* (a continuum of cosmic consciousness, in terms of James), Bucke, *cosmic consciousness*, Bergson, *insight*, Husserl, *transcendental phenomenology*, Whitehead, *category of eternal objects*, Popper, *the third world, the world of intelligibles*, Assagioli, *subpersonality*, Hegel, *self-developing spirit*, Plato, *the world of ideas*. Differences in the manifestations of the unconscious can be described by introducing the idea of multidimensional *psychological space*. This is again nothing more than a metaphor, but it is convenient in that it allows us to present various manifestations of the unconscious as its projections onto psychological subspaces of lesser dimensions. Freudian vulgar and all-embracing hypersexuality is nothing more than a projection of the entire variety of the psychological world onto a peculiarly chosen psychological subspace. However, we proceed here from the ideas of Plato: recall his "shadows in the cave." Perhaps the famous Oedipus complex was also a shadow in the cave of Freudian sexually traumatized consciousness.

2. From the familiar, though apophatic sounding, term "the unconscious" we pass to a metaphorically rich concept of *semantic field*. Human consciousness turns out to be a specific state of this field. Expanding the idea, we introduce the concept of *Semantic Universe* and *Nature* as its manifestation. *Semantic Vacuum* represents its unmanifested potentiality: it includes ancient concepts of Nothing, Nirvana, Fullness of Time.

3. The manifested semantic universe is seen by us as *structured not by logic, but by number*, as it had been expressed by Pythagoras and Plotinus. Such manifestations of world semantics as taxons of animals and plants, human individualities, and specific features of cultures may be said to be given by probability distribution functions constructed over

one and the same continuous semantic field. A vision of the World via the probability distribution functions is actually the numerical vision of the World. However, another thing is also of interest: according to modern ideas, the stability of the physical World and its fitness for the evolution of life is determined by the stability of numerical values of the so-called *fundamental physical constants*. The set of these constants may be said to be necessary and sufficient for the existence of our World. The existence of *principal states* — nuclei, atoms, stars, and galaxies — is possible only in this world (Rozental', 1980). This makes us feel that the Universe is dominated by the *principle of expediency*, or, in other words, that the numerical values of these constants have been biologically selected. Thus it turns out that from the concepts broadly accepted in modern physics (opposed by the "bootstrap" conception, mentioned in Chapter 1) it follows that the physical world is arranged through number.

4. In this book we were constantly asserting the similarity between our ideas and the physical vision of the world. However, there is also a significant, and perhaps even principal, difference between them. The Texts of physicists invariably contain Time. The physical world is revealed through wave processes stretched on the above-mentioned fundamental physical constants regulating them. The process of world existence — its expansion and collapses, passage through singularity and restoration — is also a wave process (Davies, 1977). The world of physical reality, from microcosm to macrocosm, is a huge oscillating hierarchy.

The world of semantics is quiet: it lacks both wave processes and constants arranging it. It is free in its peace. Its being is in its non-being. The probabilistic logic I have developed, based on an expanded interpretation of the Bayesian theorem, does not contain Time. The world of semantics is a world of a different order. Only when we describe its physical manifestation does there arise the necessity of introducing Time. The psychological Time is given by Doing realized in the world of physical reality. Time is divided into three categories — past, present, and future — only when in our description the two realities contact each other.

In other words, Time is the grammar of the language of the world containing a definite set of fundamental physical constants. The world of semantics is a metaworld; it is described in a language which does not contain any limiting constants and has no idea of the principal states. The semantic world is also arranged through number, but in a different manner than the physical world.

5. If we compare consciousness and brain activity, a certain analogy with a computer seems relevant. Logical constructions performed by a computer do not require for their comprehension the categories of space and time, though they are necessary for the description of the work of the computer. Watching the computer work, we see quite clearly that

logic cannot be described by motion, though it is produced by motion. Here logic is of interest for us because, taken independently, it is an extra-temporal reality. From what is said above it becomes evident that quantum-mechanical concepts can be applied to the description of brain activity but not to that of the semantic world which, like logic, is also an extra-temporal reality.

6. The analogy with logic is naturally far from being complete. Introducing the concept of the semantic field, we resort to the idea of *psychological space*. This is an abstract, *probabilistic* space on which not physical events, but only distribution functions, are localized. Earlier, for the sake of simplicity, we confined ourselves to the consideration of a one-dimensional semantic field. If this limitation is removed, the idea of the expanded consciousness typical for the state of meditation will be interpreted not only as a change in the distribution function, but much more significantly as an expansion of the dimensions of the semantic space. We can also pose the following question: in what way can a possible change in the metrics of the semantic space be interpreted? Perhaps this signifies an entrance into other semantic worlds, analogous to physics in which the coordinated change of the numerical values of the fundamental constants can be thought to produce another physical world.

Note that the meaning of *multidimensionality* of the semantic space can be revealed only by setting a probabilistic measure on it. If, for example, we pass from a one-dimensional space to a two-dimensional one, we get an opportunity to speak of a two-dimensional function of the probability distribution. There emerges a new parameter: coefficient of pair correlation linking two random variables μ_1 and μ_2 which characterize different, probabilistically related manifestations of the same personality. In a five-dimensional space, we shall naturally have to deal with a five-dimensional personality characterized by 10 pair correlation coefficients. We thus deepen the conception of doubles which we mentioned several times in Chapter 16. We would like to emphasize here that in our model the idea of the multi-dimensional Ego appears after we start to consider the probabilistic space emerging after the introduction of a probabilistic measure.

The multidimensional nature of a personality proves to be the manifestation of its fullness: its individual manifestations, acquiring the character of the doubles, act as mutually complementary elements. Actually, sometimes versatility seems to have only one side, and then it may frighten and repel us. For example, Nietzsche's brilliantly expressive *Also sprach Zarathustra* repels many readers (this is what happened to me in my youth). However, *Zarathustra* is but one of Nietzsche's doubles which allowed him to see a lot of things with striking clarity. We can comprehend many things only after having identified ourselves with this, only after feeling this as part of ourselves. We can go even further and take a risk of asserting Judas to be a double of Christ. During the Last Supper Christ told Judas, "What you are going to do, do quickly" (John 13:27).

Tillich (1951–63) discussed the problem, quite painful for Christianity, which was once posed by Kierkegaard: can a man sacrifice himself for the sake of the truth? Acting in this way, he becomes responsible for those who sacrificed him. This is perhaps also true of Christ and his permission to Judas, one of his closest disciples, to betray him. However, if metaphorically Judas is but Christ's double, this problem loses its poignancy.

The passage into the depths of one's unconscious represents the expansion of one's consciousness which is often accompanied by such a distinct personalization of one's doubles that the latter are given individual names. For example, Jung (1965) personalized his interaction with the unconscious by three figures: the masculine figure of Elijah, an old man with a white beard; the feminine anima, the young blind girl Salome; and the Black Serpent, the hero's double often occurring in myths. Jung, a psychiatrist, made the following remark:

> It is of course ironical that I, a psychiatrist, should at almost every step of my experiment have run into the same psychic material which is the stuff of psychosis and is found in the insane. This is the fund of unconscious images which fatally confuse the mental patient. But it is also the matrix of a mythopoetic imagination which has vanished from our rational age. (p. 188)
>
> The years when I was pursuing my inner images were the most important in my life—in them everything essential was decided. It all began then; the later details are only supplements and clarifications of the material that burst forth from the unconscious, and at first swamped me. It was the *prima materia* for a lifetime's work. (p. 199)

Note that in the literature devoted to the experience of expanding consciousness, one constantly comes across the indications of meeting spiritual (non-materialized) guides. This again can be interpreted as an expansion of the semantic space of one's personality accompanied by the projection of one's double onto a separate spiritual essence. However, are many of those who dared expand their personality able to preserve their unity in the variety of their experience (what Jung *was* able to do) without disintegrating into numerous independent illusory superrealities?

Above we several times spoke of astral epidemics causing mass social phenomena of a spontaneous nature whose manifestations are irrational and thus remain inexplicable. Here we could refer to such harmless phenomena as a fashion for specific behavior and such disasters as wars, or

Nazism. One of the possible explanations of these phenomena is the idea of the reanimation of latent double states whose roots go back into the ethnogenetic or even phylogenetic human past.

This naturally poses a question of the possible dimensions of the semantic space. Enumerate the coordinate axes of this space by the series of natural numbers and assume the possibility of different semantic loading of these axes. Consider all the possible subspaces of this set of axes. Each subset creates a personality (or hyperpersonality) of a definite image. The set of such personalities will have the power of a continuum (recall that a continuum is the power of all the subsets of natural numbers). The *image*[3] that is thus formed is that of inserted lattices of semantic (or, if you like, psychological) spaces leaving the boundaries of common notions. This image is versatile: it reflects both our idea of the *ultimate reality* and that of the *illusory nature of a personality*, as well as, however, of its participation in the *whole*.

This may seem grotesque. But, wishing to perceive the world as transfinite in its potentiality, we cannot act otherwise. The numerical description of the world has its own logic. The world of the psyche cannot be finite in the numerical description: We do not know how to choose the border number. Ancient thinkers avoided this difficulty by introducing the sacred numbers 3, 7, 8, 12, and even 360 (gnostics). Transfinite analysis may lead to a mythic image of the human psyche. However, the mathematics may be a revealing clue about the potential complexity of human personality.

7. In my earlier book (Nalimov, 1981a) an attempt was made to reveal the probabilistic mechanism of comprehending verbal meanings which we use on the deep levels of consciousness. Here another step forward is made: the grammar of the probabilistic comprehension proved transferred on the surface level of our consciousness. This provoked the emergence of a language enabling us at least partially to comprehend the unconscious. And while physical models are metaphors, ours is but a hint.

[3] Here we make use of highly abstract mathematical notions to form an image elucidating the psychological reality. The power of the set A is such that its property is inherent to any equally powerful set B. Two sets are considered equally powerful if their elements are in a mutual one-to-one correspondence. For example, it may be readily shown that the sets of all the points of spaces R^n (R is the set of all real numbers, n is a natural number) have the power of a continuum. At the same time, there can exist sets which may be regarded both in abstract and semantic aspects. Grünbaum (1962) emphasized Russell's statement that

> . . . there are continuous manifolds, such as that of colors (in the physicist's sense of spectral frequencies), in which the individual elements differ qualitatively from one another and have inherent magnitude, thus allowing for metrical comparison of the elements themselves (p. 16)

Here color acts as a semantics, psychologically given on the limitless variety. Note that this semantics proves to be different for different cultures.

8. Our approach allows us to discover the psychological premises of *solipsism* (from the Latin *solus*, the unique, and *ipse*, self), the philosophical teaching asserting that the reality of the world is contained in the consciousness of the thinking individual. This latter, in its consistent form, used always to arouse the amazement of many scholars. Recall Schopenhauer's assertion that complete solipsists could be found only among the inhabitants of an asylum. As a matter of fact, solipsism is nothing more than an awkward attempt brought about by the persistent desire to express the inwardly felt idea of the world integrity in the language of European philosophy. If we reject rigid personalization and start regarding individuals only as formations conditioned by sliding probability distribution functions given on the semantic field single for the whole animate Nature, then even the ideas of extreme solipsism are no longer perceived as an absurdity. It was Fichte who to a certain extent approached the possibility of such comprehension: in his *science-teaching* he asserted that individual Ego in the long run coincided with self-realization of the consciousness of the whole of mankind. But even this deficient conception of holisticity was hard to make comprehensible. The acutely felt awareness of *integrity* in which everyone is the carrier of all could in no way break through the language sieve of Western thought of modern time. It became a caricature.

9. The idea of the temporal integrity of consciousness was specifically reflected in the philosophical hermeneutics of Ricoeur [his views are compactly described by Rasmussen (1971)]. If we recognize that the principal task of philosophy is the study of man, then, according to Ricoeur, this task can be accomplished by interpreting the mythosymbolic language, which is of an extra-temporal nature. The symbolics of the myth is immanent in man and invariant with respect to the variety of its cultural manifestations. Ricoeur, analyzing myths, tried to comprehend the nature of evil as a human facet.

My approach, in contrast to philosophical anthropology, presupposes the analysis of myths and symbols borrowed not from the historical past but from the depths of consciousness of contemporary man, which is natural and legitimate from the viewpoint of the transpersonal nature of symbols.

Discussing the mechanism of interpreting texts, Ricoeur emphasizes the fact that this is the process of self-interpretation and self-cognition. In my approach, the mechanism of interpreting texts consists in generating within the depths of consciousness individual filters $p(y|\mu)$ determining personal values on the semantic field μ with respect to the text y. The dynamics of the evolution of values reveals the deep levels of consciousness.

Also significant is the proposition of Ricoeur stating that the symbol gives rise to an idea which, brought to its limit, in its turn generates another symbol. This cyclic process can be illustrated by my work, which started with mythosymbolic constructions obtained in experiments subjected to logical analysis and was completed by philosophical constructions made in the language of new symbols—probabilistic structures. The ideas of Ricoeur are naturally linked with the phenomenology of Husserl. Husserl would call my experimental research *archaeology* of meaning, since it made excavations in the depths of consciousness.

10. One may ask: in what way is the integrity of consciousness manifested in human physiology? We are not ready to answer this question in detail. The mechanisms of the interaction of nerve nets responsible for conscious activity remain mysterious as yet. This is true not only of humans but also of animals, whose memory mechanism is still unrevealed. Here two approaches can be mentioned. One of them is *localizational*: information is believed to be located in definite cells. This enables the researcher to regard the human brain as a biocomputer. Despite a number of experimental facts which seem to support this approach, it is hard to imagine how a brain, being only a biological device, can cope with the accuracy and speed which is typical of a computer.[4] The other approach is *distributive* (it stems from the widely known papers by Karl Spencer Lashley): it regards information as being distributed over a large area of nerve nets so that information relating to different events intersects in each local point. This approach comes close to the modern holographic theory of transpersonal consciousness (Anderson, 1977), holographic memory theory (Pietsch, 1981), and the ideas of Bohm (Bohm and Welwood, 1980) on the holographic theory of the universe. The distributive approach is further developed by Cooper and Impert (1981), who base their work on both new experimental data and its mathematical analysis. Perhaps my approach, proceeding from the interaction of distribution functions, will also be supported and applied physiologically?

C. Questioning as a Revelation of the Semantic Universe

1. *Questioning* is the interaction of knowledge included in the assertive part of the *question* with the knowledge to which the question is addressed. The progress of science goes through the hierarchy of questions. The arrangement is regulated by hypotheses that allow the researchers to formulate meaningfully the assertive part of the questions. In my earlier

---

[4] The well-known book by Lilly (1974) is an odd attempt to present a human being as an automaton acting according to a bioprogram.

book (Nalimov, 1981*b*) I tried to show that a mathematical model in science was nothing more than a question posed to Nature by the researcher. In contemporary physics the concept of a *device*, or instrument, is revealed through its identification with a question:

> A device is none other than the materialized "question" of consciousness, the "question" addressed to the external object. As a result of interaction between the object and device we get an answer to the question (an answer reflecting the relation of the object to the device, and, in the long run, to ourselves). (Grib, 1980)

Note that, whereas in the early stages of scientific progress Instruments (e.g., Galileo's telescope) were merely enhancements of the human senses and capacities, modern instruments, such as a radio telescope probing a neutron star, are devices with a substantial knowledge of physics implicitly built in. The instrument contains knowledge put in it by scientific theories. In a scientific experiment this knowledge interacts with that of the external world.

A model based on the Bayesian theorem, as was cursorily mentioned above (in Chapter 8), can also be regarded as a formulation of a question, emerging under the conditions of fuzzy semantics. Then $p(y|\mu)$ is the assertive part of the question proper addressed to the initial knowledge $p(\mu)$, and $p(\mu|y)$ is the answer. In probabilistic semantics the Bayesian formula can act both as a syllogism and a question. This accounts for the unique significance of this formula.

The semantic universe is revealed through questions posed to it. A human being proves to be the psychosomatic device by means of which questioning is materialized and turns into Doing.

Man is a carrier of both types of knowledge: that to which the question is related and that which is contained in the question. Knowledge (or information) is a piece of selective manifestation.

Man regarded as a selective manifestation of the semantic field is also knowledge. This knowledge is dialectical. Its dialectical nature is manifested through our free will which allows us to choose freely what knowledge a question should contain.

Thus man turns out to be a unique device possessing free will. And free will is the fire cast upon the world.

D. Continuum—a Model for Semantic Integrity: an Urge to Divide the Continuum— a Model for a Conflict

The concept of the semantic continuum is a model for semantic integrity of the World. The incessant desire to split the continuum gives rise to conflicts which are the moving force of history.

To elaborate this idea, I am going to consider, at least in an obviously simplified form, the mathematical outlook of splitting the continuum.

If we are not afraid of metaphorical argumentation, the Dedekind axiom of continuity can be interpreted as follows. According to this axiom, when splitting the continuum we must indicate the point of division, not the interval between the discrete points, as can be done when a discrete series is split. The division point can be referred either to one subset or to the other: it is the upper bound of one subset and the lower bound of the other. This is exactly what happened when we dichotomously divided good and evil, truth and falsity, idealism and materialism. The main trouble was to find the place for the dividing point: its reference to one or the other of the divided parts confused the entire reasoning. Then another dividing point was being looked for, and the same happened. At last, the problem was solved by the auto-da-fe.

Further elaboration of the ideas of splitting the continuum is the theorem by Sierpinski asserting that ". . . no continuum can be decomposed into the union of the countable family of disjoint closed[5] sets." At the same time we know that the union of two continua having a common point is a continuum.

Now let us turn to humans. Man, on the logically structured level of his activity, invariably turns to isolated, clear-cut semantic blocks out of which opposing concepts are constructed. These blocks cannot have common semantic points; otherwise the law of the excluded middle, one of the major laws of Aristotelian logic, could not have been fulfilled.

Wishing to refine his outlook, man invariably tends to further delimit himself from the opposing conception (or, on a broad scale, ideology). Such a demarcation from the viewpoint of formal logic (proceeding from the discretely given semantics) may become clear-cut only when both outlooks are represented as two logically well-elaborated and opposing conceptions. But any conceptualization is based on a division of the semantic field into opposing concepts (closed subsets, as a mathematician would say), and this actually gives rise to still new common points, which in no way strengthens his position but, on the contrary, weakens it. Thus any refinement proves to be fraught with self-destruction. From the viewpoint of a metaobserver, all of human history with its ceaseless ideological oppositions is a vain attempt to overcome the impossibility of splitting the continuum into disjoint closed semantic sets. To solve this problem, people had always to resort to Power. But human consciousness, due to its participation in the semantic continuum, is still uncontrollable:

> The human mind is not meant to be governed, certainly not by any

[5] A closed set in a topological space is a set containing its limit points. Roughly speaking, it is a set containing its boundary. Here is an instance of a closed set: segment $[a,b]$ containing its initial and final points; a set consisting of a finite number of points, etc.

book of rules yet written; it is supposed to run itself, and we are
obliged to follow it along, trying to keep up with it as best we can.
(Thomas, 1980)

We might say, if a bit too schematically, that a person posing a question, on the unconscious level gets an answer as a probabilistically given preference function constructed on the semantic continuum. Then conceptualization takes place on the conscious, logically structured level: the continuum is cut into separate blocks corresponding to the maximum probability concentration. Clear-cut conceptualization oppositions create the polarization without which the passionate temperament of individuals (passionarity[6] in the terminology of Gumilev, 1979) that provides society with its energy could not have been realized. But a person is never separated from his unconscious: the latter sooner or later liberates the person from the power of what it has generated on the conscious level.

Let us consider as an illustration one of the episodes of the Middle Ages, the Crusades. There the polarization was distinct: two worlds, of Christianity and Islam, were sharply opposed. Each of them knew for sure what and where the evil was, the unconditional evil.

However, even then there seemed to emerge doubts as to the legitimacy of the polarization. Here is an example:

The knights of the Templar order crossed their swords with the warriors of the Moslem order of Assassins. The former were in white clothes, with red crosses on them, the latter—also in white clothes, but with red belts. Not only was this resemblance striking, but also the complete congruence of the *structure* of the orders and their *teachings.* (Sède, 1962)

How could this be discovered! And, when discovered, it perhaps gave impetus to the seven-year trial (1307–1314) which was the first of all the subsequent ideological–political trials. The emotional furor echoed down the ages.

The quotation cited below emphasizes the striking similarity of the two opposing visions of the world:

The principal source of the acrimony underlying the Christian-Moslem relationship is a historical equivalent of sibling rivalry. Christians somehow hate to admit that in many ways their faith stands closer to Islam than to any other world religion . . . Both faiths are the offspring of an earlier revelation through the Law and the Prophets to the people of Israel. Both honor the Virgin Mary and Jesus of Nazareth. Both received an enormous early impetus from an

---

[6] We are apt to ascribe mythological significance to passionarity, explaining the emergence of the high level of energy that makes actions passionate as the result of collision with invisible carriers of energy (see p. 53).

apostle—Paul for Christianity and Muhammed for Islam—who translated a particularistic vision into a universal faith. The word "Allah" . . . is not an exclusively Moslem term at all. It is merely the Arabic word for God, and is used by Arabic Christians when they refer to the God of Christian faith. (Cox, 1981)

Imagine for a moment that at the height of the struggle between the two religions, during the Crusades, there appeared a metaobserver–Logician who would say (in the contemporary language):

. . . What is the meaning of your fight? Your faiths are based on the same thing: indivisible semantic field. The two preference functions dividing you are not very much separated from each other on this field. What you regard as opposition are merely different weights ascribed to various areas of this field, the latter being such that no logical operations can be deduced from it.[7]

The Logician, extinguisher of passionarity, would have been reckoned as a heretic in both religions despite the fact that both cultures are far from being alien to logic.

From the viewpoint of a metaobserver, passionarity looks like an obsession. But, without it, persons or nations might lose their energy. And what happens then? Slackness seeks comforts (which a passionary does not need) or starts resorting to external stimulants. In a society void of passionarity, its islands keep emerging constantly, and they are often perceived as instances of senseless aggression on the verge of madness. But if passionarity is invariably suppressed in the bud what will follow? We must acknowledge passionarity to be immanent to people. A selective manifestation of the whole, man tends to discover the entrance for the selectivity and thus acquires energy.

Western culture originated from the myth of the Fall. There are many different interpretations of this myth. But it immediately gains the status of the basic premise of culture if we view it as the urge toward dichotomous splitting which makes actions passionate, in contrast to the more contemplative societies of the Orient. To eat from the tree of good and evil is to pose a question aimed at dividing the whole into parts. The dichotomous pair "good–evil" turned into a symbol of behavior inscribed on the banner of European culture. The temptation of questioning was called the Fall, the temptation which made Adam a person able to act. Recently, a Catholic theologian told me that the greatest victory of the devil in our time was that he made people believe he did not exist. This is a curious instance of the dialectics of Christian thinking: the urge toward division was called the Fall, and its rejection, the devil's victory. Thus,

---

[7] The requirement of σ-algebra entering the axiomatics of probability theory.

quite suddenly and despite the original myth, the rejection of division has become a devil's intention.

So, what is the meaning of History? We only know that History is generated by the right and faculty of people to pose questions to the semantic universe and to transform the responses obtained, through their logical comprehension, into discrete concepts which sometimes take the shape of personalized images. Then History starts to resemble Demonology.

History as a Game again represents the dialectics of the open end, generated by the opposition of the unconscious and the logically structured. The indivisibility of one level semantically manifested through probabilistic weighting given on the integrity of the whole is opposed by the endless attempts to divide. The perpetual interaction of these two essences generates an exciting game situation.

Perhaps the boundless urge toward dividing the indivisible, and each time anew, can be likened to the image of many-armed Dancing Siva. But why are we involved in this game?

Mentally we can imagine the possible exit from this game: it is represented by the culture of the probabilistic vision of the world. In Chapter 1, I attempted to show that such culture must not necessarily become that of Non-doing. But rejection of dividing may give birth to emotional extinction. History, or at least the history of the Western World, cannot be imagined without this division. On the other hand, the progress of technology seems to necessitate the smoothing of game situations.

I would like to conclude this section by the quotation from Wittgenstein (1955):

> The sense of the world must lie outside the world. In the world everything is as it is and happens as it does happen. In it there is no value—and if there were, it would be of no value. (6.41)

E. What Is the Meaning of Everything Said Above?

1. My probabilistic model remains and must remain an open-ended model. Like any realistic model, it does not actually explain anything but only reconciles us to the observed facts (e.g., Grof's records do not any longer seem scientifically impossible), and, what is most important, it makes us face the new mysteries of life. No knowledge can or should reveal all the mysteries. On the contrary, behind the old mysteries of the world we should be able to discern new, more profound ones. If there *is* progress of true knowledge, it lies here. All the rest is the mastery of the World. Science itself stops caring only for the mastery of the world when

it not so much explains facts as makes us face new, inexplicable facts. Perhaps this accounts for the attractiveness of contemporary physics.

2. Completing this work, I notice with amazement that everything said above is nothing more than a response to what had earlier been said in the Bhagavad-gita, and then by the gnostics, Plotinus,[8] Eckhart, Boehme, Leibniz, Kant, Jung, Tillich, and partly by Heidegger, though I have not planned this book as to be a response to these ideas. Strange as it may seem, the chain of succession unites thinkers seemingly quite alien to one another. It is noteworthy that Plotinus is followed only by German philosophers.

3. Now we see quite distinctly that the first thinker of modern time in European culture who paid attention to the unconscious was Kant, not Freud. Kant's idea of the a priori given categories and forms of sensual perception is directly addressed to the unconscious. But Kant was a logician, not a psychologist, and his ponderous reasoning was incomprehensible for psychologists. Nowadays it has become clear that the observations made by Kant can be expanded. What is given to us a priori is not rigidly fixed in our unconscious. We know that the concept of Time may be radically different in different countries. Moreover, in our own culture it proved to be flexible enough to enable physicists to produce its various images. The category of causality also turned out to be less rigid than it had been assumed to be in Kant's epoch. After twenty centuries of resistance, it allowed Europeans to develop a probabilistic vision of the world; as for the East, this category seems to have never been all-embracing there. This category in its absolute form exists only in primitive cultures with their magic vision of the world.

4. At the same time, the concept of Time as a form of sensual contemplation of the world seems to be firmly and deeply imprinted in our consciousness. But also deep is the human urge to live through the Fullness of Time and come close to Ultimate Reality (in terms of Tillich). Therefore, people are open to perceive the idea of Nothing. This idea is one of the greatest gains of mankind. Its meaning lies in the idea that we must feel the integrity of the world in its depths which remain unmanifested in time.

5. The major part of what has been said in this book may be regarded as the elaboration of ideas implicitly contained in the following four basic postulates:

• The certainty that man is a specific psychosomatic device interacting with a reality inaccessible for physical devices.

[8] The fragment of Bhagavad-Gita quoted as the epigraph to this chapter strikingly resembles assertions by Plotinus concerning the holisticity of the world manifested in its manifoldness through the numerical distribution (see Chapter 4 of this book).

- The idea of existence of the semantic field (axiom of the continuous nature of consciousness).
- Describing the semantic world without the category of Time.
- The idea that theoretico-probabilistic description of semantic phenomena can be qualitative. (In a broad context it is possible to say that there is an axiom asserting that mathematics can be used only metaphorically to simulate the semantic World.)

6. Naturally this book does not exhaust the contents of the above postulates, but I am not going to discuss this here. I consider another thing more important than that, namely, to consider alternatives of our axiomatics. The third axiom can evidently be rejected, as other linguistic means can be sought for expanding the axiom of continuous nature. Perhaps, quantum logic can be made use of (Grib, 1980)—it is also directed at describing one manifestation of the World in the opposition "continuous versus discrete." The description of the unconscious made in this language, if meaningful at all, will naturally look different from mine, since the world will be perceived through Time, and then it will be necessary to discover in this world the fundamental constants determining its stability. We shall have to find the analogues for such fundamental principles of quantum mechanics as the principle of superposition and the principle of identity. If someone finds my interpretation of the second axiom absolutely unacceptable he will naturally have to turn to the only possible alternative: the axiom of discrete consciousness. However, this latter is nothing more than representation of consciousness as a biocomputer—it is not fruitful in any way. A radical solution would be an axiomatics ignoring the opposition "discrete versus continuous" in consciousness. But how can this be done? An analogy with geometry seems relevant. The fifth postulate in Euclidean axiomatics had always provoked distrust. At last two alternatives emerged: the geometry of Riemann and that of Lobachevsky. But the radical solution was an emergence of the new geometry, topology—a structure of axioms ignoring the problem of parallel lines. However, Euclid and Riemann, one of the founders of topology, are separated by a whole epoch, roughly speaking by twenty centuries.

7. My approach on the whole is one more attempt to revive *natural philosophy*,[9] directing it toward viewing the world through the entire rich experience acquired by humanity. The structures of natural philosophy

---

[9] Natural philosophy is the application of scientific ideas for the speculative (not directly comparable by experiment) interpretation of nature in its holisticity. In the epoch of the Renaissance, Bruno, Campanella, Cardano, and Paracelsus were natural philosophers; later, Schelling attempted to generalize contemporary natural science in this key. Natural philosophic theories close to our time are the theory of emergent evolution, the holistic philosophy of Whitehead, biocosmism of Vernadsky, and the theocosmism of Teilhard de Chardin.

have never lost their attractiveness, but it is becoming more and more difficult to construct them because the experience of human interaction with the world is increasing, as well as its conceptual formulation. If it is possible at all to seize at one glance, it can be done only in old age. The structures of natural philosophy are always open to criticism since they try to embrace too much and therefore simplify and schematize things. Stern science cannot forgive any simplification and thus dooms itself to division. And so division, as preservation of purity, becomes the principle of scientific knowledge, which forbids natural philosophy. But if this prohibition is not violated, now can a *Weltanschauung* coordinated with science be possible?

8. So what is the meaning of all that has been said in this book? We are listening to the sounding of the world. The rhythm of the Universe is the Liturgy of the World. The rhythm of revealing ideas. The cyclic change of cultures. And again, as in the olden days, we have apocalyptic visions: if we are ready to accept singularity in cosmological solutions of Einstein's gravitational equations as a specific state of the world when the density of matter and space–time curvature become infinite and the matter compressed into a super-hot point, then in the semantic world, in the days when culture collapses, the continuum of ideas also seems to be compressed into a single point. And when the field of ideas is compressing to a point, the measure of value for these ideas, expressed by the probability distribution function, tightens to a straight line, forming for the probability density the infinite splash of singular intensity[10] (by force of the normalizing condition, the area under the curve is to be unity).

The unrevealed potentiality into which the entire past and future are compressed becomes extremely important. And the point of compression itself becomes extremely hot and ready for a new explosive revelation through the emergence of a new probabilistic space. Preparing ourselves intensively for the new, we want to see it through the old and eternal embodied in our consciousness, and in the history of our cultures—not only in what has been realized but in their unrealized, romantic tendencies. We wish to see how what we now see as non-real, compressed into a point, will open up in the probabilistic spaces. That is the meaning of all that was said above.

The entire past of mankind was invariably accompanied by an *expansion of the life space*. Rome, the world Empire, spread throughout the world two opposing principles which determined the dynamics of culture

---

[10] Mathematically, we record this as $\delta(x) = 0$, when $x \neq 0$ and $\delta(0) = \infty$, and by force of normalization

$$\int_{-\infty}^{+\infty} \delta(x)\, dx = 1$$

(We are dealing here with Dirac's δ-function, as a physicist would say).

—Aristotelian logic borne by Hellenism and the religious mysticism of Judeo-Christianity. The discovery of America enabled the emergence of what seemed impossible in the Old World, and colonialism completed Roman tendencies—it drew the entire variety of cultures into one orbit. As a completion, the conquest of Space is under way in the urge to make it also fit for dwelling. In contrast, we see the *new* as an expansion of the space for *human existence*—the entrance into new psychological spaces. But is our consciousness mature enough not to pollute these new spaces?

References

Abel R.   Language and the electrone. *Akten des XIV. Internationalen Kongresses für Philosophie*, 2–9 September 1968, Vienna. Vienna: Herder & Co., 1969. p. 351–6.

Alleau R.   *La science des symboles*. Paris: Payot, 1976. 292 p.

Allen M, Gawain Sh & Bernoff N.   *Reunion; tools for transformation*. Berkeley, CA: Whatever Pub., 1978. 77 p.

Anderson R M.   A holographic model of transpersonal psychology. *The Journal of Transpersonal Psychology*, 9:119–28, 1977.

Annales Historiques de la Revolution Française.   Sommaire: la Franc-Maconnerie et la révolution française. 197:373–539, 1969.

Appel K E.   Religion. (Arieti S, ed.) *American handbook of psychiatry*. New York: Basic Books, 1959. v. II.

Assagioli R.   *Psychosynthesis*. New York: Viking Press, 1971. 323 p.

Bal'mont K D.   *Zmeinye tsvety* (Serpent's flowers). Moscow: Scorpion, 1910. 248 p.

Bal'mont K D.   *Krai Ozirisa* (The land of Osiris). Moscow: Kushnerov Publ., 1914. 323 p.

Bakhtin M M.   *Tvorchestvo Fransua Rable i narodnaya kul'tura srednevekov'ya i Renessansa* (Works by Fransua Rablé and folk culture of the Middle Ages and the Renaissance). Moscow: Khudozhestvennaya literatura, 1965. 525 p.

Barbarin G.   *Le secret de la grande pyramide ou la fin du monde adamique*. Paris: J'ai Lu, 1969. 192 p.

Bardo thödol.   (Evans-Wentz W Y, ed.) *The Tibetan Book of the dead*. New York: Oxford Univ. Press, 1960. 249 p.

Bellah R N.   *Beyond belief; essays on religion in post-traditional world*. New York: Harper & Row, 1976. 298 p.

Belyi A.   *Simvolizm; kniga statei* (Symbolism; collection of articles). Moscow: Musaget, 1910. 633 p.

Berdyaev N.   *Samopoznanie; opyt filosofskoi avtobiografii* (Self-knowledge; an experience of philosophical autobiography). Paris: YMCA Press, 1949. 377 p.

Berg L S.   *Nomogenesis; or evolution determined by law*. Cambridge, MA: MIT Press, 1969. 477 p.

Bernshtein N A.   Na putyakh k biologii aktivnosti (On the way to biology of activity). *Voprosy Filosofii* 10:65–78, 1965.

Blavatsky H P.   *Isis unveilled: a master-key to the Mysteries of ancient and modern science and theology*. New York: J. W. Bouton, 1877. 2 vols.

301

Blavatsky H P.   *An abridgment of the secret doctrine.* Wheaton, IL: Theosophical Publishing House, 1966. 260 p.

Blokhintsev D I.   *Printsipial'nye voprosy kvantovoi mekhaniki* (Principal problems of quantum mechanics). Moscow: Nauka, 1966. 159 p.

Boas G.   The fixation of symbols. (Bryson L, Finkelstein L, Maciver R M, McKeon R, eds.) *Conference on Science, Philosophy and Religion in Their Relation to the Democratic Way of Life.* 13th. Symbols and values: an initial study. September 1952, New York. New York: Harpers, 1954. p. 215-28.

Boehme J.   *The signature of all things, and other writings.* London: James Clarke & Co., 1969. 295 p.

Böhlig A & Wisse, F, eds.   *Nag Hammadi codices, III, 2 and IV, 2: The gospel of the egyptians* (the holy book of the great invisible spirit). Leiden: Brill, 1975. 236 p.

Bohm D.   *Wholeness and the implicate order.* London: Routledge & Kegan Paul, 1980. 224 p.

Bohm D & Welwood J.   Issues in physics, psychology and metaphysics: conversations. *The Journal of Transpersonal Psychology* 12:25-36, 1980.

Boldyreva S A.   Reflection of hallucinations in the drawings of schizophrenic children of preschool age. *Zhurnal Nevropatologii i Psikhiatrii* 69:1575-80, 1969.

Boldyreva S A.   *Risunki detei doshkol'nogo vozrasta, bol'nykh shizofreniei* (Pictures by children under school age suffering from schizophrenia). Moscow: Meditsina, 1974. 159 p.

Boon H, Davrou Y & Macquet.   *La sophrologie, une révolution en psychologie, pedagogue, medicine?* Paris: Retz-C.E.P.L., 1976. 256 p.

Boorstein S.   Troubled relationship: transpersonal and psychoanalytic approaches. *The Journal of Transpersonal Psychology* 11:129-40, 1979.

Born M.   *Natural philosophy of cause and chance.* Oxford, England: Clarendon Press, 1949. 215 p.

Bregman L.   Spiritual dimensions to psychotic experience. *The Journal of Transpersonal Psychology* 11:59-74, 1979.

Brink T L.   Flying dreams: the relationship of creativeness, handedness, and locus of control factors. *Journal of Altered States of Consciousness* 5:152-7, 1979/80.

Browne P F.   Arbitrariness of geometry at the aether. *Foundations of Psychics* 6:457-71, 1976.

Brune J.   Idéologie de la demythisation. (Castelli E, ed.) *Demythisation et idéologie*: actes du colloque organisé par le Centre international d'études philosophiques de Rome. 4-9 janvier 1973, Rome. Paris: Aubier, 1973. p. 405-19.

Brushlinsky A V.   *Myshlenie i prognozirovanie* (Thinking and forecasting). Moscow: Mysl', 1979. 229 p.

Bryson L, Finkelstein L, Maciver R M & McKeon R, eds.   *Conference on Science, Philosophy and Religion in Their Relation to the Democratic Way of Life.* 13th. Symbols and values: an initial study. September 1952. New York. New York: Harpers, 1954. 827 p.

Budge Sir E A T W.   *Book of the dead* (The papyrus of Ani). New York: Dover Publications, 1967. Vol. 6-8.

Bulgakov S.   *Filosofiya imeni* (Philosophy of name). Paris: YMCA Press, 1953. 278 p.

Burtt E A.   *In search of philosophic understanding.* New York: American Library, 1965. 329 p.

Capek M.   Relativity and the status of becoming. *Foundations of Physics* 5:607-17, 1975.

Capra F.   *The Tao of physics.* Boulder, CO: Shambhala, 1975. 330 p.

Capra F.   Modern physics and eastern mysticism. *The Journal of Transpersonal Psychology* 8:20-39, 1976.

Cassirer E. *The philosophy of symbolic forms*. New Haven: Yale University Press, 1957. 3 vols.

Castañeda C. *The teaching of Don Juan: a Yaqui way of knowledge*. New York: Simon & Schuster, 1968. 288 p.

Castañeda C. *A separate reality; further conversations with Don Juan*. New York: Simon & Schuster, 1971. 317 p.

Castañeda C. *Journey to Ixtlan: the lessons of Don Juan*. New York: Simon & Schuster, 1972. 315 p.

Castañeda C. *Tales of power*. New York: Simon & Schuster, 1974. 287 p.

Charpentier L. *The mysteries of Chartres Cathedral*. Wellingborough, England: Thorsons, 1972. 190 p.

Chavchanidze V V. K voprosu o prostranstvenno-vremennykh kvantovo-volnovykh protsessakh v nervnoi sisteme (On the problem of time-spatial quantum-wave processes in the nervous system). *Soobshchenie Akademii Nauk Gruzinskoi SSR* 59:37–40, 1970.

Chavchanidze V V. K kvantovo-volnovoi teorii kogerentnoi modeli mozga (On the problem of quantum-wave theory for a coherent model of brain). (Berg A I & Braines S N, eds.) *Progress biologicheskoi i meditsinskoi kibernetiki*. Moscow: Meditsina, 1974. 486 p.

Chekhov M A. *Put' aktera* (To the actor on the technique of acting). New York: Harper, 1953. 201 p.

Chew G F. "Bootstrap": a scientific idea? *Science* 161:762–5, 1968.

Chitrabhanu G S. *The psychology of enlightenment: meditation on the seven energy centers*. New York: Dodd, Mead, 1979. 91 p.

Chudakov V N. *Fiziko-matematicheskie osnovy teorii myshleniya* (Physical and mathematical principles in theory of thinking). Khar'kov: Khar'kov Univ., 1977. Part I.

Colodny R G, ed. *Paradigms and Paradoxes*. Pittsburgh: University of Pittsburgh Press, 1972. 446 p.

Cooper J C. *An illustrated encyclopedia of traditional symbols*. London: Thames & Hudson, 1978. 208 p.

Cooper L N & Impert M. Seat of memory. *The Sciences* 21:10–3; 28–9, 1981.

Corney C. My sister, my self. The secret language of identical twins. *Washington Post* 17 July 1979, p. B1; B11.

Cox H. Understanding Islam. *Atlantic Monthly* 247:73–80, 1981.

Davies P C. *Space and time in the modern universe*. Cambridge: Cambridge Univ. Press, 1977. 232 p.

Dawkins R. *Selfish Gene*. London: Oxford Univ. Press, 1976. 224 p.

Denisov L. *Zhytie prepodobnogo otsa nashego Serafima Sarovskogo* (Life of Saint Seraphyme Sarovsky). Moscow: Stupin Publ. House, 1904. 206 p.

Dinkler E. *Signum crucis. Aufsätze zum Neuen Testament und zur christlichen Archäologie*. Tübingen: Mohr, 1967. 403 p.

Dinkler E. Beobachtungen zur Ikonographie des Kreuzes in der nubischen Kunst. (Michałowski K, ed.) *Colloque nubiologique international, 2d, Musée national de Varsovie, 1972*. Nubia: récentes recherches: 19–22 juin 1972, Varsovie. Varsovie: Musée national, 1975. p. 22–9.

Dolgin, J L, Kemnitzer D S & Schneider D M, eds. *Symbolic anthropology: a reader in the study of symbols and meanings*. New York: Columbia Univ. Press, 1977. 523 p.

Doob L W. *Patterning of time*. New Haven: Yale University Press, 1971. 472 p.

Dostoevsky F M. *Prestuplenie i nakazanie* (Crime and punishment). Moscow: Nauka, 1970. 808 p.

Duffey G H. Tachyons and superluminal wave groups. *Foundations of Physics* 5:349–54, 1975.

Dusen W Van.   Hallucination as the world of spirits. (White J, ed.) *Frontiers of consciousness*. New York: Julian Press, 1974. p. 53–71.

Dychtwald K.   Sexuality and the whole person. *The Journal of Humanistic Psychology* 19:47–61, 1979.

Eckhart M.   *Meister Eckhart*. New York: Harper & Row, 1941. 333 p.

Edmonds J D, Jr.   Extended relativity: mass and the fifth dimension. *Foundations of Physics* 5:239–49, 1975.

Efron R.   Biology without consciousness and its consequences. (Colodny R G, ed.). *Logic, laws and life, some philosophical complications*. Series in the philosophy of science. Pittsburgh: Univ. of Pittsburgh Press, 1977. Vol. 6.

Eiseley L C.   *The firmament of time*. New York: Atheneum, 1960. 182 p.

Eliade M.   *Occultism, witchcraft, and cultural fashions*: essays in comparative religions. Chicago: University of Chicago Press, 1976. 148 p.

Emmons M.   *The inner sources: a guide to meditative therapy*. San Luis, CA: Impact Publ., 1978. 291 p.

Episcop Feofan.   *Sobranie pisem Ep. Feofana* (Collection of letters by Bishop Feofan). Moscow: 1898, iss. I–VI.

Fedotov G P.   *Svyatye drevnei Rusi X–XVII stoletie* (The Saints of old Russia X–XVII centuries). New York, 1959. 243 p.

Feigenberg I M.   *Mozg, psikhika, zdorov'e* (Brain, psyche, health). Moscow: Meditsina, 1972. 111 p.

Feyerabend P K.   *Against method: outline of an anarchistic theory of knowledge*. London, NLB; Atlantic Highlands, NJ: Humanities Press, 1975. 339 p.

Figner V.   *Zapechatlennyi trud. Vospominaniya* (Memorable experience. Reminiscences). Moscow: Mysl', 1964. 2 vols.

Fine T L.   *Theories of probability. An examination of foundations*. New York: Academic Press, 1973. 263 p.

First E.   Visions, voyages, and new interpretation of madness. (White J, ed.) *Frontiers of consciousness*. New York: Julian Press, 1975. p. 43–52.

Fraenger W.   *Hieronymus Bosch*. Dresden: Verlag der Kunst, VEB; 1975. 516 p.

Frankl V E.   *Man's search for meaning: an introduction to logotheraphy*. New York: Pocket Books, 1963. 226 p.

Fraser J T.   *Of time, passion and knowledge: reflections on the strategy of existence*. New York: George Braziller, 1975. 529 p.

Fraser J T.   *Time as conflict; a scientific and humanistic study*. Basel: Birkhäuser, 1978. 356 p.

Fromm E.   *The forgotton language*. New York: Rinehart, 1951. 263 p.

Gale R M.   *The language of time*. New York: Humanities Press, 1968. 247 p.

Gale R M, ed.   *The philosophy of time, a collection of essays*. London: Macmillan, 1968. 514 p.

Gallagher E.   The value of symbolism, as suggested by St. Augustine's "De Magistro." (Bryson L, Finkelstein L, Maciver R M & McKeon R, eds.) *Conference on Science, Philosophy and Religion in Their Relation to the Democratic Way of Life*. 13th. Symbols and values: an initial study. September 1952. New York. New York: Harpers, 1954. p. 109–20.

Galvin R M.   Probing the mysteries of sleep. *Atlantic Monthly* 243:53–61, 1979.

Gardner M.   *The ambidextrous universe: mirror asymetry and time-reversed worlds*. New York: Charles Scribner Sons, 1979. 293 p.

Garfield E.   Negative science and "The outlook for the Flying Machines." *Essays of an information scientist*. Philadelphia, PA: ISI Press, 1980. Vol. 3. p. 155–72. Reprinted from: *Current Contents* (26):5–16, 27 June 1977.

Gawain Sh. *Creative visualization*. Berkeley, CA: Whatever Pub., 1978. 156 p.

Gerson W. *Le Nazisme, société secrète*. Paris: Productions de Paris, 1969. 367 p.

Gibbs-Smith C H. *Flight through the ages*: a complete, illustrated chronology from the dreams of early history for the age of space exploration. New York: Crowell, 1974. 240 p.

Gill J G. The definition of freedom. *Ethics* 82:1-20, 1971.

Ginsburg S. *The mathematical theory of context-free languages*. New York: McGraw Hill, 1966. 232 p.

Ginsburg V L. *Sovremennaya astrofizika* (Astrophysics of to-day). Moscow: Nauka, 1970. 191 p.

Gödel K. An example of a new type of cosmological solutions of Einstein's equations of gravitation. *Review of Modern Physics* 21:447-50, 1949a.

Gödel K. A remark about the relationship between relativity theory and idealistic philosophy. (Schilpp P A, ed.) *Albert Einstein: philosopher-scientist*. Evanston: The Library of Living Philosophers, 1949b. p. 566-72.

Gold C & Gold E J. *Beyond sex*. Nevada City, CA: Inst. for the Development of the Harmonious Human Being, 1978. 184 p.

Goldsmith E. *Ancient pagan symbols*. Detroit: Goley Research Co., 1976. 220 p.

Goldstein J. *The experience of insight*. Santa Cruz: Unity Press, 1976. 169 p.

Goleman D. The Buddha on meditation and states of consciousness. Part II. A typology of meditation techniques. *The Journal of Transpersonal Psychology* 4:151-210, 1972.

Goleman D. *The varieties of the meditative experience*. New York: Irvington Publishers, 1977. 130 p.

Govinda L A. *Creative meditation and multi-dimensional consciousness*. Wheaton, IL: Theosophical Pub. House, 1976a. 294 p.

Govinda L A. *Psycho-cosmic symbolism of the Buddhist stúpa*. Berkeley, CA: Dharma Publishing, 1976b. 102 p.

Grib A. Metodologischeskoe znachenie kvantovoi teorii dlya psikhologii (Methodological impact of quantum theory on psychology). (Pavinsky P P & Mostepanenko A M, eds.) *Kvantovaya mekhanika i teoriya otnositel'nosti*. Leningrad: Izd-vo Leningrad Univ., 1980. p. 130-45.

Grof S. *Realms of the human unconscious: observations from LSD research*. New York: Viking Press, 1975. 257 p.

Group for the Advancement of Psychiatry. Committee on Psychiatry and Religion. *Mysticism: spiritual quest or psychic disorder*? New York: Group for the Advancement of Psychiatry, 1976. p. 705-825.

Grünbaum A. The nature of time. (Colodny R G, ed.) *Frontiers of science and philosophy*. Pittsburgh: University of Pittsburgh Press, 1962. Vol. 1. p. 149-88.

Grünbaum A. *Philosophical problems of space and time*. Boston: D Reidel, 1973. 884 p.

Guénon R. *Le Theosophisme; histoire d'une pseudo-religion*. Paris: Nouvelle Librairie nationale, 1921. 310 p.

Guénon R. *L'Esotérisme de Dante*. Paris: Gallimard, 1957. 74 p.

Guilyarov A N. *Filosofia v ee sushchestve, znachenii i istorii* (Philosophy in its essence, meaning and history). Kiev, 1919. Part II. 209 p.

Gumilev L N. *Etnogenez i biosfera zemli* (Ethnogenesis and biosphere of the earth). Vol. 1. A link between nature, environment and society. Vol. 2. Passionarity. Vol. 3. Age of ethnos. Moscow: VINITI, 1979. 3 vols. Deponirovannye rukopisi. (Manuscripts are deposited in All Union Institute of Scientific Information) N 1001-79, N 3734-79, N 3735-79.

Hadamard J. *An essay on the psychology of invention in the mathematical field*. Princeton, NJ: Princeton Univ. Press, 1949. 145 p.

Hankins T L. *Sir William Rowan Hamilton*. Baltimore: Johns Hopkins Univ. Press, 1980. 474 p.

Heidegger M. *Sein und Zeit*. Tübingen: M. Niemeyer, 1960. 437 p.

Hennell T. *The witnesses*. New Hyde Park, NY: University Books, 1967. 251 p.

Holden A V. *Models of the stochastic activity of neurones*. New York: Springer-Verlag, 1976. 368 p.

Hölderlin F. *Sämtliche Werke*. Stuttgart: W. Kohlhammer, 1954–62. 6 vols.

Holland J L. *Making vocational, choices: a theory of careers*. Englewood Cliffs, NJ: Prentice-Hall, 1973. 150 p.

Hutten E H. *The language of modern physics. An introduction to the philosophy of science*. New York: Macmillan, 1956. 278 p.

Ivanov V V & Toporov V N. Invariant i transformatsiya v mifologicheskikh i fol'klornykh tekstakh (Invariant and transformation in mythology and folklore texts). *Tipologicheskie issledovaniya po fol'kloru*. Moscow: Nauka, 1975. p. 44–76.

Jaspers K & Bultman R. *Myth and christianity; an inquiry into the possibility of religion without myth*. New York: Noonday Press, 1958. 116 p.

Jerome J. The body athletic. *Esquire* 93(3):17–8, 1980.

Jonas H. *The gnostic religion; the message of the alien god and the beginning of Christianity*. Boston: Beacon Press, 1958. 302 p.

Jung C G. *Psychology and alchemy*. London: Routledge & Paul, 1953. 563 p.

Jung C G. *Psychology and religion*. New Haven: Yale University Press, (1938) 1962. 131 p.

Jung C G. *Memories, dreams, reflections*. New York: Vintage Books, (1963) 1965. 418 p.

Jung C G. *Psychological types*. Princeton, NJ: Princeton University Press, 1971. 617 p.

Kant I. *Critique of pure reason*. London: Macmillan, 1929. 681 p.

Kant I. *Prolegomena zu einer jeden kunftigen Methaphysiks*. Leipzig: Reclam 1979. 191 p.

Kantorovich A. Structure of hadron matter: hierarchy, democracy, or potentiality? *Foundations of Physics* 3:335–49, 1973.

Kazaryan V P. *Ponyatie vremeni v strukture nauchnogo znaniya* (Time concept in the structure of scientific knowledge). Moscow: Moscow State Univ. Press, 1980. 274 p.

Keen S. Some ludicrous theses about sexuality. *The Journal of Humanistic Psychology* 19:15–22, 1979.

Kleene S C. *Introduction to metamathematics*. Amsterdam: North-Holland, 1952. 550 p.

Kohr R L. Dimensionality in meditative experience: a replication. *The Journal of Transpersonal Psychology* 9:193–203, 1977.

Kornfield J. Intensive insight meditation: a phenomenological study. *The Journal of Transpersonal Psychology* 11:11–58, 1979.

Kropotkin P A. *The great French revolution 1789–1793*. New York: Putnam & Son, 1909. 610 p.

Kuhn T S. *The structure of scientific revolution*. Chicago: Chicago Univ. Press, 1970. 210 p.

LaFarge J. Some lessons of religious symbolism. (Bryson L, Finkelstein L, Maciver R M & McKeon R, eds.) *Conference on Science, Philosophy and Religion in Their Relation to the Democratic Way of Life*. 13th. Symbols and values: an initial study. September 1952. New York. New York: Harpers, 1954. p. 121–6.

Laing R D. *The politics of experience*. New York: Pantheon Books, 1967. 138 p.

Lavrov.L I. *Istoriko-etnograficheskie ocherki Kavkaza* (Essays on historical ethnography of Caucasus). Leningrad: Nauka, 1978. 183 p.

Lee D. Lineal and nonlineal codification of reality. (Dolgin J L, Kemnitzer D S & Schneider M, eds). *Symbolic anthropology: a reader in the study of symbols and meanings*. New York: Columbia Univ. Press, 1977. p. 151–64.

Leibniz G W. *Leibnizens mathematische Schriften*. Halle: H. W. Schmidt, 1849–1863. 6 vols.

Leonov Yu P.   *Teoriya statisticheskikh reshenii i psykhofizika* (Theory of statistical decisions and psychophysics). Moscow: Nauka, 1977. 226 p.

Lestienne R.   Do we need to reformulate physics (some reflections on the work of David Bohm). *Scientia* (Milano) 67:69–85, 1973; 108:87–101, 1973. (Engl.)

Ligou D.   Structures et symbolisme maçonniques sous la révolution. *Annales Historiques de la Revolution Française* 197:511–23, 1969.

Lilly J C.   *Programming and metaprogramming in the human biocomputers, theory and experiments*. New York: Abacus Press, 1974. 60 p.

Lizerand G, ed.   *Le dossier de l'affaire des Templiers*. Paris: Société d'edition "Les Belles Lettres," 1964. 229 p.

Ludwig A M.   Altered states of consciousness. *Archives of General Psychiatry* 15:225–34, 1966.

Lytton E G E.   *Vril: the power of the coming race*. Blauvert, NY: R. Steiner Publ., 1972. 248 p.

Marutyan T A.   *Khram Avan* (The temple of Avan). Erevan: Ayastan, 1976. 204 p.

Mayorov G G.   *Teoreticheskaya filosofiya Gotfrida B. Leibnitsa* (Theoretical philosophy of Gotfried B. Leibniz). Moscow: Moscow Univ. Press, 1973. 264 p.

McCollum P.   Spacetime code: preliminaries and motivations. *Foundations of Physics* 8: 211–28, 1978.

McKeon R.   Symbols, myths, and arguments. (Bryson L, Finkelstein L, Maciver R M & McKeon R, eds.) *Conference on Science, Philosophy and Religion in Their Relation to the Democratic Way of Life*. 13th. Symbols and values: an initial study. September 1952. New York. New York: Harpers, 1954. p. 13–38.

Meschkowski H.   *Mathematik und realität*. Mannheim, 1979.

Metzger B M.   *An introduction to the Apocrypha*. New York: Oxford Univ. Press, 1957. 274 p.

Meyen S V.   Plant morphology in its nomothetical aspects. *Botanical Review* 39:205–60, 1973.

Meyen S V.   *Sledy trav indeiskikh* (Traces of Indian herbs). Moscow: Mysl', 1981. 160 p.

Meyen S V & Nalimov V V.   Veroyatnostnyi mir i veroyatnostnyi yazyk (Probabilistic vision of the world and probabilistic language). *Khimiya i Zhizn'* 6:22–7, 1978.

Meyendorf I F.   O Vizantiiskom isikhazme i yego roli v kulturnom i istoricheskom razvitii Vostochnoi Evropy v XIV veke (On Byzantine hesychasm and its role in cultural and historical evolution of Eastern Europe in the XIVth century). *Trudy Otdela Drevnerusskoi Literatury* 29:291–305, 1974.

Miguel A P.   *La escatologia musulmana en la Divina Comedia*, Madrid, 1919.

Milner D, ed.   *Explorations of consciousness. A sequel to the loom of creation*. Sudbury, Engl.: Neville Spearman, 1978. 439 p.

Misner G W, Thorne K S & Wheeler J A.   *Gravitation*. San Francisco: W. H. Freeman, 1973. 1279 p.

Molchanov Yu B.   *Chetyre kontseptsii vremeni v filosofii i fizike* (Four conceptions of time in philosophy and physics). Moscow: Nauka, 1977*a*. 192 p.

Molchanov Yu B.   Trudy "Mezhdunarodnogo obshchestva po izucheniyu vremeni" (Transactions of the "International Society on time study"). *Voprosy Filosofii* 5:159–66, 1977*b*.

Monod J.   *Chance and necessity: an essay on the natural philosophy of modern biology*. New York: Random Press, 1972. 199 p.

Moody R A.   *Life after life*. Boston: G. K. Hall, (1975) 1977. 245 p.

Moody R A.   *Reflection on life after life*. Harrisburg, PA: Stackpole Books, 1977. 140 p.

Morris J.   Meditation in the classroom. *Learning* 5:22–7, 1976.

Murdock M H.   Meditation with young children. *The Journal of Transpersonal Psychology* 10:29–44, 1978.

Murphy M & White R A. *The psychic side of sports*. Reading, MA: Addison-Wesley, 1978. 227 p.

Nalimov V V. *In the labyrinths of language: a mathematician's journey*. Philadelphia, PA: ISI Press, 1981. 246 p.

Nalimov V V. *Faces of science*. Philadelphia, PA: ISI Press, 1981. 297 p.

Nalimov V V & Barinova Z B. Sketches of the history of cybernetics. Predecessors of cybernetics in ancient India. *Darshana International* 14(2):35–72, 1974.

Nalimov V V & Golikova T I. *Logicheskie osnovaniya planirovaniya eskperimenta* (Logical foundations of experimental design). Moscow: Metallurgiya, 1981. 151 p.

Nalimov V V, Kuznetsov O A & Drogalina J A. Vizualizatsiya semanticheskikh polei verbal'nogo teksta sredstvami gruppovoi meditatsii (Visualization of semantic fields of verbal texts by means of group meditation). *Bessoznatel'noe: Priroda, Funktsii, Metody Issledovaniya* 3:703–10, 1978.

Nalimov V V & Meyen S V. Probabilistic vision of the world. *International Congress of Logic, Methodology and Philosophy of Science, 6th. Abstracts*, Sect. 7:253–7, 1979.

Needham J. *Science and civilization in China*. Cambridge, England: Cambridge Univ. Press, 1954–76. Vol. 2.

Negley G. The failure of communication in ethics. (Bryson L, Finkelstein L, Maciver R M & McKeon R, ed.) *Conference on Science, Philosophy and Religion in Their Relation to the Democratic Way of Life*. 13th. Symbols and values: an initial study. September 1952. New York. New York: Harpers, 1954. p. 647–55.

Noyes R, Jr. Dying and mystical consciousness. (White J, ed.) *Frontiers of consciousness*. New York: Julian Press, 1974. p. 347–60.

Nys E. *Idées modernes: droit international et franc-maçonnerie*. Bruxelles: M. Weissenbruch, 1908. 124 p.

Oster G. Phospenes. *Scientific American* 222(2):83–7, 1970.

Ozhegov S I. *Slovar' russkogo yazyka* (Explanatory dictionary of Russian). Moscow: Sovetskaya Entsiklopediya, 1972. 846 p.

Palou J. *La franc-maçonnerie*. Paris: Payot, 1964. 349 p.

Panchenko A I. *Sovremennye filosofskie diskussii po osnovam fiziki*. Teoriya otnositel'nosti i problema edinstva nauchnogo znaniya (Contemporary philosophical discussions on foundations of physics. Theory of relativity and the problem of integration of scientific knowledge). Moscow: Izd-vo AN USSR, 1980. 62 p.

Panke W W & Richards W A. Implication of LSD and experimental mysticism. (Tart Ch T, ed.) *Altered states of consciousness*. New York: John Wiley & Sons, 1969. 575 p.

Papus. *Kabbala, nauka o boge, vselennoi i cheloveke* (Cabbala, science on God, universe and man). Peterburg: Bodganovski Publ., 1910. 272 p.

Pauli W. Der Einfluss archetypischer Vorstellungen auf die Bildung naturwissenschaftlicher theorien bei Kepler (Influence of archetypical notions on the construction of scientific theories by Kepler). *Naturerklärung und Psyche*. Zurich: Rascher, 1952. p. 109–94.

Pauwels L & Bergier J. *Le matin des magiciens* (The morning of the magicians). Briarcliff Manor, NY: Stein & Day, 1977.

Paz O. On translation. *UNESCO Courier* 29:36–40, Jan. 1975.

Pietsch P. *Shufflebrain. The quest for hologramic mind*. Boston: Houghton Mifflin, 1981. 273 p.

Plotinus. *The Enneads*. London: Faber & Faber, 1956. 635 p.

Podgoretskii M I. Sushchestvuet li kvantovaya teoriya izmerenii (Does there really exist a quantum theory of measurement). *Budushchee nauki*. Moscow: Institut Filosofii AN USSR, 1978.

Pomerants G S. Ikonologicheskoe myshlenie kak sistema i dialog semioticheskikh sistem

(Iconological thinking as a system and dialogue of semiotic systems). *Istoriko-filosofskie issledovaniya*. Moscow: Nauka, 1974. 511 p.

Popenoe C. *Books for inner development: the Yes! guide*. New York: Random House, 1976. 383 p.

Popper K R. *Conjectures and refutations. The growth of scientific knowledge*. New York: Basic Books, 1962. 412 p.

Popper K R. *The logic of scientific discovery*. London: Hutchinson, 1965. 479 p.

Prior A N. *Papers on time and tense*. Oxford: Clarendon Press, 1968. 166 p.

Ram D. *Journey of awakening: a meditator's guidebook*. New York: Bantam Books, 1978. 395 p.

Rambach P. *The secret message of tantric Buddhism*. New York: Rizzoli Int. Publs., 1979. 169 p.

Rapoport A. *Semantics*. New York: Thomas J. Crowell Co., 1975. 465 p.

Rasmussen D M. *Mythic-symbolic language and philosophical anthropology: a constructive interpretation of the thought of Paul Ricoeur*. The Hague: Martinus Nijhoff, 1971. 158 p.

Ravenscroft T. *The spear of destiny: the occult power behind the spear which pierced the side of Christ*. New York: Putnam Books, 1973. 362 p.

Reich C A. *The greening of America*. New York: Random House, 1970. 399 p.

Restivo S P. Parallels and paradoxes in modern physics and eastern mysticism. Part I: A critical reconnaissance. *Social Studies of Science* 8:143–82, 1978.

Restivo S P. Physics, mysticism and society: A sociological perspective on distinguishing and relating alternate reality. *Social Studies of Science* 11:1, 1979.

Rogers J. *Dreams*. New York: Baraka Press, 1976a. 34 p.

Rogers J. *Inner worlds of meditation*. New York: Baraka Press, 1976b. 76 p.

Rogers J. *Awakening into light*. New York: Baraka Press, 1976c. 83 p.

Roxburgh L W & Tavakol R K. Conventionalism and general relativity. *Foundations of Physics* 8:229–36, 1978.

Rozental' I L. Fizicheskie zakonomernosti i chislennye znacheniya fundamental'nykh postoyannykh (Physical laws and numerical values of fundamental constants). *Uspekhi fizicheskikh nauk* 131(2):239–56, 1980. (Soviet Physics. Uspekhi 23(6):296–305, 1980.)

Rozman D. *Meditating with children*. Boulder Creek, CA: University of Trees Press, 1975. 77 p.

Rozman D. *Meditation for children*. Millbrae, CA: Celestial Arts, 1976. 151 p.

Rudolph K. *Die Gnosis: Wesen und Geschichte einer spätantiken Religion*. Göttingen: Vandenhoeck & Ruprecht, 1977. 435 p.

Russell N, Jr. Dying and mystical consciousness. (White J, ed.) *Frontiers of consciousness*. New York: Avon Books, 1974. p. 396–410.

Sall M J. Demon possession or psychopathology? *Journal Psychology and Theology* 4(4): 286–90, 1976.

Samarin W J. *Tongues of men and angels; the religious language of pentecostalism*. New York: Macmillan, 1972. 277 p.

Sampath G & Srinivasan S K. *Stochastic models for spike trains of single neurons*. Berlin: Springer-Verlag, 1977. 198 p.

Sangharakshita Bhikshu. *A survey of Buddhism*. London: Shambhala, 1980. 484 p.

Schayer S. *Contributions to the problem of time in Indian philosophy*. Krakow: Nakladen Polskij Akademii Umiejetnosci, 1938. 76 p.

Scheidweiler F. The Gospel of Nicodimus. Acts of Pilate and Christ's Descent into Hell. (Hennecke E, ed.) *Bible. N.T. Apocryphal books. New Testament Apocrypha*. London: Lutterworth Press, 1963. p. 444–83.

Schlegel R A.　Lorentz-invariant clock. *Foundations of Physics*. 7:245–53, 1977.

Scholem G.　*The messianic ideas in judaism*. New York: Schocken Books, 1971. 376 p.

Séde Gérard de.　*Les Templiers sont parmi nous*. Paris: R. Julliard, 1962. 302 p.

Skhimnik Illarion.　*Na gorakh Kavkaza*. Beseda dvukh startsev pustynnikov o vnutrennem uedinenii s Gospodom, nashykh serdets cherez molitvy Iisusovu ili dukhovnaya deyatel'nost' sovremennykh pustynnikov (On mountains of the Caucasus. Colloque of two hermits (startsev) on Jesus prayer and spiritual assiduity). Baltolapashinks: 1910.

Smuts J C.　*Holism and evolution*. New York: Macmillan, 1936. 358 p.

Solomon D L & Walter C, eds.　*Mathematical models in biological discovery*. Berlin: Springer-Verlag, 1977. 240 p.

Stepanyan N S & Chakmachyan A.　*Dekorativnoye iskustvo srednevekovoi Armenii* (Decorative art of medieval Armenia). Leningrad: Avrora, 1971. 61 p.

Stevenson I.　*Cases of the reincarnation type. Ten cases in India*. Charlottesville: Univ. Press of Virginia, 1975. Vol. 1.

Stevenson I.　Research into the evidence of man's survival after death. A historical and critical survey with summary of recent development. *The Journal of Nervous and Mental Disease* 165(3):152–70, 1977.

Stine G H.　The bionic brain. *Omni* 1(10):84–6; 121–2, 1979.

Stuart C I J, Takahashi Y & Umezawa H.　Mixed-system brain dynamics: neural memory as a macroscopic ordered state. *Foundations of Physics* 9:301–27, 1979.

Symbolisme, Le (collection of articles in special issues).　*Les Etudes Philosophiques* 3: 291–352, 1971.

Tart C T.　*Altered states of consciousness. A Book of Reading*. New York: John Wiley & Sons, 1963. 600 p.

Tart C T.　Science, states of consciousness and spiritual experiences. (Tart C T, ed.). *Transpersonal Psychologies*. New York: Harper & Row, 1975. p. 9–58.

Tart C T.　Is the transpersonal illusory? Spiritual and transpersonal aspects of altered states of consciousness. Symposium report. *The Journal of Transpersonal Psychology* 11:59–74, 1979.

Tarthang T.　*Time, space and knowledge*: a new vision of reality. Emeryville, CA: Dharma Publishing, 1977. 306 p.

Tarthang T.　*Openness mind*. Emeryville, CA: Dharma Publishing, 1978. 160 p.

Taylor E.　Psychology of religion and Asian studies: the William James legacy. *The Journal of Transpersonal Psychology* 10:67–79, 1978.

Teilhard de Chardin P.　*The phenomenon of man*. New York: Harper & Row, 1965. 320 p.

The way of a pilgrim; and, The pilgrim continues his way. New York: Seabury Press, 1965. 242 p.

Thomas L.　The attic of the brain. *Discover* 1(2):32–3, 1980.

Thompson Sir D'Arcy W.　*On growth and form*. Cambridge, England: Cambridge Univ. Press, 1943. 1116 p.

Thurman H.　*Mysticism and the experience of Love*. Wallingford, PA: Pendle Hill, 1961. 23 p.

Till W C.　*Das Evangelium nach Philippos*. Berlin: Walter de Gruyter, 1963. 95 p.

Tillich P.　*The courage to be*. New Haven: Yale Univ. Press, 1952. 197 p.

Tillich P.　*Biblical religion and the search for ultimate reality*. Chicago: Univ. of Chicago Press, 1955. 84 p.

Tillich P.　*Systematic theology*. Existence and the Christ. Chicago: Univ. of Chicago Press, 1951–63. Vol. II.

Tillich P.　The significance of the history of religions for the systematic theology. *The future of religions*. New York: Harper & Row, 1966. p. 80–94.

Tompkins P.　*Secrets of the Great Pyramid*. New York: Harper & Row, 1971. 416 p.

Toporov V N.   Ob odnom klasse simvolicheskikh tekstov (On one class of symbolic texts). *Balanco-Balto-Slavica*. Sympozium po strukture teksta. (Predvaritel'nye materialy i tezisy.) Moscow: 1979, 116–30.

Vaughan F.   Transpersonal psychotherapy: context, content and process. *The Journal of Transpersonal Psychology* 11:101–10, 1979.

Veereshwar S A.   Love. *The Journal of Humanistic Psychology* 19(2):3–13, 1979.

Vernadsky V I.   *Razmyshleniya naturalista. Prostranstvo i vremya v nezhivoi i zhivoi prirode* (Naturalist's reflections. Space and time in animate and inanimate nature). Moscow: Nauka, 1975. Vol. 1.

Vernadsky V I.   *Razmyshleniya naturalista. Nauchnaya mysl'kak planetarnoe yavlenie* (Naturalist's reflections. Scientific idea as a planetary phenomenon). Moscow: Nauka, 1977. Vol. 2.

Vinogradov V V.   *Problema avtorstva i teoriya stilei* (The problem of authorship and the theory of style). Moscow: Khudozhestvennaya literatura, 1961. 613 p.

Walsh R.   Initial meditative experiences. Part I. *The Journal of Transpersonal Psychology* 9:151–92, 1977.

Walsh R.   Meditation research: an introduction and review. *The Journal of Transpersonal Psychology* 11:161–74, 1979.

Watts A.   *The way of zen*. New York: Random House, 1974. 252 p.

Weinberg S.   *The first three minutes; a modern view of the origin of the universe*. New York: Basic Books, 1977. 188 p.

Welwood J.   Meditation and the unconsciousness: a new perspective. *The Journal of Transpersonal Psychology* 9:1–26, 1977a.

Welwood J.   On psychological space. *The Journal of Transpersonal Psychology* 9:97–118, 1977b.

Welwood J.   Befriding emotions: self-knowledge and transformation. *The Journal of Transpersonal Psychology* 11:141–60, 1979.

White L M.   Recovery from alcoholism: transpersonal dimensions. *The Journal of Transpersonal Psychology* 11:117–28, 1979.

Whorf B L.   Science and linguistics. (Carroll J, ed.) *Language, thought and reality*. London: Chapman & Hall, 1956. p. 207–19.

Wilber K.   *The spectrum of consciousness*. Wheaton, IL: Theosophical Pub. House, 1977. 374 p.

Wilber K.   A development view of consciousness. *The Journal of Transpersonal Psychology* 11:1–21, 1979.

Wilber K & Meadow M J.   Spiritual and transpersonal aspects of altered states of consciousness. A Symposium report. *The Journal of Transpersonal Psychology* 11:59–74, 1979.

Wild J.   Christian rationalism (Aquinas, Gilson, Maritain). (Earle W, Edie J M & Wild J, eds.) *Christianity and Existentialism*. Chicago: Northwestern Univ. Press, 1963. p. 40–65.

Wittgenstein L.   *Tractatus logico-philosophicus*. London: Routledge & Keegan Paul, 1955. 207 p.

Zadeh L A.   Fuzzy set as a basis for a theory of possibility. *Fuzzy Sets and Systems* 1: 3–28, 1978.

Index of Names

Index of Subjects

317